ON WHAT CANNOT BE SAID

ON WHAT CANNOT BE SAID

Apophatic Discourses
in Philosophy, Religion, Literature,
and the Arts

VOLUME 2. MODERN AND
CONTEMPORARY TRANSFORMATIONS

Edited with Theoretical and Critical Essays by

William Franke

University of Notre Dame Press

Notre Dame, Indiana

Manufactured in the United States of America

Reprinted in 2015

Library of Congress Cataloging-in-Publication Data

On what cannot be said : apophatic discourses in philosophy, religion, literature,
   and the arts : vol. 2: Modern and contemporary transformations / edited with
   theoretical and critical essays by William Franke.
      p.   cm.
   Includes bibliographical references.
   ISBN-13: 978-0-268-02885-5 (cloth : alk. paper)
   ISBN-10: 0-268-02885-0 (cloth : alk. paper)
   ISBN-13: 978-0-268-02883-1 (pbk. : alk. paper)
   ISBN-10: 0-268-02883-4 (pbk. : alk. paper)
   1. Mysticism.   2. Negative theology.   3. Speeches, addresses, etc.   I. Franke,
William.
   BL625.O54   2007
   120—dc22

                                                        2006036923

   ∞ *The paper in this book meets the guidelines for permanence and durability*
   of the Committee on Production Guidelines for Book Longevity of the Council
   on Library Resources.

If that be simply perfectest
Which can by no way be expresst
But negatives, my love is so.
To All, which all love, I say no.

—John Donne, "Negative Love"

Comme certaines musiques
Le poème fait chanter le silence,
Amène jusqu'à toucher
Un autre silence,
Encore plus silence.

—Eugène Guillevic, "Art poétique"

CONTENTS

Preface: Apophasis as a Mode of Discourse   1

Introduction: Modern and Contemporary Cycles of Apophasis   9

FRAGMENTS AND FINITUDE

1. Hölderlin, Poems: "What Is God?," "The Root of All Evil,"
   "In My Boyhood Days," "Exhortation," "Brevity"   53
2. Schelling, "The Stupor of Reason," from *The Philosophy of Revelation,*
   Berlin Introduction, Lecture VIII   62
3. Kierkegaard, *Fear and Trembling,* from Problema III   74
4. Dickinson, Poems 1668, 1563, 581, 1700, 288, 420, 985, 1004,
   1071, 1251, 1452   84
5. Hofmannsthal, *The Lord Chandos Letter*   90
6. Rilke, *Duino Elegies* 9 and 8; *Sonnets to Orpheus* I.1, 3, 5   102
7. Kafka, "On Parables" and "The Silence of the Sirens"   113
8. Benjamin, "The Task of the Translator"   121

NEW APOPHATIC PHILOSOPHIES

9. Rosenzweig, from *The Star of Redemption*: God and His Being or
   Metaphysics; Esthetic First Principles; The Proper Name;
   Liturgy and Gesture; The Star or the Eternal Truth   139
10. Wittgenstein, "A Lecture on Ethics" and *Tractatus* 6.4–7   166
11. Heidegger, "Words," from *On the Way to Language*   180
12. Weil, "He Whom We Must Love Is Absent"   202

DEPICTING, COMPOSING, REPRESENTING NOTHING

13. Malevich, "God Is Not Cast Down"   211

14. Schoenberg, *Moses and Aaron,* Act II, scenes 4–5,
    and Act III (fragment)   246

15. Adorno, "Music and Language: A Fragment," from
    Quasi una fantasia, and *Negative Dialectics,* III.iii.12   260

16. Cage, "Lecture on Nothing," from *Silence*   271

17. Jankélévitch, "Music and Silence," from *Music and the Ineffable*   283

18. Beckett, from *The Unnamable* and "Texts for Nothing," #8   308

19. Steiner, "Silence and the Poet," from *Language and Silence*   323

20. Philip, from *Looking for Livingstone: An Odyssey of Silence*   344

THE UNUTTERABLY OTHER

21. Bataille, from *Inner Experience*   361

22. Jabès, from *El, or the Last Book* and *The Book of Resemblances*   376

23. Celan, selected poems:

    "Below," "An Eye, Open," "With All My Thoughts,"
    "Dumb Autumn Smells," "Psalm," "It Is No Longer," "Mandorla,"
    "Etched Away," "Once," "The Trumpet Part," "The Poles"   387

24. Levinas, from *Otherwise than Being or Beyond Essence*   406

25. Blanchot, "How to Discover the Obscure?" from
    The Infinite Conversation   427

26. Derrida, from "Sauf le nom (Post-Scriptum)," in *On the Name*   443

27. Marion, from *God Without Being*   460

Permissions and Acknowledgments   477

PREFACE

Apophasis as a Mode of Discourse

The critical revolution of recent decades has changed how we approach the reading and understanding of texts. We have become increasingly sensitized to the fact that we need not—and cannot—always take discourse at its word. For the word often, if not always, covers over more than it makes manifest, conceals as the very condition by which it reveals. We have therefore been relearning to read for what words do not and perhaps cannot say. This entails attending especially to the ruptures and interruptions, to the silences and ellipses, that displace discourse and break the circuits of sense. These gaps open discourse to the non-sense or surplus of sense that it embodies and bears witness to, even without being able to say it. The motivations of discourse lie to a great extent in what cannot be said, and to read for this unsayable that is betrayed especially by impasses to saying is to recognize the moment of apophasis, of silence and *un*saying, as constitutive of saying and its meanings.

"Apophasis" is the word used by Plato and Aristotle simply for a negative proposition or denial. But etymologically it suggests even stronger negative meanings such as "away from speech" (*apo:* away from; *phasis:* speech or assertion) or *un*saying. Among the Neoplatonists, "apophasis" takes on the connotation of a negation of discourse *simpliciter,* for they concentrate on the inability of discourse per se to affirm anything whatsoever about ultimate reality, for them "the One." Ever since these ancient and endless speculations, the intrinsic limits of discourse, with its failure to attain its object and to articulate the ultimately real, as well as the silence that follows as a consequence, have been a perennial preoccupation, especially at certain junctures, of the Western intellectual tradition. The great variety of discourses—and inflections of discourses—that have resulted can be considered together as different expressions of an apophatic mode.

As a discursive mode, apophasis arises in the face of what cannot be said. It bespeaks an experience of being left speechless. There are no words for what is experienced in this form of experience, no possibility of a positive description of it. One falls back on saying what it is not, since whatever *can* be said is *not* it. By their very failure, however, conspicuously faltering and foundering

1

attempts at saying can hint at what they inevitably fail to express, at what cannot be said at all. In this way, the unsayable and discourse about it turn out to be inseparable. Indeed, according to at least one view, what cannot be said can *only* (not) be said: apart from this failure, it would be altogether nought. Certainly it has no objective content or definition, for that *could* be said. Nevertheless, it can be discerned in perhaps all that is said as what *un*says saying, as what troubles or discomfits discourse.

By reading for what cannot be said, we look past expressions themselves to their limits and even beyond, and thereby cull intimations of what they do not and cannot express. The unsayable is inaccessible to direct interpretation, but it can be read in everything that *is* said, if reading means a sort of interpretive engagement that coaxes the text to betray secrets it cannot as such say. The unsayable shows up in texts as their limit of opacity. Everything said, however clear and transparent, is said *from* somewhere, which is indirectly intimated yet cannot itself be fully divulged or exhaustively illuminated in and by its own saying. It necessarily remains opaque and off-limits. Rather than discarding this as the inevitable part of non-intelligibility that is best neglected in whatever *is* said, certain new methods of reading have been bent upon recognizing this as the unsayable that is essential to the meaning of everything said. Such methods can be illuminated by an apophatic tradition reaching all the way back to its ancient theological matrices, for they are in an at least indirect line of descent from these sources.

This book presents exemplary texts of "apophatic" discourse, discourse that in various ways denies and takes itself back. As a newly emerging logic, or rather a/logic, of language in the humanities, this new (though also very old) quasi-epistemic paradigm for criticism, as well as for language-based disciplines and practices in general, can help us learn to read in hitherto unsuspectedly limber and sensitive ways. It can sharpen our critical awareness of what we are already doing even if we do not fully understand how and why. For we have become increasingly attuned to the unsaying and the unsayable within discourse that is covertly undoing its own purported purposes and programs. To this extent, we are reading differently than in the past, yet this very difference has been bequeathed by the past, if we care to know about it, and we can learn to know our own minds and their mysterious ways much better if we do. For what present generations have experienced characterizes also a recurrent, cyclical movement of culture, spirit, and intellect from time immemorial. Most immediately and directly, certain modern and contemporary models have shaped our sensibility for deciphering in discourse these limits of language and what it cannot say.

How do we identify the particular touchstones that can help us understand more accurately the sorts of reading and insight that are enabled and enhanced by this acute attention to what cannot be said? By what criteria are these exemplary texts to be chosen? Claims concerning the inadequacy of language to describe experience are, of course, encountered in all kinds of discourse: literary, religious, artistic, and philosophical alike. But the mode of apophasis need be invoked only where precisely this struggle with language in the encounter with what it cannot say demonstrably engenders the experience in question. The experience of apophasis, as an experience of not being able to say, is quintessentially linguistic: the experience itself is intrinsically an experience of the failure of language. It is not an experience that is otherwise given and secured and perhaps even approximately conveyed—with provisos regarding the accuracy of the description and apologies for the results actually achieved. In apophasis, strictly construed, unsayability or the failure of language is itself basic to the experience—and, indeed, the only experience that admits of description or objectification at all.

And yet the experience in question is *not* fundamentally experience of language or of any other determinate object, for this *could* be adequately expressed. The experiencing subject is affected by "something" beyond all that it can objectively comprehend, something engendering affects that it cannot account for nor even be sure are its own. This entails a sort of belief in, or an openness to, something—that is, to something *or other* that is surely no *thing*—that cannot be said and that refuses itself to every desire for expression. There is not even any "what" to believe in, but there is passion—for nothing, perhaps, certainly for nothing that can be said: and yet that passion itself is not just nothing. The apophatic allows for belief before any determinate belief, and for passion before any object of passion can be individuated: all definitions are only relative, approximate delimitations of what is not as such any object that can be defined. Apophatic thought thus relativizes every verbal-conceptual formulation and orients us toward the unformulated non-concept, no-word that is always already believed in with in(de)finite passion in every defined, finite confession of belief.

Thus apophaticism is not nihilism. Authors of apophatic discourse may sometimes embrace an agnosticism as to whether language has any meaning at all, but their apophaticism is not nihilistic, if that means somehow *concluding* all under Nothing, as if "Nothing" were the final answer, rather than making the admission of the inadequacy of all our names and saying an overture opening toward . . . what cannot be said—and toward the inexhaustible discourses that fail to say it. This is typically an opening toward immeasurably

more—or immeasurably less—than can be said. In either case, what *is* said
serves to guide an asymptotic approach to the infinite of what cannot be said.
I have privileged believers in apophasis as some kind of extra-logical, supra-
rational revelation or liberation—though this deliverance may be of the most
minimalist, desolate sort. There is strictly no saying what the apophatic writer
believes in, but there clearly is a passion of belief—or unbelief: indeed, every
formulated, *expressed* belief must be *dis*believed and abjured in order to keep
the faith in what cannot be said. Just as for mystic writers, who typically cannot define what they believe in or desire, so for apophatic writers the sense of
their belief in . . . what they can neither know nor say nevertheless permeates
all that they do say and write.

It goes without saying that many extremely important and appropriate
texts have been omitted. For example, my representation of recent French
apophaticism, an area that actually receives considerable attention here, nevertheless begs to be extended to embrace many other writers such as Maurice
Merleau-Ponty and Michel Foucault.[1] Even more tempting are Jacques Lacan's
linguistic formulations, which constantly strain beyond their own words toward something that withdraws from articulation, as Lacan himself is well
aware: "There is nowhere any last word unless in the sense in which *word* is *not
a word*. . . . Meaning indicates the direction in which it fails."[2] Also powerfully
expressing these currents in French thought and criticism are Luce Irigaray,
Hélène Cixous, and Julia Kristeva, the last especially in her analysis of the unspeakably abject in *Pouvoirs de l'horreur.*

Feminist discourse has been exceptionally fecund in reflection about silence and its significances. Originally, these reflections tended to revolve

---

1. Especially interesting are Foucault's "Le langage à l'infini," *Tel Quel* 15 (1963):
44–53, and "Préface à la transgression," *Critique* 195–96 (1963): 751–769, as well as "La
pensée du dehors," *Critique* 229 (1966): 523–546. For madness as a silence within the discourse of rationality, see Foucault, *Folie et déraison* (Paris: Plon, 1971), and, further, James
Bernauer, "The Prisons of Man: An Introduction to Foucault's Negative Theology," *International Philosophical Quarterly* 27/4 (December 1987): 365–380. Especially pertinent
by Merleau-Ponty is "Le langage indirect et les voix du silence," in *Signes* (Paris: Gallimard, 1960), pp. 49–104. Other texts are treated by Bernard P. Dauenhauer, "Merleau-
Ponty's Elucidation of Silence," in *Silence: The Phenomenon and Its Ontological Significance* (Bloomington: Indiana University Press, 1979), pp. 115–126.

2. Jacques Lacan, "A Love Letter," in *Feminine Sexuality: Jacques Lacan and the
École Freudienne*, ed. J. Mitchell and J. Rose (New York: Norton, 1982 [1966]), p. 150, cited
in Michael A. Sells and Richard E. Webb, "Psychoanalysis and the Mystical Language of
'Unsaying,'" *Theory & Psychology* 5/2 (1995): 195–215, here p. 199. See further *Lacan and
Theological Discourse*, ed. Edith Wyschogrod, David Crownfield, and Carl A. Raschke
(Albany: SUNY Press, 1989).

around the silencing of female voices and focused sharply on class, color, and sex as motives for the silencing of women writers. Tillie Olsen's *Silences*, for example, stated emphatically that it was not about the natural silences intrinsic to the creative process but rather about "the unnatural thwarting of what struggles to come into being, but cannot."[3] There was frequently a determined effort to divorce the topic of enforced silences of women from any sort of empty, abstract, metaphysical, Romantic concept of the ineffable. Recently, however, feminists have shown a growing interest in silence as more than just negative, more than a lack due to externally imposed interdictions. Apophasis is being discovered in its multivalent potency as gendered in complex ways. Feminine discourse has become sensitive and attentive not only to the silencing of female voices but also to the subversive strategies that cultivate and exploit silence.[4] Silence plays an ambiguous role as an imposed restriction but also an elected source of unlimited power, for example, in the creative silences of a poet like Emily Dickinson.

Of late, a wealth of creative literature by and on women has addressed the paradoxical poverty yet power of their silences. M. Nourbese Philip, in *Looking for Livingstone: An Odyssey of Silence*, and Monica Ochtrup, in *What I Cannot Say / I Will Say*, turn this predicament into the empowering premise of a highly potent new poetry.[5] Although these writers do not necessarily regard the apophatic tradition as their own and rarely cite it, with the exception of references to Wittgenstein, it is doubtful that such literature would have been possible in the state in which we find it without the diffuse presence of apophasis as an element in postmodern culture. Clearly this literature is propelled by a sense of the crisis of language. Its denial and even defiance of *Logos*, interpreted, at least implicitly, as patriarchal authority par excellence, resonates, whether deliberately or not, with the apophatic in its many historical manifes-

---

3. Tillie Olsen, *Silences* (New York: Dell, 1978), p. 6.
4. See Jeanne Kammer, "The Art of Silence and the Forms of Women's Poetry," in *Shakespeare's Sisters: Feminist Essays on Women Poets*, ed. Sandra Gilbert and Susan Guber (Bloomington: Indiana University Press, 1979), pp. 153–164, as well as essays in *Feminist Measures: Soundings in Poetry and Theory*, ed. Lynn Keller and Cristanne Miller (Ann Arbor: University of Michigan Press, 1994), and *Listening to Silences: New Essays in Feminist Criticism*, ed. Elaine Hedges and Shelley Fisher Fishkin (Oxford: Oxford University Press, 1994).
5. On these writers, see Cristanne Miller, "M. Nourbese Philip and the Poetics/Politics of Silence," pp. 139–160, and Dorothea Steiner, "Silence Pretended, Silence Defended: A Look at Monica Ochtrup's Poetry," pp. 309–327, in *Semantics of Silence in Linguistics and Literature*, ed. Gudren M. Grabher and Ulrike Jessner (Heidelberg: Universitätsverlag C. Winter, 1996).

tations. In theology itself, particular attention is now being devoted to how women's voices in the pulpit can find the most effective registers for letting silence speak.[6]

Social sciences, too, are producing a daunting bibliography on the subject of silence. The topic is approached from many disciplines, including psychology, linguistics and pragmatics, anthropology and ethnography, discourse and narrative analysis, and systems and communications theory focusing on all manner of media, as well as on "natural" human conversation and interaction.[7] While not usually interrogating the apophatic directly in its fundamental motivations, these discourses nevertheless reflect upon and illuminate it. They belong to the explosion of new, broadly or tendentially apophatic approaches in every sector of contemporary culture.

Some of the widest and richest areas that I have been barely able to touch upon here are found in the fine arts. Performing arts, such as contemporary theater and dance, have been obsessed with the expressiveness of eluding and even eliminating all determinate form and significance from gesture and movement so as to communicate by the naked, silent power of physical presence—or absence. Aesthetic form and definition are negated for the sake of the sheer evocativeness of neutrality, indeterminacy, and non-statement. Throughout the last century the arts have been especially prolific in negative theologies. The selections of readings and their introductory essays in the anthology begin to suggest some of these directions in contemporary apophasis.

In the case of some of the selections, we are in possession of compact treatises on the subject at hand. In others, I am merely trying to suggest by select samplings the powerfully apophatic thrust or quality of writing diffusely operating throughout an author's *oeuvre*, though perhaps nowhere specifically brought into focus as such. The selections vary widely in length and consistency, and the introductions, similarly, are not uniform in purpose or approach. Beyond offering a minimum of context for an informed reading, the introductions to each reading do not adhere to a common mold. They do,

6. See, for example, *Silence in Heaven: A Book of Women's Preaching*, ed. Heather Walter and Susan Durber (London: SCM, 1994).

7. Representative samples of a much larger field of these applications to social sciences can be found in Adam Jaworski, ed., *Silence: Interdisciplinary Perspectives,* Studies in Anthropological Linguistics 10 (Berlin–New York: Mouton de Gruyter, 1997). Also contributing to these directions of research are the essays in *Perspectives on Silence*, ed. Deborah Tannen and Muriel Saville-Troike (Norwood, N.J.: Ablex, 1985), and *The Regions of Silence: Studies on the Difficulty of Communicating*, ed. Maria Grazia Ciani (Amsterdam: J. C. Gieben, 1987); and Robin Patric Clair, *Organizing Silence: A World of Possibilities* (New York: SUNY Press, 1998).

however, attempt to sound the significance of each text, and of its author's thought and expression in general, for our understanding of the all-important issue of the unsayable. This goal is given precedence over exposition in strict conformity with the commonly accepted views of the current scholarship on each author. Each selection is interpreted in a way that serves to substantiate the theory of apophatic discourse and to elaborate the vision of what cannot be said that the book as a whole creates and advocates. The general introduction to this volume offers a more consolidated exposition of this theory and vision in historical terms.

The territory traversed is vast. Accordingly, I have reduced many of the selections to minimum proportions. They exemplify the sort of discourse typical of a certain author by tendering a few golden nuggets, while the introductions indicate where a full-loaded vein may be mined. The anthology, in this way, rather than attempting to engulf all relevant material within its own covers, becomes a guide to a much larger literature outside itself. Some texts are introduced only by references to the already existing publications. These decisions may have been influenced by issues of publication rights and expenses, but also by the ready availability and familiarity of many relevant works. Especially in these cases, situating the work within the field outlined here is the essential purpose and service of this anthology-cum-history-and-theory of apophasis.

This volume comprises new and often radical currents of thinking from the last two hundred years about the limits of language and what may or may not lie beyond them. It is the sequel to a volume presenting ancient, medieval, and early modern classic readings in apophasis. It thus continues a novel venture in canon formation begun with that volume, by pursuing the project into the modern and contemporary periods and extending it from philosophical, religious, and literary texts into criticism and the arts. The two volumes were conceived and elaborated as a unity, and both are indebted to all those acknowledged in the preface to volume 1.

A NOTE ON TRANSLATIONS

In quoting foreign language texts, I generally prefer to translate quotations directly from the originals, even where English translations exist; unless specific English language editions are cited, the translations are my own. The original language editions cited in my introductions are ones that I have used in the preparation of each volume, not necessarily those from which the translators have worked.

INTRODUCTION

Modern and Contemporary Cycles of Apophasis

I

Periodically in intellectual history, confidence in the *Logos*, in the ability of the word to grasp reality and disclose truth, flags dramatically. Discourses in many disciplines and fields suddenly become dubious and problematic as language enters into a generalized crisis and the currency of the word goes bust. The cyclical collapse of verbal assurance fosters cultures that can be characterized as "apophatic," that is, as veering into widespread worries about the reliability of words and even into wholesale refusal of rational discourse. This type of culture, in its retreat from language, becomes pervasive notably in the Hellenistic Age in a spate of Hermetic philosophies and Gnosticisms. All in various ways are repudiations of the Greek rational enlightenment. It rises to prominence again toward the end of the medieval period with the surpassing of Scholasticism as an all-encompassing rational system. The thinking of Meister Eckhart is exemplary at this juncture. Eckhart engendered hosts of scions and satellites who carried his inspiration forward into Baroque mysticism, which likewise bursts the measures of reason and word that had been dictated by Renaissance rhetorical norms. Something similar happens yet again with Romanticism in its revolt against the Enlightenment—*Aufklärung*—on the threshold of the period with which the present volume is concerned. Such eruptions arguably have continued with an intensifying rhythm ever since.

A particularly dense and destiny-laden nodal point of this history is Viennese culture at the turn of the twentieth century. It pivots on figures such as Hugo von Hofmannsthal, Ludwig von Wittgenstein, Robert Musil, Rainer Maria Rilke, Gustav Klimt, Karl Kraus, and Arnold Schoenberg. The catastrophe of an entire historical epoch was here felt in all its extremity and was expressed with the utmost acuteness and often pathos too. Hofmannsthal's "Letter of Lord Chandos" (1901) witnesses emblematically to the collapse of cultural values that had guided Western civilization since classical antiquity.

9

The failure of classical reason, the bankruptcy of bourgeois culture, and the general demise of civilization are registered as events that radically invalidate and undermine the value of language. The great discourse which the West had entertained for centuries, based on confidence in reason, suddenly seemed to have become null and void, and even somewhat obscene. No longer able to carry on this conversation, many of the most sensitive and honest intellects of the time found themselves faced with an imperative of silence. Freud's discovery of the unconscious as what unsays language by its "slips" is symptomatic of the widespread emphasis specifically on the linguistic dimensions and derivation of the disaster. Franz Kafka, from the Jewish quarter in Prague, is thoroughly imbued with this *Mitteleuropean* mood of doom that presided over the declining Hapsburg Empire. Though living at different times and places, Walter Benjamin and Samuel Beckett are both responding to this same experience of collapse. So are numerous leading beacons, Jewish and non-Jewish, across all arenas of art and culture: they are indelibly marked by the specific form of apophatic crisis that was given expression by these late-nineteenth-century and early-twentieth-century Viennese writers and artists.[1]

Beckett is linked to precisely this ambience of the crisis of language through his involvement with the linguistic skepticism of the Austrian philosopher of language Fritz Mauthner. As a young man, Beckett read Mauthner's *Beiträge zu einer Kritik der Sprache* (1901) aloud to James Joyce, whose eyesight was failing him. The nominalist philosophy of language expressed with great stylistic vehemence in Mauthner's work in fact turns out to bear close affinities to the representations of language in Beckett's texts.[2] Mauthner's views were formed, like those of Kafka and Hofmannsthal, in the context of the fall of Austro-Hungarian civilization—a metonymy for general European decline and the demise of the West—and the consequent cultural hollowing-out that resulted in mendacious verbal manipulation and a rigid insistence on empty formalities in the attempt to stave off the inevitable collapse. Beckett's

---

1. See Alan Janik and Stephen Toulmin, *Wittgenstein's Vienna* (New York: Simon & Schuster, 1973). The story of this epoch is told suggestively by Franco Rella in *Il silenzio e le parole: Il pensiero nel tempo della crisi* (Milan: Feltrinelli, 1988 [1981]) as it revolves around the now largely forgotten Otto Weininger and his *Geschlecht und Charakter* (1903), which was followed by the definitive silence of its author's suicide at the age of twenty-three.

2. See Linda Ben-Zvi, "Samuel Beckett, Fritz Mauthner, and the Limits of Language," *PMLA* 95 (March 1980): 183–200. Beckett thus serves as a bridge to the postwar Parisian culture of shock at the unspeakable in the wake of Nazi atrocities, as detailed, for example, by May Daniels in *The French Drama of the Unspoken* (Edinburgh: Edinburgh University Press, 1953).

distrust of language and his resulting determination to write in an apophatic vein shapes, from this early period, his sense of his mission as a writer: "The experience of my reader shall be between the phrases, in the silence, communicated by the intervals, not the terms, of the statement, between the flowers that cannot coexist, at the antithetical (nothing so simple as antithetical) seasons of words, his experience shall be the menace, the miracle, the memory, of an unspeakable trajectory."[3]

This culture of crisis leveraged from linguistic collapse continued to evolve, with a new wave of apophatic expression by post-Holocaust writers in Germany and Austria, as well as by French thinkers of "difference" a generation later. It lives on in various tendencies within postmodern culture—across its many channels of expression—that issue in an evacuation of the real. Contemporary America has emerged as a leading venue for a new apocalyptic apophaticism. American abstract art was once in the vanguard of this tendency. Now discourses of silence are conspicuously gaining ground in humanities and social science disciplines in the American academy. Apophatic discourse, paradoxically, is assuming the role of a common language, a *koiné*, like Hellenistic Greek, for many expressions of the postmodern predicament. This "language" of apophatic discourse, which is rather a constant reminder of the lack of any adequate language, is also proving to be the key to interpreting postmodern culture's unsuspected, only recently rediscovered precursors in tradition. We can now appreciate certain cyclical cultural crises of the past as intimately bound up with typically apophatic failures of language.

The proximate intellectual precedent for all these various forms of apophaticism in Western thought over the last two centuries can be found in the rebellion against Hegel and his System that was staged by his Romantic contemporaries and post-Romantic opponents. This suggestion may appear paradoxical, at first, since the history of German speculative mysticism—one of the most fertile seedbeds for apophatic thought from Meister Eckhart and Nicholas of Cusa through Jakob Böhme and Silesius Angelus—is often taken to culminate in Hegel.[4] But precisely the apophatic emphasis of this tradition

---

3. *A Dream of Fair to Middling Women*, ed. Eoin O'Brien and Edith Fournier (New York: Arcade Publishing, 1992), p. xiii. This first novel of Beckett was written in 1932, when the author was twenty-six years old, though it was published only sixty years later.

4. See, for example, F.-W. Wentzlaff-Eggebert, *Deutsche Mystik zwischen Mittelalter und Neuzeit: Einheit und Wandlung ihrer Erscheinungsformen*, 3rd ed. (Berlin: Walter de Gruyter, 1969), and Marco Vannini, *Il volto del Dio nascosto: L'esperienza mistica dall'Iliade a Simon Weil* (Milan: Mondadori, 1999). The argument for viewing Hegel as a proponent of negative theology is also made by Rowan Williams, "The Mystery of God

is erased by Hegel. Hegel's main premise is that everything that is real *can* be said. He eliminates anything that is supposed to lie definitively and irretrievably beyond the grasp of Logos. The whole line of apophatic speculation stemming from Eckhart and ultimately Plotinus, based on being or existence as exceeding verbal and conceptual grasp, passes rather through the later Schelling. The discovery of existence as radically open, for lack of any rational or sayable ground, was further developed in original ways, under the direct influence of Schelling, by Søren Kierkegaard, and then in currents reaching from Kierkegaard to Dada, Expressionism, and Existentialism, each in different ways assaulting the word by a reality gone mad beyond saying.[5]

The predominantly German strain of apophatic speculation that gathers in Schelling, together with Jewish thought in the tradition of the Kabbalah, flows into the work of Franz Rosenzweig and Walter Benjamin. Franz Kafka unites the same elements and produces texts that are seminal for subsequent apophatic writing. However, it is Rosenzweig who most convincingly elaborates an original apophatic philosophy in a contemporary key that is attuned to language as the paradigm of all knowledge. By gathering together the German and Kabbalistic philosophical and religious traditions, and responding to the crisis of language that shook European civilization in the years leading up to the Great War, with its epicenter in Vienna, Rosenzweig emerges as arguably the preeminent apophatic thinker of modern times. The second section of this introduction offers a new exposition of his thought from this perspective.

It is essential to recognize how extensively and incisively Jewish thinkers, writers, and artists have contributed to apophatic tradition and culture throughout Western intellectual history. This contribution is particularly intense through modern times up to the present. The biblical interdiction on images to represent God acknowledges the transcendence of an unrepresentable deity. This God, nevertheless, remains at the root of a great genealogical tree that branches all the way to the twentieth century. It is a vigorous growth that even the Holocaust was not able to truncate so much as stimulate. Still, the imagery of cutting and rupture has deeply scored recent apophatic expression, especially that of Jewish provenance. Images of tearing and rending, as well as of shattering into fragments and destroying—for example, the

---

in Hegel's Philosophy," in *The via negativa* (*Prudentia*, Supplementary Number 1981), ed. D. W. Dockrill and R. Mortley (Aukland, New Zealand: Prudentia, 1981), and by Quentin Lauer, S.J., "Hegel's Negative Theology," *Journal of Dharma: The International Quarterly of World Religions* 6 (1981): 46–58.

5. An emblematic figure here is Hugo Ball. See *Dionysius DADA Areopagita: Hugo Ball und die Kritik der Moderne*, ed. Bernd Wacker (Munich-Vienna: Schöningh, 1996).

vase of pure language breaking into the babel of historical languages envisioned by Benjamin, or the conceit of the broken vessels of Creation relayed by Edmond Jabès from the Lurian Kabbalah—give this literature and this philosophical reflection their characteristic accent.

Poets, particularly Jabès and Paul Celan, use the imagery of cutting and splitting of the word and its meaning to convey this sense of openness toward what hurts and haunts the word. Meaning cannot be contained within or communicated intact by a word that has been torn apart and rent asunder. Rather, an aura of what the word cannot say hangs over the desert landscape left by the Holocaust and its concentration camps. Bodies and souls alike are just such words, rent and wracked and thereby opened to what is no longer meaning of any definable sort and yet remains superlatively significant as beyond the reach of meaning.

Celan's poems reflect on and resonate provocatively with both Jewish and Christian traditions of apophasis and negative theology. Especially characteristic is his insistence on images such as the "prayer-sharp knives of my silence" ("ihr / gebetscharfen Messer / meines / Schweigens," from ". . . Rauscht der Brunnen") and "grass, written asunder" ("Grass, auseinander geschrieben," from "Engführung") on the terrain of a concentration camp. Such images suggest a breaking open of meaning to what cannot be defined and so remains unlimited in meaning that relates to an experience that is cryptically evoked as nameless and indescribable. The limits and failures of language are a recurrent trope and theme. Language is brought into check as it issues from "the mouth stammered true" ("wahr- / gestammelten Mund," from "Hohles Lebensgehöft"). In poem after poem, Celan explores in linguistically amazing and original ways the modes of inexpressibility. The experiences to which the poetry alludes but leaves locked and indecipherable are at the extreme limits of possibility and cannot be represented. They are best conveyed or witnessed to by linguistic annihilations.

For Jabès, every human word and letter bespeaks the absence of God. As part of the totality of language, a word evokes the plenitude of meaning that it is missing. For it is but a fragment of the infinite, which it cannot re-present. Voided of absolute presence, "the word is a world of emptiness" ("Le verbe est univers du vide").[6] It cannot represent what it has been broken off from, the infinite that is its hidden root ("l'infini est racine cachée," El, p. 121). The human word in no way contains this original wholeness, yet it is a

---

6. Quotations are from Edmond Jabès, El, ou le dernier livre (Paris: Gallimard, 1973), p. 93.

reminiscence: for in its very brokenness it exceeds all determinations of mean-ing and evokes an anteriority to sense. As wounded and bleeding, moreover, the word disperses significance that is in fact without limit because it is with-out any definition that does not at the same time give way and *un*define itself in the flood of infinite meanings in which it issues, or to which it is exposed. This deluge becomes inevitable, once the semantic skin that contains mean-ing has been violated and broken open. Every finite, determinate sense is swamped in the ocean of other possible meanings that pour into it.

The discrete, circumscribed sense attributed to language is like a decoy that prevents or protects us from contemplating its gaping wounds ("les béantes plaies d'un / leurre que le sens attribué à nos mots—et à / nos maux—empêche autrui, comme nous, de contempler," *El*, p. 99). When their sense shatters, as it does in Jabès's texts, words are opened to an uncharted and un-chartable region or dimension. An openness to the infinite is enacted beyond all boundaries of the senses of words. It is discovered in the abyss of the un-sayable divine Name as the emptiness at the core of every word. The Hebrew name for God, "El," happens to reverse the masculine definite article in French—"le"—designating substantive things in general, and this, in a certain manner, builds it implicitly into everything that is said in that language.

In the post-Holocaust period, from within and beyond Jewish culture, many have emphasized the brokenness and shattering of meaning as necessary to opening it up to the indefinable, the unsayable. The incidence of alterity, that is, of confrontation with what is unassimilable and unsayable, and what therefore interrupts the circuit of the self and the same, is the starting point for Emmanuel Levinas's thinking on the topics of externality and infinity. In close conjunction with Levinas, Blanchot has worked out his thought of "dés-aster," of the dis-order of the universe as a coming undone and falling apart. Closely intertwined with these ideas are also Bataille's and Derrida's dis-integrative, heterogeneous biases and outlook.

Both German speculative and Jewish mystical elements, transmitted es-pecially through the writings of Rosenzweig, Benjamin, and Levinas, are part of the most important and direct background for recent French thinkers of al-terity, or difference. These writers have taken up many of the characteristic concerns and turns of apophatic thinking. They have placed a vigorous new accent particularly on the theme of the Other. This emphasis is an original de-parture in thinking through the problem of the unsayable that is less meta-physical or ontological and more fundamentally ethical—and sometimes overtly political—in orientation. This orientation is programmatic in Levinas, who, together with Bataille, opens up the path pursued by Derrida and Blanchot. These deontologized approaches to the unsayable focus not on the ground of being, the *Urgrund*, but on absolute alterity as what is beyond saying. It is because of radical difference, which cannot be mediated in any way, that nothing can be said in the face of the Other.

With Levinas as the connecting link, the French thinkers of alterity are in deep continuity with Rosenzweig. The key motif of Rosenzweig, and perhaps of Jewish thinking generally, is that of separation. Recognizing separateness is the first step toward any possible knowledge, or rather the first step toward *un-knowing*, a step that both lames and empowers. Certainly words are impotent to reach what is radically separate. However, Rosenzweig also concentrates on how to interpret *discourses* concerning unassimilable difference: they unite in being surpassed by what lies beyond discourse. While emphasizing separateness and alienation, Rosenzweig also envisions unity in a "new" form.[7] This too, I argue, is what cannot be said. Indeed, there is more than can be said to unity, too. Throughout Western intellectual history, Jewish thinkers have taken an important lead in exploring the Divine Name, in which all names unite, as the prime instance of what cannot be said. This reflection, too, lies at the heart of Rosenzweig's thinking. The configuration of writers and thinkers of difference that has just been sketched is, to a considerable extent, working out the destiny of Jewish apophaticism in a radically secular cultural context today, and all are indebted to Rosenzweig in this undertaking. But Rosenzweig also anticipates another, very different perspective that has recently emerged—one that is increasingly being called "post-secular."[8]

II

Innovative and rebellious as he was, Rosenzweig nonetheless extends traditional theological reflection on pure being, or existence per se, viewed in a creationist framework, as quintessentially what cannot be said. This line of

---

7. See Franz Rosenzweig, *Der Stern der Erlösung* (Frankfurt a.M.: Suhrkamp, 1988 [1921]), pp. 424–425.

8. See, for example, *Post-Secular Philosophy: Between Philosophy and Theology*, ed. Phillip Blond (New York: Routledge, 1998). Other collections offering significant probings in related directions include *The Otherness of God*, ed. Orrin F. Summerell (Charlottesville: University Press of Virginia, 1998), and *Silence and the Word: Negative Theology and Incarnation*, ed. Oliver Davies and Denys Turner (Cambridge: Cambridge University Press, 2002).

reflection developed from Neoplatonic speculations on the One as irreducibly beyond the reach of words. Although the One was placed originally "beyond Being," in the course of tradition this came to mean that it was beyond qualified being, that is, beyond being *this* or *that* being; in contrast, the unsayable One could be identified with unqualified, that is, pure being. This move to equating the absolute, unsayable principle, or the One, with pure being was already evident in Porphyry, among the Neoplatonists, and it became standard Christian doctrine with Saint Augustine. It continued through medieval Scholastic philosophy, which conceived God as Being itself, *ipsum esse*, and on into Renaissance Neoplatonism.

Rosenzweig, however, adds a sharply existentialist and even "empiricist" accent: he interprets pure being in totally immanent terms as the actual and factual. In a letter in which he first spells out the blueprint or "original cell" of his "new thinking," he defines the distinguishing mark of revelation, over against mere human knowledge, as "the relation of pure facticity."[9] Pure facticity cannot be deduced by reason; it is simply there, to reason's utter astonishment. The world as Creation is such a revelation. The principle that brings it into being is not accessible to reason. The world, together with its unaccountable order, is revealed thereby as a miracle. But to know the world purely as a fact is to know nothing about it. For all that knowing and saying can tell, the world as pure fact is nothing. The fact *that* the world is tells us nothing about *what* anything is.

This facticity eluding knowledge is found not only, nor even primarily, in the created world. "God," too, is factual. We know nothing of God ("von Gott wissen wir nichts"). But all the richness of factual existence, understood in relation to *what* or *whom* we know nothing about, informs the maximally positive concept ("höchst positiver Begriff") of God's reality ("die Wirklichkeit Gottes") toward which Rosenzweig strives in *The Star of Redemption*. This is a concept not directly of God or his essence but of our relation to the God of whom we have no conception. It begins from the not-nothing of our ignorance of God. Even our ignorance of God, an ignorance that fundamentally characterizes and conditions human existence, is *not nothing*. It is a powerful determination of our existence toward that which we do not know, that of which we know nothing except that we do not and cannot know it. Everything

---

9. "die Offenbarung ist eben das Verhältnis der 'reinen Tatsächlichkeit' schon selbst." "'Urzelle' Des *Stern der Erlösung*," Brief an Rudolf Ehrenberg, November 18, 1917, in *Franz Rosenzweig: Der Mensch und sein Werk. Zweistromland: Kleinere Schriften zu Glauben und Denken, Gesammelte Schriften* (Dordrecht: Nijhoff, 1984), vol. 3, p. 136.

in our existence is thereby directed toward and defined in terms of what cannot be known or said.

In this manner, the nothing of God ("das Nichts Gottes") from which we begin, God's nothingness to us, becomes the absolute facticity ("absolute Tatsächlichkeit") of existence. This beginning, from negation, of our knowledge of God and therefore also of our own reality actually begins, without saying so, from existence as positively given (following the lead of Schelling's "positive philosophy"). But by simply negating our knowledge of God and reality, we do not try to hang any concept on this unaccountable givenness or assert it. Rather, our *discourse* begins by negating itself—with the denial that this discourse is in any way a knowledge of God or of any reality. The positively given and factual, which is originally articulated only by the negation of our knowledge of it, is not defined and delimited but is opened to its infinity and lack of any definable ground. Only what it is *not* has been specified, while its own intrinsic meaning and purport are rendered totally open and indeterminate, so far as words and concepts are concerned. And yet, even while remaining undefined and unsayable, this meaning becomes fully concrete and specific in actual human existence. When any given individual confronts this positive existence as nothing knowable or sayable, it is no longer the general concept Nothing, the Nothing for all, but rather takes on concrete and singular significance in the life-and-death struggle of a particular person in their own unique existence.

This sort of reasoning, already found in Schelling's "positive" philosophy, could be viewed as an existential version of the ontological argument. It starts from the nothing of any conceptualization of God. Yet this very nullity is itself something. We conceive of something which we cannot conceive. That is an extraordinarily revealing fact about human existence as standing in relation to what is not given or manifest to it. Our conceiving and saying relates itself to what cannot be conceived or said. The capacity for such relating (without concepts and language) can be verified as an existential fact by every individual who attempts, for example, to conceive of "God," and the tradition of discourses on what cannot be said documents this curiously contradictory, yet superlatively revealing predicament as a historical fact.

The nothing from which Rosenzweig begins is a nothing of knowledge and, in every case, of an individual existing in unknowing. But the negation of any determinate, knowable object already entails an affirmation of something greater than is—or ever could be—known or said. There is no object for this affirmation, and so logic cannot pick it up and deal with it. Yet the "grammatical method" expounded by Rosenzweig finds this affirmation within negation itself, just as it discerns a "Yes" silently accompanying every word that is said: to say a word is, after all, to affirm what it says—even though this is merely a determinate way of negating the Infinite that it does not and cannot say. A word is a delimitation, a negation, but as a pure act of positing, that is, before conceptual determination, the word is infinitely positive. The gesture of naming, taken in and for itself, posits what is undefined and infinite, so long as it is not determined as to *what* it names.

Rosenzweig invents, in effect, an apophatic logic or rather grammar that begins not from a given object but from what cannot be said, from an indeterminate Nothing in terms of speech and concepts. Such are his "elements": they are called "God," "Man," and "World" only proleptically. In themselves, they are nameless and without identity in a protocosmos from which they will be forced to emerge only with the advent of language. More primordial than any linguistic fabrication, they swim in a linguistically amorphous state. At the level of these elemental proto-realities, there are no objects and therefore no *Logos*—no logic and no words. Nevertheless, the web of words is the only basis for projecting back to the pre-*res* of this protocosmos. And only on this basis do the elements become objects, first of all objects of discourse. To this extent, language is prior to things as logical objects capable of being adjudged real or true, even though Rosenzweig loathes the linguistic idealism that denies the miracle of created reality in order to treat everything as the invention merely of language. While any *determinate* reality presupposes language, this reality is itself already a result: it is a linguistic delimitation of a positively, infinitely Unsayable that as such knows nothing of language.

In fact, Rosenzweig calls his method not a logic at all but rather a "grammar," since it is based on the nature and dynamics of language, not on the laws of conceptual thinking. Logic requires determinate objects—A and B, x and y—to be given before it can proceed. By contrast, for language there are no givens entirely outside its scope: whatever it touches becomes, in some sense, language, and to this extent it conjures its elements out of nothing but itself. In language, the original presentation of the elementary terms is itself a linguistic production: a named object, as opposed to a logical object, already has a contour that is inextricably linguistic. Without its name, this element is . . . nothing—nothing that can be said, anyway. It is precisely this original nothing, what language does not and cannot grasp objectively and as separate from itself, that constitutes the element which Rosenzweig's "new thinking" discovers. He begins with the original Nothing—*for knowledge and language*—of the elements God, World, Man. We know—and so can say—nothing of them. This is the Archimedean point for everything Rosenzweig then goes on to say.

Since language does not have an object that is given to it in a wholly external manner, in the way that logic does, but rather always has a hand in fashioning its own object, it always remains in touch with the nothing, no-thing, or no-linguistically-determinate-thing lurking below the surface of the things that it dextrously handles with names. Precisely this Nothing is the "ground," or rather background, to which Rosenzweig constantly calls attention in expounding the elements of his new *linguistic* thinking. Because language remains conversant with the nothing of its elements, a linguistic thinking is able to keep in view, peripherally at least, the Nothing underlying every revelation, every articulation of being and essence. From beyond all manner of verbal determinations in which our experience consists, language can recall and call forth the unrepresentable, unsayable sea of Nothing on which it skims. Only this skipping and skidding of language temporally demarcates the eternal abyss of Nothing—that is, nothing sayable—by giving it positive inflections through delimitation and qualification. Otherwise this abyss remains imperceptible.

Rosenzweig characterizes his thought as a "speaking thinking" ("das sprechende Denken"), as against the "thinking thinking" ("das denkende Denken") of virtually all earlier philosophy. Whereas thinking-thinking knows its own thought before expressing it and must simply complete the outward expression of itself in speech, speaking-thinking does not know what it is going to say, for it is open to time and the other. It does not know where it is going, for it depends in its inmost core and content on what the other will say. In this sense, speaking is time-bound; it is given its cue by the other and lives from the life of the other. Whereas thinking aspires to be timeless, to make its beginning and end coincide, speaking "does not know in advance where it will end up; it allows itself to be given its theme from the other. It lives fully from the life of the other . . . while thinking is always alone."[10]

The thinker knows his thought before he expresses it, and the time that this expression takes cannot add to the thought except in accidental and distracting ways. In conversation, by contrast, I do not know what the other will say, nor even what I will say, or whether I will say anything at all. In Rosenzweig's view, this openness to the Other in speaking is the origin of thought.

---

10. "Das Neue Denken, Einige nachträgliche Bemerkungen zum 'Stern der Erlösung,'" in *Gesammelte Schriften*, vol. 3, p. 151: "weiß nicht im voraus, wo es herauskommen wird; es läßt sich seine Stichworte vom andern geben. Es lebt überhaupt vom Leben des anderen . . . während Denken immer einsam ist." A translation can be found in *Franz Rosenzweig's "The New Thinking,"* trans. and ed. Alan Udoff and Barbara E. Galli (Syracuse: Syracuse University Press, 1998).

Of course, this Other is what can never be expressed in language. But speaking nevertheless stays in touch with this Other that it cannot say—precisely *because* it cannot say it. The otherness that cannot be said is also the origin of time, of division into distinct tenses that do not comprehend one another. Language transpires in time, present time, but it is open to other times, past and future, that are not sayable and that, as such, remain unsayably other. This unsayable otherness can be phantasized in story or myth, making an image of the irretrievable past, or again in ritual and hymn, which intimate an eternal future that likewise cannot per se be made present in language. The perennial past is commemorated especially in the traditions of paganism, while Judaism and Christianity reveal images of the eternal future that is by its nature unsayable.[11]

In fact, this what-cannot-be-said as it appears nevertheless in the images of pagan myth and Judeo-Christian religion turns out to be the whole point of Rosenzweig's philosophy. These pagan and biblical figures are a sort of discourse, not logical but apophatic in nature, concerning the always-perduring ("immerwährende") past and the eternal future of reality as a whole. These dimensions are glimpsed from language and are even elaborately articulated by Rosenzweig, but in a language of pure projection, a speech of the unspeakable that is in different ways like the languages of art and ritual or religion.

In Judaism and Christianity, "the secret of God, the world, and man that is only experienceable, not expressible, along the way of life becomes expressible."[12] Deeply considered, this revelation of life in religion is the invention of a language for the unsayable. Judeo-Christian religion emerges as a compelling interpretation of human ways of relating to the all-pervasive, all-important Unknown. It discloses life in its intrinsic openness and mystery. To know nothing of God is a way of being in relation to the whole of life and existence as infinite and unknowable. This unknowing is far more vital and potent than any positive knowing; in fact, all positive knowing is contained proleptically therein and can only be a working out and an articulating of a relation to some virtual wholeness that is as such unsayable—a relation to "God," "Man," or "World" as what we can know absolutely nothing about.

The existence of the universe exceeds any logic that can account for it. It is "metalogical." It is simply given as a miraculous fact—Creation. Likewise, hu-

---

11. Cf. Stéphane Moses, *Système et révélation: La philosophie de Franz Rosenzweig* (Paris: Seuil, 1982).

12. "in ihrem Gott, ihrer Welt, ihrem Menschen wird das auf der Bahn des Lebens nur erfahrbare, nicht aussprechbare Geheimnis Gottes, der Welt, des Menschen aussprechbar." "Das Neue Denken," p. 155.

manity is discovered as "metaethical," as having a unique self or character that is simply there in its singularity and that cannot be communicated in the common language or be subsumed under ethical norms. It is represented by the isolation of the tragic hero of Greek drama in his or her truly unspeakable, unthinkable individuality ("wahrhaft 'unausprechliches' 'unausdenkbarer' Individualität," *Stern der Erlösung*, p. 53). Rather than deny such an irreducible individual existence and dissolve it into a set of character traits, Rosenzweig admits it as an unrevealed, undiscloseable, and unspeakable reality. This is the facticity of existence that cannot be expressed. This positive facticity of existence also has a "metaphysical" dimension; it is "metaphysical" when apprehended as the mystery enshrined in the unsayable Name of God.

For Rosenzweig, knowledge and its articulation in language, namely, the whole intricate network of mutual relations and disclosure of things, is a veiling of the separate, unspeakable reality of each of the elements—God, World, Man—which are *not* as such all one, or *not* any All. In the relations of Creation, Revelation, and Redemption, these elements are disclosed and articulated in relation to one another, but in themselves they remain pure enigma. Each is an ineffable mystery that no concept can grasp. We experience only the bridges between them; our experiences are such "over-bridgings" ("Brückenschläge"). Rosenzweig insists on the separation of his elements because only thus can they remain fundamentally unknown fragments that do not fit into any pre-existing All. And as such they are inarticulable. In relation to one another, they become disclosed and articulable as part of an overarching system—a revelation, a language. In their separateness, they resist language. And this separateness is their truth, not the factitious constructions of language, in which everything communicates with everything else and all is one.

There is, for Rosenzweig, a present of disclosure, a "revelation to Adam." Apart from religion and its revelations, language itself naturally is a disclosure of life in the present. This is what Part II of the *The Star of Redemption* expounds. But this presentation of language between his discussion of the ever-enduring night of paganism in Part I and the eternal future of Judeo-Christianity in Part III contextualizes it in such a way that these prior and posterior truths of origin and of eschatology are precisely what it does not and *cannot* say. The dumbness of the protocosmos (Part I) and the silent ritual intimating eternity of the hypercosmos (Part III) underlie and overlay every articulation in the present of the cosmos (Part II).

Being as it occurs in existence—and that means in language—is always significant of something other than what we actually see and experience. It is hemmed in and conditioned by a protocosmos or Pre-world ("Vorwelt") and a hypercosmos or Over-world ("Überwelt"). It is precisely the limit of language, the unsayableness at the limit of existence, that betokens these other, unsayable realms. To speak of a "realm" is, of course, improper, since the unsayable neither *is* nor *is not*, and "realm" seems to reify what cannot in itself be concretely characterized. Yet this limit is experienced in everything in the linguistically reified world that we *do* experience, and it suggests a correspondence of this world to an other world which, however, never appears objectified as such. The only manifestation of this other world is in the pre-language of myth (paganism) and in the post-language of ritual (Judeo-Christian religion). It is out of these limits of experience that Rosenzweig interprets a Pre-world and Over-world in the opening and closing parts of his work.

What is revealed in language, the "organon of revelation," is existence, but also, indirectly, the unsayable "realms" of the protocosmos and hypercosmos—the irretrievable past and the unimaginable future. Revelation is always totally in the present, but this is a vanishing present. It vanishes into the eternal past and eternal future, which remain in themselves and as such unrevealed. They are the unsayable par excellence. Nevertheless, languages of the unsayable exist for them, namely, story or myth and hymn or ritual. These are the fundamentally improper languages of art and religion, languages that intimate what is not linguistically expressible.

Rosenzweig also develops a "negative cosmology" and "negative psychology," which are parallel to the negative theology that he actually disavows—or rather reverses, in order to insist on the positive result at which he aims. This reversal, however, is still complicit with negative theology as it can be rediscovered in the traditions of discourse on what cannot be said. In either case, something inexpressible is exposed. Rosenzweig insists that unknowing and the limits of language for him are not the end of thought but only the beginning. However, this holds true for apophaticism and negative theology in general, even if they are often accompanied by a rhetoric exalting limits for their own sake. The infinite possibilities opened by apophatic discourse have always been what motivate this "negative," that is, eminently positive quest—it negates the finite and articulable only in order to open them to the infinite.

Rosenzweig furnishes the essential elements for a thoroughgoing apophatic revolution of thought capable of proposing novel answers to the fundamental questions of philosophy and, beyond that, of life. He rethinks the positivity of existence as given in experience on the basis of the negativity of knowledge as constituted in human discourse. All knowing is more fundamentally an unknowing, for language can have any meaning at all only on the basis of what it cannot say. Such is the meaning of recognizing the Name of God as the source and foundation of language, and thereby of knowledge, for the divine Name represents the quintessence of the unnameable and un-sayable.

In the *Parmenides* commentary tradition of Neoplatonism, the One as unsayable was generally deemed beyond being. In certain monotheisms, pure, positive being as such became the unsayable par excellence. Rosenzweig and other Jewish thinkers, by contrast, emphasize that the revelation of the Word is more original than any revelation of being. Correspondingly, there is an un-sayable of language prior to the unsayability of pure being and prior to the un-sayability of the being-transcendent One. This is explored in theories of the divine Name as the transcendent source of language. Speaking and relation-ship between persons, not perception or intellection of things in the world, are taken to be the fundamental situation in which reality is first disclosed. But here, too, there is an infinite, indefinable instance, in this case of language rather than of being, upon which all that is sayable depends and from which it devolves: the Name of God. The Name of God, which cannot itself be said, is latent in every part of language and alone guarantees the power of language to speak and mean. But it withdraws itself from speech and meaning as an absent foundation, as an abyss—the unsayable, the undiscloseable. It marks the gap in reality that leaves us speechless.

Rosenzweig's work thus juxtaposes the ontological approach to unsaya-bility that characterizes the Greek tradition from Parmenides to Heidegger with another approach through language and the problematic of the divine Name that stems from Judeo-Christian tradition: alongside the unsayability of existence, the emptiness of language and the ineffability of the Divine Name testify to the apophatic at the center of all we say and express. Indeed, language exposes perhaps yet more intractable grounds for inexpressibility than are found in existence. The Divine Name is without content; it names nothing determinate or articulable. It is not even considered to be pronounceable in Hebrew tradition. When language is explored thus to its empty core, it testifies to . . . what cannot be said.

The unnameable Name of God is a constant reminder that we relate to God, or to the source and ground of all that is, in a way that no language of ours can grasp. In this regard, the divine Name is paradigmatic of the proper name in general. Proper naming, as revealed exemplarily by the Name of God, marks the site of the unnameable in the midst of every naming and thus at the foundation of language. Pure proper naming can only be a naming of noth-ing, at least of nothing that is sayable. Any kind of semantic content ascribed to it violates the nature of the proper name and is idolatrous in relation to God. The Names of God were taken in traditional metaphysical discourse to comprise the categories of being. But they also have a profoundly apophatic significance as ciphers of namelessness, which is brought out by the speculative traditions that Rosenzweig both transmits and elaborates.

Rosenzweig does not present his philosophy expressly as apophatic. Nevertheless, he effectively gives a philosophical rationale for the sorts of theosophies that traditionally have been overtly apophatic in purport and intent, and which he does expressly acknowledge as akin to and as crucial precedents for his own thought. Theosophy, to his own astonishment proves integral and necessary, alongside theology and philosophy, to his project. Theosophy is precisely the triangulation of *theo*logy and philo*sophy*. It affords a "scientific" knowledge pointing beyond words, whereas any approach based on words—"philology"—cannot but remain silent about the mystery in question: "With theology and philosophy, thereby completing the trinity of the sciences—I am stunned and repulsed by this thought—theosophy keeps company. The rest is philo-logy, i.e., silence."[13]

Rosenzweig forges a strangely hybrid discourse for the quasi-theological, quasi-philosophical non-object of his thinking. Loquacious and eloquent, it is different from reasonable, "normal," philosophical discourse, as well as from any average theological language, and its difference has to do with what it does not and cannot say. It is ingeniously resourceful, nevertheless, in inventing ways to talk about the protocosmos and hypercosmos that by rights are purely antithetical to language.

Wittgenstein, like Rosenzweig, discovered the religious, together with the ethical and aesthetic, as the unsayable at the limit of language. However, he did not appropriate the positive content of religious revelation as indirectly articulating and expressing this Inexpressible, in the way Rosenzweig does. On the contrary, it remained mute for him. Hence his famous injunction: "About that of which we cannot speak we must remain silent." Although he realizes that what we cannot speak about is what inspires art, religion, and ethics, he does not recognize these discourses as languages for the unsayable: it remains for him simply and strictly inexpressible. He is focused on the moment of collapse of logical sense (and thus of language, for him) vis-à-vis the unsayable. Wittgenstein considers the value-discourses of ethics, art, and religion as forms of nonsense rather than of language. He recognizes something

---

13. "'Urzelle' des *Stern der Erlösung*," pp. 137–138: "Zu *Theologie* und *Philosophie* gesellt sich, so das Dreieck der Wissenschaften abschließend—ich bin selber noch erstaunt und widerwillig gegen diesen Gedanken—die Theosophie. Der Rest ist Philologie, d. h. Schweigen."

miraculous about them, but he does not, like Rosenzweig, follow up the various "theosophical" attempts to lend language beyond rational discourse to this unsayability. For Wittgenstein, the way of exploring this *terra incognita* is not available to philosophy. One needs other means and methods: those of art, ethics, and religion.

Heidegger, like Wittgenstein and contemporaneously with Rosenzweig, undertook a rethinking of philosophy in linguistic terms—and he, too, discovered the apophatic dimension of language. Rosenzweig's realization of the "linguistic turn," however, has a special twist to it in that the biblical tradition, out of which he thinks, was based all along on revelation by the Word rather than on the purely intellectual contemplation of being or the pure empirical intuition of sense-perception. Whereas the Greek tradition, especially as Heidegger rediscovered it, was a thinking of being, Rosenzweig's Judeo-Christian tradition in its deepest sources and inspiration is already a thinking of the word. Here the unsayable at the origin of all possibility of saying is not fundamentally Being or the transcendent One but the Word in its transcendent instance, paradigmatically, the unnameable Divine Name. This provides different motives for unsayability, even though the ineffability of the Name and that of Being or the One are tightly intertwined from early on in the Western tradition.

Beings have their unsayable origin in Being itself, as Heidegger demonstrates, but there is also an unsayable instance within language. The revelation of the word itself reveals something unsayable. This unsayable is a stranger to being and is perhaps much more radically unsayable or, more properly, unnameable. This, for Rosenzweig, is to forsake Athens for Jerusalem: the latter, not the former, is claimed as cultural source of a true and eternal tradition. It means beginning from responsibility to the Other rather than listening for intimations of the disclosure of Being, as in the presocratic thought revived by Heidegger. The relevant watchwords are not those of perceiving or conceiving things, but rather of relating to others and to the absolutely Other. This, according to Rosenzweig, is the interruption interjected by Hebraism into the philosophical tradition of the West as a perennial challenge, particularly since Christianity appeared on the Hellenistic scene, reviving the biblical prophets' proclamation of a transcendent, divine Word. This specifically Hebraic inspiration was vigorously reasserted by Maimonides in the Middle Ages, and it still is asserted in various forms of poetry and theory today. We have seen that this is a distinct approach, distinct from apophasis vis-à-vis pure Being. What it approaches, however, may turn out to be indiscernibly inexpressible in any language whatever.

III

Rosenzweig's work is continued directly by Levinas. The language of Levinas's philosophy is apparently very different, for he does not adopt the systematic terms and structures of his predecessor. Yet he was acutely aware of his unsayably great indebtedness to Rosenzweig.[14] The claim of a distinctively Hebraic thinking that is fundamentally a thinking of language rather than of being unites these two philosophers in a radical critique of all philosophy governed by Logos. As a thinking and saying *of being*, the Logos always has its object before it. The Logos of philosophy is nothing but what it *can* say. It says *what is*, and in doing so forgets what is before being and saying. Logos is purely a knowing and is circumscribed by this knowing. Language, in contrast, originates in an unknowing and retains the traces of what precedes being and is radically other to itself: it is open toward what it cannot comprehend or say. Language is always already open toward an other in and with which it originates as address or call. It is not grounded on anything manifest and given like being. From this perspective, Levinas's philosophy in its entirety reads as a highly original development of the seminal insights of Rosenzweig.

Levinas's thought turns on the idea of an alterity that withdraws from the world of reckonable, commensurable, articulable values and meanings, and this means essentially from all that can be expressed in language. Levinas probes human reality in ways that burst asunder the schemata of philosophy and of any Logos. Nevertheless, it is precisely language that announces this absolute, incommensurable alterity. Following cues of Heidegger concerning "das Sagen," Saying, and even more directly Rosenzweig's ideas about language, Levinas interprets language fundamentally not as system or sign but as "address." This "address" of language as such—language defined as transcending all manifest linguistic forms and as simply the naked appeal of the Other—Levinas calls the Face of the Other. The Face of the Other speaks as an irrecusable ethical appeal that obligates me even before I am free to choose.

Although not in any manifest phenomenon of language, of words or sounds, the Face speaks. It calls those who see it to unconditional responsibility in relation to the Other. It does this by undoing the normal function of language to thematize or to categorize beings in some way: "The face is a living

---

14. In the preface to *Autrement qu'être et au de-là de l'essence* (Paris: Livre de Poche, 1990 [1974]), Levinas avows that his debt to Rosenzweig is too pervasive to be specified, though he does manage to say more about it in his preface to Stéphane Mosès's study of Rosenzweig, *Système et révélation*.

presence, it is expression. The life of the expression consists in undoing the form wherein the being, exposing itself as theme, by that very token is dissimulated. The face speaks. The manifestation of the face is already discourse."[15] This is discourse, however, before articulate language. It is naked appeal and obligation. It means something that breaks out of the web of references in which the language of Being consists. It is an absolute, an ethical imperative that cannot be reduced to any words. "Speech" arises from the Face of the Other in that this Face resists being understood in terms of any other context or totality and calls us to unconditional ethical responsibility (p. 211ff.).

For Levinas, the face-to-face of relation of one human being with another is an origin for the intelligibility of things that does not presuppose any prior disclosedness of beings. Our being in relation to others, blindly and helplessly, without any conscious control or conceptual mastery, precedes all sense and intelligibility of objects that we are able to grasp and conceptualize. It is the hidden ground or precondition or, better yet, *in*condition for anything making sense or being significant to humans. This ethical situation also translates the underlying sense of the Word of God. The constant message of the Bible is responsibility for the other: not to forget the widow, the orphan, and the stranger within your gates, as the prophets relentlessly insist. The Word of God speaking in the Face of the Other has a sense or significance beyond being and transcending all that can be said. It is a *signifyingness* that no being can contain, nor any saying confer. They can only reduce it to their own immanent terms, losing the ethical significance of relation to transcendence.

Levinas presents this inherently ethical thinking as more originary than the originally Hellenic thinking of being. Hebraism thus takes on universal significance. It lays claim to harboring the deepest root of philosophical thought, which emerges, like all forms of human sense, out of relation to the Other—to human others and thereby also potentially to a transcendent Other. It begins from transcendence rather than immanence—from the transcendence of the Other, that is, the other person, rather than from the immanence of Being. Before any Logos that discloses Being, and beyond the reach of language and Logos and disclosure, the unsayable, undiscloseable Other orients and gives meaning to all possibilities of discourse. In this sense, Levinas's thought is originarily attuned to the unsayable.

---

15. Levinas, *Totalité et infini: Essai sur l'extériorité* (Paris: Livre de Poche, 1971 [1961]): "Le visage est une présence vivante, il est expression. La vie de l'expression consiste à défaire la forme où l'étant, s'exposant comme thème, se dissimule par là même. Le visage parle. La manifestation du visage est déjà discours" (p. 61).

And yet, paradoxically, Levinas finds this unsayable precisely in Saying. The Face itself, in its very muteness, is a Saying, an appealing for ethical responsibility and justice. As such, the Face speaks. Levinas interprets the message that speaks to me from the Face as the *Dire* (Saying) in contrast to the *Dit* (Said). Not any visible phenomenon but a Saying that cannot itself be said is the ethical import of the Face. It claims me by its naked vulnerability and neediness and makes me its unconditional servant, a "hostage." This is a Saying which can never be said, for that would reduce its absoluteness to common terms of rationality. It is to this extent apophatic: there is an unbridgeable distance, beyond logical or analogical mediation, between Saying and the Said.

Levinas devised this vocabulary at least partly in response to Derrida's objections to his *Totality and Infinity* (*Totalité et infini*, 1961). Derrida pointed out that it was not possible for Levinas to escape the language of being so long as he was still saying all this in philosophical language. In his later work, *Otherwise than Being or Beyond Essence* (*Autrement qu'être et au-delà de l'essence*, 1974), Levinas maintained that the ethical instance beyond being, as what cannot be said, is nevertheless betrayed by the "indiscretion" of what is said. This indiscretion of the Said provides the language that makes it possible to say that which is otherwise than being, the "outside" or the "ex-ception" to being. By dint of such indiscretion, the Other occurs as an event within being. But this translation of Saying into the Said is inevitably a betrayal of the unsayable. *Traduction* cannot but be *trahison*: "Betrayal at the price of which all shows itself, even the unsayable, and which renders possible indiscretion with regard to the unsayable that is probably the very task of philosophy."[16]

Philosophy's task, as Levinas understands it, is to foster and presumably to interpret this indiscretion with regard to the unsayable. This means "reducing" the Said that betrays and covers over Saying in a way that lets us discern the Saying: "The unsayable Saying lends itself to the Said, to the ancillary indiscretion of abusive language that vulgarizes or profanes the unsayable, but lets itself be reduced, without effacing the unsayable in the ambiguity or in the enigma of the transcendent, where the out-of-breath spirit retains an echo that becomes remote."[17] Thus, this unsayable Saying ("le Dire indicible") is

---

16. "Trahison au prix de laquelle tout se montre, même l'indicible et par laquelle est possible l'indiscrétion à l'égard de l'indicible qui est probablement la tâche même de la philosophie" (*Autrement qu'être et au-delà de l'essence*, p. 19).

17. "Le Dire indicible se prête au Dit, à l'indiscrétion ancillaire du langage abusif qui divulgue ou profane l'indicible, mais se laisse réduire, sans effacer l'indicible dans l'ambiguïté ou dans l'énigme du transcendant où l'esprit essoufflé retient un écho qui s'éloigne" (ibid., p. 76).

signaled only in the indiscretion and abuse of language, and only in disappearing like a fading echo. Description becomes necessarily tenuous, but clearly there is some trace in language of something not yet altogether effaced. It is figured as an unsayable Saying, which is betrayed by what is said.

The ineffable transcendence discovered in the ethical relation to the Other cannot be comprehended and articulated, but rather dis-articulates me from my origin as self-conscious subject and freely choosing agent. It is an "an-archic" ("pre-originary") openness of the self to the Other. This disarticulation or unsaying is the indiscretion of the Said that betrays the Saying that is within it. This deformation of language is essentially apophasis, or at least its effect. In fact, in a vocabulary of precisely apophatic resonance, Levinas calls it "a saying that must also unsay itself" ("un dire qui doit aussi se dédire," *Autrement qu'être*, p. 19).

Levinas stresses that testimony or witness forms a positive counterpart to the negation of representability that characterizes the transcendent as such. His various terms for absolute ethical responsibility (for instance, proximity, substitution) on the part of a subject, who in this regard bears witness to an alterity that cannot be directly perceived, supply a positivity in the place left empty by the denial of representation in purely negative theology. He writes of "negation of the present and of representation which finds in the 'positivity' of proximity, responsibility, and substitution a difference with respect to the propositions of negative theology."[18] Levinas here evokes a stereotyped caricature based on what the label "*negative* theology" prima facie suggests. But as concretely developed by any of its eminent practitioners, negative theology has always been accompanied by some positive form of witness, such as Levinas himself also outlines. Pseudo-Dionysius the Areopagite intertwines negative with affirmative theology and braids them into a mystical theology that suspends and surpasses the negative-positive polarity in the experience of a "luminous darkness." Generally, prayer, poetry, and even sacramental rites step in as witness where affirmations by predicative propositions prove impossible. Elaborating on the "hyper" or "plus quam," more-than-positive propositions of Pseudo-Dionysius, John Scott Eriugena's negative theology actually consists in "hyper-phatic" super-affirmations. Something similar can be shown for proponents of negative theology all through apophatic history down to Jean-Luc Marion. And while both Levinas and Rosenzweig make a show of rejecting the tradition of negative theology, both depend on it (or

---

18. "Négation du présent et de la représentation qui trouve dans la 'positivité' de la proximité, de la responsabilité et de la substitution une différence par rapport aux propositions de la théologie négative" (ibid., p. 237).

unwittingly imitate it) to articulate a reversal that is not dialectical but quin-tessentially apophatic—not a negation of something definite that is posited, but an evocation of what is not and cannot be posited as such or in words.[19]

In reality, Levinas's discourse of the ethical is deeply indebted to the apophatic tradition. This is evident even from his own descriptions of its an-tecedents:

> In Greek philosophy one can already discern traces of the ethical breaking
> through the ontological, for example, in Plato's idea of the 'good existing
> beyond being' (*agathon epekeina tes ousias*). . . . And similarly, supra-
> ontological notions are to be found in the Pseudo-Dionysian doctrine of
> the *via eminentiae*, with its surplus of the divine over being, or in the Au-
> gustinian distinction in the *Confessions* between the truth that challenges
> (*veritas redarguens*) and the ontological truth that shines (*veritas lucens*),
> and so on.[20]

The genealogy alluded to here is clearly inscribed into key junctures in Levinas's *oeuvre*. The programmatic statement in the preface to *De l'existence à l'existant* presents the relation to the Other as a movement toward the Good and cites the Platonic topos of the Good beyond Being as the guiding light, or *Leitmotif*, of his researches: "The Platonic formula placing the Good beyond being is the most general and the most empty indication that guides them."[21] This motif recurs in all of Levinas's major subsequent writings.[22] In his essay "La trace de l'autre" Levinas adds Plotinus to the list of his predecessors, quot-ing Plotinus to the effect that Being is the trace of the One.[23] In this essay Le-vinas also makes reference to the One of the first hypothesis of Plato's *Par-

---

19. Kevin Hart, in *The Trespass of the Sign: Deconstruction, Theology and Philosophy* (Cambridge: Cambridge University Press, 1989), chapter 6, brings out the broader sense of "negative theology" that exempts it from the critique of metaphysics, contrary to the assumptions underlying Levinas's statements against negative theology.

20. Levinas, "Dialogue with Emmanuel Levinas," in *Face to Face with Levinas*, ed. Richard A. Cohen (Albany: SUNY Press, 1986), p. 25.

21. Levinas, *De l'existence à l'existant*, 2nd ed. (Paris: Vrin, 1984 [1st ed. 1948]): "La formule platonicienne plaçant le Bien au-delà de l'être est l'indication la plus générale et la plus vide qui les guide."

22. Imposing full-scale studies of Levinas's thought turn on the importance of this orientation. See Thomas Wiemer, *Die Passion des Sagens: Zur Deutung der Sprache bei Emmanuel Levinas und ihrer Realisierung im philosophischen Diskurs* (Freiburg and Mu-nich: Alber, 1988), and Antje Kapust, *Berührung ohne Berührung: Ethik und Ontologie bei Merleau-Ponty und Levinas* (Munich: Wilhelm Fink Verlag, 1999), p. 11.

23. "La Trace de l'autre," in *En découvrant l'existence avec Husserl et Heidegger* (Paris: Vrin, 1974), pp. 187–202. An English translation, "The Trace of the Other," can be

menides as "neither similar nor dissimilar, neither identical nor non-identical," as beyond all possibility of being revealed. Everything that can be expressed, that *is* and that makes up the world of things that exist, is a trace of this One— or Other—that is irrevocably beyond Being but nevertheless determines the significance of everything that is, and even the very "signifyingness" of human subjectivity.

Levinas refers to the One that *is not,* the One that is before being, in Plato's *Parmenides* and in Plotinus as adumbrating a transcendence beyond all binary oppositions. It is beyond the opposition between transcendence and imma- nence and is rather a "third way" between transcendence and immanence. This is the radically Other of ethical experience, which is an Other absolutely alien to every possibility of representation and expression. It bears a signifi- cance, or better a "signifyingness" that is anterior to every language and is rather the presupposition of any language.

Of course, these precedents, insisted on by Levinas himself, do not di- minish the radical nature of his break with the tradition of the thinking of Being. They merely show that the break was there all along, inherent in this tradition itself. It is accomplished by the apophatic and negative theological countercurrents within this tradition that render its terms equivocal—as they must be, given the fundamental inadequacy of language in treating what it cannot say.

For Levinas, language is ethical transcendence. He is the philosopher who, after Rosenzweig, most deliberately supplants the thinking of being by a thinking of the word. The word comes from beyond being. Nevertheless, it is a word that must remain unspoken, unsaid, and even unsayable, if it is to be Saying itself. Language as communication opens a dimension that is beyond being and therefore beyond being said. Traditionally, this beyond-all-that- can-be-said, which is Saying itself, was meditated on as the Name of God. Le- vinas clearly suggests in a passage at the climax of *Autrement qu'être,* where his own philosophical activity comes to consciousness of itself as a labor of love, that his thought as a whole can be understood as an attempt to interpret the inevitable mistranslation of the ineffable Name of God into articulate speech. His overturning of the discourse of being issues in a discourse on the Name of God. Again, this is a translation that is necessarily a betrayal:

> God—unique proper name that does not enter into any grammatical category—does it enter without difficulty—into the vocative?—and thus,

---

found in *Deconstruction in Context: Literature and Philosophy,* ed. Mark C. Taylor (Chicago: University of Chicago Press, 1986), pp. 345–359.

not thematisable and which, even here, is a theme only because in a Said everything before us is translated, even the ineffable, at the price of a betrayal that philosophy is called to reduce . . . [24]

The indiscretion of language that is the only means by which the Other can be translated/betrayed is epitomized by the Name of God. This is "perhaps" only a word—perhaps there is nothing to which it corresponds—yet it maintains itself in an ambiguity and an enigma that marks the openness of language to what it cannot comprehend. This word like perhaps no other opens language to the *fortior mei*, the stronger-than-I, that enables it to be witness and inspiration, a testimony to what is absolutely beyond language. This word marks the hole in the middle of language at the point where language would be grounded and founded as a whole, if that were not made impossible by the dependence of language on what escapes and exceeds it. For Levinas, the language of being, which turns on the unsayable of Saying, must be elucidated in terms of the Name of God as the submerged non-essence and incondition of all language. The approach to the unsayable through being thereby collapses into an approach through language, just as it did for Rosenzweig. And again we find ourselves focusing on the exceptional status of the Divine Name.

Levinas describes the ambiguity in the *Said* that permits *Saying* to be glimpsed behind it as "the resonance of every language 'to the name of God,' inspiration by the prophetism of all language" ("la résonance de tout langage 'au nom de Dieu', inspiration au prophétisme de tout langage," *Autrement qu'être*, p. 237). All language, by being addressed to the Other, prophesies the coming of the incommensurable, the strange and unassimilable that crushes and ruptures the self-enclosure and sufficiency of the self and the same. In this way, all language "resonates" to the unnameable Name of God: it invokes what it cannot say or absorb, that before which it can only grow dumb in awe. The ambiguity of whatever can be said consists in the "oscillation" between visible presence in the Face and the transcendent Other that it reveals as not present, not said (p. 246).

---

24. "Dieu—nom propre et unique n'entrant dans aucune catégorie grammaticale—entre-t-il sans gêne—dans le vocatif?—et, ainsi, non thématisable et qui, ici-même, n'est thème que parce que, dans un Dit, tout se traduit devant nous, même l'ineffable, au prix d'une trahison que la philosophie est appelée à réduire" (*Autrement qu'être*, pp. 252–253).

Rosenzweig, Levinas, and also Benjamin are heirs to much fundamental reflection on the topic of the unsayable that has revolved around the mysteries of naming and in particular of the Divine Name. In monotheistic traditions, a great deal of thought has been devoted to the question of how any possible naming, and consequently language as such, is grounded on the unnameable Name of God. The Divine Name serves as the absolute paradigm of what cannot itself be said but nevertheless (un)grounds the possibility of language and thus renders possible the saying of all that can be said. At this limit of the sayable, certain remarkable, even "mystical" (Wittgenstein) or "magical" (Benjamin) properties of language are discovered. Here alone, at the limits of language, is it possible to relate to things as a whole, or better, as unlimited, as infinity. Whatever can be said and articulated is no longer whole in the sense of in-tact (untouched) and ab-solute (unsevered)—as is betrayed by the words themselves, since they are produced by negation. The said is no longer able, therefore, to contain immanently, or in anticipation, all that is and that can be articulated. It is the infinite, indivisible power, or rather potential, of what cannot be said that enables us, by the verbal alchemy of negation, to gather an intimation of all that *is* before its emergence into distinctness as determinate being. Thus, at this limit of silence represented by the unpronounceable Divine Name, inquiry necessarily entails an attempt to pry into the mystery of language and its formative—which means also its delimiting—role with respect to the world and its component parts and limits. This seems to be the only possible path of approach to the unworldly or perhaps otherworldly—to what is beyond the bounds of any world that we can know and describe.

Both the unnameable Name of God in revealed religions and the One in Neoplatonic discourse play the role of the unsayable source of all saying, and indeed of all being. Agreement on an inarticulable first principle, recognized as supreme principle and source of all, allowed the integration of Neoplatonism into monotheistic apophatic traditions and especially into their mystical offshoots, such as Islamic Sufism, Jewish Kabbalah, and Christian mysticisms. This marriage of philosophy and faith, each in its own way beholden to what cannot be said, was the secret cement that held together the very diverse and even conflictual culture of the Middle Ages in a sort of tenuous synthesis. It came apart, or at least went underground, during the Renaissance—except in a few authors such as Giordano Bruno (1500–1550), who preserved the remembrance of what cannot be said, despite cataclysmic upheavals in the Western conception of the physical and geographical universe, and interpreted these outward dislocations as the verification of the crisis inscribed in language itself.

The historical interdependence of apophatic and metaphysical approaches to the question of the unsayable and especially of the Names of God suggests a vital connection that deserves to be reactivated. Apophasis opens avenues for reinterpreting the metaphysical tradition in ways that elude Heideggerian and post-Heideggerian critiques of metaphysics. It makes possible a rewriting of the history of Western thinking from the standpoint of what it could never say but nevertheless hinted at indirectly, by developing alternative modes of expression for what evades statement in propositional discourse. From this perspective, the deconstruction of metaphysics was already in full swing among the Neoplatonists in the ancient world. Heidegger's history of metaphysics largely ignores this Neoplatonic phase of Greek thinking, in which the ontological difference between Being and beings, which opens a space even for the "beyond" of Being, was never forgotten but remained a main preoccupation of philosophy—though a concern refractory to discourse. In this way, the deeper apophatic meaning of metaphysical traditions turns out to render them, if not immune to attacks, at least capable of absorbing them, and of being resurrected on a new ground—or rather, groundlessness.

Jean-Luc Marion's intervention in the contemporary discussion concerning the Names of God has just such a bearing. Marion answers criticisms from postmodern deconstructionist and antimetaphysical thinkers by showing that traditional Christian discourses on the divine Names by church fathers such as John Chrysostom, Gregory of Nyssa, Dionysius, and Theophilus already harbor a complete deconstruction of the metaphysics of presence. God is recognized by these early Christian theologians writing in Greek, who borrowed but also purged concepts of Greek metaphysics, as unnameable. Procedures of "de-naming" ("de-nomination," akin to Derrida's "dé-négation"), or of rendering anonymous, are key to this Christian-theological rethinking of the concept and reality of God in terms of naming and unnaming.

Marion considers his way to be a "third way" beyond affirmation and negation. The failure of the name is not due to the lack of a phenomenon that gives an experience of God—quite the opposite. The excess of the intuition of divine self-giving to any possibility of being conceptualized or named is what most concerns Christian theologians in the apophatic tradition from its Greek patristic roots. This experience expresses itself in terms of stupor and terror, testifying to an insupportable excess in the intuition of God. It is the basis for the negative theology made canonical by Dionysius, in which God can never be properly known or named according to his essence. What exceeds name and concept Marion understands in terms of a phenomenology of the "gift," and the "gift" he understands fundamentally in terms of the Eucharist. Eucharistic Christianity (Catholicism), as a positive testimony of apophatic negativity, thus points to a new horizon for apophatic expression.

Just as the experience of Judaism as cult and praxis within the broader Judeo-Christian tradition permitted Rosenzweig to think apophatically in a manner that opened a path for a modern philosophy of the unsayable, so Marion begins from a form not only of thought but of life that silently embodies the unsayable in an actual human practice. Marion's analysis of apophasis is rooted essentially in the Christian experience of the Eucharist, that is, of corporeal assimilation into community in the body of Christ. As the most concrete of theological mysteries, the Eucharist is also the least comprehensible. It is the greatest challenge ("défie") to thought, defying rational expression. Christ's gift of his body in the Eucharist resists all conceptual explications, whether these are cast in terms of "transubstantiation" or invoke the idea of the unity of the community in a single eucharistic consciousness. The Eucharist is an action, or rather passion, of the body offered up to be informed and deformed by a love that it cannot master or articulate verbally. The eucharistic "present" is possible only with the abandonment of conceptualization. The beaten, bloody body of Christ bears signs of love that become the witness to self-sacrifice and self-opening to the inexpressibly other. Practiced at the levels both of ritual actions and of consequent acts of charity, the Eucharist exceeds verbalization. It involves an emptiness of conceptual content that is filled with activity and action-producing passion or affect realized as a self-giving beyond rational motivation and comprehension.

In the experience of the Eucharist, Christian faith thus becomes exemplary of openness to genuine otherness: experience as such is revealed as eucharistic, that is, as open to the gift of the Other. In Marion's eucharistic phenomenology of the gift, the temporalities of ritual re-memoration and eschatological expectation interpenetrate and dispossess the present. The Eucharistic present—the "gift"—is not the presence of "substance" (for traditional Catholics) nor the unity of "consciousness" in the present moment of community (for certain Protestants), but the continual self-giving of love: a bodily breaking and exceeding of self in the gift of self to the other. This theology of the Eucharist entails a refounding of phenomenology, which is really an *un*founding of it by incorporation of the lessons of negative theology.[25] The

25. Marion pursues his refounding of phenomenology in terms of the idea of the gift in *Réduction et donation: Recherches sur Husserl, Heidegger et la phénomenologie* (Paris: Presses Universitaires de France, 1989).

purpose is not to suppress anything positive but to liberate the phenomenon from the falsifications that language inevitably effects.

The future of apophasis, indeed the future as such belongs, beyond all that is said, to what is actually done. It is ironic that a traditional form of life such as Catholicism should point a way out of postmodern impasses of reflection and towards the limitless expanses opened by apophasis. Marion's thought is a timely reminder that there is a decisively negative theological side to Christian theology, though it has often been muted by the strong claims of incarnate revelation.[26] This negative side comes back to life in times like the present, when many theologians are skeptical about language and sensitive to the danger of idolatry (about which Jewish theology had always been exceptionally vigilant). No less radically than in Jewish theology of the unnameable Name, the divine names, particularly as employed in eucharistic practice, designate what one does not and cannot know or name. Any name of God serves not as a means for humans to affirm or deny anything about God, but rather as a means for them to *be* named—to be called, or summoned beyond themselves to a life in God. "The Name—we must inhabit it without saying it, but rather letting ourselves be said, named, called in it. The name is not said, it calls."[27] In some respects, this is exactly the conclusion that Levinas, pursuing insights opened up by Rosenzweig, reaches on the basis of Jewish tradition. We are called by an unsayable Saying to respons-ibility that precedes every Said, every possible formulation in words.

---

26. Incarnation, of course, can also become a modality of apophasis. The essays in *Silence and the Word: Negative Theology and Incarnation,* ed. Davies and Turner, explore indirect ways in which incarnation can connive with apophasis rather than oppose it. Critiquing George Steiner's "language-silence dualism," Graham Ward, in "'In the daylight forever?': Language and Silence," argues for a quasi-transcendence that recognizes silence as incarnate in language. Like Marion, he points to a "eucharistic" dimension of apophasis, for example, in Derrida's use of *kenosis,* the self-emptying of God in the incarnate Word, which becomes an allegory for deconstruction; or in the angelology of Michel Serres, which makes the messages descending apparently from nowhere upon the modern city's communication networks incarnate in the technological mediators of those tidings—the medium itself becomes the message.

27. Jean-Luc Marion, "Au Nom: Comment ne pas parler de 'Théologie Négative,'" *Laval théologique et philosophique* 55/3 (1999): 339–363: "Le Nom—il faut y habiter sans le dire, mais en s'y laissant nous-mêmes dire, nommer, appeler. Le Nom ne se dit pas, il appelle" (p. 363).

IV

In the preceding sections, this historical introduction has hewed close to the philosophical and theological ground-concepts and infrastructures of apophatic thought, as formulated by some of its major exponents, that serve to stake out decisive turnings and successive stages in the modern and contemporary history of apophatic discourse.[28] But, as a number of references have already suggested, in addition to and in conjunction with these traditions of apophatic thought in philosophy and theology, artists and poets in all ages have given compelling testimonies to what cannot be said. The modern and contemporary periods have been especially prodigal in apophatically-pitched discourses and productions in all the arts.

Among countless poets of the unsayable, a few distinguish themselves for the programmatic way in which the theme of the unsayable emerges at the center of their work and at the core of their act of making poetry. Dante, in his culminating work, the *Paradiso*, and with him Rumi and John of the Cross, stand as maximum medieval classics in this genre. Friedrich Hölderlin, Emily Dickinson, Rainer Maria Rilke, T. S. Eliot, Paul Celan, and Wallace Stevens (for example, in "Notes Toward a Supreme Fiction") serve as further canonical representatives of this vein of poetry in modern literature. While perhaps most poets, especially in modern and postmodern times so traumatized by the crisis of language, touch on the theme of the unsayable, and while many have made enduring contributions, these poets in particular may serve as touchstones of a latently apophatic vocation perhaps of poetry per se as we are able understand it today, at least in its most extreme ambitions and aspirations.

The idea of poetry as apophatic expression uttering "thoughts too deep for words" is already a commonplace in the most familiar Romantic poetry. Wordsworth's *Prelude* turns on ineffable moments of insight, interruptive of time. And his "Ode on Intimations of Immortality from Early Childhood" says of such moments that they "have power to make / Our noisy years seem moments in the being of the eternal Silence." A related conception governs Coleridge's "Frost at Midnight," whose fitfull, nervous mode conveys the sense of contact with inexpressible calm and stillness:

---

28. *Flight of the Gods: Philosophical Perspectives on Negative Theology*, ed. Isle N. Bulhof and Laurens ten Kate (New York: Fordham University Press, 2000), somewhat analogously traces the "minimalist" echoes of the history of negative theology in contemporary thinkers.

'Tis calm indeed! so calm, that it disturbs
And vexes meditation with its strange
And extreme silentness.

A transcendent power of silence speaking in the immanence of excessive sensation is enshrined perhaps most exquisitely of all in Keats's "Ode on a
Grecian Urn." This "still unravished bride of quietness," this "foster child of silence," can express a tale more sweetly than Keats's rhymes can, precisely
because it does not speak. Its melodies are the more ravishing in that they remain "unheard." The poem is most expressive in illustrating all that it does not
and cannot say by projecting it onto the urn as silent artifact. This container
for death gathers into its rapturous silence the sacrifice of life actually depicted
on it in the shape of the "mysterious priest" leading a heifer to the "green altar."
The sensuous liveliness of the scenes appearing on the urn's surface interprets
a higher intensity of life that mysteriously speaks from the inanimate urn,
giving voice to its muteness and emptiness. In this respect, Keats's Romantic
lushness of description already enfolds the sense of unattainability—and the
consequent resort to "negative capability"—that have become keynotes of
contemporary apophatic poetry.

The themes of apophatic plenitude, or of the power and richness of silence, are pervasive in modern poetry, and post-Romantic poetry generally
registers an increasing consciousness and accentuation of the crisis of language that is embodied in such silence. Baudelaire, Rimbaud, and Mallarmé
with good reason have been treated as founders of a distinctively negative
modern lyric style.[29] Nevertheless, the focus on style for its own sake and on
language itself fights shy of the apophatic passion for what lies beyond language. There is no denying the powerfully apophatic thrust of Mallarmé's poetic project, yet there is perhaps an important nuance of difference between
him and the chief exemplars of this type of discourse: he is focused on his
"grande oeuvre" rather than on anything beyond it, much less on the beyond
of every work.

Mallarmé has enormous standing as the poet of pure language that
evacuates reality, the poet par excellence of the "nothing" ("rien"), the word
with which his collected poems begin (in "Salut") and end (in "À la nue acca-
blante tu"). His poems ideally aim to be approximations to the nothing of si-

29. See Hugo Friedrich, *Die Struktur der modernen Lyrik* (Hamburg: Rowohlt
Taschenbuch Verlag, 1956), especially "Negative Kategorien," p. 19ff., "Das Sagen des
Ungesagten; einige Stilmittel," and "Die Nähe des Schweigens," pp. 88–90.

lence. Words for him, especially written words, are forms of silence. His ideal would be a mute, silent poem of blanks—"poème tu, aux blancs."[30] He famously wrote, "I have created my work only by *elimination*, and all acquired truth was born only from the loss of an impression . . ."[31] Yet the "Nothing, which is the truth" and "Destruction" as his "Beatrice" do not elude him but tend rather to validate a science of form that can become a sort of nihilistic knowledge or truth. By contrast, the apophatic, negative-theological posture does not know what it believes (and disbelieves). Mallarmé (or at least certain epistemological assumptions commonly assigned to this name) knows the truth and knows that it is Nothing.

Consequently, for Mallarmé the silent and unsayable does not open up as a realm of the unknown to be explored. There is for him no realm of the beyond, no beyond of language. His characteristic posture or attitude is one of making exquisitely precise formal determinations rather than of opening consciousness beyond all determination of form to unlimited *un*knowing. In Mallarmé's art, the accent falls on an act of delimitation and not on the *un*delimiting of every possible act of "poiesis." Both gestures pivot on the Nothing, but the one states this Nothing and instrumentalizes it for the sake of its statement—for art's sake—while the other unstates *itself* and surrenders wholly to the Nothing that it cannot state or say.

Caution, therefore, is advisable before amalgamating Mallarmé with any negative theology and its corresponding poetics, although certain powers of apophasis are brilliantly refracted in his work. Mallarmé also has strong affinities with formalist poetics, whereas apophasis exalts formlessness, or the beyond of form, in its quest for the ground beyond all sounding. Compared to Mallarmé, Maurice Maeterlinck and the Belgian symbolists perhaps give a greater sense of the immaculate riches that surface only as tainted by expression in the form of words. In Maeterlinck's own imagery, there is a realm into which the diver delves, but from which only pieces of reflecting glass can be brought back, not the unspeakable treasures of the fathomless depths.[32]

---

30. "Crise de Vers," in *Oeuvres complètes*, ed. Henri Mondor and G. Jean-Aubry (Paris: Pléiade, 1951), p. 367.

31. Letter to Eugène Lafébure, May 17, 1867, in Mallarmé, *Correspondance*, ed. Henri Mondor, 8th ed. (Paris: Gallimard, 1959), pp. 245–246. In a letter to Henri Cazalis of May 14, 1867, Mallarmé writes of his unrecountable ("inénarrable") experience of Eternity and of a "Conception Pure" (p. 240).

32. Cf. Rosmarie Waldrop, *Against Language? 'Dissatisfaction with Language' as Theme and as Impulse Towards Experiments in Twentieth Century Poetry* (The Hague: Mouton, 1971), p. 17ff.

Marjorie Perloff, in *The Poetics of Indeterminacy*, distinguishes a "Symbol-ist mode," running through Baudelaire, Eliot, and the great Romantics, from an anti-symbolist mode, turning on indeterminacy and undecidability, that she traces from Rimbaud. Borrowing a phrase from John Ashbery, she dubs this second current "the other tradition."[33] Apophatic poetics as I construe them share much in common but do not simply coincide with Perloff's po-etics of indeterminacy. Perloff opposes her poetics of indeterminacy to Sym-bolist poetics in that there is no longer any grounding for images in a real world or in any kind of reference beyond text and image themselves. What I am suggesting instead is that indeterminacy is encountered precisely in the (necessarily futile) effort to approach and appropriate—to name or say—the ground or object of which discourse is speaking. The idea of a grounding of language in something outside it is still operative and indeed paramount, however elusive and even "impossible" such grounding becomes.

Rimbaud serves as founding figure for Perloff's "other tradition," but not necessarily for apophatic poetics as I understand them. Rimbaud, like Mallarmé, pushed poetry to the limits of language as radically as anyone ever has, and he ends his career in literal silence more consistent than any self-proclaimed poet or prophet of silence. Moreover, Rimbaud is much more the mystic than Mallarmé: "un mystique *à l'état sauvage*," as Paul Claudel char-acterized him.[34] Nevertheless, he does not leave the impression of having been absorbed into a Beyond more powerful and captivating than the world of words, but rather of having simply forsaken this whole world *as* nothing and of having done so *for* nothing else—not for any mystically intuited "other" re-ality that cannot be said.

Rimbaud's *Illuminations* bears a title that might well hail from the apophatic tradition, yet the apparent blocking of external referentiality for his "illuminations" isolates the text as artifact imploding into itself. At least, Perloff reads him this way—"Indeed, external reference seems peculiarly ir-relevant in the case of these poems" (p. 45)—although I am not sure she is right to do so. Do not Rimbaud's words also explode outward into an infinity or "Éternité" such as never has been nor ever could be articulated or even imagined? Continual contradictions do not necessarily block meaning *tout court*; they can, on the contrary, break open all finite, determinate meanings into the infinite.

---

33. Marjorie Perloff, *The Poetics of Indeterminacy: Rimbaud to Cage* (Princeton: Princeton University Press, 1981), p. vii.

34. Claudel's preface to Rimbaud's *Poésies complètes* (Paris: Gallimard, 1960), p. 5.

These especially tricky cases aside, it is not difficult to discern a genre of poems about their own impossibility and about the impediments to their being written. The genre would comprise examples such as Coleridge's "Dejection: An Ode," Yeats's "The Circus Animals' Desertion," Gerard Manley Hopkins's "To R.B.," and Dylan Thomas's "On No Work of Words."[35] It is hard to resist adding T. S. Eliot's *Four Quartets*, self-described as "a raid on the / inarticulate" and an "intolerable wrestle / With words and meanings." "Burnt Norton," on the "still point of the turning world" and the descent into the darkness of the "World not world" (sections II and III), and "East Coker," with its evocations of the dark night of the soul (section III), are deliberate transmissions of negative theology. The same vein of apophatic tradition stemming from John of the Cross is further mined by Geoffrey Hill in *Tenebrae* (1979).

Another poet who has gained considerable recognition as peculiarly adept at exploiting silences and the failures of language is Elizabeth Bishop.[36] Indeed, negative poetics, the language of failure, and the failure of language, are strongly asserted throughout a wide range of contemporary American poetry.[37] The tendency has been to lose faith in language and in the self that constructs itself in language, paradigmatically in Walt Whitman's "Song of Myself"—which, however, pivots in the end on something in him, he knows not what, a mystery "without name—it is a word unsaid" (sec. 50). Contemporary poetry simply radicalizes the apophatic predicament that is seldom hard to find in poetic expressions of nearly every age. The so-called deep image school, numbering poets such as James Wright, Robert Bly, Galway Kinnell, and Mark Strand, is especially attuned to poetry as a resonating of silence and of what cannot be said in words. Exceptionally talented at feeling out verbal forms that convey a sense of the unsayable is W. S. Merwin, who avows in "The

---

35. See Dwight Eddins, "Darkness Audible: The Poem of Poetic Failure," *Style* 34/3 (Fall 2000), special issue entitled "Go Figure: Troping the Unspeakable," pp. 402–420.

36. See Jerome Mazzaro, "Elizabeth Bishop and the Poetics of Impediment," *Salgamundi* 27 (1974): 118–144. See also Margaret Dickie, "The Love Poetry of Elizabeth Bishop: Silent and Silenced," in *Semantics of Silences in Linguistics and Literature,* ed. Gudrun M. Grabher and Ulrike Jessner (Heidelberg: Universitätsverlag C. Winter, 1996), pp. 271–291, and in the same volume, Josef Raab, "Elizabeth Bishop's Autobiographical Silences," pp. 291–308.

37. See, for example, Paul A. Bové, *Deconstructive Poetics: Heidegger and Modern American Poetry* (New York: Columbia University Press, 1980), and Charles Altieri, *Painterly Abstraction in Modernist American Poetry: The Contemporaneity of Modernism* (Cambridge: Cambridge University Press, 1989). For a comparable approach to European authors, see Marjorie Perloff, *Wittgenstein's Ladder: Poetic Language and the Strangeness of the Ordinary* (Chicago: University of Chicago Press, 1996).

Piper" that all he has learned up to "now" is how to be able to say what he cannot say:

> It has taken me till now
> to be able to say
> even this
> it has taken me this long
> to know what I cannot say.[38]

Merwin exquisitely expresses, though with little or no reference to the wider apophatic tradition, an apophatic sensibility that has become pervasive in contemporary poetry. The poet finds that he "cannot call upon words" now that "all my teachers are dead except silence."[39] His poetic task is to interpret "This silence coming at intervals out of the shell of names." In a striking image, he writes that "my words are the garment of what I shall never be / Like the tucked sleeve of a one-armed boy." Merwin explores the language of imagination as a dimension of emptiness that nevertheless reveals the real counterpunctually. His poems consistently suggest that the real is precisely what language is not and cannot say. Realities are summoned powerfully to mind, precisely by the failure of our attempts to represent them. The real is revealed only as the antithesis of ourselves and our representations in language: "Everything that does not need you is real," and thus the problem is "Not that heaven does not exist but / That it exists without us." In a short prose piece, Merwin drives home the irony that saying always misses and must miss its putative object in order to testify to its origin in the unnamed:

> To say what or where we came from has nothing to do with what or where we came from. We do not come from there, any more, but only from each word that proceeds out of the mouth of the unnamed.
> And yet sometimes it is our only way of pointing to who we are.[40]

Similar apophatic emphases are patent in the poetry of other Western languages and cultures. French poets following Rimbaud—the initiator in 1870 of an "epistemic break," as George Steiner maintains in *After Babel*—and

---

38. W. S. Merwin, *Selected Poems* (New York: Atheneum, 1988), p. 154. See Thomas B. Byers, *What I Cannot Say: Self, Word, and World in Whitman, Stevens, and Merwin* (Urbana: University of Illinois Press, 1989).

39. W. S. Merwin, *The Lice: Poems* (New York: Atheneum, 1967), p. 50. The following Merwin quotations are from this volume, pp. 37, 62, 34–35.

40. W. S. Merwin, *The Miner's Pale Children* (New York: Atheneum, 1963), p. 132.

the heirs of Surrealism have been at loggerheads with language in myriad ways. Distinguished examples among contemporary French poets most attuned to the apophatic include Bernard Noël, Eugène Guillevic, and Jean-Louis Chrétien. In "Approches," Guillevic effectively suggests that silence is not just the emptiness that surrounds us like the night, but also something with an unmanifest density of its own that mysteriously engenders desire from within: "There is not just silence alone / to edify our night. // There is also that which makes us / want to live on silence":

> In n'y a pas que le silence
> Pour édifier notre nuit.
>
> Il y a ce qui nous fait
> Vouloir vivre de silence[41]

Hölderlin, Rilke, and Celan form an axis of poets who are preoccupied in fundamental ways with the unsayable, and who bequeath this focus to new generations of poets writing in German.[42] Hermetic poetry of the "absolute Metaphor," for example, in Ingeborg Bachmann or Gottfried Benn, eventually gives place to the taciturnity of the "laconic poem."[43] Saying the least possible, or almost nothing, asserts itself as the least compromised form of communication. Hence Günter Eich's quip: "Every poem is too long!" ("Jedes Gedicht ist zu lang!") and Eugene Gomringer's composition:

> silence silence silence
> silence silence silence
> silence   silence
> silence silence silence
> silence silence silence[44]

---

41. Eugène Guillevic, *Du silence / Von der Stille*, French-German ed., trans. Monika Fahrenbach (Tübingen: Narr, 1997). See also *Art poétique: Poème* (Paris: Gallimard, 1989), p. 81, and *Inclus* (Paris: Gallimard, 1973), #108, p. 123.

42. See Otto Lorenz, *Schweigen in der Dichtung: Hölderlin—Rilke—Celan. Studien zur Poetik deiktisch-elliptischer Schreibweisen* (Göttingen: Vandenhoeck & Ruprecht, 1989). For recent German-language poetry revolving around the breakdown of language, see Michael Braun and Hans Thill, *Das verlorene Alphabet: Deutschsprachige Lyrik der neunziger Jahre* (Heidelberg: Wunderhorn, 2000).

43. Cf. Karl Krolow, "Über das lakonische in der modernen Lyrik," in *Schattengefecht* (Frankfurt a.M.: Suhrkamp, 1964).

44. Eugene Gomringer, *konkrete poesie* (Stuttgart: Reclam, 1972). My translation.

Modern Spanish-language lyric by poets such as Gerardo Diego ("Callar"), Jorge Luis Borges, Jorge Guillén ("Una Puerta"), Antonio Machado, Miguel Unamuno, Alfonsina Storni, Pedro Salinas ("Sí, por detrás de las gentes"), and Octavio Paz has likewise been affected by an apophatic turn focusing on the limits of expression and a longing to step outside and beyond language.[45] However, it is José Ángel Valente who distinguishes himself as true heir to John of the Cross. In a similar spirit, Demetrio Vázquez Apolinar concentrates on poetry as the negation of thought and its verbal expression.[46] In each of these very different linguistic and cultural worlds, a great part of modern poetry has been bent on destroying or eluding language in order to let what is other to language break out or break free.

In contemporary poetry, as in other fields, a significant portion of the culture of the unsayable takes its orientation from Kafka and Beckett, whose works often explicitly recall or play off currents of negative theology. The word is turned to absurdity by always waiting upon what can never arrive, and meanwhile the bases of its sense shift out from under it—even simply through the silent action of a "pause," as in Beckett's *Endgame* and *Waiting for Godot*. Or again, the word revolves around an absolute, yet empty, indeterminate center that commands all, but in ways that never are or could be intelligibly expressed and thus dealt with logically, as in Kafka's *The Castle* and *The Trial*.

Similarly inspired by a fascination with what escapes every form of "language" in whatever media are creative originators in the fine arts, such as Arthur Schoenberg and John Cage, Paul Klee and Kasimir Malevich. Masterly theoretical treatises on painting and music by Malevich and Vladimir Jankélévitch, respectively, explore the far-reaching ramifications of apophasis in these nonverbal modes. These sensuous channels of expression are discovered as lending themselves handsomely to attempts to escape from or deny articulate speech.

Jankélévitch conceives music as a kind of silence, the silence of all other sounds. Music imposes silence upon the ordinary rumble and murmur of the world, which includes especially the droning on of words. By its special order-

---

45. Poetry of the ineffable in Spanish is discussed by Emma Sepúlveda-Pulvirenti, *Los Límites del Lenguaje: Un Acercamiento a la Poética del Silencio* (Madrid: Torremozas, 1990). See also Janet Pérez, "Functions of the Rhetoric of Silence in Contemporary Spanish Literature," *South Central Review* 1/1–2, Spring–Summer (1984).

46. See especially José Ángel Valente, *Variaciones sobre el pájaro y la red. Precedidas de La piedra el centro. Ensayos sobre mística* (Barcelona: Tusquets, 1991), and Demetrio Vázquez Apolinar, *El habla del Ángel* (Mexico: Gobierno del Estado de Guanajuato, 1992).

ing of sound in time, music interrupts the normal continuum of sounds and silences it in order to let something else become audible. This "something else" is its own intricate structuration of sound, of course, but also, more profoundly, something other than sound altogether. As a form of sound able to silence the generality of sound, music becomes a relation to the inaudible. To the extent that what music silences is speech, this is a relation to the ineffable. All noise must cease in order for music to take place. But this is especially true of words: "Music is the silence of words, just as poetry is the silence of prose."[47]

For Jankélévitch, musical silence, or music as silence, is not the void. By inaugurating an audible order more refined than the chaos and confusion of ordinary sound in the world, including the relatively ordered sound of speech, music alludes to an order above and beyond, an order without any disturbance of sound—a void of sensible sound that is a fullness of what these sounds cover over. Sensations of music are apt to suggest this "suprasensible" silence, and in fact Jankélévitch interprets music quite generally as being about this essential silence. Music uniquely renders it perceptible, inasmuch as it silences speech and circumambient noise. This deeper silence is not merely lack and absence but more like the pure potential of sound.

Jankélévitch emphasizes that the relation between the full and the void is reversed by music: the void is plenitude inasmuch as it is the vehicle for something completely different from plenitude in the vulgar sense of being fully charged with phenomenal content. Such a void is a "silence within silence" that cannot be represented but that music intimates, not only by silencing noise but also through techniques such as *pianissimo*—by approaching a silencing of itself, by becoming almost nothing, by nearly disappearing. *Pianissimo* is "the *nearly* insensible form of the supra-sensible" ("la forme *presque* insensible du supra-sensible," *La Musique*, pp. 175–176). Music has a propensity to erase even itself as erasure of talk and random noise. And this releases a silence unseen, unheard, but gestured toward in the self-suppression of music as found especially in composers such as Gustave Fauré and Claude Debussy.

Jankélévitch expounds his view of music expressly in terms of the unsayable "je ne sais quoi" of apophatic theology. He takes this phrase from John of the Cross, the poet of "la musica callada" ("silent music"), and he illustrates his theories with ample citations from Plotinus and Pseudo-Dionysius the Areopagite, as well as from Silesius Angelus and other mystics.[48] He maintains

---

47. Vladimir Jankélévitch, *La Musique et L'Ineffable* (Paris: Seuil, 1983), p. 172: "La musique est le silence des paroles; tout comme la poésie est le silence de la prose."

that the distinguishing feature of the human being is not its ability to speak, according to the canonized notion of classical humanist anthropology, but rather its ability to hear and conjure silence. Yet the silence we can talk about and objectively experience is relative. For silence per se, without relation to any order of sound, cannot be perceived. The absolute Nothing, taken for itself, is an abstraction: we hear Nothing only as lurking in and around sounds that attenuate and tend *toward* elimination of themselves. It is always some particular relation to Nothing that is experienced, never the Nothing pure and simple. And musical forms furnish ways of enabling this nothing of absolute silence to register.

In visual forms of expression, apophatic negation has been the privileged modality particularly of abstract art. Twentieth-century abstract painting has pioneered the exploration of the empty and void as perhaps the only authentic (non)objects of artistic expression. This historically path-breaking movement was guided by negative theologies such as those formulated in Judeo-Christian theosophical traditions.[49] In the work of a founding figure like Wassily Kandinsky, the drive to abstraction was influenced by the Russian orthodox cult of the icons as visually signifying something invisible and transcendent. From a different direction, but in the same spiritual dimension, feeling after the same space of the unrepresentable, the likewise seminal work of the Dutchman Piet Mondrian was powerfully influenced by the trenchant iconoclasm of Protestant religious outlooks. The whole development of abstract expressionism from Malevich through Mark Rothko and beyond follows an apophatic—or "aphairetic" ("stripping away")—logic. It is spellbindingly rendered by Barnett Newman's monochrome fields slit by stripes or "zips." It is given also a verbal formulation, parallelling his pictures, by the American painter Ad Reinhardt. Reinhardt's statements on his Black Paintings, which occupied him almost exclusively during the last period of his life (1954–1967), recount a mystic journey into the resonant, numinous potency of a nothingness that cannot be expressed. All external representation, and even internal, conscious reflection, must be forsaken as idolatrous:

---

48. These ideas are also alluded to in Jankélévitch's general philosophy, as expounded in numerous works, including *Le Je-ne-sais-quoi et le Presque-rien* (Paris: Presses Universitaires de France, 1957).

49. A reading of modern and postmodern art in this key is offered by Mark C. Taylor, *Disfiguring: Art, Architecture, Religion* (Chicago: University of Chicago Press, 1992), chapters 1–4.

.   .   .   .
Leave temple images behind
Risen above beauty, beyond virtues, inscrutable, indescribable
Self-transcendence   revealed yet unrevealed

Undifferentiated unity, oneness, no divisions, no multiplicity
No consciousness of anything
No consciousness of consciousness

All distinctions disappear in darkness
The darkness is the brilliance   numinous, resonance
.   .   .   .[50]

This language resonates powerfully with discourses of apophasis in traditional sources such as Plotinus (the oneness beyond thought and consciousness) and Pseudo-Dionysius (the luminous darkness, the "divine dark"). For Reinhardt too, the total abstraction from representation, in perfect blackness, results in

Triumph over time, death, oblivion 'a fragrance of eternity'
Totality, unity, finality   wordless essence[51]

The deliberate and explicit iconoclasm of this sort of endeavor to evoke an unrepresentable All by the elimination of particular representation is carried from painting into architecture by Le Corbusier. This crucial founder and theorist of the new architecture vaunted himself as the inventor of "l'espace indicible." His experience of this "unsayable space" in architecture was expressly modeled on religious paradigms of negative theology.[52] The minimalist philosophy of "less is more" proceeded to build form by elimination through the experimental styles of De Stijl and Bauhaus, leading to a sort of apocalypse of emptiness in the architecture of Mies van der Rohe. In his

---

50. Ad Reinhardt, *Art-as-Art: The Selected Writings of Ad Reinhardt*, ed. Barbara Rose (New York: Viking Press, 1975), p. 90.

51. Ibid., p. 92. A sustained reading of Reinhardt's work and thought in terms of negative theology is developed by Mark C. Taylor, "Think Naught," in *Negation and Theology*, ed. Robert P. Scharlemann (Charlottesville: University Press of Virginia, 1992), pp. 25–38.

52. See interviews in *Le Corbusier et l'architecture sacrée*, ed. François Biot (Lyon: La Manufacture, 1985), p. 96, and in *L'architecture d'aujourd'hui*, special issue of *Architecture religieuse* (June–July 1961), p. 3. I owe these references to Uwe Bernhardt's essay "Eine Poesie der offenen Welt," now included in his book *Le Corbusier et le projet de la modernité* (Paris: L'Harmattan, 2002).

buildings, which sometimes appear suspended as if over a void, Mies carried the aesthetic of "purism" to its extreme consequences.

Architecture historian Manfredo Tafuri expounds the work of Mies in terms that, in effect, elicit from it an apophatic aesthetic. Tafuri observes that architectural features such as the uninflected, absolute regularity of continuous glass facades and the "curtain wall" create a building that is scrupulously designed to "say nothing." Of van der Rohe's Seagram Building (1954–1958) on Park Avenue in Manhattan, Tafuri writes: "In the interior of chaos the perfect silence is disquieting. Here the absoluteness of the object is total. The maximum of formal structurality is matched by the maximum absence of images. That language of absence is projected on an ulterior 'void' that mirrors the first void and causes it to resonate. . . ." This second void is the plaza between the skyscraper and Park Avenue, which is laid between two symmetrical fountains and reflects horizontally the vertical (non)significance of the building. Together, the building and the plaza form "two voids answering each other and speaking the language of the nil, of the silence which—by a paradox worthy of Kafka—assaults the noise of the metropolis." In this intepretation, the proximity of architecture to negative theology could hardly be more patent, and it becomes explicit in the art historian's language, including, finally, the term "Renunciation—the classical *Entsagung*."[53]

More recently, architectural emptiness, or the organizing of space around absence, has been called upon to express unspeakable annihilation in the Holocaust monuments designed by Daniel Libeskind. The Berlin Jewish Museum and other works of his are described by Libeskind, in a number of theoretically suggestive writings, as architectural realizations of the void of the Holocaust.[54] At this juncture, the unspeakable in the arts intersects with the psychology of trauma as an experience that cannot be verbally worked through and so compulsively repeats itself.[55]

These contemporary discourses of the apophatic share at least a generic affinity with, and in many cases an actual common genesis from, the matrices

53. Manfredo Tafuri, *Modern Architecture*, trans. Robert Erich Wolf (New York: Rizzoli, 1976), vol. 2, p. 312. Tafuri is also quoted by Mark Taylor, who describes Mies's architecture from an apophatic, or more precisely "aphairetic" perspective, in *Disfiguring*, p. 140f.

54. See especially Daniel Libeskind, *Between Zero and Infinity: Selected Projects in Architecture* (New York: Rizzoli International Publications, 1987), and *Radix-Matrix: Architecture and Writings* (New York: Prestel, 1997).

55. See Daniel Libeskind, "trauma / void," in *Trauma: Zwischen Psychoanalyse und kulturellem Deutungsmuster*, ed. Elisabeth Bronfen, Birgit R. Erdle, and Sigrid Weigel (Köln: Böhlau, 1999), pp. 3–26. For theories of trauma emphasizing themes of silence and

of negative theology. In the historical perspective the volumes of the present work provide, such discourses can be seen to share a preoccupation with what cannot be said that decisively marks Western culture through the entire course of its development. From the contemplation of the One to the thought of difference, the idea of what cannot be said unifies and divides. It unifies in order to divide all that can be said from the unsayable. It divides in order to open— breaking discourse into a silence that is no longer beholden to the divisiveness of significance. Thanks to the idea of what cannot be said, or of the "apophatic difference" of the sayable from the unsayable—a difference which remains infinite and indefinable—it becomes possible to tolerate differences remaining open infinitely.

This introduction, with its wide-ranging probes into disparate histories, has aimed to give some sense of the wider field from which the representative authors of the anthology have been chosen. It has also aimed to summarily present some of the chief forms in which the underlying intellectual and existential—or relational—problem that gives rise to apophaticism has expressed itself in the Occident. We have discerned the lineaments of traditions of apophasis that follow hard on the heels of *Logos* in its triumphal march through history, escorted by the phalanxes of philosophy. Along the way, murmurs arise from the margins reminding us of what philosophy must choose to forget in order to achieve completion and comprehend everything within its language. At historical moments of crisis, especially of crisis for language, insurgent skepticism, and the collapse of reigning paradigms of discourse, these shadowy traditions show up more prominently because the object of philosophy's contemplation—articulable reality, the *Logos* of being—in its presumptive blinding splendor suddenly darkens. In these circumstances of tottering philosophical confidence, the undercurrents of apophasis resurface. What had gone unheard now clamors for attention and can no longer be suppressed. This has been happening especially in the amazing contortions of culture we are living through at present. It has also enabled the traditions of our past to be re-read in a new light with acute attention to the fundamental apophatic elements that were always there, lurking in the background of the dominant philosophical outlook. These elements were oftentimes nervously ignored, and thereby loomed the more ominously. They are now emerging again into the foreground, as the unspeakable restlessly seethes on all sides round.

---

survival, see Cathy Caruth, *Unclaimed Experience: Trauma, Narrative and History* (Baltimore: Johns Hopkins University Press, 1996), and Dominick LaCapra, *Writing History, Writing Trauma* (Baltimore: Johns Hopkins University Press, 2001).

FRAGMENTS
AND FINITUDE

1. HÖLDERLIN (1770–1843)

"Was ist Gott?," "Würzel Alles Übels," "Da ich ein Knabe war," "Ermunterung," "Die Kurze," in *Sämtliche Werke und Briefe*, 2 vols., ed.
Günter Mieth (Berlin: Aufbau-Verlag, 1995), vol. 1.

Trans. Michael Hamburger, *Friedrich Hölderlin: Poems and Fragments* (Ann Arbor: University of Michigan Press, 1967), pp. 71, 81–83,
161–163, 45. Translation of "Was ist Gott?" is my own.

Grossly underappreciated in his own time and throughout the nineteenth century, Friedrich Hölderlin was bitterly disappointed in his unsuccessful efforts
to achieve recognition as Germany's national poet and prophet. He met with
crushing defeat in his personal life as well, with its intense loves and idealism.
He became mentally unstable and was committed to institutions. Clinically
mad for the latter half of his life, though not without occasional flashes of
poetic creativity, he spent his last thirty-six years convalescing in the tower of
a kind friend, Ernst Zimmer, on the Neckar River in Tübingen. He was a living
emblem of the close kinship between poetry and madness that was diagnosed
early on by Plato in the *Phaedrus*. Partly on this basis, he later became a chief
beacon for modern poets in illustrating the impossible attempt of poetry to
say the unsayable.

Hölderlin pioneered a distinctively modern apophaticism. Lamenting
the withdrawal of the gods, he assumed a vocation as poet of following in their
track toward the now empty heavens. Ingeniously, he sought to discover the
traces of the gods conserved in the hollows of his own poetic language. His
most characteristic poetic rhetoric opens up the classical plenitude and symmetry of well-rounded, harmonious phrases by means of breaks, ellipses, and
anacoluthons—an apophatic rhetoric in which language is stymied and silenced.[1] The greater part of his most important work, whether odes and

---

1. Hölderlin's late technique of "paratactic composition," based on additive form
and lists, breaking up syntactic connection, has been stressed by Eric L. Santner, *Friedrich
Hölderlin: Narrative Vigilance and the Poetic Imagination* (New Brunswick, N.J.: Rut-
gers University Press, 1986), following Theodor W. Adorno, "Parataxis: Zur späten Lyrik
Hölderlins," in *Noten zu Literatur* (Frankfurt a.M.: Suhrkamp, 1981). See also Hans Frey,
Dichtung, Denken und Sprache bei Hölderlin (Zürich: W. Kunz, 1951).

hymns, novel or tragedies, consists of failed drafts and fragments of works that he could not complete. Emblematically, his fragmentary hymn "Wie wenn am Feiertage . . ." founders on the impossible attempt to grasp divine lightning in language. The "fire from heaven" ("Feuer vom Himmel") for Hölderlin is something that defies human reception and expression.[2]

The gods are what language cannot say—"divine names are lacking" ("es fehlen heilige Namen")—so it is only the silences and misfirings of language left behind by an excess of divinity with respect to emotion, and of emotion with respect to speech, that hint at the Highest:

> Nenn' ich den Hohen dabei? Unschickliches liebet ein gott nicht,
>   Ihn zu fassen, ist fast unsere Freude zu klein.
> Schweigen müssen wir oft; es fehlen heilige Namen,
>   Herzen schlagen und doch bleibet die Rede zurück?
>   ("Heimkunft")

> Do I thereby name the Most High? A god does not love what is unseemly,
>   To grasp him, our joy is too small.
> We must often keep silent; divine names are lacking,
>   Hearts beat and yet speech remains behind?

This inability of ours to name the Highest, and our consequent silence, alone preserve the place and memory of the gods. But while we wait for inspiration and watch, the times seem empty of signs: "Speechless and cold, in the wind / the weathercocks clatter" ("Sprachlos und kalt, im Winde / klirren die Fahnen," from "Hälfte des Lebens").

Yet perhaps this apparently sterile speechlessness can itself speak. Hölderlin also imagines an ideal past, when there was no need at all for language, when the gods were present in silence. In "Da Ich ein Knabe war . . . ," he describes this as a natural and original state of intimacy with the gods, of being kissed by sun and moon, "Helios" and "Luna." This was before he called the gods by their names ("Zwar damals rieff ich noch nicht / Euch mit Nahmen . . ."), for naming evokes their nearness *as lost*: it negates the immediacy of pure nature and love, the divine presence. In particular, the names of divinities learned from study of the Greek tongue alienate, even while invoking,

---

2. These words are from Hölderlin's Letter 236, of December 4, 1801, to Casimir Ulrich Böhlendorff. Mieth, vol. 2, p. 926. All quotations of Hölderlin's works are from this edition.

the gods. It is by becoming silent again and by simply showing things in their very being, rather than signifying them through the difference between word and object, that human speech might again become the Name of God. This would be the speechless, natural language of the gods in which words, the blossom of the mouth ("die Blume des Mundes," from "Germanien"), bloom like flowers:

> Nun, nun müssen dafür Worte, wie Blumen, entstehen.
> ("Brot und Wein")

> Now, now words for this must spring up like flowers.

Hölderlin thus looks forward prophetically to a pentecostal future, where language will again approach an all-embracing divine silence. Poets, by their language, keep open this dimension of silence, which would otherwise be drowned out in the in-between time of lack ("Wozu Dichter in dürftiger Zeit?"). It is the very failing of language, as in Hölderlin's poems, that becomes the expression of this utopia projected into the future, which is also understood as a return to the speechlessness of the state of nature: "divinely present nature / has no need of speech" ("Die göttlichegegenwärtige Natur / Bedarf der Rede nicht," *Der Tod des Empedokles*, First Draft, lines 1628–1629). In the vision of this tragedy, Empedocles' wordless teaching is like Nature or the nameless God in the experience of a child ("In Tagen des Frühlings, namlos aber ist / In ihnen der Gott . . ."). When this silence returns, it will itself be a language ("wenn die Stille kehrt, auch eine Sprache sei . . . ," from "Friedensfeier"), a new poetic language as the medium of a utopian community. But so long as man's spirit does not know how to keep silent and wants to express what is not to be expressed ("Aussprechen will Unauszusprechendes," *Der Tod des Empedokles*, Second Draft, line 176), it plays dangerously with the fire from heaven.

Hölderlin often is heard, as in "Ermunterung," crying out for the return of the divinity that has vanished and grown silent among humans, whose hearts are dumb. But actually speechlessness is the sign that holds open the place of the silent language to come. In the utopian society that Hölderlin envisages, human language will celebrate the Name of God and indeed identify itself with this Name, precisely by not saying it. It must be incarnate in the unity of a people, a *Volk*, in the intimate communication of their unexpressed communion. The God of this "new church" ("neue Kirche") must not be named, except insofar as guarding silence itself names him. Hölderlin's hero Hyperion declares:

Den Einen, dem wir huldigen, nennen wir nicht; ob er gleich uns nah ist,
wie wir uns selbst sind, wir sprechen ihn nicht aus. Ihn feiert kein Tag;
kein Tempel ist ihm angemessen; der Einklang unserer Geister, und ihr
unendlich Wachstum feiert ihn allein.[3]

The One, whom we worship, we do not name; because he is as near to us
as we are to ourselves, we do not express him. No day is his solemnity; no
temple is designated for him; the harmony of our spirits and their endless
growth alone celebrate him.

The Name of the Highest is thus shrouded in silence ("Vom Höchsten will ich
schweigen"). Similarly, if Hyperion should speak of his beloved, he must forget what she is as a whole ("Ich muß vergessen, was sie ganz ist, wenn ich von
ihr sprechen soll"). The divisions between man and man, man and woman,
and human and divine often become unendurable for Hyperion in his passion
for inexpressible oneness. His strongest impulse is to undo individuation and
deny difference, by transcending language through what amounts to a negative theology.

Hölderlin anticipates this growing silent of language in his poetry, especially when it breaks off in fragments. This happens thematically in "Die
Kürze," a song about its own necessary brevity.[4] The immediate, happy experience of nature as infinite and divine withdraws ("hinweg ist's"). His language accordingly shrinks to desolation. But the future language, where God is
present as spirit in human speech ("der Gott, der Geist / Im Menschenwort,"
from "Ermunterung"), is realized, paradoxically, by the fragment. The fragment breaks off into and absolutizes a mere part. The part is different from the
whole, which cannot be gathered from it and articulated as such, but the whole
is nevertheless one with the fragment. Indeed, in the absense of the whole, the
fragment itself becomes one and all—albeit a oneness that cannot be articulated. This is the paradoxical logic of the fragment: it *is* that of which it is only
a part. But it is this whole as broken open at the edges, as lacking in closure and
completion—like the decapitated bust of a Greek god. An analogous type of

3. "Hyperions Jugend," chapter 5, in *Hyperion, oder der Eremit in Griechenland*
(Mieth, vol. 1, pp. 545–546). For *Hyperion* as an extended meditation on the ineffable, see
Andreas Siekmann, "Die ästhetische Funktion von Sprache, Schweigen und Musik in
Hölderlins *Hyperion*," *Deutsche Vierteljahresschrift* 54/1 (1980): 47–57.

4. See Christiaan L. Hart Nibbrig, *Rhetorik des Schweigens: Versuch über den Schat-
ten literarischer Rede* (Frankfurt a.M.: Suhrkamp, 1981), pp. 94–95.

paradox is illustrated again when Hölderlin offers no unitary solution to the theological problem of reconciling the pagan pantheon with Christian monotheism: Christ is the one true God and also the brother of Dionysius (in "Der Einzige")—equivocally the whole or just a part of the godhead.

The pervasive apophatic theme in Hölderlin's works continues into the late hymns, such as "Patmos," where language as sign is emptied and dispersed, as if it were "the throw of a sower of seeds" ("Es ist der Wurf des Säemanns"). With Christ's death and the disappearance of the Face of the Highest, God's presence is literally disseminated—God is the infinite dispersion of whatever lives ("Unendlich hin zerstreut das Lebende Gott")—and German poetry must dedicate itself to interpreting its remains and traces in the form of the letter of Holy Writ ("heiliger Schrift"). The hymn "Germanien" exemplifies Hölderlin's obsession with the vocation of German letters to renew the speaking of the gods, but in a different way, one in which truth may be made manifest and yet remain "unuttered," since it must remain "innocent" ("Doch ungesprochen auch, wie es da ist / Unschuldige, muß es bleiben"). The return to pre-Christian religions enables Hölderlin to circumvent the Church's idolatrous language, denounced in Letter 173 to his mother, so as to recover an ur-Christian experience—the theophany inspiring praise and thanks that human language now can approach only by silence. And this recovery is the office of the poet.

The tremendous insight of Hölderlin's long poem "Patmos"—the name of the isle on which St. John the Divine received his revelation—into a God who is manifest precisely through the loss of presence, or the averting of the divine Face, is also condensed in the fragmentary poem "Was ist Gott?" from the same peak period of 1800–1805:

Was ist Gott? unbekannt, dennoch
Voll Eigenschaften ist das Angesicht
Des Himmels von ihm. Die Blitze nämlich
Der Zorn sind eines Gottes. Je mehr ist eins
Unsichtbar,   schicket es sich in Fremdes. Aber der Donner
Der Ruhm ist Gottes. Die Liebe zur Unsterblichkeit
Das Eigentum auch, wie das unsere,
Ist eines Gottes.

What is God? unknown, yet
Full of attributes is the face
Of heaven from him. The lightning namely

The wrath are a god's. The more a thing
Is invisible,   it sends itself into foreignnness. But thunder
Is the Fame of God. The love of immortality
Property, too, like ours,
Are a god's.

About fifty poems survive from the period after 1806, the period of Hölderlin's madness or "Umnachtung," even though this was above all a period of
silence. Testimonies of visitors concur in describing him as taciturn and dis-
inclined to more than minimal conversation. This final withdrawal from language can be read as the logical outcome of Hölderlin's whole undertaking as
poet and as the goal toward which his works were striving all along. His poetic
and existential trajectories both, in their progression toward muteness, culminate thus in an inexorable drawing of language toward resolution in silence.[5]

---

5. Just such a reading is carried out in detail by Thomas E. Ryan, *Hölderlin's Silence* (New York: Peter Lang, 1988).

From *Poems and Fragments*

The Root of All Evil (Würzel Alles Übels)

Being at one is god-like and good, but human, too human, the mania
    Which insists there is only the One, one country, one truth and
    one way.

In My Boyhood Days . . . (Da ich ein Knabe war)

In my boyhood days
  Often a god would save me
    From the shouts and the rod of men;
      Safe and good then I played
        With the orchard flowers
          And the breezes of heaven
            Played with me.

And as you make glad
The hearts of the plants
When toward you they stretch
Their delicate arms,

So you made glad my heart,
Father Helios, and like Endymion
I was your darling,
Holy Luna.

O all you loyal,
Kindly gods!
Would that you knew how
My soul loved you then.

True, at that time I did not
Evoke you by name yet, and you
Never named me, as men use names,
As though they knew one another.

Yet I knew you better
Than ever I have known men,
I understood the silence of Aether,
But human words I've never understood.

I was reared by the euphony
Of the rustling copse
And learned to love
Amid the flowers.

I grew up in the arms of the gods.

Exhortation (Ermunterung)
Second Version

Echo of Heaven, heart that are hallowed, why,
    Why do you now fall silent, though living still,
        And sleep, you free one, by the godless
            Banished for ever to Night's deep dungeons?

Does not the light of Aether, as always, wake?
    And Earth, our ancient mother, still thrive and flower?
        And here and there does not the spirit,
            Love with a smile wield her laws as ever?

You only fail! Yet heavenly powers exhort,
    And silently at work, like a stubble field,
        The breath of Nature blows upon you,
            She the all-brightening, soul-inspiring.

O hope, now soon, now soon not the groves alone
    Shall sing life's praise, for almost the time is come
        When through the mouths of mortals, this, the
            Lovelier soul will make known her coming,

Allied with men more lovingly then once more
    The element will form, and not rich or full
        But when her pious children thank her,
            Endless the breast of our Earth unfold then,

And once again like blossoms our days will be
    Where heavenly Helios sees his own light shared out
        In quiet alternation, finding
            Joy in the joy of those mortal mirrors,

And he who silent rules and in secret plans
    Things yet to come, the Godhead, the Spirit housed
        In human words, once more, at noontide,
            Clearly will speak to the future ages.

Brevity (Die Kurze)

'Why so brief now, so curt? Do you no longer, then,
   Love your art as you did? When in your younger days,
     Hopeful days, in your singing
       What you loathed was to make an end!'

Like my joy is my song.—Who in the sundown's red
   Glow would happily bathe? Gone it is, cold the earth,
     And the bird of the night whirs
       Down, so close that you shield your eyes.

2. SCHELLING (1775–1854)

Philosophie der Offenbarung, Vorlesung VIII. In *Sämtliche Werke,* ed. Karl Friedrich August Schelling (Stuttgart: Cotta, 1856–71), vol. 13, pp. 160–171.

My original translation as "The Stupor of Reason," from *The Philosophy of Revelation,* Berlin Introduction, Lecture VIII. Emphasis in translation is my own.

Friedrich Wilhelm Joseph von Schelling is best known, along with Hegel and Fichte, as one of the three pillars of German idealist philosophy. However, late in life he developed a way of thinking completely contrary to idealism. In this last phase, he evolved a "philosophy of revelation" that grows out of theosophical matrices and focuses on what withholds itself from thought—what cannot be rationally grounded and must instead be positively given or revealed. This was Schelling's answer to the Hegelian System, in which *Logos*-philosophy had reached unsurpassable perfection as a total articulation of all that is. Whereas Hegel rationalized everything by the *Logos,* fully identifying the real and the rational, Schelling attempted to think that which exceeds the furthest reaches of rational comprehension.

Schelling's *Philosophy of Revelation* interprets Christian Trinitarian and Christological mysteries as transcending the capacity of reason to understand, and as therefore inducing a break in systematic thought. In the "Berlin Introduction" to this work, moreover, Schelling dwells particularly on the "stupor of reason," on reason's being literally dumbstruck before the fact of existence—*that* anything is at all, apart from any determinations as to *what* things are. He inquires into what is not said or sayable in any system: "that before which thought grows dumb" ("das, vor dem das Denken verstummt"), that which arrests and silences reason ("das wovor di Vernunft stille steht").[1] He becomes thereby a key link in the tradition of apophatic thought, bringing Christian

---

1. An influential reading of the late Schelling's thought as pivoting on the "stupor of reason" is Luigi Pareyson, "Stupore della ragione e angoscia di fronte all'essere," in *Ontologia della libertà: Il male e la sofferenza* (Turin: Einaudi, 1995).

mysticism and Jewish Kabbalah into touch with modern philosophy. He was to have a decisive influence, especially on Rosenzweig.

Schelling delivered his *Philosophy of Revelation* as lectures in Berlin in 1841 at the age of sixty-six, after several decades of virtual silence following his 1809 essay on human freedom (*Die menschliche Freiheit*), in which he first discovered a principle that reason could not comprehend, and the 1811 *Weltalter* fragment, in which he formulated the idea of a past that cannot be made contemporaneous with any present in terms that remain current today in Levinas, Derrida, and Blanchot. Schelling's lectures attracted considerable public notice, and the audience numbered among other luminaries Kierkegaard, Jules Michelet, Friedrich Engels, Jacob Burckhardt, and Karl Rosenkrantz. Although Kierkegaard was deeply impressed, at least at first, nearly everyone seems to have been dissatisfied by Schelling's unusual manner of philosophizing, with its confusing mix of theosophies and Christian orthodoxy. Yet in recent times these lectures have been recognized as "one of the profoundest works of modern religious thought."[2] While this assessment was distinctly a minority view when it was written, recent years have seen a prodigious resurgence of interest in the late Schelling among continental philosophers. In the view of some, everything in continental philosophy today that does not stem from Hegel passes through Schelling.[3]

In the section excerpted below and translated into English for the first time, Schelling begins by outlining the limits of "negative," dialectical, Hegelian philosophy in order to reach the concept of the necessarily Existing that precedes all conceptions. Schelling's own "positive philosophy" then starts from the purely existing rather than from the negations of thought. Schelling is following suggestions of Kant, who had acutely analyzed the limits of reason, before Hegel absorbed everything, without remainder, into the infinity of spirit.[4]

---

2. Emil L. Fackenheim, "Schelling's Philosophy of Religion," *University of Toronto Quarterly* 22/1 (1952): 1–17, gives a lucid, concise account of the importance of the lectures in the development of Schelling's thought and in post-Enlightenment philosophy after the demise of idealism and the ensuing crisis of reason. See also Fackenheim's "Schelling's Conception of a Positive Philosophy," *The Review of Metaphysics* 7 (1954): 563–582, and, further, John Burbidge, "Reason and Existence in Schelling and Fackenheim," in *Fackenheim: German Philosophy and Jewish Thought*, ed. Louis Greenspan and Graeme Nicholson (Toronto: University of Toronto Press, 1992), pp. 90–117.

3. See the essays in *Le dernier Schelling: Raison et positivité*, ed. Jean-François Courtine and Jean-François Marquet (Paris: Vrin, 1994), and Courtine, *Extase de la raison: Essais sur Schelling* (Paris: Galilée, 1990).

4. An important background for Schelling's philosophy of religion, as well as for modern negative theology generally, is Kant's "Critique of Every Theology Founded on

Schelling's late philosophy rejects the principle of identity at the foundation of the idealism that he himself had elaborated in his youth. By insisting on the limits of reason, he rejects the identity of finite spirit (Man) with infinite spirit (God), or of experience with reality. This identity, as Fackenheim points out, was the common assumption of Hegel's rational Absolute and Schleiermacher's absolute of religious feeling alike.

In rediscovering the "infinitely Existing" ("das unendlich Existirende") as the "abyss of reason," as that which thought cannot think or say even though it is presupposed by all thought, Schelling is, in effect, reiterating the principle of unlimited being—unqualified, infinite existence—that was exalted by medieval apophatic tradition and that he associates particularly with Spinoza's philosophy. Like Meister Eckhart, he recognizes this unsayable principle as the generating source, indeed the Creator, of every determinate, finite being. What cannot be conceived or articulated is thus acknowledged as prior to, and as ungraspably, indefinably present in, everything that demonstrably, expressly is.

Specific Principles of Reason," *Critique of Pure Reason*, pt. 2, Transcendental Dialectic, Book II, chapter iii, section vii. Reason also is confronted with what exceeds conceptual comprehension in the experience of the sublime; on this, see Kant's *Critique of Judgment*, sections 23–27.

from *The Philosophy of Revelation,* Berlin Introduction, Lecture VIII

The Stupor of Reason

Note well that the starting point is only the necessarily existing. I do not say, the necessarily existing being or essence. That would be to say too much. One must think of this necessarily existing as only existing, nothing else.

Negative philosophy can also reach this concept of necessary existing that precedes all concepts, or rather it leads us in its final conclusion—which is nothing but a correction of the ontological argument—to this concept of the *pure*, the *merely* existing. For this reason, it might seem as if the beginning of positive philosophy is, after all, furnished by negative philosophy, and that positive philosophy, after all, is grounded by negative philosophy. But it is not so. For precisely with this *pure, mere* existence without any previous potency, with the, in this sense, existing, philosophy happens upon something that requires no grounding at all, something whose nature excludes every grounding. For it would not be the existing, what itself is absolutely First, if one could arrive at it by way of anything else. For in that case, this Other would be the First. The nature of the merely existing is precisely to be independent of every idea, and so also of the last idea of negative philosophy. The merely existing thereby frees itself from the presupposition that it only accidentally had in the preceding philosophy, and even so did positive philosophy, as I expressed it, drop the concept and retain only *pure* being, being without all What, and so free itself from negative philosophy. With this principle, that of the merely existing, positive philosophy *could* even wholly of itself begin, even when preceded by no rational philosophy.

For I at least have no knowledge that anyone disputed the right of Spinoza to begin from the infinitely existing, since we could name infinitely existing also that whose being is delimited by no preceding power. The simply, the merely existing is precisely that through which all that could derive from thought is struck down, that before which thought grows dumb, before which reason itself bends, since thought has to do precisely with possibility, with potential; and where this is excluded, thought has no hold. The infinitely existing is therefore, because it is such, also secure against all thought and doubt.[1] That cannot be principle which is vulnerable to collapse. Only what is secured against every subsequent possibility and so indubitably Is can be principle, the never-able-to-perish, the always and necessarily

---

1. It would be a contradiction to place before the first in thought an *other* first in *thought*, but it is not contradictory to subordinate to the first-in-*being*—and to that extent all thought-surpassing and over-flying—this first-in-thought or to think of the latter as posterior to the former. For there is being not because there is thought, but there is thought because there is being.

remaining that stays on top, no matter what happens or comes about in the sequel.

What has in mere thinking once begun can also continue in mere thinking and never go further than the *idea*. What needs to reach reality must also begin from reality, that is, from *pure* reality, and so from the reality that precedes every possibility. It could be objected: a reality that precedes every possibility cannot be *thought*. This one can in a certain sense admit and say: precisely therefore is it the *beginning* of all real thinking—for the *beginning* of thinking is not yet itself thinking. A reality that precedes possibility is also a reality that comes before thought; but precisely therefore it is the first proper *object* of thinking (*quod se objicit* [that which is thrown in its way]). The question of what relation it could have to reason is that much more important, however, if reason knuckles under to it ["wenn sie vor ihm sich beugt"]. In any case, it has for itself already a relation to reason, but, as the expression used just now suggests, a negative relation.

One can find oneself in difficulty with the infinitely existing when one has to explain whether it is also to be called an idea, a concept of reason. At first, it seems irrefutable that it is called an idea, for at first no proposition, no affirmation seems to be bound to it. This merely existing is in its way also the existing itself, αὐτὸ τὸ ῎Ον, if, that is, we take ῎Ον [Being] in a verbal sense. To this extent, one cannot predicate being of it *attributively;* what *elsewhere* is the predicate is here the subject, is itself in the place of the subject. Existence, which in everything else is accidental, is here the essence. The *quod* [that] is here in the place of the *quid* [what]. It is thus pure idea, and yet it is not idea in the sense that the word has in negative philosophy. The merely existing is being in which all ideas, and that means all power, is excluded. We will be able therefore to name it only the reversed idea, the idea in which reason is placed *outside* of itself. Reason can posit being in which there is yet nothing of a concept, of a What, only as an absolute *Outside-itself* (of course, only, thereafter, *a posteriori*, to win it back as its content, and so at the same time return back into itself): reason, therefore, in this positing, is placed outside itself, is absolutely ecstatic. And who has not felt the ecstasy of Spinozism and of all teachings that move from the necessarily existing![2]

2. The mystic wants to know ecstatically also the *what.*

Kant names the unconditional necessity the *sustainer of all things*, as he says, which we indispensably need (Kant has undoubtedly before his eyes that familiar argument: if anything at all exists, and at least *I myself* exist, so must there be also something that necessarily, that groundlessly exists)—Kant names the unconditioned necessity of being that precedes all thought the true abyss for human reason. "Even eternity," he continues, "however frightfully sublime even a Haller might picture it, makes a far less vertiginous impression on the spirit, since eternity only measures the duration of things, but does not *sustain* them. One cannot *do without* this thought, yet no more can one endure it, that a being that we represent as the highest of all possible beings should say to itself: I am from eternity to eternity, outside me is nothing except what is something only through my will, *but where am I then from?* Here everything sinks beneath us, and the greatest perfection, like the smallest, wavers without any stay before the face of speculative reason, which at no cost to itself can let the one as well as the other disappear without obstacle."[3] I report these words because they express Kant's deep feeling for the sublimity of this being that comes before all thought, in the place of which, in our times, has been set indeed likewise being as the beginning of philosophy, but only as a mere moment of thought, whereas in this inevitable thought, impressed most deeply into human nature, the discussion is about being that is before all thought.

We can produce *a priori* in mere thought everything that our experience presents, but it is so also *only* in thought. If we wanted to transform this into an objective proposition, and so say that everything even in itself is only in thought, then we would have to return to the standpoint of Fichtean idealism. If we want something existing outside thought, then we must begin from a being that is absolutely independent from all thought, one that comes before all thought. The Hegelian philosophy knows nothing of this being, it has no room for this concept. Kant, for his part, thinks the necessarily existing insofar as it is already at the same time *God*. At the beginning of the positive philosophy we must still ignore this and take it as the *merely* existing; we forgo the concept *God*, precisely because it is a contradiction to posit, on the one hand, the merely existing and, on the other, to posit it as already *something* with a *concept*. For either the

---

3. Kant, *Kritik der reinen Vernunft*, Hartensteinsche ed., pp. 470–471.

concept must precede, and then being would have to be the consequence of the concept, and it would no longer be unconditioned being; or else the concept is the consequence of being, and then we would have to begin from being, without the concept, and this is exactly what we want to do in positive philosophy. But exactly *that* in God in virtue of which he is the groundlessly existing Kant names the abyss for human reason; what else is this but that before which reason stands still, mute [wovor die Vernunft stille steht], that by which reason is swallowed up, that over against which reason is at first nothing and can do nothing?

Kant still distinguishes the groundless necessity of existence in God from eternity, but absolute eternity, eternity insofar as it is not already *over against* time, but before and above all time—absolute eternity is itself also nothing other than just this existence, in which we know no *prius*, no beginning. For that is eternal which no concept comes before, that in relation to which thought has no *freedom*, as it does in relation to finite being, to precede it with thought, which philosophy can comprehend *a priori*.

One would completely misunderstand Kant if one wished to see in the position in question a rejection of that idea (of groundless, necessary existing); what he wishes to express is rather only its conceptual incomprehensibility; for he is himself penetrated by the ineluctable necessity of reason to admit a groundless existing. And incomprehensible—yes, so is it, this existence, if one interprets the incomprehensible as the not *a priori* comprehensible. Negative philosophy deals with this last, the *a priori* comprehensible, positive philosophy with the *a priori* incomprehensible; but it deals with this only in order to transform even this *a priori* incomprehensible into something comprehensible *a posteriori;* with God the *a priori* incomprehensible becomes comprehensible.

As long as reason makes an object of itself (and this orientation was given and deeply impressed upon it by Kant), it can find as its immediate content only the infinite power of being. Hereby reason sees itself placed in an *a priori* position in relation to all being, but only in relation to finite being; and it can itself not come to stability with this, cannot itself bring this to a conclusion, without making recourse to the above-being, which however has a completely different *prius*, namely, not potential but being, and specifically *that* being for which thought can find no ground or beginning. If reason is the object of itself, if thought orients itself to the content of reason, as in negative philosophy, this is all something accidental; reason is not thereby in its pure substantiality and essentiality. If, however, it is in *this latter* element (and so does not draw back into itself, does not seek its object in itself), so only the infinite *actus* can correspond to the infinite potential of knowing. In accordance purely with its *nature*, reason posits only the infinitely existing; on the other hand, in positing this, it is as if without motivation, as if petrified, *quasi attonita* [as if astonished]; but it freezes toward the being that dominates all only in order, through this submission, to realize its true and eternal content, which it cannot find in the sensible world as really known, which it therefore now also possesses *eternally*.

The infinitely existing is thus the *immediate* concept of reason, at which reason free from itself, that is, reason that is not its own object, has no need to arrive first through the otherwise so natural and inevitable inference, of which Kant in his naive way says: "It is something extraordinarily remarkable that when one presupposes that something exists, one cannot avoid the consequence that something also exists in a necessary manner." Kant calls this a natural, even if not therefore a *certain* inference, and he is fully right to apply his criticism to the cosmological proof, which wants to ascend regressively from condition to condition up to the unconditioned. But the directly, the *immediately* posited concept of the necessarily existing is one precisely that excludes all criticism. The criticism of a concept places the possibility of its object in question. But it would, as already remarked, be senseless to ask if a necessarily existing *could* [exist], although that is what was asked. For if it *could* exist it would therefore not be the necessarily existing. It is the necessarily existing precisely because it excludes all *preceding* possibility, because it comes before all potential. One can subject to criticism the concept of the necessarily existing as the result of an argument, namely, of the cosmological argument, but no one has been able to subject to criticism the concept directly, immediately established by Spinoza, just as no one can escape it, but everyone must submit to it. Only in this concept, not in the system itself, lies the presumable irrefutability of Spinozism.

Not less absurd than the question whether the necessarily existing *could* exist is the question: *what essence* could a necessarily existing have, how must this essence be constituted in order that it be able to be a necessarily existing. This happens essentially in the ontological argument, where first one proves the ineluctable assumption of a necessarily existing essence and then seeks to show that the necessarily existing essence could only be, at the same time, the most perfect of all, that is, God. It is absurd to ask, what being *could* a necessarily existing be, for then I assume that the necessarily existing is preceded by an essence, a what, a possibility, while I must rather posit it as *merely* existing, in which as yet nothing of an essence, a "what" can be conceived.

In the manner in which the old metaphysics handled the concept, the deception arises always from the fact that one already ascribes an essence (namely divinity) to the pure concept of the necessarily existing, in which however yet nothing of any essence should be thought, rather than letting the *concept* completely fall away in order to get to the merely existing. Kant in his critique of the cosmological argument says that the whole task of the transcendental ideal turns on finding either a concept for absolute necessity or absolute necessity for the concept of any thing whatever. He continues, "If one can know the one, so must one know the other also; for reason knows as absolutely necessary only that which is necessary on the basis of its *concept*" (*op. cit.*, p. 470). Concerning now this last point, I deny that any essence can be recognized as necessary on the basis of its concept; for should this essence be God, then it can be seen on the basis of the concept not that he necessarily exists but that he *can only be* the necessarily existing, or in other words that he necessarily is the necessarily existing, if he exists, but it does not follow that he does exist. If, however, the discourse is about the simply-necessarily existing, then again one cannot say that existence follows from its concept, for its concept is exactly that it is *merely* existing; existence here is not the consequence of the concept or of the essence, but rather existence is here itself the concept and itself the essence.

Concerning the other member of the Kantian either-or (the first was that for the concept of some essence necessary existence was sought, as happens in the ontological argument, the second that conversely for absolute necessity the concept was sought)—concerning this second member, it would really be the affair of positive philosophy, namely, to attempt to get from the necessarily existing (as a yet conceptless *prius*) to the *concept*, to the essence (of God) as *posterius*. This, as one can see, is exactly the opposite way from that of the ontological argument; but in order to set out on it, one must first be resolved about the concept of the merely, the simply existing and have given up the false dependency upon the idea of God in which this concept in the former metaphysics was held. For the necessarily existing is not the necessarily existing because it is God; for then it would be precisely not the necessary, the groundless existing, because in the concept of God a *ground* for the necessary existence would have been found. The necessarily existing is precisely not the consequence of a preceding concept but the existing *from itself*, as has already been said, *a se, sponte, ultra*, without any preceding ground. Here is the knot of the former metaphysics that is only to be loosed by keeping the two concepts separate. This solution was the more congenial to Kant in that he, on one side, recognized the undeniability of the necessarily existing as an immediate concept of reason, and on the other recognized the concept of the highest being as the ultimate, permanent content of reason. In this manner, Kant has the absolutely *immanent* concept, that of the highest essence (for *all else is only* relatively immanent, inasmuch as it can go over into being) and the absolutely *transcendent* concept (that of the necessarily existing) only as unlinked *next* to each other, *both* as concepts of reason, without being able to elucidate their standing next to each other. Here there is really a gap in Kant's critique. But both concepts must definitely bound each other, for the first (that of the highest essence) is the end of negative philosophy, the other (that of the necessarily existing) is the beginning of positive philosophy. Both concepts accordingly are linked in the latter as in the former, but in a different way in each; in the negative in such a way that one says, the highest being, *if it exists*, can be being only *a priori*, therefore it must be the necessarily existing, the *being* that is before its concept, before every concept. This is the only truth that remains from the ontological argument. In positive philosophy, they are linked in *this* manner, that one says: the necessarily existing (namely the simply-necessarily existing) *is*— not necessarily, but *factically* the necessarily necessarily-existing essence or God; and this is proved *a posteriori* in the manner already indicated: if the necessarily existing is *God*, then this and that consequence follow—we mean to say, so *a, b, c,* etc., become *possible;* but based on our experience, *a, b, c,* etc., really exist, so—the necessary conclusion—the necessarily existing is *really* God.

I have called the merely existing, without antecedent potential, the "absolutely transcendent concept." Since Kant there has been so much talk of immanent knowledge and immanent thinking in a favorable sense, but of transcendent, by contrast, in an unfavorable sense, that one cannot name the latter without some kind of apprehension or fear. But this fear is justified only from the standpoint of the old metaphysics, which we have overcome. Consider the following. Everything transcendent is really something relative, it *is* only in relation to something, which will be transcended. If I pass from the *idea* of the highest essence to its *existence*, this is a transcending; I have first posited the idea, and now I wish to pass over from it into existence; so there is here a transcendence. If, however, I *set out* from that which precedes every concept, then here I have overstepped nothing, and rather, if one calls this being the transcendent, and I proceed from it to the concept, so have I overstepped the transcendent and am thus become immanent again. The transcendence of the old metaphysics was merely relative, that is, hesitant and partial, whereby one wished to remain with one foot in the concept. The transcendence of positive philosophy is absolute, and for just that reason none, in the sense in which Kant forbad it. If I have first made myself immanent, that is, sealed myself up in pure thought, then transcendence is at least possible; but if I begin from the transcendent (as does positive philosophy), then there is nothing that I have overstepped. Kant denies transcendence to metaphysics, but he denies it only to dogmatic reason, that is, to reason that from *itself* through inferences would reach existence; but he does not proscribe (for he did not think of it, this possibility never presented itself to him) passing, conversely, from the *merely*, that is, the infinitely *existing* to the concept of the highest *Essence* as *posterius*. Meanwhile, as we said previously, reason can place that merely existing (ἀπλῶς ΄Ον) *absolutely* outside itself precisely because there is in it no such concept, because it is the opposite of all concepts; however, reason posits it only with a view to making what is outside and above reason once more into contents of reason: it becomes this precisely inasmuch as it is *a posteriori* God (is recognized as God). Reason posits conceptless being in order to pass from it to the concept and posits the transcendent in order to metamorphose it into the absolutely immanent, and in order at the same time to have this *absolutely* immanent as an existence, which is possible only by this way, for it has the absolutely immanent already also in negative philosophy, but not as an existence.

Pure or infinite potential (the beginning of negative philosophy) is in content *identical* with thinking and can therefore, because it does not go toward thinking (because it is identical with it), only proceed forth from thinking. By contrast, the *merely* existing is that which is not identical with thinking, indeed is content at first to exclude it; however precisely therefore can and must first be brought to reason—*because* it is originally outside reason. God is not, as many think, the transcendent, he is the transcendent made immanent (that is, that which is made the content of reason). In overlooking this lies the great misunderstanding of our time. As I already said, the being that is *a priori* inconceivable, because mediated by no preceding concept, becomes in God a conceivable, or in God comes to its concept. The infinitely existing, which reason cannot hide in itself, becomes immanent to reason in God.

We have so far designated negative philosophy primarily as the science of reason. This can create the appearance that positive philosophy is a science opposed to reason. But the true relation is the following: in the first, reason sets out from its immediate but chance content, from which arbitrariness it gradually frees itself, in order to reach a process necessary to its permanent content. But it reaches this without at the same time reaching it really; it remains at the level of the mere idea. *Positive* philosophy sets out from what is absolutely outside reason, but reason subjects itself to this only in order to return back immediately into its rights. As was already said earlier, the science of reason cannot prove its last idea, which is precisely the content of reason remaining within reason, as it can everything else coming to it in experience, and yet precisely *this* concept has the distinction that it cannot be indifferent concerning the real existence of that which is required in it, whereas in relation to everything previous it was indifferent to the philosophical subject whether it existed. Here it is said: *Tua res agitur.* Now precisely therefore reason, which cannot verify this last idea in experience, must turn itself to the being that is itself outside and over experience, to the being that relates to it as the *pure* faculty of knowing, in the same way as the being that is presented in experience relates to the powers of sensible representation.

[Schelling goes on to demonstrate that reason cannot know "that" things exist but must accept this fact on the authority of the senses. And so ends the eighth Lecture of his introduction to *The Philosophy of Revelation.*]

3. KIERKEGAARD (1813–1855)

Fear and Trembling, from Problema III. Trans. Howard V. Hong and Edna H. Hong (Princeton: Princeton University Press, 1983), pp. 112–120.

Søren Kierkegaard is widely recognized as a precursor of twentieth-century existentialism. After Hegel had claimed essential knowledge of the totality of the real by bringing all to the light and judgment of Logos, Kierkegaard felt it incumbent on himself, his own particular self, to speak up for an existence that could not be gathered into and digested by any logical essence and which he understood as religious in nature. His own existence thus became the fulcrum for penetrating philosophical reflections that continue to prove compelling for thinkers today. It was an existence aspiring to emulate the Christian and also Romantic ideal of the "Knight of Faith" ardently in search of an authentic Christianity, in outspoken opposition to the compromised Christianity of a state church comfortably ensconced in bourgeois Danish society.

Kierkegaard thus endeavored to open up an exteriority to reason against Hegel's all-encompassing identification of the real and the rational. Although much later Levinas would object to Kierkegaard's approach as too "subjective," Levinas was similarly pursuing the exception to the uniform rule of logic and homogeneous consciousness. Kierkegaard thus prefigures the widespread revolts against the Hegelian System and its apparent banishing of all possibility of something unsayably singular or other that have continued to erupt in contemporary philosophy, notably among French thinkers of difference in the wake of Levinas.[1]

In *Either/Or, A Fragment of Life* (1843), Kierkegaard elaborates his theory of three different spheres or stages of existence: the aesthetic, the ethical, and the religious. The aesthetic entails an experience of the identity of All in the immediacy of the moment of sensation. The ethical is based on a rational me-

---

1. Kierkegaard is so presented by Mark C. Taylor in *Altarity* (Chicago: University of Chicago Press, 1987). A thoroughgoing apophatic reading of Kierkegaard is proposed by David R. Law, *Kierkegaard as Negative Theologian* (Oxford: Clarendon Press, 1993).

diation of All by universal law. Both fall infinitely short of the religious sphere, for neither confronts the purely and absolutely incommensurable; both the aesthetic and the ethical absorb all possible experience into their own self-enclosed forms of existence. Only the religious sphere of existence is fundamentally riven asunder and therefore open and exposed to something not itself, the radically Other. The religious alone confronts the absolutely unsayable.

Kierkegaard's *Philosophical Fragments* (1844), a polemic against the Hegelian System from its very title, identifies the religious as Absolute Paradox. The religious form of existence involves an absolute relation to the absolute that cannot be comprehended in any universal (ethical) terms, and yet is not simply the particularity of the aesthetic phase: it is rather a higher immediacy of incommensurable individuality. This paradoxical relation is analyzed in depth with respect to the silence it imposes and that betokens it in Problema III of *Fear and Trembling* (1843), which asks: "Was it ethically defensible of Abraham to conceal his purpose from Sarah, from Eleazar, from Isaac?" Abraham, under the divine injunction to sacrifice his son, represents the paradox of an individuality higher than any universal ethical rule that could explain such an action or divine command. This forces him to be silent. And it makes his case absolutely different from all forms of "aesthetic concealment," where it is noble for the protagonists to keep secret some divine decree or demonic destiny that nevertheless they *could* in principle divulge in order to exonerate themselves, were it not for their heroic decision to bear the blame and suffer uncomplainingly without any relief of exculpation.

The long movement of Problema III suggests many different reasons for keeping silence, but the climax of the passage, which is here excerpted, defines Kierkegaard's thought about the most essential silence. It concludes the exegesis of the story of Abraham and Isaac from Genesis 22 that underlies *Fear and Trembling* as a whole. Signed pseudonymously "Johannes *de silentio*," the work is also implicitly a commentary on tacit, Abraham-like sacrifices in Kierkegaard's own personal life: his sacrifice of his engagement with Regine Olsen, and his own father's sacrifice of him, the last of seven children, by making him the *confidant* of the pious father's troubles in life to such an extent that Søren would later avow, "I was born old, I never had a childhood."

Fear and Trembling, from Problema III (conclusion)

But now to Abraham—how did he act? For I have not forgotten, and the reader will please remember, that I got involved in the previous discussion to make that subject an obstacle, not as if Abraham could thereby become more comprehensible, but in order that the incomprehensibility could become more salient, for, as I said before, I cannot understand Abraham—I can only admire him. It was also pointed out that none of the stages described contains an analogy to Abraham; they were explained, while being demonstrated each within its own sphere, only in order that in their moment of deviation they could, as it were, indicate the boundary of the unknown territory. If there is any question of an analogy, it must be the paradox of sin, but this again is in another sphere and cannot explain Abraham and is itself far easier to explain than Abraham.

So Abraham did not speak, he did not speak to Sarah, or to Eliezer, or to Isaac; he bypassed these three ethical authorities, since for Abraham the ethical had no higher expression than family life.

Esthetics allowed, indeed demanded, silence of the single individual if he knew that by remaining silent he could save another. This alone adequately shows that Abraham is not within the scope of esthetics. His silence is certainly not in order to save Isaac; in fact, his whole task of sacrificing Isaac for his own and for God's sake is an offense to esthetics, because it is able to understand that I sacrifice myself but not that I sacrifice someone else for my own sake. The esthetic hero was silent. Meanwhile, ethics passed judgment on him because he was silent on account of his accidental particularity. It was his human prescience that led him to remain silent. Ethics cannot forgive this. Any human knowing of that sort is only an illusion. Ethics demands an infinite movement, it demands disclosure. The esthetic hero, then, can speak but will not.

The authentic tragic hero sacrifices himself and everything that is his for the universal; his act and every emotion in him belong to the universal; he is open, and in this disclosure he is the beloved son of ethics. This does not fit Abraham; he does nothing for the universal and is hidden.

Now we are face to face with the paradox. Either the single individual as the single individual can stand in an absolute relation to the absolute, and consequently the ethical is not the highest, or Abraham is lost: he is neither a tragic hero nor an esthetic hero.

Here again it may seem that the paradox is the simplest and easiest of all. May I repeat, however, that anyone who remains convinced of this is not a knight of faith, for distress and anxiety are the only justification conceivable, even if it is not conceivable in general, for then the paradox is canceled.

Abraham remains silent—but he *cannot* speak. Therein lies the distress and anxiety. Even though I go on talking night and day without interruption, if I cannot make myself understood when I speak, then I am not speaking. This is the case with Abraham. He can say everything, but one thing he cannot say, and if he cannot say that— that is, say it in such a way that the other understands it—then he is not speaking. The relief provided by speaking is that it translates me into the universal. Now, Abraham can describe his love for Isaac in the most beautiful words to be found in any language. But this is not what is on his mind; it is something deeper, that he is going to sacrifice him because it is an ordeal. No one can understand the latter, and thus everyone can only misunderstand the former. The tragic hero does not know this distress. In the first place, he has the consolation that every counterargument has had its due, that he has given everyone an opportunity to stand up against him: Clytemnestra, Iphigenia, Achilles, the chorus, every living person, every voice from humanity's heart, every cunning, every alarming, every incriminating, every commiserating thought. He can be sure that everything permitted to be said against him has been said ruthlessly, mercilessly— and to fight against the whole world is a consolation, to fight against oneself is frightful. He does not have to fear having overlooked anything, so that later on he perhaps must cry out as King Edward IV did on hearing of the murder of Clarence.[1]

Wer bat für ihn? Wer kniet' in meinem Grimm
Zu Füssen mir und bat mich überlegen?
Wer sprach von Bruderpflicht? Wer sprach von Liebe?

---

1. [Editors' note:] Shakespeare, *King Richard the Third, Shakspeares dramatische Werke*, Schlegel and Tieck, III, p. 278.

[Who sued to me for him? Who (in my wrath)
Kneel'd at my feet and bid me be advis'd?
Who spoke of brotherhood? Who spoke of love?]

The tragic hero does not know the dreadful responsibility of loneliness. Moreover, he has the consolation that he can weep and lament with Clytemnestra and Iphigenia—and tears and cries are relieving, but groanings that cannot be uttered are torturing. Agamemnon can quickly concentrate his whole being in the certainty that he is going to act, and then he still has time to comfort and encourage. This Abraham cannot do. When his heart is moved, when his words would provide blessed comfort to the whole world, he dares not to offer comfort, for would not Sarah, would not Eliezer, would not Isaac say to him, "Why do you want to do it, then? After all, you can abstain." And if in his distress he wanted to unburden himself and clasp to himself all that he held dear before he proceeded to the end, the terrible consequence might be that Sarah, Eliezer, and Isaac would take offense at him and believe him to be a hypocrite. Speak he cannot; he speaks no human language. And even if he understood all the languages of the world, even if those he loved also understood them, he still could not speak—he speaks in a divine language, he speaks in tongues.

This distress I can understand very well. I can admire Abraham. I have no fear that anyone reading this story will be tempted rashly to want to be the single individual. But I also confess that I do not have the courage for it and that I would gladly renounce every expectation of proceeding further if it were even possible, be it ever so late, that I should come that far. At every moment, Abraham can stop; he can repent of the whole thing as a spiritual trial; then he can speak out, and everybody will be able to understand him—but then he is no longer Abraham.

Abraham *cannot* speak, because he cannot say that which would explain everything (that is, so it is understandable): that it is an ordeal such that, please note, the ethical is the temptation. Anyone placed in such a position is an emigrant from the sphere of the universal. But even less can he say the next thing. To repeat what was sufficiently developed earlier, Abraham makes two movements. He makes the infinite movement of resignation and gives up Isaac, which no one can understand because it is a private venture; but next, at every moment, he makes the movement of faith. This is his consolation. In other words, he is saying: But it will not happen, or if it does, the Lord will give me a new Isaac, that is, by virtue of the absurd. The tragic hero, however, comes to the end of the story. Iphigenia submits to her father's resolve; she herself makes the infinite movement of resignation, and they now have a mutual understanding. She can understand Agamemnon, because the step he is taking expresses the universal. But if Agamemnon were to say to her, "Although the god demands you as a sacrifice, it is still possible that he would not demand it, that is, by virtue of the absurd"—then he would instantly be incomprehensible to Iphigenia. If he could say this by virtue of human reckoning, Iphigenia would very likely understand him, but as a result Agamemnon would not have made the infinite movement of resignation and thus would not be a hero; then the soothsayer's declaration is a sailor's yarn, and the whole event is a vaudeville.

So Abraham did not speak. Just one word from him has been preserved, his only reply to Isaac, ample evidence that he had not said anything before. Isaac asks Abraham where the lamb is for the burnt offering. "And Abraham said: God himself will provide the lamb for the burnt offering, my son."

I shall now consider in more detail these last words by Abraham. Without these words, the whole event would lack something; if they were different words, everything perhaps would dissolve in confusion.

It has frequently been the subject of my pondering whether a tragic hero, culminating either in a suffering or in an action, ought to have last words. As far as I can see, it depends on the sphere of life to which he belongs, whether his life has intellectual significance, whether his suffering or action is related to spirit.

It goes without saying that the tragic hero, like any other man who is not bereft of speech, can say a few words in his culminating moment, perhaps a few appropriate words, but the question is how appropriate is it for him to say them. If the meaning of his life is in an external act, then he has nothing to say, then everything he says is essentially chatter, by which he only diminishes his impact, whereas the tragic conventions enjoin him to complete his task in silence, whether it consists in action or suffering. In order not to wander too far afield, I shall take the most pertinent example. If Agamemnon himself, not Calchas, should have drawn the knife to kill Iphigenia, he

would only have demeaned himself if in the very last moment he had
said a few words, for the meaning of his deed was, after all, obvious to
everybody, the process of reverence, sympathy, emotion, and tears
was completed, and then, too, his life had no relation to spirit—that
is, he was not a teacher or a witness of the spirit. However, if the
meaning of a hero's life is oriented to spirit, then the lack of a statement would diminish his impact. What he has to say is not a few appropriate words, a short declamatory piece. Instead, the significance
of his statement is that he consummates himself in the decisive moment. An intellectual tragic hero like that ought to have and ought
to retain the last word. He is required to have the same transfigured
bearing proper to every tragic hero, but one word is still required.
If an intellectual tragic hero like this culminates in a suffering (in
death), he becomes immortal through this last word before he dies,
whereas the ordinary tragic hero does not become immortal until
after his death.

Socrates can be used as an example. He was an intellectual tragic
hero. His death sentence is announced to him. At that moment he
dies, for anyone who does not understand that it takes the whole
power of the spirit to die and that the hero always dies before he dies
will not advance very far in his view of life. As a hero Socrates is now
required to be calm and collected, but as an intellectual tragic hero he
is required to have enough spiritual strength in the final moment to
consummate himself. He cannot, as does the ordinary tragic hero,
concentrate on self-control in the presence of death, but he must
make this movement as quickly as possible so that he is instantly and
consciously beyond this struggle and affirms himself. Thus, if Socrates had been silent in the crisis of death, he would have diminished
the effect of his life and aroused a suspicion that the elasticity of irony
in him was not a world power but a game, the resilience of which had
to be used on an inverted scale in order to sustain[2] him in pathos at
the crucial moment.

2. [Kierkegaard's note:] There can be various opinions as to which of
Socrates' statements may be regarded as decisive, inasmuch as Plato has poeti-
cally volatilized Socrates in so many ways. I suggest the following: the verdict
of death is announced to him, and in that same moment he dies, in that same
moment he triumphs over death and consummates himself in the celebrated
response that he is surprised to have been condemned by a majority of three
votes. He could not have bantered more ironically with the idle talk in the

These brief suggestions are indeed not applicable to Abraham if one expects to be able to find by means of some analogy an appropriate final word for Abraham, but they do apply if one perceives the necessity for Abraham to consummate himself in the final moment, not to draw the knife silently but to have a word to say, since as the father of faith he has absolute significance oriented to spirit. I cannot form in advance any idea of what he is going to say; after he has said it, I presumably can understand it, perhaps in a certain sense understand Abraham in what was said without thereby coming any closer to him than in the preceding exposition. If there were no final lines from Socrates, I could have imagined myself in his place and created some, and if I had been unable to do so, a poet would have managed it, but no poet can find his way to Abraham.

Before considering Abraham's final words more closely, may I first point out the difficulty for Abraham to manage to say anything at all. As explained above, the distress and anxiety in the paradox were due in particular to the silence: Abraham cannot speak.[3] Thus it is a self-contradiction to demand that he speak, unless one wishes him out of the paradox again, so that he suspends it in the decisive moment and thereby ceases to be Abraham and nullifies all that preceded. Thus, if Abraham were to say to Isaac in the decisive moment: You are the one intended—this would simply be a weakness. For if he could speak at all, then he ought to have spoken long before this, and the weakness then would be that he had not had the spiritual maturity and concentration to think through the whole agony beforehand but had shoved something aside in such a way that the actual agony was more than that in thought. Moreover, by speaking thus, he would have turned away from the paradox, and if he actually wished to speak with Isaac, he would have had to change his position to one of spiritual trial, for otherwise he could say nothing, and in that case he would not even be a tragic hero.

---

marketplace or with the foolish comment of an idiot than with the death sentence that condemns him to death. [From the editors' note on Socrates' trial:] Plato, *Apology* 36a. . . . Now the reading is more commonly "thirty votes."

3. [Kierkegaard's note:] If there is any analogy at all, it is one such as provided by the death scene of Pythagoras, for in his final moment he had to consummate the silence he had always maintained, and for this reason he *said*: It is better to be killed than to speak. See Diogenes, VIII, para. 39. [Editors' note:] Diogenes Laertius, *Vitis*, II. Loeb edition, II, p. 355.

But a final word by Abraham has been preserved, and insofar as I can understand the paradox, I can also understand Abraham's total presence in that word. First and foremost, he does not say anything, and in that form he says what he has to say. His response to Isaac is in the form of irony, for it is always irony when I say something and still do not say anything. Isaac questions Abraham in the belief that Abraham knows. Now, if Abraham had replied: I know nothing—he would have spoken an untruth. He cannot say anything, for what he knows he cannot say. Therefore he answers: God himself will provide the lamb for the burnt offering, my son! From this we see, as described previously, the double-movement in Abraham's soul. If Abraham in resignation had merely relinquished Isaac and done no more, he would have spoken an untruth, for he does indeed know that God demands Isaac as a sacrifice, and he knows that he himself in this very moment is willing to sacrifice him. After having made this movement, he has at every moment made the next movement, has made the movement of faith by virtue of the absurd. Thus he is not speaking an untruth, because by virtue of the absurd it is indeed possible that God could do something entirely different. So he does not speak an untruth, but neither does he say anything, for he is speaking in a strange tongue. This becomes still more evident when we consider that it was Abraham himself who should sacrifice Isaac. If the task had been different, if the Lord had commanded Abraham to bring Isaac up to Mount Moriah so that he could have his lightning strike Isaac and take him as a sacrifice in that way, then Abraham plainly would have been justified in speaking as enigmatically as he did, for then he himself could not have known what was going to happen. But given the task as assigned to Abraham, he himself has to act; consequently, he has to know in the crucial moment what he himself will do, and consequently, he has to know that Isaac is going to be sacrificed. If he has not known this for sure, he would not have made the infinite movement of resignation; then his words certainly are not untruth, but he is also very far from being Abraham, and he has less significance than a tragic hero—indeed, he is a man devoid of resolution who cannot make up his mind one way or the other and for that reason always speaks in riddles. A vacillator like that, however, is merely a parody of the knight of faith.

Here again it is apparent that one perhaps can understand Abraham, but only in the way one understands the paradox. I, for my part, perhaps can understand Abraham, but I also realize that I do not have the courage to speak in this way, no more than I have the courage to act as Abraham did; but by no means do I therefore say that the act is of little importance, since, on the contrary, it is the one and only marvel.

And what was the contemporary age's verdict on the tragic hero? That he was great and that it admired him. And that honorable assembly of noble-minded men, the jury that every generation sets up to judge the past generation—it gave the same verdict. But there was no one who could understand Abraham. And yet what did he achieve? He remained true to his love. But anyone who loves God needs no tears, no admiration; he forgets the suffering in the love. Indeed, so completely has he forgotten it that there would not be the slightest trace of his suffering left if God himself did not remember it, for he sees in secret[4] and recognizes distress and counts the tears and forgets nothing.

Thus, either there is a paradox, that the single individual as the single individual stands in an absolute relation to the absolute, or Abraham is lost.

---

4. [Editors' note:] See Matthew 6:6.

4. DICKINSON (1830–1886)

Poems 1668, 1563, 581, 1700, 288, 420, 985, 1004, 1071, 1251, 1452. In *The Poems of Emily Dickinson*, ed. Thomas H. Johnson (Cambridge, Mass.: The Belknap Press of Harvard University, 1955).

Emily Dickinson lived an outwardly uneventful life in her family's house in Amherst, Massachusetts, but she was inwardly travailed by feverish spiritual and artistic ferment. In her struggle with the rigid Puritanism of her social ambience, poetry became her passageway to a freer, more personal faith. Her exploration of modes of negation in poetic language enabled her to discover what are, in effect, negatively theological forms of belief.

Dickinson's highly original writing makes her a maddeningly difficult poet, one whom eminent critics confess baffles them. Yet her poems become startlingly accessible when read according to their apophatic grammar and rhetoric: the words and phrases fall into place—the place they make for what they necessarily leave unsaid but allow to show up, distinctly silhouetted in their hollows and shadows. The poems selected here generally thematize a negative method of thought and perception, but they are merely the most explicit representatives of a poetic corpus that is, throughout, profoundly apophatic in nature and inspiration and that rewards being read as such, while it stiffly resists readings that ignore this orientation.

Dickinson's poetry is pregnant with the sense that unsayability itself can signify and that the poem's very failing to say what it strives to say may harbor its most powerful significance. She says as much in one of her poems:

> If I could tell how glad I was
> I should not be so glad –
> But when I cannot make the Force
> Nor mould it into Word
> I know it is a sign
> That new Dilemma be
> From mathematics further off
> Than from Eternity.
>
> (Poem 1668)

This incapacity of speech, or apophasis, is a sign of how far removed from "mathematics," that is, from any rationally calculable, articulable knowledge, is the intimation of the Eternity that Dickinson dwells on but cannot express. Still, her "hindered Words"—a good expression for apophatic rhetoric—are the key to telling of this Nothing (nothing that can be said, which is nevertheless everything), and thereby to renovating the world:

> By homely gift and hindered Words
> The human heart is told
> Of Nothing –
> "Nothing" is the force
> That renovates the World –
> (Poem 1563)

As so often, something indicated as missing makes the poem and clinches its significance.

Dickinson's poetry continually approaches and even coincides with characteristic themes of negative theology. In various ways, she articulates the principle that the Nothing is the All, the Absolute (Poem 1071). Even more acutely, she says that this is so because the All *is not:* it is "The Missing All" (Poem 985). This is exactly the status of the Neoplatonic One, which is no thing, but which everything that is anything emanates from and deeply depends on and indeed *is* (to the extent that it really is at all). In this sense, the One is All. On the basis presumably of this sort of "intuition" and not of "terms" (Poem 420), Dickinson feels her way to the same kind of vocabulary that was used by the Neoplatonic negative theologians:

> I found the words to every thought
> I ever had – but One –
> And that – defies me –
> As a Hand did try to chalk the Sun
>
> To Races – nurtured in the Dark –
> How would your own – begin?
> Can Blaze be shown in Cochineal –
> Or Noon – in Mazarin?
> (Poem 581)

It is impossible to find the right word for the One, if it is thought strictly as without any determination or multiplicity. In like fashion, the sun, symbolically the source of all, cannot itself be delineated or illuminated, since everything visible can be delineated or illuminated only by *its* light. Absolute brightness cannot be perceived apart from the colors or dyes that alone make it visible by toning down its total intensity, so as to bring it within the range of finite perception. A similar idea was expressed by another celebrated poetic Platonist in the familiar verses: "Life like a dome of many-colored glass / Stains the white radiance of eternity" (Shelley, "Adonis"). But Shelley's flowing eloquence and rhetorical grandeur are far removed from Dickinson's laconic anti-rhetoric, with its hard-edged, rare-dye quality that safeguards a peculiarly apophatic effect of the mystery of the unsaid. Whereas Shelley's language becomes transparent like light, Dickinson's poetry, with its rare words and rhythmic arrests—marked especially by her idiosyncratic use of dashes for spacings within and between lines—tends toward verbal viscousness and opacity.

Dickinson's poems offer some of the most poignant expressions anywhere in literature of how linguistic negation becomes the positive source of all that is and that can be said. They oftentimes place this experience in an aesthetic dimension of beauty, enchantment, and rapture, exclaiming, for example:

> To tell the Beauty would decrease
> To state the Spell demean –

However, this Spell is itself but the sign of something yet more indefinite and inarticulable:

> There is a syllable-less Sea
> Of which it is the sign –
> My will endeavors for its word
> And fails, but entertains
> A Rapture as of Legacies –
> Of introspective Mines –
>   (Poem 1700)

There is no adequate expression for this experience that issues in a "syllable-less Sea." Yet the rapture left as a result or "legacy" of such experience testifies to interior riches that cannot be put into words and thus be exteriorized or objectified; these riches nevertheless remain lodged in "introspective Mines"—where "Mine(s)" perhaps also suggests something irreducibly private and personal, even though this very expression crystallizes the subjective sensation as a grammatical fact.

While her poems often proved impossible for her contemporaries to penetrate, they have won immense appreciation in more recent critical appraisals, particularly those attuned to the poetics of the unsayable. Readings of Dickinson pointing in this direction have insisted on compression and abbreviation as features that distinguish her style, especially as against the stylistic canons of her own time. Cristanne Miller's analysis of Dickinson's versification shows ellipsis—the omission and deletion of logical and syntactical links—to be its governing principle.[1] Carla Pomarè finds in this elliptical technique the means of producing the silence that paradoxically gives Dickinson her distinctive voice. Margaret Freeman, analyzing Dickinson's poetry in terms of cognitive principles of discourse, similarly stresses omissions and absences as the signifying elements that grant the poetry its power, a power "through silence to capture the true essence of intimacy."[2]

----

1. Cristanne Miller, *Emily Dickinson: A Poet's Grammar* (Cambridge, Mass.: Harvard University Press, 1987).

2. Carla Pomarè, "A 'Silver Reticence': Emily Dickinson's Rhetoric of Silence," pp. 211–222, and Margaret H. Freeman, "Emily Dickinson and the Discourse of Intimacy," pp. 191–201, both in *Semantics of Silence in Linguistics and Literature*, ed. Grabher and Jessner.

Poems of Emily Dickinson

288

I'm Nobody! Who are you?
Are you – Nobody – Too?
Then there's a pair of us?
Don't tell! they'd advertise – you know!

How dreary – to be – Somebody!
How public – like a Frog –
To tell one's name – the livelong June –
To an admiring Bog!

420

You'll know it – as you know 'tis Noon –
By Glory –
As you do the Sun –
By Glory –
As you will in Heaven –
Know God the Father – and the Son.

By intuition, Mightiest Things
Assert themselves – and not by terms –
"I'm Midnight" – need the Midnight say –
"I'm Sunrise" – Need the Majesty?

Omnipotence – had not a Tongue –
His lisp – is Lightning – and the Sun –
His Conversation – with the Sea
"How shall you know"?
Consult your Eye!

985

The Missing All – prevented Me
From missing minor Things.
If nothing larger than a World's
Departure from a Hinge –
Or Sun's extinction, be observed –
'Twas not so large that I
Could lift my Forehead from my work
For Curiosity.

1004

There is no Silence in the Earth – so silent
As that endured
Which uttered, would discourage Nature
And haunt the World.

1071

Perception of an object costs
Precise the Object's loss –
Perception in itself a Gain
Replying to its Price –
The Object Absolute – is nought –
Perception sets it fair
And then upbraids a Perfectness
That situates so far –

1251

Silence is all we dread.
There's Ransom in a Voice –
But Silence is Infinity.
Himself have not a face.

1452

Your thoughts don't have words every day
They come a single time
Like signal esoteric sips
Of the communion Wine
Which while you taste so native seems
So easy so to be
You cannot comprehend its price
Nor its infrequency

5. HOFMANNSTHAL (1874–1929)

"Ein Brief," in *Gesammelte Werke in Einzelausgaben*, ed. Herbert Steiner (Frankfurt a.M.: Fischer, 1945), pp. 7–20.

Trans. Michael Hofmann, *The Lord Chandos Letter* (London: Syrens, 1995), pp. 3–20.

Hugo von Hofmannsthal's literary forgery, the *Letter* of the invented Lord Philipp L. Chandos, is addressed to a historical figure, Francis Bacon, author of the *Organum Novum* (1620). A nominalist belonging to the empiricist tradition that stretches from William of Ockham to David Hume, Bacon cherished the Renaissance dream of a universal and perfect language, a *characteristica* conformable to the exact qualities of things. But this dream of human mastery of the world through language shatters in Chandos's experience. The *Letter* delineates the predicament of a writer who finds words completely inadequate and counterproductive when confronted with real natures. The concrete substance of things overflows and overwhelms any formal, verbal significances that words can establish. Everything presents itself to Chandos with an immediacy and absoluteness that incapacitates language as an instrument for comprehending the world. And without the word as mediation, the immediate presence or revelation ("Offenbarung") of things becomes ungraspable and unfathomable.

This state of verbal impotence issues in a feverish sort of consciousness in a medium or material that is fluid, without definite identities, and more immediate and irresistible than words ("eine Art fieberisches Denken, aber Denken in einem Material, das unmittelbarer, flüssiger, glühender ist als Worte"). Chandos can no longer get a handle on any distinct, individual entity as a whole ("Ganze"), for anything whole has become an "unnameable something" ("unnennbares Etwas"). Moreover, the knowing subject itself disintegrates in this breaking through of the unsayable, of reality as unmasterable by language.

The *Letter*'s pseudonymity thinly veils the fact that it witnesses to a crisis and turning-point in Hofmannsthal's own life. His amazingly precocious and highly acclaimed career as a poet, the pseudonymous "Loris," came to a halt abruptly in 1900, when he was twenty-six years old—the age of the fictive author of the *Letter*. At this point Hofmannsthal abandoned the cosmopolitan language of lyric poetry and turned to prose in his native Austrian dialect. By the same token, the device of antedating the *Letter* by three centuries to the threshold of the seventeenth century, the age of science par excellence, scarcely disguises its pertinence to Hofmannsthal's own peculiar historical moment in 1902. The breakdown of verbal order as illustrated by the English Lord's quandary is emblematic of the collapse of an aristocratic (or high-bourgeois) culture in its death throes all over Europe at the turn of the twentieth century.

The *Letter* has usually been read as an inaugural testimony of modern language skepticism, but Otto Lorenz, among others, argues that theological motivations for silence, based on Christian mystical tradition, are just as decisive. Lorenz finds a negative-theological *Deus absconditus* clearly alluded to at the end of the *Letter* in the reference to an "unknown Judge" of the dead to whom the author will finally be accountable to answer in a language of mute things.[1] Rainer Nägele, in contrast, reading the *Letter* in the context of Hofmannsthal's later works, maintains that, unlike his Lord Chandos, Hofmannsthal seeks to save himself from this loss of language ending in silence by renouncing his lyrical and magical conception of language in exchange for a social one. By this account, Hofmannsthal would have found a way to the social ("Weg zum Sozialen"), a non-mystical way ("nichtmystischen Weg").[2]

Yet social discourse per se is no less undermined than are lyrical and mystical language by Chandos's crisis. Moreover, the peculiar confessional notes "To Myself" ("Ad Me Ipsum"), from which Nägele quotes the phrases cited, also explicitly mention the *Lord Chandos Letter* as illustrating the situation of "the mystic without mysticism" ("Chandos-brief: Die Situation des Mystikers ohne Mystik"). This describes precisely an apophatic self-negation of mystic discourse. Such negation is, nonetheless, a "way into existence" ("Weg in die Existenz"). This mystical way ("Der mystische Weg") brings about the "decency of silence" as its result ("Der Anstand des Schweigens als Resultat").[3]

J. B. Bednall weighs in the balance both the mystical, specifically apophatic tendency of Hofmannsthal, which persists even after the *Letter*, and his great sense of social responsibility. Hofmannsthal seems to have found in the Austrian dialect and especially light comedy a more authentic idiom that

---

1. Lorenz, *Schweigen in der Dichtung*, p. 22.
2. Rainer Nägele, "Die Sprachkrise und ihr dichterischer Ausdruck bei Hofmannsthal," in *German Quarterly* 43 (1970): 720–732. Citation, p. 730, borrowing terms from Hofmannsthal's own "Ad me Ipsum," in *Aufzeichnungen* (1959).
3. Hofmannsthal, "Ad me Ipsum," in *Aufzeichnungen, Gesammelte Werke in Einzelausgaben*, ed. Steiner, p. 215. See, further, Werner Metzler, *Ursprung und Krise von Hofmannsthal's Mystik* (Munich: Bergstadt-Verlag, 1956).

avoided the inveterate lies of language and its pretensions to general truth and universality. This unmistakably non-universal language expressed in local color and nuance the silent strength and "mute patience," the immemorial verbal practice of his "folk" ("Stummes Dulden und Tun . . . Urkräfte geweckt: das Volk").[4]

---

4. Hofmannsthal, "Die Idee Europa," quoted by J. B. Bednall, "From High Language to Dialect: A Study in Hofmannsthal's Change of Medium," in *Hofmannsthal: Studies in Commemoration*, ed. F. Norman (London: University of London, 1963), p. 114. Jost Bomers, in *Der Chandosbrief—Die Nova Poetica Hofmannsthals* (Stuttgart: Poeschel Verlag, 1991), also brings to focus the *Letter*'s importance as apophatic expression.

The Lord Chandos Letter

This is the letter which Philip Lord Chandos, younger son of the Earl of Bath, wrote to his friend Francis Bacon, later Lord Verulam and Viscount St Albans, to apologise for his renunciation of all literary activity.

It was kind of you, my dear, honoured friend, to overlook my two years of silence, and to write to me as you did. It was more than kind to express your anxiety, and your dismay at the intellectual torpor into which I seemed to you to be falling, with the good humour and the lightness of touch of which only great men are capable, steeped as they are in life's perils, but not demoralized by them.

You close with the aphorism from Hippocrates: 'Qui gravi morbo correpti dolores non sentiunt, iis mens aegrotat,' and conclude that I need medical attention not only to curb my illness, but even more to sharpen my awareness of my inner condition. I would like to answer you as your concern merits, would like to open my heart to you, and don't quite know how to set about it. I hardly know if I am still the person to whom your precious letter is addressed: am I, at twenty-six, the same person who, at nineteen, wrote that 'Second Paris', that 'Daphne's Dream', that 'Epithalamium', those pastoral plays tumbling along under the splendour of their words, which a heavenly Queen and a few all-too-generous Lords and gentlemen are gracious enough to recall? And is it I who at twenty-three in the stone arcades of the grand piazza of Venice found within himself that sequence of Latin sentences whose conception and construction enraptured his spirit more than the buildings of Palladio and Sansovino, rising out of the sea? And, if otherwise I am the same, could I have removed from my incomprehensible mind all the scars and traces of the product of my most concentrated thinking, to the extent that in your letter which is lying in front of me, the title of that little treatise looks at me blankly and coldly, so that I could not grasp it straight away as a familiar patterning of words, but could only apprehend it one word at a time, as though these words of Latin, thus connected, had met my gaze for the very first time? But of course it is me, and all these questions are rhetoric, rhetoric which is good for women or for the House of Commons, but whose powers, so overestimated in our time, are not sufficient to penetrate the innermost core of things. But I must reveal to you my own innermost self, the peculiarity, the freakishness, if you like, the disease of my mind, if you are to understand that an unbridgeable gulf separates me as much from whatever literary works might appear to lie before me, as from those that are behind me, and which, so alien do they appear to me, I hesitate to call my own.

I don't know which to admire more: the intimacy of your benevolence, or the unbelievable sharpness of your memory, when you recall to me the various little plans I busied myself with in those shared days of fine enthusiasm. Really, I did want to portray the first years of the reign of our late glorious sovereign, Henry VIII. The notes that my grandfather, the Duke of Exeter, left about his negotiations with France and Portugal provided me with a kind of foundation. And from Sallust there flowed in those lively, fortunate days, as through freely flowing pipes, the understanding of form, of that deep, true, inner form which can only be guessed at, beyond the limitation of rhetorical art, form, of which one could no longer say that it ordered content, but which penetrates it, suspends it and achieves truth and poetry at the same time, an interplay of eternal forces, something as glorious as music and algebra. That was my favourite plan.

What is man, to harbour projects!

I toyed with other plans as well. Your kind letter permits them too to float into view. Each one of them freighted with a drop of my blood, they dance in front of me like sad mosquitoes in front of a drab wall, on which the sun of happier days no longer shines.

I wanted to take the fables and mythological tales of the ancients, in which painters and sculptors take such endless and thoughtless delight, and interpret them as the hieroglyphs of an arcane, inexhaustible wisdom, a breath of which, as though from behind a veil, I sometimes thought I felt.

I remember that project. Its motive was sensual and intellectual pleasure of some kind: as the hunted deer longs for water, I longed to enter the naked, shining bodies of those sirens and dryads, of Narcissus and Proteus, Perseus and Actaeon: I wanted to disappear into them and to speak for them with tongues. I wanted. I wanted so much besides. I thought of compiling a collection of 'Apophthegmata', like Julius Caesar's: you will recall Cicero mentioned it in a letter. In it I thought of juxtaposing the most memorable sayings that I had managed to collect in my association with the learned men and the clever women of our time, or with egregious commoners, or with cultivated and excellent persons in the course of my travels: to these I would add fine maxims and reflections from Classical and Italian literature, and whatever else I might encounter in the way of intellectual gems in books, manuscripts or conversation; in addition, the ordering of some especially fine processions and festivals, remarkable crimes and cases of madness, descriptions of the greatest and most curious architecture in the Netherlands, France and Italy, and much else besides. The whole work was to bear the title, 'Nosce te ipsum'.

To be brief: in the enduring drunkenness that was my state of mind at that time, all existence was one single entity: there was no contradiction between the intellectual and the physical world, or between higher and bestial existence, art and non-art, solitude and company; in all of them I felt Nature, in the ravings of madness as much as in the extreme refinements of a Spanish ceremonial; in the oafishness of young farmers no less than in the sweetest allegories; and in all Nature I felt myself; in my hunting-lodge, when I drank the warm frothing milk that a straw-haired peasant had milked into a wooden bucket from the udder of a beautiful, gentle-eyed cow, then that to me was no different from when, sitting on the windowseat of my studio, I drew sweet and foaming intellectual nourishment from a folio volume. The one was like the other; neither conceded anything to the other, either in terms of a celestial, dreamlike nature or of physical vigour, and so it went on, through the whole breadth of life, on all sides of me; everywhere I was in the thick of it, and never was I aware of any falsehood. Or I suspected all was symbolic, and every creature was the key to another, and I felt I was the man capable of seizing them all in turn, and using each one to disclose as much as it could disclose of the others. That is the explanation for the title I thought to give my encyclopaedic work.

To someone susceptible to such thoughts, it may appear as the well-conceived plan of a divine providence that my mind should have been obliged to shrink from such swollen arrogance into the extreme of despondency and impotence that is now its lasting condition. But such religious conceits have no power over me; they belong to those spiders' webs through which my thoughts go speeding off into emptiness, whereas so many of their fellows are caught in them, and come to rest. For me, the mysteries of belief have taken the form of a lofty allegory, which hangs over the fields of my life like a shining rainbow, at a constant distance, always ready to withdraw, in case I should suddenly be inclined to run to it and wrap myself in the hem of its coat.

But, my dear friend, even mundane things shrink from me in the same way. How should I try to describe for you these strange mental tortures, the branches of fruit-trees withdrawing from my outstretched hands, the murmuring water receding from my thirsting lips?

In short, my condition is this: I have quite lost the faculty to think or speak on any subject in a coherent fashion.

To begin with, it gradually became impossible for me to converse on any higher or general subject, and to use those words which all men use constantly and unhesitatingly. I felt inexplicably loath even to say 'Mind' or 'Soul' or 'Body'. I found myself incapable of passing an opinion on the affairs at Court, events in Parliament, or whatever else. And this not through caution or regard—you know I am candid to the point of recklessness: but those abstractions which the tongue has to pronounce in making any judgement fell apart like rotten mushrooms in my mouth. It happened that I wanted to draw the attention of my four-year-old daughter, Katharina Pompilia, to a childish lie she had perpetrated, and to point out to her the necessity of always being truthful, but the abstractions rushing into my mouth suddenly took on such scintillating colours, and flowed together into one another, that I mumbled the rest of the sentence as well as I could—as if I had suddenly been taken ill, and indeed, I had turned pale and there was a strong pressure on my brow—and left the child, slammed the door behind me, and only started to feel restored on horseback, doing a sound gallop on the deserted meadow.

Gradually, though, this incapacity spread everywhere like a corrosive rust. Even in familial and domestic conversation, all those judgements which normally are given with an easy, sleepwalking assurance, became so questionable to me that I could no longer take part in such conversations. I was filled with an inexplicable rage which I was only barely able to conceal when I heard things like: this matter has gone well or badly for so-and-so; Sheriff N. is a bad, Preacher T. a good man; the leaseholder M. is to be pitied, his sons are wastrels; someone else is enviable, because his daughters are good housekeepers; this family is rising, that one is falling. All these seemed to me to be quite untenable, mendacious and full of holes. I was compelled to view everything that came up in such a conversation as from an awful proximity: the way I had once seen a piece of skin on my little finger under a magnifying-glass to look like a field with furrows and hollows, so it was now with men and their actions. I was no longer able to grasp them through the simplifying regard of habit. Everything fell into pieces in front of me, the pieces into more pieces, and nothing could be contained in a single concept any more. Individual words swam around me; they melted into eyes, which stared at me, and which I had to stare back at: they are like whirlpools, it gives me vertigo to look down at them, they turn without cease, and transport you into nothingness.

I attempted to rescue myself from this condition in the intellectual world of the Classics. Plato I avoided; I was terrified of his perilous metaphorical flights. I decided to stay mostly with Seneca and Cicero. I hoped to cure myself with that harmony of limited and orderly concepts. But I was unable to reach them. Their concepts I could well understand: rising before my eyes like majestic fountains with golden balls, I saw the wonderful play of their equivalences. I could float around them and see how they played together; but they were only concerned with each other, and the deepest, most individual part of my thought was excluded from their dance. In their company, I was overcome by a feeling of terrible solitude; I felt like someone who had been locked into a garden full of eyeless statues; I fled back into the open.

Since then, my existence has been one that, I fear, you will hardly be able to comprehend, so devoid of mind and thought is it; an existence that, admittedly, is hardly any different from that of my neighbours, my relatives, and the majority of the landowning nobility of the kingdom, and one that is not without its moments of joy and liveliness. It will not be easy for me to give you an idea of these good moments; the words that might do it have deserted me. For it is something that has never been named and that it is probably impossible to name, which manifests itself to me at such moments, taking some object from my everyday surroundings, and filling it like a vessel with an overflowing torrent of higher life. I cannot expect you to understand me without examples, and I must beg you to excuse the silliness of these examples. A watering-can, a harrow left abandoned in a field, a dog in the sun, a poor churchyard, a cripple, a small farmhouse, any one of these can become a vessel for my revelations. Each of them, and a thousand others like them, things which otherwise the eye passes over with natural indifference, can suddenly take on for me in a moment, which I am quite incapable of producing of my own will, an exalted and moving appearance, to express which all words seem to me inadequate. Yes, it can even be the fixed imagining of an absent object on which this inexplicable choice may fall, and this is then filled to the brim with a gently and abruptly rising tide of divine feeling. Thus, not long ago, I had given instructions for the milk-cellars of one of my leasehold farms to be liberally strewn with rat-poison. Towards evening, I rode out, and, as you may imagine, thought nothing further of it. There, as I trotted over the deeply-churned ploughland, with only a brood of quails scattering around me, and the big sun sinking far away over the undulating fields, a cellar suddenly opens up inside me, filled with the death-struggle of this population of rats. It was all there within me: the cool, fusty air of the cellar, filled with the sweetish, sharp smell of the poison, and the shrillness of the death-cries, rebounding off the mouldy walls; the cramps of impotence knotted into each other, and the scurrying desperations; the demented search for a way out; the cold look of fury when two meet in a blocked-up crack. But what am I doing with words, when I have renounced them! You remember, my friend, the wonderful description in Livy of the last hours before the destruction of Alba Longa? How they wander through the streets they are seeing for the last time . . . how they say goodbye to the stones on the ground. I tell you, my friend, this was in my mind, and the burning of

Carthage as well; but it was more, it was more godlike, more bestial; and it was present, fully and exaltedly present. There was a mother whose dying little ones were quivering around her, and who didn't look at them, nor at the implacable stone walls, but sent her glances into empty air, or through the air into endlessness, gnashing her teeth as she looked!—When a slave stood, full of helpless terror, near Niobe as she stiffened in death, he must have gone through what I went through when inside me the soul of this animal bared its teeth against its terrible doom.

Forgive me this description, don't think, however, that what I felt was pity. If you were to think that, then I would have chosen my example very badly. It was much more and much less than pity: a terrible empathy, a flowing across into those creatures, or a feeling that a fluid of life and death, of dreaming and waking, had flowed into them for a moment—from where? For what could it have to do with pity, what with rational human processes of thought, if on another evening I find a half-empty watering-can under a nut-tree, left there by a gardener's lad, and if that watering-can and the water in it, which is dark from the shadow of the tree, and a water-boatman, who is rowing across the surface of the water, from one gloomy bank to the other, if this combination of things of no consequence shakes me with such presence of infinity, shakes me from the roots of my hair to the marrow in my heels, so that I want to break out into words, of which I know that, if I found them, they would force down those cherubim in whom I don't believe, and I then turn away from this place silently, and weeks later, when I catch sight of that nut-tree, I pass it with a shy, sidelong glance, because I don't want to dispel the aftermath of the miracle that still surrounds the tree, I don't want to drive away the unearthly tremors that still pulse around the nearby foliage. In these moments, a trifling creature, a dog, a rat, a beetle, a shrivelled apple-tree, a cart-track winding over a hillside, a mossy stone, is more to me than the most beautiful and abandoned lover on the happiest night. These mute and sometimes inanimate creatures raise themselves towards me with such a fullness and presence of love, that my charmed eye is unable to find a dull spot anywhere in the vicinity. Everything, everything in my memory, everything my most confused thoughts have touched on, seems to be something. Even my own weight, and my otherwise dull brain appears to me to be something; I feel an enchanting, quite limitless counterpoint within me and around me, and among the substances playing against one another, there is none into which I could not flow. At such a time, I feel as though my body consisted entirely of ciphers, which reveal everything to me. Or as though we could enter into a new, intuitive relationship with the whole universe, if we began to think with our hearts. But when this extraordinary spell fades from me, I am unable to say anything about it; I could as little describe in sensible words what this harmony weaving me and the whole world together consisted of and how I perceived it, as I could describe in detail the inner movements of my intestines or the congestion of my blood.

Apart from these extraordinary occurrences, of which, by the way, I can hardly say whether they should be called physical or spiritual, I lead a life of almost unbelievable emptiness, and find it difficult to conceal from my wife the deadness that is inside me, and from my household my indifference to the business of ownership. The good, strict upbringing I owe my late father, and my old habit of leaving no hour of the day without occupation, alone, it seems to me, give my life the appearance of stability, and the demeanour suited to my estate and person.

I am rebuilding a wing of my house, and every now and then I manage to talk to the architect about the state of the work; I look after my land, and my tenants and stewards probably find me more taciturn than before, though no less kind. None of them, as they stand bare-headed outside their doors as I go riding by in the evening, will have an inkling that my eye, which they are accustomed to catch respectfully, is wandering with silent longing over the rotten planks, beneath which they go to look for earthworms to bait their hooks, that it dips through their small, barred windows into their fusty rooms, where the low bed in the corner seems always to be waiting for somebody to die or to be born; that my eye rests for a long time on ugly young dogs, or on the cat which stalks lightly among the flower-pots, and that among all the poor and coarse objects of an agricultural way of life, it is looking for the one whose improbable form, whose lying or leaning somewhere, unremarked by anyone, whose mute being can be the source of that mysterious, silent, boundless enchantment. For my nameless feeling of bliss is more likely to break forth at the sight of a single, distant shepherd's fire, than of the whole starry firmament; at the chirping of a last, dying grasshopper, as the autumn wind drives wintry clouds across the

barren fields, rather than the majestic drone of an organ. And sometimes in my thoughts I compare myself to the orator, Crassus, of
whom it is reported that he conceived such an inordinate affection
for a tame muraena, for a silent, red-eyed, dull fish in his ornamental
pond, that it became the talk of the town; and when Domitius once
upbraided him in the Senate for shedding tears at the death of this
fish, in order to make him out for a fool, Crassus answered him:
'What I did for the death of my fish, you did neither for the death of
your first wife, nor your second.'

I don't know how often Crassus with his muraena comes to my
mind as an image of myself, reflected across the abyss of the centuries. But not for the answer he gave Domitius. The answer brought
the laughers round to his side, and resolved the matter as a joke. But I
am affected by the matter itself, which would have remained the way
it was, even if Domitius had cried bloody tears of honest grief for his
wives. Then Crassus would still be confronting him, with his tears for
his muraena. And it is about this figure, whose ridicule and contempt
in the midst of the Senate that discussed the most lofty affairs and
that ruled the world is so apparent, that an unnameable something
makes me think in a way that seems to me entirely foolish when I try
to put it into words.

The image of Crassus is sometimes in my mind at night, like
a splinter around which everything festers, pulses and seethes. Then
it seems that I myself am in ferment, bubbling, simmering, sparkling.
And the whole thing is a kind of fevered thinking, but thinking in a
medium which is more immediate, more fluid and glowing than
words. It is like a whirlpool again, but not like those of language that
lead into bottomless emptiness, but somehow into myself, and the
deepest seat of peace.

My friend, I have troubled you unduly with this protracted
account of the inexplicable condition which usually remains locked
inside me.

You were so kind as to express your dissatisfaction with the fact
that no book of my authorship comes to you any more, 'to com-
pensate you for the want of my company'. At that moment, I felt with
a positive certainty which was not without some pain for me, that
in the next year, and the year thereafter, and in all the years of my
life I shall write no English and no Latin book: and this for a reason
whose—to me—distressing strangeness I leave it to your boundless

intellectual superiority to place with an undazzled vision there where it belongs in the array of spiritual and physical manifestations that are harmoniously spread out before you: namely, because the language in which it might perhaps have been given to me not only to write, but also to think, is neither Latin nor English nor Italian nor Spanish, but a language of which I do not know even one word, a language in which dumb things speak to me, and in which I may once, in my grave, have to account for myself before an unknown judge.

I wish it had been given to me, in the last words of this presumably last letter I shall write to Francis Bacon, to concentrate all the love and gratefulness, all the unmeasured admiration for the greatest benefactor of my spirit, and the foremost Englishman of my time that I hold in my heart, and will keep there until it breaks in death.

AD 1603, this 22nd August.

Phi. Chandos

6. RILKE (1875–1926)

Duineser Elegien 9 and 8; *Die Sonette an Orpheus* I.1, 3, 5, in *Sämtliche Werke*, ed. Ernst Zinn (Wiesbaden: Insel-Verlag, 1955–66).

Trans. A. Poulin, Jr., *Duino Elegies and The Sonnets to Orpheus* (Boston: Houghton Mifflin, 1977), pp. 61–67, 55–59, 85, 89, 93.

Born in Prague, Rainer Maria Rilke lived in the cultural world of the late Hapsburg Empire and epitomizes its intense passion for the arts. Aesthetic cultivation and refinement were a driving force throughout the poet's life, yet like other Viennese contemporaries, he obsessively confronted the limit where aesthetic sense can no longer articulate itself and must become speechless. In fact, just such a predicament was divulged by Rilke as the principle of his poetics in a dedication to the Polish translator of his *Duineser Elegien*: "Happy they who know that behind all languages lies the unsayable" ("Glücklich, die wissen, daß hinter aller Sprachen das Unsägliche steht").[1] The Elegies suggestively illustrate this principle. Completed in 1922, they were originally inspired and largely written in 1912 during Rilke's stay at the Duino castle of Princess Marie von Thorn und Taxis-Hohenlohe. Together with the *Sonnets to Orpheus*, all apparently written in February 1912 as the outcome of the poet's crisis of self-doubt and despair concerning his means of expression, they are commonly taken to represent the peak of his poetic production.

Rilke's poetry is situated constantly at the edge of what is sayable. In the ninth of his ten Duino Elegies, he seems to turn sharply away from the Unsayable, leaving out-of-reach things—"the stars"—alone as *better* unsayable ("*die* sind *besser* unsäglich"). In effect, he follows Wittgenstein's advice. He enjoins rather an adherence to the earth and to objects that can be named—house, bridge, fountain, gate, and so on. Saying such things appears to be our reason for being here ("Sind wir vielleicht *hier*, um zu sagen Haus, / Brücke, Brunnen, Tor, Krug, Obstbaum, Fenster . . ."). Accordingly, he celebrates the here and now that can be said: "*Here* is the time for the *sayable, here* is its home" ("*Hier* ist des *Säglichen* Zeit, *hier* seine Heimat").

---

1. Cited in Nibbrig, *Rhetorik des Schweigens*, p. 168.

Yet this acceptance of the condition of finitude, with its orientation toward the things that can be said, turns out to be not a renunciation so much as an indirect realization of something unsayably other and infinite. For human finitude transforms all things after its own image in an infinite process of metamorphosis. In our very evanescence is lodged our cosmic task: by saying the things that are and that vanish, we give them the present-perfect status of eternally having been, *once*, once and no more, never again, yet irrevocably having been. Our finite consciousness, by its very finiteness, thanks to our transitory being, refracts the finite objects it can grasp and say into the eternity that it cannot say but nevertheless somehow glimpses in the poem. In fact, all that the poet now says has been enabled by his wrestling with his "angels," his strife with what surpasses earth and everything nameable, a combat terrible beyond his comprehension and expression.

Rilke thus turns away from the other world "over there" ("hinüber") as beyond human reach, yet discloses it in doing so. He discloses the sayable world of things as a reflex of this other, uncanny (*unheimlich*) region from which he has drawn away: the "invisible Earth" and the infinite "we," unknown to ourselves, indirectly become through his poetry, by what it backs off from, the burden of the language of even ordinary things. In the last line of the ninth Elegy, Existence bursts forth in his heart as beyond reckoning, as without number, as countless or excessive—"Überzähliges"—an expression that by a sort of *double entendre* reads also as meaning "more than can be told," since it contains both "over" ("Über") and "tell" ("erzähl"), in addition to a plural form of "number" ("Zahl").

The eighth Elegy, by contrast, turns away from human saying and naming. It eulogizes the worldview of the dumb animal ("ein stummes") as free and open, a pure space ("den reinen Raum") in which flowers eternally bloom ("in den die Blumen / unendlich aufgehen"). This view is free from the trammels of human self-consciousness, which is blocked by objects in correlation to a subject hemmed in by death. Free from death ("Frei von Tod"), the brute beast's horizon is unlimited, in effect "God," whereas *we* see only death. Our world is not open and infinite but is produced by negation, which we are never and nowhere without ("niemals Nirgends ohne Nicht," lines 14–18). The fate of being always "over against" ("gegenüber sein"), defined by opposites, oppresses us. To the animal, its being is rather infinite, ungraspable ("sein Sein ist ihm / unendliche, ungefaßt," lines 38–42). Free of time and its oppositions, which make us live our lives forever taking leave ("so leben wir und nehmen immer Abschied"), the animal lives with its gaze trained on the Open ("das Offene"), with its demise always in back of it and God before it ("seinen

Untergang stets hinter sich und vor sich Gott"). It sees All and itself *in* All ("dort sieht es Alles / und sich in Allem") precisely because it and its reality are unarticulated. A human being can approach this mystic state perhaps only as a child who is lost in silent stillness ("Als Kind / verliert sich eins im Stilln").

The *Sonnets to Orpheus* continue this meditation on the threshold of speech as revealed from the animal kingdom. The negation of saying stands at the origin of the poetics of even that most natural of poets, Orpheus, as Rilke imagines him. The first composition is a programmatic poem that presents poetry as a deciphering of silence. The image for Orpheus's singing is one of hearing—"a tall tree in the ear"—rather than of voice. This image signifies an organic wholeness unbroken by voice: what is heard here is an all-pervading silence ("Und alles schwieg"), and this silence is heard as origin of all significant sound, not to mention articulate speech, before any gesture ("Wink") or inflection ("Wandlung") of meaning. Pre-articulate beasts feel this power of silence. Their own sounds reduce themselves to an inarticulate interior dimension of the "heart" ("Brüllen, Schrei, Geröhr / schien klein in ihren Herzen"). This silent power is thereby unveiled as broader than humanity and any of the universalities achieved by Logos or concepts. Orpheus's silent song contains all that can be said and even more that is supremely meaningful, as the dumb beasts can best attest. It is also described as a pure transcendence or "rising over" ("O reine Übersteigung!").

Hearing requires silence; we must become dumb like beasts to be receptive to Orpheus. Then his song grows like a tree in our ear. This happens in the silence and speechlessness of nature, in which an interior space or void opens, thanks to the void created by silencing human language. By not being endowed with speech, Orpheus's animals are more attuned to silence, though this may itself be a language:

> Fische sind stumm . . . , meinte man einmal. Wer weiß?
> Aber ist nicht am Ende ein Ort, wo man das, was der Fische
> Sprache wäre, *ohne* sie spricht?
>   (*Sonnets to Orpheus*, II, xx)

> Fish are dumb . . . one used to think. Who knows?
> But isn't there a place at last where perhaps what fish
> speech would be is spoken—*without* them?

Conversely, it is the silencing of common human language, language as we know it, that enables dumbness and silence themselves to wax eloquent. There is another language, a mysterious and revelatory language that is sounding and can be heard if we can ever quiet our conventional speech down enough. The sonnet preceding the one just cited defines this as a language that can be heard only by the godly and that can be said only in singing ("Nur dem Auf-singenden säglich / Nur dem Göttlichen hörbar," II, xix).

Rilke was fascinated by the idea of "the kind of speech that may be pos-sible THERE, where silence reigns." After writing the Elegies and Sonnets, he talked confidentially of "a language of word-kernels, a language that's not gathered, up above, on stalks, but grasped in the speech-seed. Would it not be in this language that the perfect Hymn to the Sun would have to be composed, and isn't the pure silence of love like heart-soil around such speech-seeds? Oh, how often one longs to speak a few degrees more deeply!"[2]

Some of Rilke's most purely apophatic poems are his *Vergers*, written in French. Here the themes of silence and nothingness, of search for an absent god, become fully explicit and obsessive:

> Si l'on chante un dieu,
> ce dieu vous rend son silence.
> Nul de nous ne s'avance
> que vers un dieu silencieux. . . .[3]
>
> (no. 9)

> If one sings a god,
> this god grants you his silence.
> None of us advances
> except toward a silent god. . . .

---

2. Rilke is quoted by J. R. von Salis, in *Rainer Maria Rilkes Schweizer Jahre*, p. 139. See *Duino Elegies*, ed. J. B. Leishman and Stepher Spender (New York: Norton, 1939), p. 18. See, further, Joachim W. Storck, "Poesie und Schweigen: Zum Enigmatischen in Rilkes später Lyrik," *Blätter der Rilke-Gesellschaft* 10 (1983): 107–121.

3. Rilke, *Sämtliche Werke* (Wiesbaden: Insel, 1963), vol. 2, p. 520.

Duino Elegy 9

Why, when this short span of being could be spent
like the laurel, a little darker than all
the other green, the edge of each leaf fluted
with small waves (like the wind's smile)—why,
then, do we have to be human and, avoiding fate,
long for fate?

        Oh, not because happiness,
that quick profit of impending loss, really exists.
Not out of curiosity, not just to exercise the heart
—that could be in the laurel, too . . .

But because being here means so much, and because all
that's here, vanishing so quickly, seems to need us
and strangely concerns us. Us, the first to vanish.
Once each, only *once. Once* and no more. And us too,
once. Never again. But to have been
once, even if only *once,*
to have been on *earth* just *once*—that's irrevocable.

And so we keep on going and try to realize it,
try to hold it in our simple hands, in
our overcrowded eyes, and in our speechless heart.
Try to become it. To give it to whom? We'd rather
keep all of it forever . . . Ah, but what can we take across
into that other realm? Not the power to see we've learned
so slowly here, and nothing that's happened here.
Nothing. And so, the pain; above all, the hard
work of living; the long experience of love—
those purely unspeakable things. But later,
under the stars, what then? That's better left unsaid.
For the wanderer doesn't bring a handful of that
unutterable earth from the mountainside down to the valley,
but only some word he's earned, a pure word, the yellow

and blue gentian. Maybe we're here only to say: *house,*
bridge, well, gate, jug, olive tree, window—
at most, *pillar, tower* . . . but to say them, remember,
oh, to say them in a way that the things themselves
never dreamed of existing so intensely. When this silent
earth urges lovers on, isn't it her secret reason
to make everything shudder with ecstasy in them?
Doorsill: how much it means to a pair of lovers
to wear down the sill of their own
door a little more, them too, after so many
before them, and before all those to come . . . gently.

This is the time for what can be said. *Here*
is its country. Speak and testify. The things
we can live with are falling away more
than ever, replaced by an act without symbol.
An act under crusts that will easily rip
as soon as the energy inside outgrows
them and seeks new limits.
Our heart survives between
hammers, just as the tongue between
the teeth is still able to praise.

Praise the world to the angel, not what can't be talked about.
You can't impress him with your grand emotions. In the cosmos
where he so intensely feels, you're just a novice. So show
him some simple thing shaped for generation after generation
until it lives in our hands and in our eyes, and it's ours.
Tell him about things. He'll stand amazed, just as you did
beside the ropemaker in Rome or the potter on the Nile.
Show him how happy a thing can be, how innocent and ours;
how even grief's lament purely determines its own shape,
serves as a thing, or dies in a thing—and escapes
in ecstasy beyond the violin. And these things, whose lives
are lived in leaving—they understand when you praise them.
Perishing, they turn to us, the most perishable, for help.
They want us to change them completely in our invisible hearts,
oh—forever—into us! Whoever we finally may be.

Earth, isn't this what you want: to resurrect
in us invisibly? Isn't it your dream
to be invisible one day? Earth! Invisible!
What's your urgent charge, if not transformation?
Earth, my love, I will. Oh, believe me, you don't
need your Springs to win me anymore—*one*,
oh, one's already too much for my blood.
I'm silently determined to be yours, from now on.
You were always right, and your most sacred
idea is death, that intimate friend.

Look, I'm alive. On what? Neither childhood nor
the future grows less . . . More being than I'll ever
need springs up in my heart.

Duino Elegy 8

Dedicated to Rudolf Kassner

All other creatures look into the Open
with their whole eyes. But our eyes,
turned inward, are set all around it like snares,
trapping its way out to freedom.
We know what's out there only from the animal's
face; for we take even the youngest child,
turn him around and force him to look
at the past as formation, not that openness
so deep within an animal's face. Free from death,
we only see it; the free animal
always has its destruction behind
and god ahead, and when it moves,
it moves toward eternity like running springs.

Not for a single day, no, never have we had
that pure space ahead of us, in which flowers
endlessly open. It is always World
and never Nowhere without No:
that pure, unguarded space we breathe,
always know, and never crave. As a child,
one may lose himself in silence and be
shaken out of it. Or one dies and *is* it.
Once near death, one can't see death anymore
and stares out, maybe with the wide eyes of animals.
If the other weren't there blocking the view,
lovers come close to it and are amazed . . .
It opens up behind the other, almost
an oversight . . . but no one gets past
the other, and the world returns again.
Always facing creation, all we see
is the reflection of the free and open
that we've darkened, or some mute animal
raising its calm eyes and seeing through us,
and through us. This is destiny: to be opposites,
always, and nothing else but opposites.

If this sure animal approaching us
from a different direction had our kind
of consciousness, he'd drag us around
in his wake. But to the animal, his being
is infinite, incomprehensible, and blind
to his condition, pure, like his outward gaze.
And where we see the future, he sees
all, himself in all, and whole forever.

And yet the weight and care of one great sadness
lies on this warm and watching creature.
Because what often overwhelms us
also clings to him—the memory
that what we so strive for now may have been
nearer, truer, and its attachment to us
infinitely tender, once. Here all is distance,
there it was breath. After that first home,
the second seems drafty and a hybrid.

Oh, blessed are the tiny creatures
who stay in the womb that bore them forever;
oh the joy of the gnat that can still leap *within*,
even on its wedding day; for the womb is all!
And look at the half-certainty of the bird
almost aware of both from birth,
like one of the Etruscan souls rising
from the dead man enclosed inside the space
for which his reclining figure forms a lid.
And how confused is anything that comes
from a womb and has to fly. As if afraid
of itself, it darts through the air
like a crack through a cup, the way a wing
of a bat crazes the porcelain of night.

And we: spectators, always, everywhere,
looking *at* everything and never *from!*
It floods us. We arrange it. It decays.
We arrange it again, and we decay.

Who's turned us around like this,
so that whatever we do, we always have
the look of someone going away? Just as a man
on the last hill showing him his whole valley
one last time, turns, and stops, and lingers—
so we live, and are forever leaving.

Sonnets to Orpheus I

1

A tree sprang up. O sheer transcendence!
O Orpheus sings! O tall tree in the ear!
And all was still. But even in that silence
a new beginning, hint, and change appeared.

Creatures of silence crowded out of the clear
freed forest, out of their dens and lairs;
and it was clear that inner silence of theirs
wasn't out of any cunning, any fear,

but out of listening. Growl, shriek, and roar
shrank in their hearts. And where there'd been
hardly a hut before to take this in,

a dugout carved from their darkest desire
with a lintel of trembling timber—
you erected temples for them in their inner ear.

3

A god can do it. But tell me, will you, how
a man can trail him through the narrow lyre?
His mind is forked. Where two heart's arteries
intersect, there stands no temple for Apollo.

Singing, as you teach us, isn't desiring,
nor luring something conquered in the end.
Singing is Being. For a god, it's almost nothing.
But when do we exist? And when does he spend

the earth and stars on our being? Young man,
your loving isn't it, even if your mouth
is pried open by your voice—learn

to forget your impulsive song. Soon it will end.
True singing is a different kind of breath.
A breath about nothing. A gust in the god. A wind.

5

Erect no memorial stone. Let the rose
bloom every year to remind us of him.
Because it's Orpheus. His metamorphosis
is in this, and this. No other name

should trouble us. Once and for all,
when there's song, it's Orpheus. He comes and goes.
Isn't it enough that now and then he's able
to outlive the bowl of roses a few days?

Oh how he has to vanish so you'll know!
Though he too were afraid of vanishing.
Even while his word's transcending being

here, he's already there, where you don't follow.
The lyre's lattice doesn't snare his hands.
And he obeys, even as he oversteps the bounds.

7. KAFKA (1883–1924)

"Von den Gleichnissen" and "Das Schweigen der Sirenen," in *Sämtliche Erzählungen*, ed. Paul Raabe (Frankfurt a.M.: Fischer, 1970), pp. 411, 350–351.

Trans. Willa and Edwin Muir, "On Parables" and "The Silence of the Sirens," in *The Complete Short Stories* (New York: Schocken, 1983), pp. 457, 430–432.

"The world of Kafka is the world of Revelation, but in the perspective where it is reduced to its Nothingness."[1] Gershom Scholem thereby suggests that Kafka's novels express the crisis of religious categories in modern secular culture. However, this "Nothingness of Revelation" (p. 175) turns into the source of a new, negative power of unlimited creativity. The very emptiness of categories like Revelation and Redemption in a traditional religious sense opens a whole new dimension that Kafka begins to explore, drawing scores of writers in his wake. Of course, this new source is, at the same time, very old. Treating Kafka as a "modern kabbalist," George Steiner reads Kafka's work as a testament of kabbalistic thought translated into a modern idiom.[2] Just as for Scholem, this means recognizing the void of silence as key to Kafka and Kafka as key to the question of silence: "In Kafka the question of silence is posed most radically. It is this which gives him his exemplary place in modern literature."[3]

Both of these critical approaches suggest how Kafka brings the Jewish sensibility for a transcendent, inexpressible God to expression in the climate of modernism. In accentuating to an extreme the absurdity of human existence, insofar as it is dependent upon an Absolute that humans can in no way grasp or fathom, Kafka's art produces a sort of black comedy. His major works of fiction are all predicated on an inscrutable mystery that surpasses human comprehension and reckoning and yet is everywhere enigmatically present and

---

1. *Walter Benjamin—Gershom Scholem: Briefwechsel* (Frankfurt a.M.: Suhrkamp, 1980), p. 157.

2. George Steiner, *After Babel* (Oxford: Oxford University Press, 1975).

3. George Steiner, "K," in *Language and Silence: Essays on Language, Literature, and the Inhuman* (New York: Atheneum, 1967), p. 123.

inescapable. From its opening words, his unfinished novel masterpiece, *The Castle*, engenders anxiety by the proliferation of expressions emanating from a secret source that proves impossible to divulge: "It was late evening, as K. arrived. The village lay deep in snow. Nothing could be seen of the castle mountain, surrounded by mist and darkness, not even the faintest appearance of light hinted at the great castle. K. stood long on the wooden bridge, which leads from the country road to the village, and looked up into the seeming emptiness."[4]

The castle looms unseen and impenetrable, in itself totally expressionless, while mysterious, endlessly interpretable expressions emanate from it into the finite world in which humans like K. stumble about, bruised and perplexed. The tenth chapter of the novel in particular focuses on the infinitely ambiguous significance of silence. When the surveyor, K., inquires of the innkeeper if he can ask her something and she is simply silent, he takes this as meaning he may not ask and is satisfied. She replies that he misinterprets even silence.[5]

The empty expressionlessness of the castle lies at the ground of all expressions in Kafka's book, and on its indecipherability hinges the ambiguous significance of everything in the surrounding twilight world. The authority represented by the castle proves to be all the more uninterpretable the more K. works to crack its code. The attempt only exacerbates his miseries. Every incident shows how futile his effort is and how grotesque the shifts to which he is put in endeavoring to combat this situation of impenetrable silence from above. A similar situation unfolds in *The Trial* (*Der Prozess*), the novel that made Kafka famous throughout Europe from the time of the Second World War. K.'s desperate, fruitless quest to find out what he is accused of itself becomes, in effect, his trial and condemnation.

In Kafka's major works in general, something enormous but elusive seems to command everything that happens in exasperatingly cryptic ways. This intangible "disaster" (in Blanchot's sense) is made manifest only by pure projection. The works turn on interpretations projected upon some seemingly

---

4. *Das Schloss* (New York: Schocken, 1935): "Es war spät abends, als K. ankam. Das Dorf lag in tiefem Schnee. Vom Schloßberg war nichts zu sehen, Nebel und Finsternis umgaben ihn, auch nicht der schwächste Lichtschein deutete das große Schloß an. Lange stand K. auf der Holzbrücke, die von der Landstraße zum Dorf führte, und blickte in die scheinbare Leere empor."

5. Cf. Peter Sprengel, "'Sie mißdeuten alles, auch das Schweigen': Zur Hermeneutik des Schweigens bei Kafka," in "*. . . wortlos der Sprache mächtig*": *Schweigen und Sprechen in der Literatur und sprachlicher Kommunikation*, ed. Hartmut Eggert and Janusz Golec (Stuttgart-Weimar: J. B. Metzler, 1999), pp. 59–82.

absolute, or at least *nearly* absolute authority and power that, rigorously and mysteriously, guards its silence. The protagonist's fate vis-à-vis this authority is totally determined by his *own interpretation*. This negative, silent, and enigmatic presence-absence exerts decisive, in effect, all-powerful influence by communicating nothing and thereby provoking the desperate effort to resist what is so indefinite as to be impossible to resist. So far as can be concretely ascertained, it is only the protagonist's own fabrication of the myth of this all-pervasive power that in fact renders it all-powerful over his life and actions.

Such is the negative power, or vacuum, at the center of Kafka's world. To cope with it and regain mastery, one would have to reduce oneself to an equal silence and stillness of purely negative power. Kafka imagines doing just that in a posthumous prose piece. He imagines discovering the world in its ecstasy through reduction of the self to perfect stillness: "You have no need to go out of the house. Stay at your table and listen. Don't even listen, just wait. Don't even wait, just be completely still and alone. The world will offer to unmask itself to you, it cannot do otherwise, it will disport itself before you ecstatically."[6]

Kafka's writing revolves obsessively around this problem of the irresistible power of passivity. Only by not expressing what it would express can his writing succeed, for all that he would write about cannot be expressed. Only the physical world can be expressed in language: "Language can be used for everything outside the sensible world only in a hinting manner, but never analogously even by approximation, since, as suits the sensible world, it deals only with possession and its relations."[7] Kafka is in the same predicament as Wittgenstein, yet in his mode of fiction he attempts nevertheless to write about the aesthetic and ethical issues for which the only language is silence. His fictive medium itself must therefore be understood as a mode of silence.

In his parable "Von den Gleichnissen" ("On Likenesses"), Kafka confronts the paradox that the likenesses or parables used by the wise actually point up only unbridgeable *un*likeness. As in Jabès's *The Book of Resemblances*, purported resemblance turns out to be an infinite distance separating its

---

6. "Es ist nicht notwendig, daß du aus dem Hause gehst. Bleib bei deinem Tisch und horche. Horche nicht einmal, warte nur. Warte nicht einmal, sei völlig still und allein. Anbieten wird sich dir die Welt zur Entlarvung, sie kann nicht anders, verzückt wird sie sich vor dir winden." *Hochzeitsvorbereitungen auf dem Lande und andere Prosa aus dem Nachlaß* (Frankfurt a. M.: Fischer, 1953), p. 54.

7. "Die Sprache kann für alles außerhalb der sinnlichen Welt nur andeutungsweise, aber niemals auch nur annährend verglichsweise gebraucht werden, da sie, entsprechend der sinnlichen Welt, nur vom Besitz und seinen Beziehungen handelt." *Betrachtung* 57 of *Hochzeitsvorbereitungen*, p. 45.

two terms of comparison. The parables or likenesses ("Gleichnissen" has both senses in German) point to something fabulous ("sagenhaftes"), a true world that is totally unlike ordinary experience, so that they cannot be followed and applied to life except by our becoming, like them, estranged from reality. But then the unreality that we *perceive* effectively changes the reality that we *are*, for our illusion of reality in this cave-world of shadow images is vanquished by self-consciousness. Still, this very victory constitutes a loss: the one who follows the parables of the wise and so becomes free, recognizing himself as a parable, wins in reality—but loses *im Gleichnis*, in the virtual, image world of simulacra and likenesses. Such transformed reality deprives those who have been enlightened by the parable of the fiction that is necessary in order for them to live what they now recognize as their unreality.[8]

This extremely significant, one paragraph work gives a key to Kafka's *oeuvre* as a whole in concluding that all comparisons mean simply that "the ungraspable is ungraspable, and we knew it" ("daß das Unfaßbare unfaßbar ist, und das haben wir gewußt"). This underscores an ironic turn in the tradition of apophatic wisdom as a wisdom that turns against itself. The negative knowledge that saves one from the contradictions of life, raising one to a level of wisdom, is viewed as gaining knowledge of the nothingness of "reality," but also as sacrificing the unencumbered free play, of our fictive, imaginary life— its wonderful "nothingness." Such wisdom does not congratulate itself on its superior insight, but negates itself and praises rather "folly." Knowledge can only be to know the vanity of knowledge vis-à-vis the unknowable.

A similar recognition of the (nearly) absolute power of the negative, along with the unmasterable ambiguities of its apprehension by humans, and hence of the negativity of all human consciousness, informs the parable of the Sirens. "The Silence of the Sirens" was written on October 23, 1917, and published posthumously. It reinterprets the myth of the Sirens: they allure humans by the irresistible seduction not of their singing but of their silence. The absolute attraction of their song can be exerted only through this zero-degree, which is its disappearance. In Homer, the voice of the Sirens is a presence so intense that all else loses significance and men forget themselves. In Kafka, it is the silence of the Sirens, the absence of any manifest presence, that effects an enthrallment more powerfully than any perceptible attractions could. It is the abyss of our own desire, unsatisfied by anything which *is*, that opens and

---

8. See the analysis of win/lose paradoxes in parable/reality by Wolf Kittler, *Der Turmbau zu Babel und das Schweigen der Sirenen: Über das Reden, das Schweigen, die Stimme und die Schrift in vier Texten von Franz Kafka* (Erlangen: Verlag Palm & Enke, 1985), pp. 157–181.

draws us to destruction. What seduces or incites desire is never at bottom anything finite and determinate; it is as infinite as desire itself and calls rather in limitless silence. Therefore the silence of the Sirens is far more enticing and threatening than any song they could sing. The Siren song is the voice of the Nothing of insatiable desire.

Kafka makes explicit that no actual object exerts this powerful force of attraction, but precisely the absence of any object. It is the infinity of desire negating all objects that draws men on to disaster in the vortex of their own limitless longing. Such is the recursive power of the unsayable that sustains endless speech, myth, narration, novels. This idea of genesis from its own unsayability is also crucial to Blanchot's notion of narrative as *récit*,[9] which he later extended to his theory of writing as disaster (*dés-astre*).

In Kafka's version, moreover, Odysseus escapes not by his cleverness but by childish innocence. He is so taken with his technical toys, the "childish means" ("kindische Mittel"), of the wax and chains, that he fails to even notice that the Sirens do not sing to him. Technology, in fact, with its superficial fascination inviting us to play, destroys the lure of religion and disenchants us with respect to the charms of art. The thrill of his own technical prowess totally absorbs Odysseus. However, if we are to give any credence to the fabled craftiness of Odysseus, we must contemplate another possibility, expressed as a sort of appendix to the parable. Perhaps Odysseus only plays at being ignorant in order to fool the gods and everyone else. In keeping with his character as established in the tradition, he would thus be the deceiver, not the deceived. It is impossible to decide between these alternatives, since what we have is not the true voice of tradition but merely a text, that is, the poor means, the artifact that enables us to escape enchantment—or to reinvent it in creating a new myth of our own.[10] Either alternative gives us truth only as negated.

In another fragment of *Hochzeitsvorbereitungen*, the impossibility of anything but a negative expression of truth is stated another way, as an inescapable contradiction between what one says and what one is: "Confession and lying are the same thing. In order to confess, one lies. That which one is one cannot express, for that is what one *is;* one can only communicate what one is not, thus the lie. Only in the chorus can there be a certain truth."[11]

---

9. Maurice Blanchot, "Le chant des sirènes," in *Le livre à venir* (Paris: Gallimard, 1959), pp. 9–17. Trans. Lydia Davis, "The Song of the Sirens," in *The Gaze of Orpheus* (Barrytown, N.Y.: Station Hill, 1981), pp. 105–109.

10. Kittler parses out these conundrums with painstaking precision.

11. *Hochzeitsvorbereitungen*, p. 343: "Geständnis und Lüge ist das Gleiche. Um gestehen zu können, lügt man. Das, was man ist, kann man nicht ausdrücken, denn

In this instance, Kafka at first links the inexpressible with the notion of an isolated individual harboring a secret interiority. This seems reminiscent of Romantic transcendentalism à la Melville. But then he inverts the value of this private, inexpressible dimension. It is no longer the truth. Only a corporate form of expression, the chorus, can bear witness to truth. Referred to any single individual, a confession lies, for in addition to being self-consciously crafted, it states something general: indeed, language can state only the general.

In his last work, the short fiction "Josephine, die Sängerin oder das Volk der Mäuse," Kafka is still representing the power of the negative as supreme. It is the lack of distinction of the voice of the singer, its virtual nonexistence as a musical value, that lends her voice its irresistible fascination: "This mere nothing of a voice asserts itself and finds its way to us; it is well to think of that." Hence the question: "Is it her singing that enchants us, or is it not rather the solemnity of the stillness by which her frail little voice is surrounded?" ("Ist es ihr Gesang, der uns entzückt oder nicht vielmehr die Feierlichkeit der Stille, von der das schwache Stimmchen umgeben ist?")[12]

More explicit statements of his impossible attempt to communicate the Incommunicable are found in the *Briefe an Milena*, where some of Kafka's most personal feelings are exposed: "I am still trying to communicate something incommunicable, to explain the inexplicable, to tell of something that I have in my bones and which can be experienced only in the bones. It is perhaps at bottom nothing but the fear, which we have talked of so often, but that fear extended to everything, fear of the greatest and smallest, crippling fear to pronounce a single word."[13]

Only Max Brod's "indiscretion" in disobeying his friend's last will and testament, which directed him to destroy all of Kafka's unpublished manuscripts, has given the world Kafka's writing in anything approaching its existing mass and amplitude. This final gesture—of attempting to cancel itself out—seals Kafka's writing as a whole under the sign of apophatic discourse that endeavors to take itself back.

---

dieses ist man eben; mitteilen kann man nur das, was man nicht ist, also die Lüge. Erst im Chor mag eine gewisse Wahrheit liegen."

12. "Josephine, die Sängerin oder das Volk der Mäuse," in *Sämtliche Erzählungen*, pp. 172–185.

13. "ich suche immerfort etwas Nicht-Mitteilbares mitzuteilen, etwas Unerklärbares zu erklären, von etwas zu erzählen, was ich in den Knochen habe und was nur in diesen Knochen erlebt werden kann. Es ist ja vielleicht im Grunde nichts anderes als jene Angst, von der schon so oft die Rede war, aber Angst ausgedehnt auf alles, Angst vor dem Größten wie Kleinsten, Angst, krampfhafte Angst vor dem Aussprechen eines Wortes." *Briefe an Milena* (New York: Schocken, 1952), p. 249. See, further, pp. 250 and 255.

On Parables

Many complain that the words of the wise are always merely parables and of no use in daily life, which is the only life we have. When the sage says: "Go over," he does not mean that we should cross to some actual place, which we could do anyhow if the labor were worth it; he means some fabulous yonder, something unknown to us, something that he cannot designate more precisely either, and therefore cannot help us here in the very least. All these parables really set out to say merely that the incomprehensible is incomprehensible, and we know that already. But the cares we have to struggle with every day: that is a different matter.

Concerning this a man once said: Why such reluctance? If you only followed the parables you yourselves would become parables and with that rid of all your daily cares.

Another said: I bet that is also a parable.

The first said: You have won.

The second said: But unfortunately only in parable.

The first said: No, in reality: in parable you have lost.

The Silence of the Sirens

Proof that inadequate, even childish measures may serve to rescue one from peril:

To protect himself from the Sirens Ulysses stopped his ears with wax and had himself bound to the mast of his ship. Naturally any and every traveler before him could have done the same, except those whom the Sirens allured even from a great distance; but it was known to all the world that such things were of no help whatever. The song of the Sirens could pierce through everything, and the longing of those they seduced would have broken far stronger bonds than chains and masts. But Ulysses did not think of that, although he had probably heard of it. He trusted absolutely to his handful of wax and his fathom of chain, and in innocent elation over his little stratagem sailed out to meet the Sirens.

Now the Sirens have a still more fatal weapon than their song, namely their silence. And though admittedly such a thing has never happened, still it is conceivable that someone might possibly have escaped from their singing; but from their silence certainly never. Against the feeling of having triumphed over them by one's own strength, and the consequent exaltation that bears down everything before it, no earthly powers can resist.

And when Ulysses approached them the potent songstresses actually did not sing, whether because they thought that this enemy could be vanquished only by their silence, or because the look of bliss on the face of Ulysses, who was thinking of nothing but his wax and his chains, made them forget their singing.

But Ulysses, if one may so express it, did not hear their silence; he thought they were singing and that he alone did not hear them. For a fleeting moment he saw their throats rising and falling, their breasts lifting, their eyes filled with tears, their lips half-parted, but believed that these were accompaniments to the airs which died unheard around him. Soon, however, all this faded from his sight as he fixed his gaze on the distance, the Sirens literally vanished before his resolution, and at the very moment when they were nearest to him he knew of them no longer.

But they—lovelier than ever—stretched their necks and turned, let their awesome hair flutter free in the wind, and freely stretched their claws on the rocks. They no longer had any desire to allure; all that they wanted was to hold as long as they could the radiance that fell from Ulysses' great eyes.

If the Sirens had possessed consciousness they would have been annihilated at that moment. But they remained as they had been; all that had happened was that Ulysses had escaped them.

A codicil to the foregoing has also been handed down. Ulysses, it is said, was so full of guile, was such a fox, that not even the goddess of fate could pierce his armor. Perhaps he had really noticed, although here the human understanding is beyond its depths, that the Sirens were silent, and held up to them and to the gods the aforementioned pretense merely as a sort of shield.

8. BENJAMIN (1892–1940)

"Die Aufgabe des Übersetzers," in *Illuminationen: Ausgewählte Schriften I* (Frankfurt a.M.: Suhrhamp, 1977), pp. 50–62.

Trans. Harry Zohn, "The Task of the Translator," in *Illuminations: Essays and Reflections,* ed. Hannah Arendt (New York: Schocken, 1968), pp. 69–82.

Although during his lifetime the work of Walter Benjamin went virtually unnoticed, except by a few friends such as Theodor Adorno and Gershom Scholem, it has been a main impetus to literary criticism and theory since the 1960s. From early on, Benjamin's thinking hinged on a theory of knowledge that rejects modern subjectivity and its autonomous reason in favor of a theological concept of language as the creator of world and self together in a unity that reason cannot grasp. Through the resources of Jewish tradition and the doctrine of Creation by the Word, Benjamin attempts to escape from the impasse where self and world, subject and object, knowledge and being, are divided by an epistemological gulf. He devises a linguistic epistemology modeled on the idea of revelation by the divine Word, in which language in its immediacy—not as an object, nor as a medium of representation, but as pure mediation of nothing but itself—is recognized as revelation and indeed as a magical disclosure of the created natures of things.

Focusing on language as the unifying principle of all knowledge in the attempt to escape the dilemmas of modern epistemology, and countering the vulgar theory of language as a mere convention and instrument for human communication, Benjamin's early thinking on language postulates that God's speech is both a knowing and a creating, at once and inseparably.[1] After and outside of that initial speaking of "language as such," mind and matter are pitted against each other; they become abstractions from the continuum of creative speaking, and true communication or understanding between them is

---

1. Walter Benjamin, "Über die Sprache überhaupt und über die Sprache des Menschen" (1916), in *Gesammelte Schriften* (Frankfurt a.M.: Suhrkamp, 1977), vol. 2, pt. 1, pp. 140–157, trans. Edmund Jephcott, "On Language as Such and on the Language of Man," in *Reflections: Essays, Aphorisms, Autobiographical Writings* (New York: Harcourt Brace Jovanovich, 1978), pp. 314–332.

no longer possible. Only language as such preserves the original unity that the individual subject's reflexive consciousness can never recover. This is an aspect of language beyond what can be expressed by a conscious subject in propositions. It withdraws from discursive and argumentative expression. It can be divined rather in the act of naming and in works of art. It makes possible a theological kind of knowing by revelation in the word, in a way that the Enlightenment belief in the autonomy of reason obscures.[2]

Language fascinates Benjamin as being an immediacy, a direct manifestation of creative power that circumvents signification. Yet this is really the case only for language as such, not for the language of signs separate from objects that is commonly spoken by human beings. Human language in its present state is fallen. It is only through the destruction of signification that immediacy of meaning, as in Adamitic speech, where word and thing are one in essence, can be registered and apprehended in human language. Hence the concept of the inexpressible ("Ausdruckslosen"), which breaks the circuit of signification, is at the center of literary-critical works such as Benjamin's essay on Hölderlin's poems.[3]

In "The Task of the Translator" (1921), which he wrote as a preface to Baudelaire's *Tableaux Parisiennes,* Benjamin distinguishes between a rational, communicable meaning ("Mitteilung," "Sinn," "Aussage") and the "manner of meaning" ("Art des Meinens"), an intention directed upon language as such ("Intention auf die Sprache als solche"). He calls the latter "pure language" ("reine Sprache"). According to Benjamin, the translation of a literary classic confers recognition upon it as belonging, independently of any extratextual world or reality, to "pure language" as a sphere of universal communicability. In being translated, the literary work achieves the status of a language that is a supreme value in itself, purely on the strength of its own verbal resources. It is marked as translatable into another language, any language, apart from—and without—what it says, since this is, strictly speaking, untranslatable, and inseparable from the socially and linguistically concrete world in which it inheres. Translation is essentially not of communicable meaning but of the un-

2. Cf. Michael Bröcker, *Die Grundlosigkeit der Wahrheit: Zum Verhältnis von Sprache, Geschichte und Theologie bei Walter Benjamin* (Würzburg: Königshausen und Neumann, 1993), p. 12.

3. Walter Benjamin, "Zwei Gedichte von Friedrich Hölderlin. 'Dichtermut'—'Blödigkeit.'" In *Illuminationen,* pp. 21–41. See also "Das Schweigen als Aura," in *Charles Baudelaire: Ein Lyriker im Zeitalter des Hochkapitalismus,* in *Gesammelte Schriften,* vol. 1, pt. 2, p. 674.

graspable, the enigmatic, and the poetic ("das Unfaßbare, Geheimnisvolle, Dichterische," p. 56).

The unsayable in language—pure language—is thereby exalted in the most unmistakable manner. Pure language emerges from the act of translation because it is what cannot be expressed directly by any single language alone. Hence translation works as a foregrounding and an apotheosis of an inexpressible layer, a sort of superstratum of pure language. In translation, language signifies a higher language than itself and thereby estranges itself from and even violates its own historical and semantic content ("sie bedeutet eine höhere Sprache als sie ist und bleibt dadurch ihrem eigenen Gehalt gegenüber unangemessen, gewaltig und fremd," p. 62). As such, it is revealed as pure—and expressionless. Pure language erases all that is sayable and said: that is how it is manifest—as the "Non-communicable" ("das Nicht-Mitteilbares") in all languages (p. 66).

Benjamin concentrates on moments where language breaks down and signifies something other, something higher than its meaning or content. He does not always figure this realm as "unsayable," but it is the negative of the sayable, of content and expression in the ordinary sense. And he does explicitly describe pure language as "expressionless": "In this pure language—which no longer means or expresses anything but is, as expressionless and creative Word, that which is meant in all languages—all information, all sense, and all intention finally encounter a stratum in which they are destined to be extinguished. . . . It is the task of the translator to release in his own language that pure language which is under the spell of another, to liberate the language imprisoned in a work in his re-creation of that work."[4]

Benjamin thus understands the unsayable or inexpressible to be language in its im-mediacy, or turned toward itself as "intent upon language as such." However, only in the fragmentariness of historical languages can this pure language be manifest to humans. It is evidenced in the impasses to expression, particularly as encountered in the attempt to translate poetry. The inexpressible is expressed only in this negative way, yet it is also understood as a higher order of being and truth. Its breaking into history and human language is

---

4. "In dieser reinen Sprache, die nichts mehr meint und nichts mehr ausdrückt, sondern ausdrucksloses und schöpferisches Wort das in allen Sprachen Gemeinte ist, trifft endlich alle Mitteilung, aller Sinn und alle Intention auf eine Schicht, in der sie zu erlöschen bestimmt sind. . . . Jene reine Sprache, die in fremde gebannt ist, in der eigene zu erlösen, die im Werk gefangene in der Umdichtung zu befreien, ist die Aufgabe des Übersetzers" (p. 67).

experienced as "messianic." In language is some greater, albeit semantically uncircumscribable being. It is glimpsed between languages—in translation. Language contains the whole of reality—but as broken, dis-articulated. The messianic moment is this break. Its unity can be experienced only as the interruption of time as continuity, with its before and after: it is realized by the shattering of time.[5]

Benjamin's mystical theology of language stands in the tradition of the Kabbalah, though his knowledge of this tradition seems to have been mainly indirect, through Jakob Böhme, the German Protestant thinker Johann Georg Hamann, and German Romantics such as Friedrich Schlegel and Novalis.[6] Benjamin used the mystical theory of language to point up a supra-rational dimension that the bourgeois understanding of language could not grasp. Nevertheless, he understood the origin of linguistic "magic" as profane and material. This linguistic magic, informed by the theosophical doctrine of the Kabbalah, is not per se mystical, though it valorizes what mystic experience perceives and rational theory denies.

Benjamin occupies an ambiguous position on the contemporary critical scene between mysticism and materialism: he "thinks" the mystical on the basis of the material. The material, in its unaccountable facticity, its simply being there, is something per se magical—the miracle of Creation. The secret of Benjamin's work, contended over by Theology and Marxism, each claiming it as their own, is its radical allegiance to both.[7] The world is a material, rational order such as Marxism posits, yet the key to its understanding has been kept secret in the custody of theological revelation. Creation of the material world by the divine Logos, the transcendent Word, means that it is inaccessible to rational comprehension as a whole and yet still thoroughly linguistic and even rational in every part. Reason becomes infinite by being shattered into infinite fragments: such reason is the divine mind as we can discover it in the materialities of our existence.

---

5. See especially Benjamin's culminating work, his "Theses on the Philosophy of History" ("Geschichtsphilosophische Thesen," in *Illuminationen*, pp. 268–281).

6. Winfried Menninghaus, *Walter Benjamins Theorie der Sprachmagie* (Frankfurt a.M.: Suhrkamp, 1988), especially Part III: "Sprachmystik und philosophie der gewöhnlichen Sprache."

7. See Henning Günther, *Walter Benjamin: Zwischen Marxismus und Theologie* (Freiburg: Walter-Verlag, 1974).

The Task of the Translator

In the appreciation of a work of art or an art form, consideration of the receiver never proves fruitful. Not only is any reference to a certain public or its representatives misleading, but even the concept of an "ideal" receiver is detrimental in the theoretical consideration of art, since all it posits is the existence and nature of man as such. Art, in the same way, posits man's physical and spiritual existence, but in none of its works is it concerned with his response. No poem is intended for the reader, no picture for the beholder, no symphony for the listener.

Is a translation meant for readers who do not understand the original? This would seem to explain adequately the divergence of their standing in the realm of art. Moreover, it seems to be the only conceivable reason for saying "the same thing" repeatedly. For what does a literary work "say"? What does it communicate? It "tells" very little to those who understand it. Its essential quality is not statement or the imparting of information. Yet any translation which intends to perform a transmitting function cannot transmit anything but information—hence, something inessential. This is the hallmark of bad translations. But do we not generally regard as the essential substance of a literary work what it contains in addition to information—as even a poor translator will admit—the unfathomable, the mysterious, the "poetic," something that a translator can reproduce only if he is also a poet? This, actually, is the cause of another characteristic of inferior translation, which consequently we may define as the inaccurate transmission of an inessential content. This will be true whenever a translation undertakes to serve the reader. However, if it were intended for the reader, the same would have to apply to the original. If the original does not exist for the reader's sake, how could the translation be understood on the basis of this premise?

Translation is a mode. To comprehend it as mode one must go back to the original, for that contains the law governing the translation: its translatability. The question of whether a work is translatable has a dual meaning. Either: Will an adequate translator ever be found among the totality of its readers? Or, more pertinently: Does its nature lend itself to translation and, therefore, in view of the significance of the mode, call for it? In principle, the first question can be decided only contingently; the second, however, apodictically. Only superficial thinking will deny the independent meaning of the latter and declare both questions to be of equal significance. . . . It should be pointed out that certain correlative concepts retain their meaning, and possibly their foremost significance, if they are referred exclusively to man. One might, for example, speak of an unforgettable life or moment even if all men had forgotten it. If the nature of such a life or moment required that it be unforgotten, that predicate would not imply a falsehood but merely a claim not fulfilled by men, and probably also a reference to a realm in which it *is* fulfilled: God's remembrance. Analogously, the translatability of linguistic creations ought to be considered even if men should prove unable to translate them. Given a strict concept of translation, would they not really be translatable to some degree? The question as to whether the translation of certain linguistic creations is called for ought to be posed in this sense. For this thought is valid here: If translation is a mode, translatability must be an essential feature of certain works.

Translatability is an essential quality of certain works, which is not to say that it is essential that they be translated; it means rather that a specific significance inherent in the original manifests itself in its translatability. It is plausible that no translation, however good it may be, can have any significance as regards the original. Yet, by virtue of its translatability the original is closely connected with the translation; in fact, this connection is all the closer since it is no longer of importance to the original. We may call this connection a natural one, or, more specifically, a vital connection. Just as the manifestations of life are intimately connected with the phenomenon of life without being of importance to it, a translation issues from the original—not so much from its life as from its afterlife. For a translation comes later than the original, and since the important works of world literature never find their chosen translators at the time of their origin, their translation marks their stage of continued life. The idea of life and afterlife in works of art should be regarded with an entirely unmetaphorical objectivity. Even in times of narrowly prejudiced thought there was an inkling that life was not limited to organic corporeality. But it cannot be a matter of extending its dominion under the feeble scepter of the soul, as Fechner tried to do, or, conversely, of basing its definition on the even less conclusive factors of animality, such as sensation, which characterize life only occasionally. The concept of life is given its due only if everything that has a history of its own, and is not merely the setting for history, is credited with life. In the final analysis, the range of life must be determined by history rather than by nature, least of all by such tenuous factors as sensation and soul. The philosopher's task consists in comprehending all of natural life through the more encompassing life of history. And indeed, is not the continued life of works of art far easier to recognize than the continual life of animal species? The history of the great works of art tells us about their antecedents, their realization in the age of the artist, their potentially eternal afterlife in succeeding generations. Where this last manifests itself, it is called fame. Translations that are more than transmissions of subject matter come into being when in the course of its survival a work has reached the age of its fame. Contrary, therefore, to the claims of bad translators, such translations do not so much serve the work as owe their existence to it. The life of the originals attains in them to its ever-renewed latest and most abundant flowering.

Being a special and high form of life, this flowering is governed by a special, high purposiveness. The relationship between life and purposefulness, seemingly obvious yet almost beyond the grasp of the intellect, reveals itself only if the ultimate purpose toward which all single functions tend is sought not in its own sphere but in a higher one. All purposeful manifestations of life, including their very purposiveness, in the final analysis have their end not in life, but in the expression of its nature, in the representation of its significance. Translation thus ultimately serves the purpose of expressing the central reciprocal relationship between languages. It cannot possibly reveal or establish this hidden relationship itself; but it can represent it by realizing it in embryonic or intensive form. This representation of hidden significance through an embryonic attempt at making it visible is of so singular a nature that it is rarely met with in the sphere of nonlinguistic life. This, in its analogies and symbols, can draw on other ways of suggesting meaning than intensive—that is, anticipative, intimating—realization. As for the posited central kinship of languages, it is marked by a distinctive convergence. Languages are not strangers to one another, but are, a priori and apart from all historical relationships, interrelated in what they want to express.

With this attempt at an explication our study appears to rejoin, after futile detours, the traditional theory of translation. If the kinship of languages is to be demonstrated by translations, how else can this be done but by conveying the form and meaning of the original as accurately as possible? To be sure, that theory would be hard put to define the nature of this accuracy and therefore could shed no light on what is important in a translation. Actually, however, the kinship of languages is brought out by a translation far more profoundly and clearly than in the superficial and indefinable similarity of two works of literature. To grasp the genuine relationship between an original and a translation requires an investigation analogous to the argumentation by which a critique of cognition would have to prove the impossibility of an image theory. There it is a matter of showing that in cognition there could be no objectivity, not even a claim to it, if it dealt with images of reality; here it can be demonstrated that no translation would be possible if in its ultimate essence it strove for likeness to the original. For in its afterlife—which could not be called that if it were not a transformation and a renewal of something living—the original undergoes a change. Even words with fixed meaning can undergo a maturing process. The obvious tendency of a writer's literary style may in time wither away, only to give rise to immanent tendencies in the literary creation. What sounded fresh once may sound hackneyed later; what was once current may someday sound quaint. To seek the essence of such changes, as well as the equally constant changes in meaning, in the subjectivity of posterity rather than in the very life of language and its works, would mean— even allowing for the crudest psychologism—to confuse the root cause of a thing with its essence. More pertinently, it would mean denying, by an impotence of thought, one of the most powerful and fruitful historical processes. And even if one tried to turn an author's last stroke of the pen into the *coup de grâce* of his work, this still would not save that dead theory of translation. For just as the tenor and the significance of the great works of literature undergo a complete transformation over the centuries, the mother tongue of the translator is transformed as well. While a poet's words endure in his own language, even the greatest translation is destined to become part of the growth of its own language and eventually to be absorbed by its renewal. Translation is so far removed from being the sterile equation of two dead languages that of all literary forms it is the one charged with the special mission of watching over the maturing process of the original language and the birth pangs of its own.

If the kinship of languages manifests itself in translations, this is not accomplished through a vague alikeness between adaptation and original. It stands to reason that kinship does not necessarily involve likeness. The concept of kinship as used here is in accord with its more restricted common usage: in both cases, it cannot be defined adequately by identity of origin, although in defining the more restricted usage the concept of origin remains indispensable. Wherein resides the relatedness of two languages, apart from historical considerations? Certainly not in the similarity between works of literature or words. Rather, all suprahistorical kinship of languages rests in the intention underlying each language as a whole—an intention, however, which no single language can attain by itself but which is realized only by the totality of their intentions supplementing each other: pure language. While all individual elements of foreign languages—words, sentences, structure—are mutually exclusive, these languages supplement one another in their intentions. Without distinguishing the intended object from the mode of intention, no firm grasp of this basic law of a philosophy of language can be achieved. The words *Brot* and *pain* "intend" the same object, but the modes of this intention are not the same. It is owing to these modes that the word *Brot* means something different to a German than the word *pain* to a Frenchman, that these words are not interchangeable for them, that, in fact, they strive to exclude each other. As to the intended object, however, the two words mean the very same thing. While the modes of intention in these two words are in conflict, intention and object of intention complement each of the two languages from which they are derived; there the object is complementary to the intention. In the individual, unsupplemented languages, meaning is never found in relative independence, as in individual words or sentences; rather, it is in a constant state of flux—until it is able to emerge as pure language from the harmony of all the various modes of intention. Until then, it remains hidden in the languages. If, however, these languages continue to grow in this manner until the end of their time, it is translation which catches fire on the eternal life of the works and the perpetual renewal of language. Translation keeps putting the hallowed growth of languages to the test: How far removed is their hidden meaning from revelation, how close can it be brought by the knowledge of this remoteness?

This, to be sure, is to admit that all translation is only a somewhat provisional way of coming to terms with the foreignness of languages. An instant and final rather than a temporary and provisional solution of this foreignness remains out of the reach of mankind; at any rate, it eludes any direct attempt. Indirectly, however, the growth of religions ripens the hidden seed into a higher development of language. Although translation, unlike art, cannot claim permanence for its products, its goal is undeniably a final, conclusive, decisive stage of all linguistic creation. In translation the original rises into a higher and purer linguistic air, as it were. It cannot live there permanently, to be sure, and it certainly does not reach it in its entirety. Yet, in a singularly impressive manner, at least it points the way to this region: the predestined, hitherto inaccessible realm of reconciliation and fulfillment of languages. The transfer can never be total, but what reaches this region is that element in a translation which goes beyond transmittal of subject matter. This nucleus is best defined as the element that does not lend itself to translation. Even when all the surface content has been extracted and transmitted, the primary concern of the genuine translator remains elusive. Unlike the words of the original, it is not translatable, because the relationship between content and language is quite different in the original and the translation. While content and language form a certain unity in the original, like a fruit and its skin, the language of the translation envelops its content like a royal robe with ample folds. For it signifies a more exalted language than its own and thus remains unsuited to its content, overpowering and alien. This disjunction prevents translation and at the same time makes it superfluous. For any translation of a work originating in a specific stage of linguistic history represents, in regard to a specific aspect of its content, translation into all other languages. Thus translation, ironically, transplants the original into a more definitive linguistic realm since it can no longer be displaced by a secondary rendering. The original can only be raised there anew and at other points of time. It is no mere coincidence that the word "ironic" here brings the Romanticists to mind. They, more than any others, were gifted with an insight into the life of literary works which has its highest testimony in translation. To be sure, they hardly recognized translation in this sense, but devoted their entire attention to criticism, another, if a lesser, factor in the continued life of literary works. But even though the Romanticists virtually ignored translation in their theoretical writings, their own great translations testify to their sense of the essential nature and the dignity of this literary mode. There is abundant evidence that this sense is not necessarily most pronounced in a poet; in fact, he may be least open to it. Not even literary history suggests the traditional notion that great poets have been eminent translators and lesser poets have been indifferent translators. A number of the most eminent ones, such as Luther, Voss, and Schlegel, are incomparably more important as translators than as creative writers; some of the great among them, such as Hölderlin and Stefan George, cannot be simply subsumed as poets, and quite particularly not if we consider them as translators. As translation is a mode of its own, the task of the translator, too, may be regarded as distinct and clearly differentiated from the task of the poet.

The task of the translator consists in finding that intended effect [*Intention*] upon the language into which he is translating which produces in it the echo of the original. This is a feature of translation which basically differentiates it from the poet's work, because the effort of the latter is never directed at the language as such, at its totality, but solely and immediately at specific linguistic contextual aspects. Unlike a work of literature, translation does not find itself in the center of the language forest but on the outside facing the wooded ridge; it calls into it without entering, aiming at that single spot where the echo is able to give, in its own language, the reverberation of the work in the alien one. Not only does the aim of translation differ from that of a literary work—it intends language as a whole, taking an individual work in an alien language as a point of departure—but it is a different effort altogether. The intention of the poet is spontaneous, primary, graphic; that of the translator is derivative, ultimate, ideational. For the great motif of integrating many tongues into one true language is at work. This language is one in which the independent sentences, works of literature, critical judgments, will never communicate—for they remain dependent on translation; but in it the languages themselves, supplemented and reconciled in their mode of signification, harmonize. If there is such a thing as a language of truth, the tensionless and even silent depository of the ultimate truth which all thought strives for, then this language of truth is—the true language. And this very language, whose divination and description is the only perfection a philosopher can hope for, is concealed in concentrated fashion in translations. There is no muse of philosophy, nor is there one of translation. But despite the claims of sentimental artists, these two are not banausic. For there is a philosophical genius that is characterized by a yearning for that language which manifests itself in translations. "*Les langues imparfaites en cela que plusieurs, manque la suprême: penser étant écrire sans accessoires, ni chuchotement mais tacite encore l'immortelle parole, la diversité, sur terre, des idiomes empêche personne de proférer les mots qui, sinon se trouveraient, par une frappe unique, elle-même matériellement la vérité.*" [The imperfection of languages consists in their plurality, the supreme one is lacking: thinking is writing without accessories or even whispering, the immortal word still remains silent; the diversity of idioms on earth prevents everybody from uttering the words which otherwise, at one single stroke, would materialize as truth.] If what Mallarmé evokes here is fully fathomable to a philosopher, translation, with its rudiments of such a language, is midway between poetry and doctrine. Its products are less sharply defined, but it leaves no less of a mark on history.

If the task of the translator is viewed in this light, the roads toward a solution seem to be all the more obscure and impenetrable. Indeed, the problem of ripening the seed of pure language in a translation seems to be insoluble, determinable in no solution. For is not the ground cut from under such a solution if the reproduction of the sense ceases to be decisive? Viewed negatively, this is actually the meaning of all the foregoing. The traditional concepts in any discussion of translations are fidelity and license—the freedom of faithful reproduction and, in its service, fidelity to the word. These ideas seem to be no longer serviceable to a theory that looks for other things in a translation than reproduction of meaning. To be sure, traditional usage makes these terms appear as if in constant conflict with each other. What can fidelity really do for the rendering of meaning? Fidelity in the translation of individual words can almost never fully reproduce the meaning they have in the original. For sense in its poetic significance is not limited to meaning, but derives from the connotations conveyed by the word chosen to express it. We say of words that they have emotional connotations. A literal rendering of the syntax completely demolishes the theory of reproduction of meaning and is a direct threat to comprehensibility. The nineteenth century considered Hölderlin's translations of Sophocles as monstrous examples of such literalness. Finally, it is self-evident how greatly fidelity in reproducing the form impedes the rendering of the sense. Thus no case for literalness can be based on a desire to retain the meaning. Meaning is served far better—and literature and language far worse—by the unrestrained license of bad translators. Of necessity, therefore, the demand for literalness, whose justification is obvious, whose legitimate ground is quite obscure, must be understood in a more meaningful context. Fragments of a vessel which are to be glued together must match one another in the smallest details, although they need not be like one another. In the same way a translation, instead of resembling the meaning of the original, must lovingly and in detail incorporate the original's mode of signification, thus making both the original and the translation recognizable as fragments of a greater language, just as fragments are part of a vessel. For this very reason translation must in large measure refrain from wanting to communicate something, from rendering the sense, and in this the original is important to it only insofar as it has already relieved the translator and his translation of the effort of assembling and expressing what is to be conveyed. In the realm of translation, too, the words ἐν ἀρχῇ ἦν ὁ λόγος [in the beginning was the word] apply. On the other hand, as regards the meaning, the language of a translation can—in fact, must—let itself go, so that it gives voice to the *intentio* of the original not as reproduction but as harmony, as a supplement to the language in which it expresses itself, as its own kind of *intentio*. Therefore it is not the highest praise of a translation, particularly in the age of its origin, to say that it reads as if it had originally been written in that language. Rather, the significance of fidelity as ensured by literalness is that the work reflects the great longing for linguistic complementation. A real translation is transparent; it does not cover the original, does not block its light, but allows the pure language, as though reinforced by its own medium, to shine upon the original all the more fully. This may be achieved, above all, by a literal rendering of the syntax which proves words rather than sentences to be the primary element of the translator. For if the sentence is the wall before the language of the original, literalness is the arcade.

Fidelity and freedom in translation have traditionally been regarded as conflicting tendencies. This deeper interpretation of the one apparently does not serve to reconcile the two; in fact, it seems to deny the other all justification. For what is meant by freedom but that the rendering of the sense is no longer to be regarded as all-important? Only if the sense of a linguistic creation may be equated with the information it conveys does some ultimate, decisive element remain beyond all communication—quite close and yet infinitely remote, concealed or distinguishable, fragmented or powerful. In all language and linguistic creations there remains in addition to what can be conveyed something that cannot be communicated; depending on the context in which it appears, it is something that symbolizes or something symbolized. It is the former only in the finite products of language, the latter in the evolving of the languages themselves. And that which seeks to represent, to produce itself in the evolving of languages, is that very nucleus of pure language. Though concealed and fragmentary, it is an active force in life as the symbolized thing itself, whereas it inhabits linguistic creations only in symbolized form. While that ultimate essence, pure language, in the various tongues is tied only to linguistic elements and their changes, in linguistic creations it is weighted with a heavy, alien meaning. To relieve it of this, to turn the symbolizing into the symbolized, to regain pure language fully formed in the linguistic flux, is the tremendous and only capacity of translation. In this pure language—which no longer means or expresses anything but is, as expressionless and creative Word, that which is meant in all languages—all information, all sense, and all intention finally encounter a stratum in which they are destined to be extinguished. This very stratum furnishes a new and higher justification for free translation; this justification does not derive from the sense of what is to be conveyed, for the emancipation from this sense is the task of fidelity. Rather, for the sake of pure language, a free translation bases the test on its own language. It is the task of the translator to release in his own language that pure language which is under the spell of another, to liberate the language imprisoned in a work in his re-creation of that work. For the sake of pure language he breaks through decayed barriers of his own language. Luther, Voss, Hölderlin, and George have extended the boundaries of the German language.—And what of the sense in its importance for the relationship between translation and original? A simile may help here. Just as a tangent touches a circle lightly and at but one point, with this touch rather than with the point setting the law according to which it is to continue on its straight path to infinity, a translation touches the original lightly and only at the infinitely small point of the sense, thereupon pursuing its own course according to the laws of fidelity in the freedom of linguistic flux. Without explicitly naming or substantiating it, Rudolf Pannwitz has characterized the true significance of this freedom. His observations are contained in *Die Krisis der europäischen Kultur* and rank with Goethe's Notes to the *Westöstlicher Divan* as the best comment on the theory of translation that has been published in Germany. Pannwitz writes: "Our translations, even the best ones, proceed from a wrong premise. They want to turn Hindi, Greek, English into German instead of turning German into Hindi, Greek, English. Our translators have a far greater reverence for the usage of their own language than for the spirit of the foreign works. . . . The basic error of the translator is that he preserves the state in which his own language happens to be instead of allowing his language to be powerfully affected by the foreign tongue. Particularly when translating from a language very remote from his own he must go back to the primal elements of language itself and penetrate to the point where work, image, and tone converge. He must expand and deepen his language by means of the foreign language. It is not generally realized to what extent this is possible, to what extent any language can be transformed, how language differs from language almost the way dialect differs from dialect; however, this last is true only if one takes language seriously enough, not if one takes it lightly."

The extent to which a translation manages to be in keeping with the nature of this mode is determined objectively by the translatability of the original. The lower the quality and distinction of its language, the larger the extent to which it is information, the less fertile a field is it for translation, until the utter preponderance of content, far from being the lever for a translation of distinctive mode, renders it impossible. The higher the level of a work, the more does it remain translatable even if its meaning is touched upon only fleetingly. This, of course, applies to originals only. Translations, on the other hand, prove to be untranslatable not because of any inherent difficulty, but because of the looseness with which meaning attaches to them. Confirmation of this as well as of every other important aspect is supplied by Hölderlin's translations, particularly those of the two tragedies by Sophocles. In them the harmony of the languages is so profound that sense is touched by language only the way an aeolian

harp is touched by the wind. Hölderlin's translations are prototypes
of their kind; they are to even the most perfect renderings of their
texts as a prototype is to a model. This can be demonstrated by com-
paring Hölderlin's and Rudolf Borchardt's translations of Pindar's
Third Pythian Ode. For this very reason Hölderlin's translations in
particular are subject to the enormous danger inherent in all translations: the gates of a language thus expanded and modified may slam
shut and enclose the translator with silence. Hölderlin's translations
from Sophocles were his last work; in them meaning plunges from
abyss to abyss until it threatens to become lost in the bottomless
depths of language. There is, however, a stop. It is vouchsafed to Holy
Writ alone, in which meaning has ceased to be the watershed for the
flow of language and the flow of revelation. Where a text is identical
with truth or dogma, where it is supposed to be "the true language"
in all its literalness and without the mediation of meaning, this text is
unconditionally translatable. In such case translations are called for
only because of the plurality of languages. Just as, in the original, language and revelation are one without any tension, so the translation
must be one with the original in the form of the interlinear version,
in which literalness and freedom are united. For to some degree all
great texts contain their potential translation between the lines; this is
true to the highest degree of sacred writings. The interlinear version
of the Scriptures is the prototype or ideal of all translation.

NEW APOPHATIC
PHILOSOPHIES

9. ROSENZWEIG (1887–1929)

Der Stern der Erlösung (Frankfurt a.M.: Suhrkamp, 1988; originally 1921), sections 16–26, 72, 174, 311, 399–406 (pp. 25–36, 87–89, 207–209, 326–329, 423–428).

Trans. William W. Hallo, *The Star of Redemption* (Notre Dame: University of Notre Dame Press, 1985), pp. 23–33, 80–81, 186–188, 295–296, 380–385.

Franz Rosenzweig resisted being treated as a thinker exclusively for the Jewish community and insisted on the general philosophical validity and purport of his thought. Nevertheless, a key turning point in his life came in 1913 when he changed his mind about his prior decision to convert to evangelical Christianity. In a flash of insight inspired by the Yom Kippur liturgy in a synagogue in Berlin, he knew that he must remain Jewish, that this was *his* truth and destiny. It was the same truth as that promulgated by Chrisitianity as the light of the world, but in a more concentrated form of silent fire. While stationed on the battlefront in the Balkans during the First World War, he incubated this truth, which hatched in the argument of his magnum opus, the *Star of Redemption* (*Stern der Erlösung*, 1921). Subsequently, he directed an institute of Jewish studies, the *Freies Jüdisches Lehrhaus*, in Frankfurt. In the last years of his life he was tragically paralyzed by incurable illness but remained intellectually lucid, producing numerous essays and translating the Hebrew Bible into German with Martin Buber.

In the introduction to the *Star*, Rosenzweig attacks philosophy for its pretense to a presuppositionless knowledge of the All. He exposes this pretense as a self-deceptive denial of death. Death is not merely a generality that philosophy can deal with by neutralizing it in the concept of "the Nothing," but is rather a terrifying reality that is ever new for each individual mortal being who faces dying for the first and only time. Death brings out the purely singular existence of the human individual ("Der Mensch in der schlechthinnigen Einzelheit seines Eigenwesens," p. 10), and this is prior to any order imposed by language. In language everything is generalized and related to everything else. But pre-linguistically, Man, as well as World and God, are radically isolated elements. Into these elements, the All of thought and being, taken by philosophy as its object, is shattered when confronted with the individual human singularized by death. Each element is a fragment, unknowable in itself, since it could be known only as part of the All—and the All cannot be known by any finite, mortal being.

In Part I of the *Star*, Rosenzweig begins from the fact that we know nothing of God, just as we *know* nothing of the world and nothing of man. To *know* anything implies grasping it in its totality, and this is impossible. But precisely this nothing of our knowledge is an eminently positive existential fact; it defines our whole way of being and is expressed in everything we experience. The nothing of our knowledge is itself an inexhaustibly rich phenomenon: our knowledge, by telling us nothing, tells the most essential thing about God, namely, his transcendence of our faculties and therefore of our discourse. God is thus "metaphysical," a positive fact that we cannot comprehend or properly state. Similarly, the World and Man in their pure facticity transcend rational comprehension. The created world has a positivity and an order that we experience but do not comprehend; we do not see its ground any more than we see the act of Creation. Its Logos transcends knowledge; it is "metalogical." So also, man in his singular individuality is "metaethical": he is governed by a vital principle—his own individual character—that escapes rational calculation.

These metaphysical, metalogical, and metaethical elements were perceived by the Greeks in their theology, cosmology, and tragedy, but for lack of revelation the Greeks were not able to give a coherent account that would make these elements intelligible in relation to one another. Only miraculously, in Revelation, are the three elements reciprocally ordered and disclosed. God has a metaphysical nature, the World has a metalogical ordinance, and Man has a metaethical character, though each is only Nothing, or inarticulable, until language reveals the relations between them. This is a general revelation of which language is the "organon," the "revelation to Adam." Yet revelation is preceded and succeeded by something that is not and cannot as such be revealed—and that is therefore nothing, so far as what can be said goes. This opaque background before and behind revelation is treated by Rosenzweig in the first and third parts of the *Star*, which are devoted, respectively, to the *Vorwelt* (the pre-world or protocosmos) and the *Überwelt* (the over-world or hypercosmos). Together they enclose the second, middle part of the work, which expounds the world (*Welt*) as revealed, as what actually exists and is definable in terms of language. By focusing attention in parts I and III on the realms beyond the limits of language, Rosenzweig's philosophy distinguishes itself from the canonical Greek-German tradition of philosophical thought centered on disclosure of being by the word, the Logos.

Rosenzweig's work, like Hegel's, is awesomely systematic and comprehensive. He moves through a repertoire of world civilizations and religions—China, India, and pagan Greece, Islam, Christianity, and Judaism—evaluating their achievements in art and culture, as well as in social and political organization, in a manner that seems in direct competition with Hegel. Yet there is a crucial difference. Everything that history reveals is not the eternal truth but rather the revelation of the *untruth* of history. The eternally true and real are what history and discourse cannot make manifest. The only articulable, systematizable knowledge is knowledge of what is *not* man, *not* world, *not* God, for these elements are all in their own nature unknowable. To this extent, everything within the purview of language and revelation is but a reference to what is not, to a pre-world of inarticulable "elements" and an eschatological post-world of equally unspeakable futurity. Rosenzweig acknowledges his derivation of this schema from Schelling's "Die Weltalter" ("The Ages of the World"). The world of revelation, which is the world of language, is but a relation to this unsayable before and after. By foregrounding these regions beyond language, Rosenzweig shows how every determination in language is but a delimitation of something that exceeds language.

All sense in language is based on negation. Simple predication asserts "so, and *not* otherwise." The positing of anything by language is never purely positive. It always negates something. In language, to be something is to negate Nothing. Language thereby projects a shadow world of inchoate origins as well as of inactual eschatology, and thus witnesses to a realm of what cannot be said as underlying or overlaying our human, linguistic, negative, failing, vanishing experience and existence. Religious revelation interprets this realm of the unsayable in everything "said" by forms of prayer and ritual, so that we can relate to it and complete our own intrinsically incomplete relations through it. Whereas religious rite and hymn are apt to disclose the future of the Kingdom of God, art and myth disclose the otherwise mute pagan past. Although art is not real communication, nevertheless it awakes the self in its hidden, incommunicable depth. This transpires in silence, for art is a language of the unspeakable.

The following excerpts begin by expounding the grammatical logic of negation inherent within language as revelation. Creation is the Yea of God to the world and to man. Revelation is God's Nay to himself in his infinite and ungraspable being in order to allow himself to be reduced to a form that man can apprehend. Man, for his part, must say Nay to his own autonomy and completeness in order to be spoken to and commanded by an authority out-side him and infinitely greater than his own. What man's Nay negates is not absolute or abstract but rather a determinate finite phenomenon, something that is itself Nought in relation to the unlimited of what encompasses it. Therefore this Nay is in and of itself already a Yea to what it cannot say or cir-cumscribe but affirms simply by allowing, through self-negation, something to be beyond itself.

In this way, Rosenzweig starts from the *nothing* of our knowledge in order to move toward the *something* of existence as given in an infinite multiplicity of "ands." The nature of existence is to be infinitely aggregative, and this means that the infinite string of "and," "and," "and" is positively given in existence as an irreducible multiplicity. This manifold is the articulation of a divine transcendence that can never be exhaustively said—it is as such the unsay-able. In contrast to the synthesis of the speculative proposition, which reveals the predicate as already contained in the subject, and vice versa, the "and" is a brute fact of addition; it can only be revealed in its immediacy. Things are re-vealed in the world as going together, as cohering, though there is no rational necessity for this. Rosenzweig thus poses the immediacy of revelation against the mediations of reason. This fact of And is like the parataxis of biblical syn-tax, both narrative and lyrical. It builds an open, unlimited chain binding new realities to the ungraspable One that is never manifest except in the binding power of this And.

And is both Yea and Nay, and both equally, for it is open to expansion, rather than simply an attempt to encompass the negative by the positive. In consequence, Rosenzweig's apophatic grammar is not based on the both-and of Hegelian synthesis, which ties all into identity. It is rather an open And, in-finitely extendible and as such an infinite, unrealizable whole—a "bad infinite" (Hegel would say), as seen from within the finite world.

Rosenzweig attempts to distance himself also from traditional negative theology. He presents his "new thinking" ("das neue Denken") as the reversal of negative theology in that it aims not at denials but at the eminently positive. Still, the moves he makes are those performed in negative theology through-out the tradition, albeit only in some of its subtler, more paradoxical, and less commonly understood forms. Despite its name, negative theology, too, is about the absolutely positive—the paradoxical coincidence of negative and positive when each is taken, in its purity, to the extreme.

In the same spirit, Rosenzweig emphasizes not the empty indeterminacy reached at the end of the process of removing all concepts, but rather the posi-tive existential plenitude that precedes all conceptual elaboration. It is, however, clear to him that the "before" as well as the "after" are extrapolations from experience that is always already mediated by concepts. His point is that conceptual indeterminacy is not the goal of this path of thinking but only a way of enabling the concrete reality of God to be revealed. He understands *all* reality as revealing, in its very nothingness to us and our discourse, an Infinite separate from us and known only as our nothing and in our unknowing. Everything that is *some*thing vanishes into nothingness, being ungrounded, but Rosenzweig understands this as the revelation of an infinite positivity that is immediately reversed and annulled by any effort to formulate and say it. The idea common to Rosenzweig and classic negative theology is to leave all concepts of God—and their inevitable vacuousness—behind, in the interest of encountering the inconceivable and unutterable reality of God in our very existence and its constitutive *un*knowing.

Rosenzweig does not make the unsayable as explicitly central to his thinking as I have done here in this free reformulation of some of the crucial axes of his thought. The time for bringing this out has first arrived now with the ripeness of apophasis as a topic in the present critical climate. But Rosenzweig deliberately argues that revelation in language always breaks open the system of language to let something other and unmasterable—and to that extent inexpressible—show through. Whatever is actually revealed is always language, and this means pure immanence, yet what is witnessed therein is radically other to and transcendent of language and revelation—it is the unsayable. Paradigmatically, this is the divine Name that alone gives meaning to language. In itself, language is the void of negation; it is without reality. And the things it refers to are also without reality. Language gathers everything together in its nothingness. Only the divine Name, the unsayable of language, can ground and orient language in the miraculous, positive existence of all things. For it is also the divine Word at the root of the Creation of things.

As so often occurs in negative theology, a reversal brings out the deeper intent and potential of what it reverses. Negative theology claims no positive knowledge of God, but it does so in order to free the relation to God from all the pretenses of finite concepts so as to allow the inconceivable reality or irreality of divinity to be fully experienced, or at least sensed, in unknowing. This is essentially what Rosenzweig's whole philosophy does. In positioning himself as opposing a certain narrow formulation of negative theology, Rosenzweig is actually renovating the deeper insight of apophatic thinking in all ages. All our knowing is a knowing of the nothingness of our knowledge, but this itself opens to a revelation of the positive relatedness of all things, of their forming an All—albeit an All that cannot be grasped by thought or word. Revelation can point towards this unity in which Man, World, and God together are All by means of unaccountable givenness and coherencies, but this All per se is not revealable or sayable (*Stern*, sec. 416).

Rosenzweig's philosophy comes directly out of life (in this sense, it is "existential" philosophy) and makes clear that all depends on a transcendence that cannot be verbally determined or articulated. This is the key to all understanding in his vision of a new All beyond words, the eternal Truth, the Face of God.

From *The Star of Redemption*

God and His Being or Metaphysics

Negative Theology

Of God we know nothing. But this ignorance is ignorance of God. As such it is the beginning of our knowledge of him—the beginning and not the end. Ignorance as the end result of our knowledge was the basic idea of "negative theology." This theology dismembered and abolished the existing assertions about God's "attributes," until the negative of all these attributes remained behind as God's essence. Thus God could be defined only in his complete indefinability. This path leads from an existing Aught to Nought; at its end atheism and mysticism can shake hands. We do not take this path, but rather the opposite one from Nought to Aught. Our goal is not a negative concept, but on the contrary a highly positive one. We seek God, and will presently seek the world and man, precisely not within a one and universal total, as one concept among many. If that were our object, then indeed the negative theology of Nicholas of Cusa or of the sage of Koenigsberg would be the only scientific goal, for then the negative would already be established as the goal at the starting point of reasoning. One concept among many is always negative, at least vis-à-vis the others. And if it lays claim to unconditional validity, then science can only serve it with unconditional—nothingness! But precisely that presupposition of the one and universal All we have given up. We seek God, and will presently seek world and man, not as one concept among many, but rather for itself, dependent on itself alone, in its absolute actuality (if the expression is not subject to misunderstanding); in other words, precisely in its "positiveness." It is for this reason that we must place the Nought of the sought-for concept at the beginning, must put it behind us. For in front of us there lies as goal an Aught: the reality of God.

The Two Ways

God is therefore initially a Nought for us, his Nought. Two paths lead from the Nought to the Aught—or, more precisely from the Nought to what is not Nought, for we seek no Aught—the path of affirmation and the path of negation. The affirmation is the affirmation of the *demonstrandum*, the non-Nought; the negation is the negation of the given, the Nought. These two ways are as different from each other, as opposite as—well, as Yea and Nay. Their end points, too, are by no means identical with the one above designated as the *demonstrandum*. Rather they differ from one another—again as Yea from Nay. The Yea applies to the non-Nought, the Nay to the Nought. Like every affirmation through negation, affirmation of the non-Nought points to something infinite; negation of the Nought, like every negation, points to something limited, finite, definite. Accordingly, we behold the Aught in twofold guise and in twofold relationship to the Nought: once as its neighbor and once as its runaway. As neighbor of the Nought, the Aught is the whole fullness of all that "is" not Nought. In God, therefore—for apart from him we know of nothing here—it is the whole fullness of what "is" in him. As a runaway who just now has broken out of the prison of the Nought, on the other hand, the Aught is nothing more than the event of this liberation from the Nought. It is entirely defined by this its one experience; in God, therefore, to whom nothing can happen from without (at least here), it is wholly and solely: action. Thus essence issues forth from Nought without ceasing, while action breaks loose from it in sharp delimitation. One inquires after origins in the case of essence; after beginnings in the case of action.

Methodology

We have good reason not to go beyond these purely formal definitions here for the time being; we do not wish to anticipate. What has
been said, however, will already become a little clearer if we regard,
solely for purposes of comparison, the opposite process, that of becoming Nought. Here, too, two possibilities are given; the negation of
the something—or, to replace this loaded expression with one today
less narrowly defined—the negation of the Aught and the affirmation of the non-Aught, the Nought. The reversal is so exact that the
Nay appears on the outbound path where the Yea appeared before,
and vice versa. For the emergence of the Nought through the negation of the Aught, German has an expression which we have only to
free from its narrower connotations in order to be able to employ it
here: *Verwesung* [decomposition, literally destruction of the essence]
designates negation of the Aught, just like the mystical term *Entwe-
sung* [sublimation; literally removal of the essence]. For the affirmation of the Nought, however, language uses the term annihilation
[*Vernichtung*]. In decomposition, in sublimation, the Nought originates in its infinite indefiniteness; neither the decomposing body
nor the disintegrating soul strives for the Nought as something positive but solely for dissolution of their positive essence, which is no
sooner accomplished than they empty into the amorphous night of
the Nought. Mephistopheles, on the other hand, who veritably wills
evil and who loves the ever-void, craves the Nought, and so the whole
is bound to come down to—"annihilation." Here, then, we behold
the Nought, if not itself as something complex—for then it would be
something definite and not Nought—yet as something accessible by
several (different) paths and in opposite directions. And now perhaps we can better understand how different origins of the definite
can exist in the undefined Nought, how the quiet stream of life can
spring from the same darkly stagnant water as the gushing geyser of
action.

Mark you, we are not speaking of a Nought in general, like the
former philosophy which acknowledged only the All as its object. We
know of no one and universal Nought, because we have divested ourselves of the presupposition of a one and universal All. We know only
the individual Nought of the individual problem, a Nought which
is therefore however not by any means defined, but only productive
of definition. In our case this is the Nought of God. God is here our

problem, our sub-ject and ob-ject. By beginning with his Nought we express just this, that he is to be for us initially nothing more than a problem. Thus we make of the Nought his presupposition and not perchance, as already noted at the beginning, the solution. We say as it were: if God exists, then the following is true of his Nought. By thus presupposing only that the Nought is the Nought of God, we are not led beyond the frame of this object by the consequences of this presupposition. To think that we have derived essence and action in general, say the essence of the world or the action directed to the world of man, in the welling forth of "essence" or the bursting forth of "action" would thus be quite wrong; it would be a relapse into the surmounted concept of the one and universal Nought. As long as we move within this hypothesizing limit of the Nought, all concepts remain within this limit; they remain under the law of If and Then without being able to step out of the magic circle. Essence, for example, can never mean anything but an essence within God; action can never refer to an object thought of as outside God. We do not get beyond pure reflections of God—as presently of the world and then of man—within himself. We have shattered the All: every fragment is now an All in itself. By immersing ourselves in this our fragmentary knowledge, we remain, in our journey into the Realm of the Mothers, slaves to the first command, the command to submerge. The ascent will come later, and with it the fusion of the piecework into the perfection of the new All.

Divine Nature

Yea is the beginning. Nay cannot be the beginning for it could only be a Nay of the Nought. This, however, would presuppose a negatable Nought, a Nay, therefore, that had already decided on a Yea. Therefore Yea is the beginning. Moreover it cannot be the Yea of the Nought, for it is the sense of our introduction of the Nought that it is not to be the result but on the contrary and exclusively the point of departure. It is not even the beginning. At most it is the beginning of our knowledge. The point is, it is really only the point of departure, and therefore simply incapable of being itself affirmed. Admittedly it is equally incapable of being negated, as already stated. It lies equally before Yea and Nay. It would be located before every beginning if it were located. But it is not "located." It is only the virtual locus for the beginning of our knowledge. It is only the marker for the positing of the problem. We are careful to avoid naming it. It is no "somber basis" or anything else that can be named with Ekhart's terms, or Boehme's or Schelling's. It does not exist in the beginning.

In the beginning is the Yea. And since the Yea cannot, as we said, refer to the Nought, it must refer to the non-Nought. This non-Nought is, however, not independently given, for nothing at all is given except for the Nought. Therefore the affirmation of the non-Nought circumscribes as inner limit the infinity of all that is not Nought. An infinity is affirmed: God's infinite essence, his infinite actuality, his Physis.

Archetypal Word

Such is the power of the Yea that it adheres everywhere, that it contains unlimited possibilities of reality. It is the arch-word of language, one of those which first make possible, not sentences, but any kind of sentence-forming words at all, words as parts of the sentence. Yea is not a part of a sentence, but neither is it a shorthand symbol for a sentence, although it can be employed as such. Rather it is the silent accompanist of all parts of a sentence, the confirmation, the "sic!" the "Amen" behind every word. It gives every word in the sentence its right to exist, it supplies the seat on which it may take its place, it "posits." The first Yea in God establishes the divine essence for all infinity. And this first Yea is "in the beginning."

Symbol

This first Yea implies a step on the road to the perfection of God; we can attempt to capture the step in familiar logico-mathematical symbols. Initially we will confine ourselves to the use of algebraic letters and the equal-sign. In the equation $y = x$, for example, y would designate the subject and the content of the statement, y that is to say, the grammatical subject, and x the predicate. Now ordinarily the affirmative protasis designates the subject, and the negating apodosis the predicate; here, however, where we are dealing with origins, it is just the other way around. The affirmation becomes the criterion of the primeval apodosis. The predicate is in the individual case always something individual, and therefore negative, but the apodosis, according to its original concept, is precisely positive: the pure Then.

This "Then" then becomes furthermore a "Thus and not otherwise," a fact that takes effect only when the "other" joins the original unicum. It is only by means of this transition to multiplicity that the apodosis turns into negation. And as the primeval apodosis occurs in the Yea, so the primeval protasis, the supposition of the original subject, occurs in the Nay. Each individual supposition of a subject is in itself merely a groundless position, but the original supposition, lying before everything individual, the presupposition, is negation, negation, that is, of the Nought. Every individual subject is simply "other," other, that is, than the Nought. In the equation which we have to erect here, the Nay will thus come to stand to the left of the equal sign, the Yea to its right. With the simple x or y we symbolize complete unrelatedness; with $y=$ we symbolize the relation of the subject to a predicate, the apodosis with a view to a protasis which is still to be assigned to it, with $= x$ we symbolize the protasis with a view to an apodosis which it still has coming to it. In this symbolic language, we would therefore have to designate God's physis, God's utter and endlessly affirmed being by A—by A and not, say, by B or C—for it is endlessly affirmed; within the sphere peculiar to it and conditioned by its Nought, nothing precedes it that it might have to follow; nothing *can* precede it, since it is posited as infinite and not as finite. It is utter actuality, dormant but infinite. As yet we do not know whether a storm will overtake this quiet ocean of the intradivine physis and make its floodwaters swell, whether whirlpool and waves will form in its own lap to bring the placid surface into turbulent commotion. For the time being it is "A," unmoved, infinite being.

Divine Freedom

Are we really ignorant as to which of the two possibilities will bring the placid surface into commotion, the storm from without or the whirlpool from within? True, we cannot tell anything from looking at the surface itself. But let us remember how this unmoved essence originated for us in the Yea, and how we just now explained by way of anticipating that the Yea always assumed the right side of the equation $y = x$, the "x" side. Thereby the decision already falls in favor of the former of the two possible sources of motion. The Yea contains nothing which strives beyond the Yea itself; it is the "then." The commotion must therefore come from the Nay.

The Nay is just as original as the Yea. It does not presuppose the Yea. This or that derived Nay may make this presupposition, but the original Nay presupposes nothing but the Nought. It is the Nay of the Nought. Now of course it is true that it bursts forth directly from the Nought, bursts forth, that is, as its negation, and no Yea precedes it; but an affirmation does precede it. In other words: while it presupposes only the Nought, the Nought it presupposes is a Nought from which the Yea had to well forth, not a Nought with which it could have let the matter rest, not the eternal void which Mephistopheles cherishes. It is the Nought which was conceived of only as a Nought of knowledge, as a point of departure for reasoning about God, as the locus for posing the problem; it was not conceived of as positively posited Nought, nor as a "somber basis," nor as the "abyss of the deity." The original Nay is preceded, though not by the Yea itself, yet by the Nought from which affirmation had to come forth. Thus the Nay, without prejudice to the immediacy of its origin, is "younger" than the Yea. *Non* is not *propter sic* but *post sic.*

Nay is the original negation of Nought. Yea could not have remained attached to Nought because the latter provided it, so to speak, with no point of contact; repelled by Nought, Yea therefore cast itself upon the non-Nought and, thus freed to infinity from its point of departure, it placed the divine essence in the infinite realm of the non-Nought. Nay, however, is intertwined in closest bodily contact with the Nought. This close contact is now possible because the Nought had been left behind as finite through the prior infinite affirmation of the non-Nought. Thus the Nay finds its opponent directly in front of itself here. But the metaphor of a pair of wrestlers is misleading. There is no pair. This is a wrestling match not of two parties but of one: the Nought negates itself. It is only in self-negation that the "other," the "opponent," bursts forth out of it. And at the moment of its bursting forth, the Nay is rescued and liberated from the self-negating intertwining with the Nought. Now it takes shape as free, original Nay.

At this point it is necessary to put the question into precise focus again. We are inquiring into God. The self-negating Nought was the self-negating Nought of God; the Nay born of this self-negation is a Nay of God. The Yea in God was his infinite essence. His free Nay, shooting forth out of the negation of his Nought, is not in itself essence, for it contains no Yea; it is and remains pure Nay. It is not a "thus" but only a "not otherwise." Thus it is always directed toward "otherwise," it is always and only the "one," the "one," that is, as the "one" in God, before which everything else that is in God becomes a mere "other." What is thus utterly "one," this utter Nay to everything that is "other" than itself—what should we call it if not freedom? God's freedom is born of the original negation of the Nought as that which is trained on everything else only *as* something else. God's freedom is intrinsically a mighty Nay.

God's essence, we have seen, was infinite Yea. That Yea left the Nought behind as something emptied of the infinite. The free Nay fought its way in original self-negation out of what had thus become finite. It bears the scars of the struggle during which it burst forth. It is infinite in its possibilities, in what it refers to, for it refers in the last analysis to everything. Everything is "other" for it, but it is itself ever "one," ever limited, ever finite, just as it first burst forth in the self-negation of the Nought-become-finite. It bursts forth into all eternity, for all eternity is merely "other" for it, is merely infinite time for it. Over against what is thus always "other" for it, it is for all time the solitary, the ever new, the ever initial. Divine freedom confronts infinite divine essence as the finite configuration of action, albeit an action whose power is inexhaustible, an action which can ever anew pour itself out into the infinite out of its finite origin: an inexhaustible wellspring, not an infinite ocean. Essence is constituted once and for all "as is"; it confronts the freedom of action, a freedom revealing itself ever anew, but a freedom for which we cannot as yet contemplate any object other than the infinity of that everlasting essence. It is not freedom *of* God, for even now God is still a problem for us. It is divine freedom, freedom *in* God and with reference to God. Even now we know, as yet, nothing about God. We are still engaged in the piecework of knowledge, still at the stage of inquiring, not of answering.

Symbol

The piece we have just gained is divine freedom. Let us attempt to capture it in a symbol even as, above, we captured the divine essence. We must place divine freedom, as original Nay, on the left side of the future equation. It is, moreover, a Nay which, as original subject, reaches beyond itself with unlimited power—albeit, as we must repeatedly emphasize, beyond itself only within God. Thus its symbol will have to be formed on the pattern "$y=$." And finally, although this freedom is finite in its ever-renewed uniqueness, it is infinite in its continuous novelty. Nothing can precede it for nothing exists beside it. It is ever unique but never a unicum. Therefore the symbol for this freedom turns out to be "$A=$." Let us now demonstrate how this symbol of divine freedom joins with that of divine essence and how we thereby first arrive at the equation and with it the first answer to the inquiry into God.

Vitality of the God

Freedom points to something infinite. As freedom it is finite; but to the extent that its concern is with an infinite, it is infinite, infinite power or, to put it bluntly, infinite caprice. Only essence is available to it as the infinite object of its craving. But essence, such as it was symbolized by a bare letter without the equal-sign, contains no explicit direction, whether an active or a receptive one, which might strive toward that force. The divine essence maintains the infinite silence of pure existence, of voiceless actuality. It exists. Thus caprice seems able to fall upon essence without being summoned or dragged in. But in approaching essence, caprice nevertheless ends up in the magic circle of its inert being. This being does not emit any force toward caprice, and yet the latter feels its own force ebbing. With every step that takes it closer to essence, the infinite power (of caprice) senses a growing resistance, a resistance which would become infinite at the goal, at essence itself. For here the "It exists" of essence is abroad throughout, its "It is thus" is stretched out inertly and would swallow up the expressions of that power. At the focal point of the infinity of the inert Yea, the infinitely weakened power of the infinitely active Nay would be extinguished. This power is now no longer the original, infinite Nay, but already that Nay on the way to exercising its power on the inert Thus of the Yea. We must therefore capture it short of the end of the movement, that is, before the inertia of Thusness can operate as infinite inertia. For at that point the infinite power of the divine act so to speak enters the magnetic field of the divine essence, and while this power is still predominant over the inertia of that essence, it is already constrained by it. We designate this point as the point of divine obligation and fate, in contrast to the point of divine power and caprice. As divine freedom takes shape as caprice and power, so divine essence takes shape as obligation and fate. An infinite movement, starting from freedom, courses over into the realm of essence, and out of it there originates, in infinite spontaneous generation, the divine countenance which shatters broad Olympus with a quiver of its eyebrows, and whose brows are nonetheless furrowed with the knowledge of the saying of the Norns. Both infinite power in the free outpouring of *Pathos* and infinite constraint in the compulsion of *Moira*—both together form the vitality of the god.

Archetypal Words

We pause here a moment in order first to comprehend, if retroactively, the evidently decisive step which we have here taken over and beyond the bare Yea and bare Nay. We took the movement which brought us from Nay to Yea as self-evident; we did not inquire after the archetypal term which, corresponding to the Yea and Nay of the first two steps, guided this third step. The archetypal Yea had been the term of the original supposition; as such it was the silent partner of the activities which each word carries on in the proposition as a whole. The archetypal Nay likewise is active in every word of the proposition, not however, to the extent that this term is a statement, but insofar as it is the subject of statements; thus its very own place in the sentence, as already demonstrated, is with the subject. As "Thus," the Yea confirms the individual word, that is, it assures it of an enduring "firm" value, independent of the relation which it assumes in regard to the other words within the sentence; the Nay, on the other hand, concerns itself precisely with this relation of the word to the sentence. As "not-otherwise" it "locates" this "locus" of the individual word, a locus which firmly fixes the peculiarity of each word over against the "others"—not its "firm" peculiarity but one dependent on the sentence as a whole, on the "other" components of the sentence. Let us take as an example initially two extreme cases, to wit, for the Yea, the statement nothing-but, the predicate adjective, and for the Nay the nothing-but subject of a statement, the subject noun. The word "free" has a specific sense regardless of whether it occurs in the sentence "man is created free, is free" or in the other sentence "man is not created to be free." This motionless sense is the work of the secret Yea. On the other hand the word "man" is something quite different in the statement that he is a citizen of two worlds and when he is called a political animal. This diversity, created each time by the other members of the sentence which the one subject confronts, is the work of the secret Nay. And now as a concluding example, one that is anything but extreme: the word "until" always means the conclusion of a successively envisioned quantity. But in "until tomorrow" it refers to a stretch of time, a stretch of time in the future, while in "distant until the stars" it refers to a stretch of space. Incidentally, it might easily seem as though the "secret Yea" therefore had to precede the "secret Nay" in reality and not merely in conceptual sequence (as a possibility or affirmation), as though the "secret Nay" were therefore less original. But this impression is dispelled by the simple consideration that those hard-and-fast meanings of the words are in reality only derived from their context in the sentence. Accordingly this "fixity" does not really exist in the individual case; on the contrary, every new sentence context into which a word enters transforms the "constant" character of the word. Language, therefore, constantly renews itself in living speech.

We have just been speaking, quite ingenuously, of sentence and context. Actually, however, Yea and Nay never prepare more than the individual word, albeit in the case of Nay, already in its relationship to the sentence. The sentence itself first comes into being, first originates by virtue of the fact that the remarking, establishing Nay seeks to gain power over the confirming Yea.[1] The sentence presupposes Yea and Nay, Thus and not-otherwise, and so does the smallest part of the sentence: the word in isolating languages, the combination of two words in agglutinative languages, the combination of stem and inflectional affix into one word in inflectional languages. Therewith we have the third of those archetypal words which, though not the equal of the other two in originality, for it presupposes both, yet for the first time helps both to a vital reality: the word "and." "And" is the secret companion not of the individual word but of the verbal context. It is the keystone of the arch of the substructure over which the edifice of the *logos* of linguistic sense is erected. We came to know a first test of strength of this third archetypal word in the aforemen-

---

1. All the key verbs of this sentence represent etymological double-entendres in the original German which are impossible to reproduce in translation. On this other level, then, the sentence may be rendered: The sentence itself first comes to stand, first stands forth, by virtue of the fact that the localizing, fast-laying Nay seeks to gain power over the firming Yea. (Tr.)

tioned answer to the inquiry into God which we had posed when we
determined the Nought of our knowledge of God.

Symbol
The equation symbolizes what is, at least for the present, conclusive
in this answer, the equation in which the paths leading to the answer
have become invisible. By looking at the equation $A=A$, one can no
longer tell whether it is constructed from A, $A=$, $=A$, or A. One can
recognize no more in it than the pure originality and self-satisfaction
of the god. He is dependent on nothing outside of himself, and appears to require nothing outside of himself:

> God ethereal reigneth free,
> But his mighty appetites
> Nature's law doth hold in check

—the law of his own nature. The interplay of forces which produced
this vital figure of a god is submerged. Just for that reason, the equation symbolizes the immediate vitality of this figure, the vitality of
the god.

Esthetic First Principles: Content

And yet there is a world where this silence is already speech—not,
of course, the speech of the soul, but speech nonetheless, a speech
before speech, the speech of the unspoken, the unspeakable. In
the exclusive seclusion of outer form, the mythical element founded
the realm of the beautiful for metaphysical theology; in the self-
containedness of inner form, the plastic component established the
work of art, the thing of beauty, for metalogical cosmology; just so,
the tragic factor in metaethical psychology lays the foundation of the
wordless understanding by which art can first become reality on the
eloquent silence of the self. What originates here is content. Content
bridges the gap between artist and observer, indeed between the artist
as a living person and the artist who sends his *oeuvre* into the world
over and beyond his own lifetime. And this content is not the
world, for in the world, though it is common to all, each one has his
own individual share, his distinctive point of view. Content must be

something immediately equal, something which men do not share with one another like the common world but rather something which is equal in all. And that is alone the human quality per se, the self. The self is what is condemned to silence in man and yet is everywhere and at once understood. It need only be rendered visible, "acted out," in order to awaken the self in every other one as well. Itself it feels nothing at the time, it remains exiled into tragic soundlessness, it stares unflinchingly into its interior; but whoever sees it awakens, as it was once again formulated with profound foresight by Aristotle, to "terror and compassion." These awake in the spectator and at once direct themselves to his own interior, making a self out of him. If they were to awake in the hero himself, he would cease to be speechless self: *phobos* and *eleos* would disclose themselves as "awe and love," the soul would acquire speech, and the newly granted word would pass from soul to soul. There is no such rapprochement here. Everything remains speechless. The hero, who arouses terror and compassion in others, remains himself an unmoved, rigid self. In the spectator, again, the same emotions at once move inward and turn him too into a self-enclosed self. Everyone remains by himself, everyone remains self. No community originates. And yet there originates a common content. The selves do not converge, and yet the same note sounds in all: the feeling of one's own self. This wordless transfer of the identical occurs, even though no bridge as yet leads from man to man. It does not occur between soul and soul: there is no realm of souls yet. It occurs from self to self, from one silence to the other silence.

This is the world of art, a world of tacit accord which is no world at all, no real, vital, back-and-forth interconnection of address passing to and fro and yet, at any point, capable of being vitalized for moments at a time. No sound punctures this silence and yet at every instant each and everyone can sense the innermost part of the other in himself. It is the equality of the human which, prior to any real unity of the human, here becomes effective as content of the work of art. Prior to any real human speech, art creates, as the speech of the unspeakable, a first, speechless, mutual comprehension, for all time indispensable beneath and beside actual speech. The silence of the tragic hero is silent in all art and is understood in all art without any words. The self does not speak and yet is heard. The self is perceived. The pure speechless glance completes in every beholder the introversion into its own interior. Art is not a real world, for the threads which are drawn from man to man in it run only for moments, only for the short moments of the immediate glance and only at the place of the glance. The self does not come alive by being perceived. The life aroused in the beholder does not arouse the beheld to life; it at once turns inward in the beholder himself. The realm of art provides the ground on which the self can grow up everywhere; but each self is in turn a wholly solitary, individual self; art nowhere creates a real plurality of selves, although it produces the possibility for the awakening of selves everywhere: the self that awakes nevertheless only knows of itself. In the make-believe world of art, in other words, the self ever remains self, never becomes—soul....

The Proper Name

Seen thus in its substantiality the I or the Thou is an individual without more ado, without the mediation of any plurality. It is not a "the" for being an "a." Rather it is an individual without category. The place of the article is here taken by the immediate determination of the proper name. With the summons by the proper name, the word of revelation entered the real dialogue. With the proper name, the rigid wall of objectness has been breached. That which has a name of its own can no longer be a thing, no longer everyman's affair. It is incapable of utter absorption into the category for there can be no category for it to belong to; it is its own category. Nor does it still have its place in the world, its moment in occurrence. Rather it carries its here and now with it. Wherever it is, there is a midpoint and wherever it opens its mouth, there is a beginning.

In the intricate world of things there was no midpoint or beginning at all; the I, however, together with its proper name, introduces these concepts of midpoint and beginning into the world. In keeping with its creation as man and at the same time as "Adam," the I is midpoint and beginning within itself. For it demands a midpoint in the world for the midpoint, a beginning for the beginning of its own experience. The I longs for orientation, for a world which does not just lie there in any old arrangement, nor flow past in any old sequence, but a world which supports the inner order inherent in the I's experience on the solid base of an external order. One proper name demands others. Adam's first deed is to give names to the creatures of the world, and this too is but prologue. For Adam names the creatures, as they step before him in creation, by categories and not as individuals. And he names them himself, thus only expressing his demand for names. The demand still remains unfulfilled, for the names which he demands are not such as he himself might give; rather, they are names which are revealed to him like his own name, names to secure a firm basis for the individuality of the individual name. For this it is not yet necessary that the whole world be full of name; but at least it has to contain name enough in order to provide a base for his own name. One's own experience depends on one's own name; it therefore needs to be grounded in creation, that creation which we previously designated as the creation of revelation, as historical revelation. Thus grounded in the world, it must therefore be grounded in space and time precisely in order to provide a ground for experience's absolute certainty of possessing its own space and its own time. Thus both the midpoint and the beginning in the world must be provided to experience by this grounding, the midpoint in space, the beginning in time. These two, at least, have to be named, even if the rest of the world still lies in the darkness of anonymity. There must be a where in the world, a still visible spot whence revelation radiates, and a when, a yet echoing moment, where revelation first opened its mouth. Both must have been one and the same at one time, though no longer today, something as united in itself as my experience is today. For it is supposed to put my experience on a firm foundation. In their after-effect, the spatial taking-place of revelation and its temporal having-transpired live on today in separate media, the former in God's congregation, the latter in God's word: at one time, however, both must have been founded at a single blow. The ground of revelation is midpoint and beginning in one; it is the revelation of the divine name. The constituted congregation and the composed word live their lives from the revealed name of God up to the present day, up to the present moment, and into the personal experience. For name is in truth word and fire, and not sound and fury as unbelief would have it again and again in obstinate vacuity. It is incumbent to name the name and to acknowledge: I believe it. . . .

Liturgy and Gesture

. . . Where there is world, there speech is also. The world is never without the word. Indeed it only exists in the word, and without the word there would be no world. But the structures of liturgy do not possess this same simultaneity with that which is to be recognized in them. Rather, they anticipate. They take something future, and turn it into a Today. Thus they are neither key nor mouthpiece for their world, but representatives. For cognition they represent the redeemed hypercosmos. Cognition takes cognizance only of them. It does not look beyond them. What is eternal, hides behind them. They are the light, by which we see light. They are the silent anticipation of a world gleaming in the silence of the future.

The protocosmos contained only the mute elements of which the course of the Star was built. The course itself was a reality but at no moment to be seen by the eyes. For the Star which runs this course never stands still even for the batting of an eye. Only what endures more than one batting can be seen by the eyes, and only that moment which has been arrested by its eternalization permits the eyes to perceive the structure in it. Structure is thus more than elemental, more than real; it is directly subject to perception. Our eyes have not yet seen the Star as long as we know only the elements and law of its course; it remains merely a material point which moves in space. Only after telescope and spectroscope have brought it to us do we know it as we know a tool of our daily use or a painting in our chambers: in familiar perceptions. Factuality is completed only in contemplation; now no more is heard of object or act.

That which can be perceived is superior to speech and exalted above it. Light does not discourse, it shines. It does not by any means seclude itself in itself, for it shines outward, not inward. But in shining outward, it does not give itself up, as does speech. Light does not sell itself, it does not give itself away, like speech, when it expresses itself. Rather it is visible by remaining wholly in itself. It does not really shine outward, it only shines forth. It shines, not like a fountain, but like a face, like an eye which is eloquent without the lips having to move. Unlike the muteness of the protocosmos, which had no words yet, here is a silence which no longer has any need of the word. It is the silence of consummate understanding. One glance says everything here. Nothing shows so clearly that the world is unredeemed as the diversity of languages. Between men who speak a common language, a glance would suffice for reaching an understanding; just because they speak a common language, they are elevated above speech. Between different languages, however, only the stammering word mediates, and gesture ceases to be immediately intelligible as it had been in the mute glance of the eye. It is reduced to a halting sign language, that miserable surrogate for communication. As a result, the supreme component in liturgy is not the common word but the common gesture. Liturgy frees gesture from the fetters of helpless servitude to speech, and makes of it Something more than speech. Only the liturgical gesture anticipates that "purified lip" which is promised for "that day" to the peoples ever divided as to language. In it, the impoverished muteness of the disbelieving members becomes eloquent, the voluble loquacity of the believing heart becomes silent. Disbelief and belief unite their prayer.

The Star or the Eternal Truth

The Eternity of Truth

God is truth. Truth is his signet. By it he is known. And will be even when one day all has come to an end by which he used to make his eternity known within Time—all eternal life, all eternal way—there where even the eternal comes to an end: in eternity. For not the way alone ends here, but life too. Eternal life, after all, endures only so long as life in general. There is eternal life only in contrast to the life of those who pave the eternal way, which is always exclusively temporal. The desire for eternity sighs forth out of the well-pits of this temporality; if it assumes the form of a longing for eternal life, that is only because it itself is temporal life. Of a truth, in truth, life too disappears. The way became vanity as the ocean of light engulfed it in its billows; life, though it does not thus become vanity, dissolves in the light. It is transformed, and having been transformed, is no more. Life has gone up in light. The mute darkness of the protocosmos had found speech in death. And something stronger, love, had overpowered death. Love had chosen life. And as the protocosmos had found its voice in death, so now life rallies in the silence of the hypercosmos and is transformed into light. God is not life: God is light. He is the lord of life, but he is no more living than dead. To say the one or the other of him, with the old [philosopher] that "God has life," or with the new one that "God is dead," reveals the identical pagan bias. The only thing which does not resist verbal designation is that neither/nor of dead and alive, that tender point where life and death touch and blend. God neither lives nor is he dead; rather he quickens the dead—he loves. He is the God of the quick and the dead, precisely because he himself is neither quick nor dead. We experience his existence directly only by virtue of the fact that he loves us and awakens our dead Self to beloved and requiting soul. The revelation of divine love is the heart of the All.

God (Theology)

The Manifest One
We learn that God loves but not that he is love. He draws too nigh to us in love for us to be yet able to say: he is this or that. In this love we learn only that he is God, not what he is. The What, the essence, remains concealed. It is concealed precisely by being revealed. A god who did not reveal himself would not permanently hide his essence from us, for nothing remains concealed from man's far-reaching learning, his capacity for conceptualization, his inquisitive intellect. But God pours forth over us in revelation; with us he turns from stationary to active God. Precisely thereby he forges the fetters of love around our free intellect, which is irresistible for everything stationary. Bound by such bonds, summoned thus by name, we move in the orbit in which we found ourselves, and along the route on which we are placed. We no longer reach beyond this except with the powerless grasp of empty concepts.

The Concealed One
If then the Manifest God dissolves in us, his concealed aspect remains with him all the more. True, we now recognize him in the dead and the living: he is the agent who creates the dead and re-creates it, transforms it until it comes to him and lets him quicken it; he is the agent who releases from himself the living, which had heard him summon it for life, and redeems it. But Creator and Redeemer we recognize in this way only after their connection in revelation. We catch sight of the Creator and the Redeemer only from the vantage point of the God of love. We can see what has been and what is to be only to the extent that the flicker of that moment of divine love shines. The purely Prior, the protocosmos created from of yore, is too dark for us to be able to recognize the Creator's hand in it. And the purely Posterior, the redeemed hypercosmos, is too bright for us to be

yet able to see the Redeemer's countenance in it; he thrones above the
annually recurring hymns of the redeemed. Only in the immediate
vicinity of that heart and center of the All, of the revelation of divine
love, is the Creator and Redeemer too manifested to us, to the extent
that such manifestation is vouchsafed at all. Revelation teaches us
to trust in the Creator, to wait hopefully for the Redeemer. Thus
it allows us to recognize Creator and Redeemer too only as him
who loves.

The First One
Thus it is the Loving God whom alone we see directly. As such a one,
however, God is not the Lord. As such he is active. He is not above his
deed. He is within it. He is one with it. He loves. Only as the Lord is
God beyond that of which he is the Lord: the Lord of life and death is
himself beyond life and death. It is beyond conceiving what he may
be as Lord of death, his essence before creation. Revelation extends
only as far back as the Creator. Its first word is "in the beginning,"
its second "there created." Before the beginning there may have been
that inner vitality of God which grew out of divine self-creation, self-
revelation, self-redemption; we could only depict it analogically, by
analogy, that is, to the authentic creation, revelation, redemption, by
allowing God to experience within himself what emanates from him.
The heathens knew of a God who had come to be in this fashion, and
this perhaps gave us a hint that we were dealing with more than a
mere analogy. But no word, no term derived from this hint. That
vitality concealed within itself concealed this God from us too. The
God-become became the God-concealed. To answer honestly what
he might be, we would have had to say: Nought. For vitality in the
Uncreated, in the realm of the dead, is nought. The heathen God is
not dead, but he is Lord of the dead and only of the dead at that, only
of Nought. This company of gods wields power only in the realm of
the dead. Elsewhere they do not rule, they only live. But as Lords
of the Nought they themselves become—Noughts. 'The gods of the
heathen are noughts,' exclaims the Psalmist. They are not dead, far
from it; the faith of their devotees testifies to that. Gods in whom a
living world believes cannot be less alive than this world itself. But
in all their vitality they are just as unsteady, just as ephemeral, just
as subordinate to the almighty Perhaps as is this world, as are these
devotees. They lack the framework of reality, the unambiguous ori-

entation, the fixed position, the knowledge of right and left, above and below, which enters the world only with revelation. For all their vitality, they are thus "Noughts." And "those who make them are like them; so are all who trust in them." They are created, they live concealed in the shelter of their celestial fortress; and this the Psalmist counters with that which distinguishes his God from these Noughts: he has 'made the heavens.'

The Last One

What God, the true God, may have been before creation thus defies the imagination. Not so that which he would be after redemption. True, here too our living knowledge tells us nothing about God's essence beyond the Redeemer. That he is the Redeemer is the last thing that we learn by our own experience: we 'know that he lives' and that our 'eyes will behold him.' But God's redemptive function assumed a special importance even within this knowledge that is manifest to us. His creative power and his revelatory wealth both befell something else, something objective, juxtaposed to them. His redemptive function, on the other hand, has only an indirect effect on anything else, redeeming man by means of the world, the world by means of man. Its direct effect is confined to the redemption of God himself. For God himself, redemption is the eternal deed in which he frees himself from having anything confront him that is not he himself. Redemption frees God from the work of creation as well as from his loving concern for the soul. Redemption is his day of rest, his great Sabbath, the day which is but adumbrated in the Sabbath of creation. It is the day when, freed from all that is outside himself, from all that is ever and again compared to him, incomparable though he is, he 'will be one and his name: One.' Redemption redeems God by releasing him from his revealed name. In the name and its revelation there is consummated that delivery of revelation which had commenced with creation. Whatever happens thereafter, happens "in the name." Sanctification of the name or desecration of the name—since revelation there is no deed which does not bring about one or the other. The process of redemption in the world takes place in the name and for the sake of the name. The end, however, is nameless; it is above any name. The very sanctification of the name occurs only so that the name might one day be muted. Beyond the word—and what is name but the collective word—beyond the word there shines silence. There where no other names any longer confront the one name, where the one name is al(l)-one and all that is created knows and acknowledges him and him alone, there the act of sanctification has come to rest. For sanctity is meaningful only where there is still profanity. Where everything is sacrosanct, there the Sacred itself is no longer sacred, there it simply exists. This simple existence of the Highest, such unimpaired reality, omnipotent and solely potent, beyond any desire for or joy in realization, this is truth. For truth is not to be recognized through error, as the masters of the school think. Truth attests itself; it is one with everything real; it does not part in it.

The One

And such is the truth which, as God's signet, announces that he is One at the time when even the eternal people of the one God sank and disappeared. The One—this one name—outlives the people that acknowledges it. It outlives even the revealed name by which this outliving and more-than-living name will become known to the future. For the sake of this outliving which will be the lot of the One in the future, the revealed name must already be silent for the present and for every present. Precisely we Jews, we who know the name, who are called by it, and on whom the name is called, who know it and acknowledge it—we are not allowed to pronounce it. For the sake of our eternity, we must anticipate the silence in which it and we together will one day sink. We must substitute for the name itself that which God is as long as he is still called upon as one name among other names, as Creator of a world of being, as Revealer of a language of souls: The Lord. We call him the Lord in place of a name. The name itself falls silent on our lips and even beneath the silently reading eyes, just as it will fall silent one day when he is al(l)-one in all the world, when he is One.

The Lord

It is the ultimate silence which keeps silent in us there. This is the true depth of the deity. God himself is there redeemed from his own word. He is silent. Though the God of the protocosmos had not himself been dead, he was, as Lord of dead matter, himself like this a Nought. From creation we learn that the meaning of the protocosmos is death. Just so we learn, from redemption, that the meaning of the hypercosmos is life. The Lord of the hypercosmos is the Lord of life. As such he is not alive, far from it. But just as the Lord of dead matter, though not himself dead, was like the dead and thus nought, or more exactly a Nought, one of many Noughts, so too the Lord of the hypercosmos, though not himself alive, is like the living. That simile of the Psalm applies to him too: like him are those who trust in him. Since that which believes in him is what lives, therefore he must resemble that which lives. But what then is the nature of this living matter? What word can capture its essence? For we are aware that we have here made the leap beyond the world of words, just as we were still standing before its portals in the protocosmos. The realms of the dead lay before that portal, and we had recognized its Lord as a Nought there. For what could be the essence of an Aught prior to the world other than the Nought? And the Lord of dead matter, though he is not part of that matter, is in essence akin to it and thus a Nought like it. What then might be the essence of living matter, lying beyond the world of words on that side just as dead matter lay before it on this? The place of the Nought would already be occupied; it is located before words. With what word, then, are we to designate that which would lie beyond words? It would have to be just as little at home among words as the Nought. The Aught is at home in the world of words. But above this world, as little a part of it as the Nought, there rests the All, to be precise the true All, the All which does not burst into pieces as in the world of the Nought, but rather the one All, the One-and-all.

This is the essence of living matter. Like death in creation, it is the last word in redemption. As such it points beyond words, like death. It designates redeemed matter as death designates uncreated matter. And as the Lord of life, God would be equal in essence to this essence. He would be the Lord of the one-and-all. And just this, this lordliness over the one-and-all, is meant by the sentence: God is truth.

10. WITTGENSTEIN (1889–1951)

"A Lecture on Ethics." In *Philosophical Occasions 1912–1951*, ed. James C. Klagge and Alfred Nordmann (Indianapolis and Cambridge: Hackett, 1993), pp. 37–44.

  Tractatus, 6.4 to 7. From *Tractatus Logico-Philosophicus*, trans. C. K. Ogden, with introduction by Bertrand Russell (London: Routledge, 1992), pp. 183–189.

In a letter to his editor, Ludwig von Ficker, that accompanied the manuscript of the *Tractatus Logico-Philosophicus* (1922) when it was first submitted for publication in 1921, Wittgenstein explained: "I once wanted to include a sentence in the foreword which now actually is not in it, which, however, I'll write to you now because it might be a key for you: I wanted to write that my work consists of two parts: of the one which is here, and of everything which I have *not* written. And precisely this second part is the important one.... All of that which *many* are *gassing* about [schwefeln über] today, I have put in place in my book by remaining silent about it."[1]

  Leaving aside speculation on the contents of this second, unwritten part and on whether it is to be found in some form in later writings of Wittgenstein, clearly the unwritten and unexpressed is key to everything that Wittgenstein did write. Indeed, in 1931 Wittgenstein remarked: "Perhaps what is inexpressible (what I find mysterious and am not able to express) is the background against which whatever I could express receives meaning."[2] And in another telling comment he relates his experience of the inexpressible to poetry: "The poem by Uhland is really magnificent. And this is how it is: if only you

---

1. Quoted by Ray Monk, *Ludwig Wittgenstein: The Duty of Genius* (New York: Macmillan, 1990), p. 178.

  2. Wittgenstein, *Culture and Value*, ed. C. H. von Wright (Oxford: Blackwell, 1980), p. 10e. "Das Unaussprechbare (das, was mir geheimnisvoll erscheint und ich nicht auszusprechen vermag) gibt vielleicht den Hintergrund, auf dem das, was ich aussprechen konnte, Bedeutung bekommt." *Vermischte Bemerkungen*, in *Werkausgabe* (Frankfurt a.M.: Suhrkamp, 1984), vol. 8, p. 472.

do not try to utter what is unutterable, then, *nothing* gets lost. But the unutterable will be—unutterably—*contained* in what has been uttered!"[3]

Paradoxically, the unutterable is contained in the poem and conveyed—completely, wonderfully, unutterably—in what is said, without saying *it*. Wittgenstein believes fervently in what poetic language can convey that logical language cannot. This delimits unsayability, which still adheres to language, albeit as what cannot be said in language. The most revealing point of this expostulation is that for Wittgenstein the unsayable is contained *in* language—in the language of the poem—rather than standing in radical opposition to it as beyond language.

Throughout his life Wittgenstein had strong mystical inclinations. The later Wittgenstein tended to resemble certain classical mystics for whom language is only an impediment—and not a positive or productive impediment—and so must simply be voided and swept out of the way altogether. *Philosophical Investigations* (1949) describes philosophy as "a battle against the bewitchment [*Verhexung*] of our intelligence by language" (109) and its results as the uncovering of "bumps [*Beulen*] that the understanding has got by running its head up against the limits of language" (119). However, even in dissolving philosophical problems into linguistic misunderstandings, Wittgenstein still sees through them (*durchschauen*) to some pregnant mystery of what cannot be said.[4]

In any case, the earlier *Tractatus* is most significant for Wittgenstein's apophaticism and its influence. Here Wittgenstein explicitly gives decisive importance to what he calls "the inexpressible" ("das Unaussprechliche") in determining the sense of the entire work. The philosophical argument of the *Tractatus* leads up climactically to this inexpressible, which it recognizes as the mystical: "There is at all events the ineffable. This *shows* itself, it is the mystical" ("Es gibt allerdings Unaussprechliches. Dies *zeigt* sich, es ist das Mystische," *Tractatus* 6.522).

Before arriving at radically apophatic conclusions in its last section, the *Tractatus* notes that while language can express reality, it cannot express that

3. Paul Engelmann, ed., *Letters from Ludwig Wittgenstein, with a Memoir* (Oxford: Blackwell, 1967), pp. 82–84.

4. Most pertinent are *Philosophical Investigations* 89–92, 66, and 523–533 (especially 531). The exegesis of these paragraphs by Leonardo Distaso, *Estetica e differenza in Wittgenstein* (Roma: Carocci, 1999), is helpful. More generally, see *Wittgenstein at Work: Method in the Philosophical Investigations*, ed. Erich Amereller and Eugen Fischer (London: Routledge, 2004).

which enables it to do so, that which it and reality have in common, namely, their logical form (4.12); we cannot step outside language to express the fact that language expresses something (4.121). The proposition cannot say, but rather *shows* the logical form of reality (see also 6.12). To this extent, the very existence of language shows something that it cannot say.

The same vision is adumbrated in somewhat more prosaic, less oracular form in the "Lecture on Ethics" delivered to a general audience, the Heretics Society, at Cambridge in 1929. This is probably the most compact and accessible exposition of Wittgenstein's ideas on what cannot be said—which happens to include no less than all ethical, aesthetic, and religious values, and even *that* the world is. Any attempt to say these things misuses language and results in nonsense. Yet this is the very purpose of value-statements—to be about what cannot be said; their purpose lies not, at any rate, in the statements of fact that alone count as making linguistic sense.

Wittgenstein operates with a strict separation between facts and values: he maintains the strict unsayability of any type of value in an absolute sense—that is, a value that cannot be reduced to facts. Such values are completely inexpressible because language states facts and nothing else. The miracles *that* the world is and that language as such exists intimate value, an ineffable mystery, precisely because they do not say it but *are* this mystery. In this way, Wittgenstein conceives the ineffable as what is obliquely or peripherally present in every saying, without itself being said. It stands, so to speak, in the shadow of saying and cannot be thematically focused, for saying and the world alike are always more, infinitely more and mysteriously other, than any "said."

A Lecture on Ethics

Before I begin to speak about my subject proper let me make a few introductory remarks. I feel I shall have great difficulties in communicating my thoughts to you and I think some of them may be diminished by mentioning them to you beforehand. The first one, which almost I need not mention, is that English is not my native tongue and my expression therefore often lacks that precision and subtlety which would be desirable if one talks about a difficult subject. All I can do is to ask you to make my task easier by trying to get at my meaning in spite of the faults which I will constantly be committing against the English grammar. The second difficulty I will mention is this, that probably many of you come up to this lecture of mine with slightly wrong expectations. And to set you right in this point I will say a few words about the reason for choosing the subject I have chosen: When your former secretary honoured me by asking me to read a paper to your society, my first thought was that I would certainly do it and my second thought was that if I was to have the opportunity to speak to you I should speak about something which I am keen on communicating to you and that I should not misuse this opportunity to give you a lecture about, say, logic. I call this a misuse, for to explain a scientific matter to you it would need a course of lectures and not an hour's paper. Another alternative would have been to give you what's called a popular-scientific lecture, that is a lecture intended to make you believe that you understand a thing which actually you don't understand, and to gratify what I believe to be one of the lowest desires of modern people, namely the superficial curiosity about the latest discoveries of science. I rejected these alternatives and decided to talk to you about a subject which seems to me to be of general importance, hoping that it may help to clear up your thoughts about this subject (even if you should entirely disagree with what I will say about it). My third and last difficulty is one which, in fact, adheres to most lengthy philosophical lectures and it is this, that the hearer is incapable of seeing both the road he is led and the goal which it leads to. That is to say: he either thinks: "I understand all he says, but what on earth is he driving at" or else he thinks "I see what he's driving at, but how on earth is he going to get there." All I can do is again to ask you to be patient and to hope that in the end you may see both the way and where it leads to.

I will now begin. My subject, as you know, is Ethics and I will adopt the explanation of that term which Professor Moore has given in his book *Principia Ethica*. He says: "Ethics is the general enquiry into what is good." Now I am going to use the term Ethics in a slightly wider sense, in a sense in fact which includes what I believe to be the most essential part of what is generally called Aesthetics. And to make you see as clearly as possible what I take to be the subject

matter of Ethics I will put before you a number of more or less synonymous expressions each of which could be substituted for the
above definition, and by enumerating them I want to produce the
same sort of effect which Galton produced when he took a number
of photos of different faces on the same photographic plate in order
to get the picture of the typical features they all had in common.
And as by showing to you such a collective photo I could make you
see what is the typical—say—Chinese face; so if you look through
the row of synonyms which I will put before you, you will, I hope, be
able to see the characteristic features they all have in common and
these are the characteristic features of Ethics. Now instead of saying
"Ethics is the enquiry into what is good" I could have said Ethics is
the enquiry into what is valuable, or, into what is really important, or
I could have said Ethics is the enquiry into the meaning of life, or into
what makes life worth living, or into the right way of living. I believe
if you look at all these phrases you will get a rough idea as to what it
is that Ethics is concerned with. Now the first thing that strikes one
about all these expressions is that each of them is actually used in two
very different senses. I will call them the trivial or relative sense on
the one hand and the ethical or absolute sense on the other. If for
instance I say that this is a *good* chair this means that the chair serves
a certain predetermined purpose and the word good here has only
meaning so far as this purpose has been previously fixed upon. In
fact the word good in the relative sense simply means coming up to a
certain predetermined standard. Thus when we say that this man is
a good pianist we mean that he can play pieces of a certain degree of
difficulty with a certain degree of dexterity. And similarly if I say that
it is *important* for me not to catch cold I mean that catching a cold
produces certain describable disturbances in my life and if I say that
this is the *right* road I mean that it's the right road relative to a certain
goal. Used in this way these expressions don't present any difficult or
deep problems. But this is not how Ethics uses them. Supposing that
I could play tennis and one of you saw me playing and said "Well, you
play pretty badly" and suppose I answered "I know, I'm playing badly
but I don't want to play any better," all the other man could say would
be "Ah then that's all right." But suppose I had told one of you a pre-
posterous lie and he came up to me and said "You're behaving like
a beast" and then I were to say "I know I behave badly, but then I
don't want to behave any better," could he then say "Ah, then that's all

right"? Certainly not; he would say "Well, you *ought* to want to behave better." Here you have an absolute judgment of value, whereas
the first instance was one of a relative judgment. The essence of this
difference seems to be obviously this: Every judgment of relative
value is a mere statement of facts and can therefore be put in such a
form that it loses all the appearance of a judgment of value: Instead
of saying "This is the right way to Granchester," I could equally well
have said, "This is the right way you have to go if you want to get to
Granchester in the shortest time"; "This man is a good runner" simply means that he runs a certain number of miles in a certain number of minutes, etc. Now what I wish to contend is that, although
all judgments of relative value can be shown to be mere statements
of facts, no statement of fact can ever be, or imply, a judgment of absolute value. Let me explain this: Suppose one of you were an omniscient person and therefore knew all the movements of all the bodies
in the world dead or alive and that he also knew all the states of mind
of all human beings that ever lived, and suppose this man wrote all
he knew in a big book, then this book would contain the whole description of the world; and what I want to say is, that this book would
contain nothing that we would call an *ethical* judgment or anything
that would logically imply such a judgment. It would of course contain all relative judgments of value and all true scientific propositions
and in fact all true propositions that can be made. But all the facts described would, as it were, stand on the same level and in the same way
all propositions stand on the same level. There are no propositions
which, in any absolute sense, are sublime, important, or trivial. Now
perhaps some of you will agree to that and be reminded of Hamlet's
words: "Nothing is either good or bad, but thinking makes it so." But
this again could lead to a misunderstanding. What Hamlet says seems
to imply that good and bad, though not qualities of the world outside
us, are attributes to our states of mind. But what I mean is that a state
of mind, so far as we mean by that a fact which we can describe, is in
no ethical sense good or bad. If for instance in our world-book we
read the description of a murder with all its details physical and psy-
chological, the mere description of these facts will contain nothing
which we could call an *ethical* proposition. The murder will be on
exactly the same level as any other event, for instance the falling of
a stone. Certainly the reading of this description might cause us pain
or rage or any other emotion, or we might read about the pain or

rage caused by this murder in other people when they heard of it, but there will simply be facts, facts, and facts but no Ethics. And now I must say that if I contemplate what Ethics really would have to be if there were such a science, this result seems to me quite obvious. It seems to me obvious that nothing we could ever think or say should be *the* thing. That we cannot write a scientific book, the subject matter of which could be intrinsically sublime and above all other subject matters. I can only describe my feeling by the metaphor, that, if a man could write a book on Ethics which really was a book on Ethics, this book would, with an explosion, destroy all the other books in the world. Our words used as we use them in science, are vessels capable only of containing and conveying meaning and sense, *natural* meaning and sense. Ethics, if it is anything, is supernatural and our words will only express facts; as a teacup will only hold a teacup full of water [even] if I were to pour out a gallon over it. I said that so far as facts and propositions are concerned there is only relative value and relative good, right, etc. And let me, before I go on, illustrate this by a rather obvious example. The right road is the road which leads to an arbitrarily predetermined end and it is quite clear to us all that there is no sense in talking about the right road apart from such a predetermined goal. Now let us see what we could possibly mean by the expression, "*the* absolutely right road." I think it would be the road which *everybody* on seeing it would, *with logical necessity,* have to go, or be ashamed for not going. And similarly the *absolute good*, if it is a describable state of affairs, would be one which everybody, independent of his tastes and inclinations, would *necessarily* bring about or feel guilty for not bringing about. And I want to say that such a state of affairs is a chimera. No state of affairs has, in itself, what I would like to call the coercive power of an absolute judge. Then what have all of us who, like myself, are still tempted to use such expressions as "absolute good," "absolute value," etc., what have we in mind and what do we try to express? Now whenever I try to make this clear to myself it is natural that I should recall cases in which I would certainly use these expressions and I am then in the situation in which you would be if, for instance, I were to give you a lecture on the psychology of pleasure. What you would do then would be to try and recall some typical situation in which you always felt pleasure. For, bearing this situation in mind, all I should say to you would become concrete and, as it were, controllable. One man would perhaps choose as his stock example the sensation when taking a walk on a fine summer's day. Now in this situation I am, if I want to fix my mind on what I mean by absolute or ethical value. And there, in my case, it always happens that the idea of one particular experience presents itself to me which therefore is, in a sense, my experience *par excellence* and this is the reason why, in talking to you now, I will use this experience as my first and foremost example. (As I have said before, this is an entirely personal matter and others would find other examples more striking.) I will describe this experience in order, if possible, to make you recall the same or similar experiences, so that we may have a common ground for our investigation. I believe the best way of describing it is to say that when I have it *I wonder at the existence of the world.* And I am then inclined to use such phrases as "how extraordinary that anything should exist" or "how extraordinary that the world should exist." I will mention another experience straight away which I also know and which others of you might be acquainted with: it is, what one might call, the experience of feeling *absolutely* safe. I mean the state of mind in which one is inclined to say "I am safe, nothing can injure me whatever happens." Now let me consider these experiences, for, I believe, they exhibit the very characteristics we try to get clear about. And there the first thing I have to say is, that the verbal expression which we give to these experiences is nonsense! If I say "I wonder at the existence of the world" I am misusing language. Let me explain this: It has a perfectly good and clear sense to say that I wonder at something being the case, we all understand what it means to say that I wonder at the size of a dog which is bigger than anyone I have ever seen before or at any thing which, in the common sense of the word, is extraordinary. In every such case I wonder at something being the case which I *could* conceive *not* to be the case. I wonder at the size of this dog because I could conceive of a dog of another, namely the ordinary size, at which I should not wonder. To say "I wonder at such and such being the case" has only sense if I can imagine it not to be the case. In this sense one can wonder at the existence of, say, a house when one sees it and has not visited it for a long time and has imagined that it had been pulled down in the meantime. But it is nonsense to say that I wonder at the existence of the world, because I cannot imagine it not existing. I could of course wonder at the world round me being as it is. If for instance I had this experience while looking into the blue sky, I could wonder at the sky being blue as opposed to the case when it's clouded. But that's not what I mean. I am wondering at the sky being *whatever it is.* One might be tempted to say that what I am wondering at is a tautology, namely at the sky being blue or not blue. But then it's just nonsense to say that one is wondering at a tautology. Now the same applies to the other experience[s] which I have mentioned, the experience of absolute safety. We all know what it means in ordinary life to be safe. I am safe in my room, when I cannot be run over by an omnibus. I am safe if I have had whooping cough and cannot therefore get it again. To be safe essentially means that it is physically impossible that certain things should happen to me and therefore it's nonsense to say that I am safe *whatever* happens. Again this is a misuse of the word "safe" as the other example was of a misuse of the word "existence" or "wondering." Now I want to impress on you that a certain characteristic misuse of our language runs through *all* ethical and religious expressions. All these expressions *seem,* prima facie, to be just *similes.* Thus it seems that when we are using the word *right* in an ethical sense, although, what we mean, is not right in its trivial sense, it's something similar, and when we say "This is a good fellow," although the word good here doesn't mean what it means in the sentence "This is a good football player" there seems to be some similarity. And when we say "This man's life was valuable" we don't mean it in the same sense in which we would speak of some valuable jewelry but there seems to be some sort of analogy. Now all religious terms seem in this sense to be used as similes or allegorically. For when we speak of God and that he sees everything and when we kneel and pray to him all our terms and actions seem to be parts of a great and elaborate allegory which represents him as a human being of great power whose grace we try to win, etc., etc. But this allegory also describes the experience[s] which I have just referred to. For the first of them is, I believe, exactly what people were referring to when they said that God had created the world; and the experience of absolute safety has been described by saying that we feel safe in the hands of God. A third experience of the same kind is that of feeling guilty and again this was described by the phrase that God disapproves of our conduct. Thus in ethical and religious language we seem constantly to be using similes. But a simile must be the simile for *something.* And if I can describe a fact by means of a simile I must also be able to drop the simile and to describe the facts without it. Now in our case as soon as we try to drop the simile and simply to state the facts which stand behind it, we find that there are no such facts. And so, what at first appeared to be a simile now seems to be mere nonsense. Now the three experiences which I have mentioned to you (and I could have added others) seem to those who have experienced them, for instance to me, to have in some sense an intrinsic, absolute value. But when I say they are experiences, surely, they are facts; they have taken place then and there, lasted a certain definite time and consequently are describable. And so from what I have said some minutes ago I must admit it is nonsense to say that they have absolute value. And I will make my point still more acute by saying "It is the paradox that an experience, a fact, should seem to have supernatural value." Now there is a way in which I would be tempted to meet this paradox. Let me first consider, again, our first experience of wondering at the existence of the world and let me describe it in a slightly different way; we all know what in ordinary life would be called a miracle. It obviously is simply an event the like of which we have never yet seen. Now suppose such an event happened. Take the case that one of you suddenly grew a lion's head and began to roar. Certainly that would be as extraordinary a thing as I can imagine. Now whenever we should have recovered from our surprise, what I would suggest would be to fetch a doctor and have the case scientifically investigated and if it were not for hurting him I would have him vivisected. And where would the miracle have got to? For it is clear that when we look at it in this way everything miraculous has disappeared; unless what we mean by this term is merely that a fact has not yet been explained by science which again means that we have hitherto failed to group this fact with others in a scientific system. This shows that it is absurd to say "Science has proved that there are no miracles." The truth is that the scientific way of looking at a fact is not the way to look at it as a miracle. For imagine whatever fact you may, it is not in itself miraculous in the absolute sense of that term. For we see now that we have been using the word "miracle" in a relative and an absolute sense. And I will now describe the experience of wondering at the existence of the world by saying: it is the experience of seeing the world as a miracle. Now I am tempted to say that the right expression in language for the miracle of the existence of the world, though it is not any proposition *in* language, is the existence of language itself. But what then does it mean to be aware of this miracle at some times and not at other times? For all I have said by shifting the expression of the miraculous from an expression *by means of* language to the expression *by the existence* of language, all I have said is again that we cannot express what we want to express and that all we *say* about the absolute miraculous remains nonsense. Now the answer to all this will seem perfectly clear to many of you. You will say: Well, if certain experiences constantly tempt us to attribute a quality to them which we call absolute or ethical value and importance, this simply shows that by these words we *don't* mean nonsense, that after all what we mean by saying that an experience has absolute value *is just a fact like other facts* and that all it comes to is that we have not yet succeeded in finding the correct logical analysis of what we mean by our ethical and religious expressions. Now when this is urged against me I at once see clearly, as it were in a flash of light, not only that no description that I can think of would do to describe what I mean by absolute value, but that I would reject every significant description that anybody could possibly suggest, *ab initio*, on the ground of its significance. That is to say: I see now that these nonsensical expressions were not nonsensical because I had not yet found the correct expressions, but that their nonsensicality was their very essence. For all I wanted to do with them was just *to go beyond* the world and that is to say beyond significant language. My whole tendency and I believe the tendency of all men who ever tried to write or talk Ethics or Religion was to run against the boundaries of language. This running against the walls of our cage is perfectly, absolutely hopeless. Ethics so far as it springs from the desire to say something about the ultimate meaning of life, the absolute good, the absolute valuable, can be no science. What it says does not add to our knowledge in any sense. But it is a document of a tendency in the human mind which I personally cannot help respecting deeply and I would not for my life ridicule it.

Tractatus Logico-Philosophicus, 6.4–7

6.4   All propositions are of equal value.

6.41   The sense of the world must lie outside the world. In the world everything is as it is and happens as it does happen. *In* it there is no value—and if there were, it would be of no value.

If there is a value which is of value, it must lie outside all happening and being-so. For all happening and being-so is accidental.

What makes it non-accidental cannot lie *in* the world, for otherwise this would again be accidental.

It must lie outside the world.

6.42   Hence also there can be no ethical propositions.

Propositions cannot express anything higher.

6.421   It is clear that ethics cannot be expressed.

Ethics is transcendental.

(Ethics and aesthetics are one.)

6.422   The first thought in setting up an ethical law of the form "thou shalt . . ." is: And what if I do not do it? But it is clear that ethics has nothing to do with punishment and reward in the ordinary sense. This question as to the *consequences* of an action must therefore be irrelevant. At least these consequences will not be events. For there must be something right in that formulation of the question. There must be some sort of ethical reward and ethical punishment, but this must lie in the action itself.

(And this is clear also that the reward must be something acceptable, and the punishment something unacceptable.)

6.423   Of the will as the subject of the ethical we cannot speak.

And the will as a phenomenon is only of interest to psychology.

6.43   If good or bad willing changes the world, it can only change the limits of the world, not the facts; not the things that can be expressed in language.

In brief, the world must thereby become quite another. It must so to speak wax or wane as a whole.

The world of the happy is quite another than that of the unhappy.

6.431   As in death, too, the world does not change, but ceases.

6.4311   Death is not an event of life. Death is not lived through.

If by eternity is understood not endless temporal duration but timelessness, then he lives eternally who lives in the present.

Our life is endless in the way that our visual field is without limit.

6.4312   The temporal immortality of the human soul, that is to say, its eternal survival after death, is not only in no way guaranteed, but this assumption in the first place will not do for us what we always tried to make it do. Is a riddle solved by the fact that I survive for ever? Is this eternal life not as enigmatic as our present one? The solution of the riddle of life in space and time lies *outside* space and time.

(It is not problems of natural science which have to be solved.)

6.432   *How* the world is, is completely indifferent for what is higher. God does not reveal himself *in* the world.

6.4321   The facts all belong only to the task and not to its performance.

6.44   Not *how* the world is, is the mystical, but *that* it is.

6.45   The contemplation of the world sub specie aeterni is its contemplation as a limited whole.

The feeling of the world as a limited whole is the mystical feeling.

6.5   For an answer which cannot be expressed the question too cannot be expressed.

The riddle does not exist.

If a question can be put at all, then it *can* also be answered.

6.51   Scepticism is *not* irrefutable, but palpably senseless, if it would doubt where a question cannot be asked.

For doubt can only exist where there is a question; a question only where there is an answer, and this only where something *can* be *said*.

6.52   We feel that even if *all possible* scientific questions be answered, the problems of life have still not been touched at all. Of course there is then no question left, and just this is the answer.

6.521   The solution of the problem of life is seen in the vanishing of this problem.

(Is not this the reason why men to whom after long doubting the sense of life became clear, could not then say wherein this sense consisted?)

6.522 There is indeed the inexpressible. This *shows* itself; it is the mystical.

6.53 The right method of philosophy would be this. To say nothing except what can be said, *i.e.* the propositions of natural science, *i.e.* something that has nothing to do with philosophy: and then always, when someone else wished to say something metaphysical, to demonstrate to him that he had given no meaning to certain signs in his propositions. This method would be unsatisfying to the other—he would not have the feeling that we were teaching him philosophy—but it would be the only strictly correct method.

6.54 My propositions are elucidatory in this way: he who understands me finally recognizes them as senseless, when he has climbed out through them, on them, over them. (He must so to speak throw away the ladder, after he has climbed up on it.)

He must surmount these propositions; then he sees the world rightly.

7 Whereof one cannot speak, thereof one must be silent.

11. HEIDEGGER (1889–1976)

"Das Wort," in *Unterwegs zur Sprache* (Pfullingen: Neske, 1959), pp. 219–238.

   Trans. Joan Stambaugh as "Words," in *On the Way to Language* (New York: Harper & Row, 1971), pp. 139–156.

Heidegger's thought defines itself as an attempt to think, at "the end of philosophy," what has been left unthought—and therefore also unsaid—throughout Western philosophical tradition.[1] He conceives this unthought, unsaid, and unsayable in terms of the limits of thinking and specifically of language: "The internal limit of all thinking . . . is that the thinker never can say what is most his own . . . because the spoken word receives its determination from the ineffable."[2] Of course, Heidegger cannot say what this ineffable is, but by driving thought relentlessly toward its grounds, he can *indicate* what exceeds thought and speech. This is the last, ineffable ground to which thinking, saying, and being belong most profoundly, and in which all would come to rest: "Thinking's saying would be stilled in its being by becoming unable to say that which must remain unspoken. / Such inability would bring thinking face to face with its matter."[3] Anything, any being that can been talked about, will prove derivative. Only an apophatic way of thinking the unthinkable and unspeakable can disclose the grounds of being that are concealed by the words of philosophy.

   Heidegger's unremitting attempt to think Being itself in its difference from beings, which tend to cover it over and cause it to be forgotten, follows a path analogous to that of negative theology in its pursuit of a God that cannot be conceived or named in terms of any of the things that are. His philosophy from early on overlaps, moreover, with the negative theological intuition of

---

1. Heidegger, "Das Ende der Philosophie und die Aufgabe des Denkens," in *Zur Sache des Denkens* (Tübingen: Max Niemeyer Verlag, 1969), pp. 61–80.
   2. Heidegger, *Nietzsche* (Pfullingen: Neske, 1961), p. 484.
   3. "The Thinker as Poet," in *Poetry, Language, Thought* (New York: Harper & Row, 1971), p. 11, trans. Albert Hofstadter from Heidegger, *Aus der Erfahrung des Denkens* (Pfullingen: Neske, 1954), p. 21: "Die Sage des Denkens wäre erst dadurch in ihr Wesen beruhigt, daß sie unvermögend würde, jenes zu sagen, was ungesprochen bleiben muß. / Solches Unvermögen brächte das Denken vor die Sache."

the *Nihil*, the *Nichts*, as that which is at the origin of all that is. This Nothing is intuited especially in the experience of anxiety. In "Was ist Metaphysik?" (1929), Heidegger speaks of how anxiety silences speech ("Die Angst verschlägt uns das Wort") and calls it "one of the essential places of speechlessness in the sense of the terror that attunes man to the abyss of nothingness."[4] Like God, Being is no thing. Thinking or listening to Being is a profound attunement to silence. This attunement Heidegger, following Meister Eckhart, eventually calls *Gelassenheit*, that is, abandon and openness to mystery ("die Gelassenheit zu den Dingen und die Offenheit für das Geheimnis").[5] Late in his career, Heidegger came to abandon the very term "Being" and to write it under erasure, that is, as crossed out by a large **X**, since any determinate expression inevitably betrays it by treating it as *a* being or as some specific sort of being.

For Heidegger, thinking requires, before all else, listening, and listening in turn requires the silence of the listener. In *Sein und Zeit*, paragraph 34 on discourse and language, following the discussions of understanding (*Verstehen*) and interpretation (*Auslegen*), Heidegger insists that hearing is constitutive of speaking ("Das Hören ist für das Reden konstitutiv"). Hearing, in fact, constitutes the fundamental openness of human being ("Das Hören konstituiert sogar die primäre und eigentliche Offenheit des Daseins . . ."). Truth is the opening and disclosing effected by language in us through hearing, but to be in the truth and to hear, we must be in silence. Our being a conversation, according to Hölderlin's dictum—"since we are a conversation / and able to hear from one another"—"means also and equiprimordially that we are a *silence*."[6]

The unspeakable meaning of the Heideggerian experience of Being is pursued in his reading of Hölderlin as the poet of the sacred that has withdrawn, leaving the trace that the poet conserves in times of lack ("dürftiger Zeit"), that is, times lacking in divine presence and revelation. The task of the poet is to preserve the trace of Being amid this nothingness by experiencing and gesturing toward an unspoken in the spoken. The poet fulfills historical destiny by "experiencing the unsaid in the said" ("im Gesagten seiner Dichtung das Ungesprochene zu erfahren").[7] This primordial kind of speaking—

---

4. *Wegmerken*, in *Gesamtausgabe* (Frankfurt a.M.: Klostermann, 1976–) vol. 9, pp. 9–12.

5. *Gelassenheit* (Pfullingen: Neske, 1959), p. 26.

6. "Das wir ein Gespräch sind, heißt zugleich und gleichursprünglich: wir sind ein *Schweigen*." Heidegger, *Holderlins Hymnen "Germanien" und "Der Rhein*," Freiburger Vorlesung Wintersemester 1934/35, in *Gesamtausgabe*, vol. 39, p. 70.

7. Heidegger, "Wozu Dichter," in *Holzwege* (Frankfurt a.M.: Klostermann, 1950), p. 252.

essentially naming, essentially poetry—"says the unsayable in such a way that it remains unsaid."[8]

In an essay on Georg Trakl, Heidegger states that every great poet has one poem out of which he makes all his poems, but that this essential poem remains unspoken ("Das Gedicht eines Dichters bleibt ungesprochen"). His first purpose in interpreting Trakl's poetry is to attempt to point to the site of this unspoken poem.[9] Heidegger defines the place from which Trakl's poetry speaks as "Die Abgeschiedenheit," the departedness. For Trakl defines himself in his poetry as "der Absgeschiedene," the departed one. He has left the community of common language and conversation, "idle talk" ("Gerede," in Heidegger's terminology), where sayings pass from mouth to mouth as currency, quite apart from authentic experience of how things really are. It is possible, then, to define silence as a peculiarly potent way of speaking, provided it is not merely the silence of the dumb but an elected reticence ("Verschwiegenheit") that "strikes down idle talk." Trakl emerges from Heidegger's exegesis as the poet of the dark enigma and of the unsayable. As Karsten Harries explains, "Poetry communicates the poet's journey away from the established community into the night. The language of poetry has its place in-between idle talk and silence. It is a recovery of silence in the midst of idle talk. . . . Thus its life resides in the tension between what has been said and what has remained unspoken."[10]

Stefan George's poetry, by contrast, fulfills an essentially Orphic function of speaking being rather than silence, yet the two modes prove to be inseparable. To reveal a thing, language must thematize certain features of it, leaving untold others in silence and obscurity. Harries links this dark side of language as concealment with the figure of the Earth in Heidegger's essay on the origin of the work of art, "Der Ursprung des Kunstwerkes" (1936): in Heidegger's terminology, the Earth, absorbing the human world back into its dark womb,

---

8. Heidegger, *Was heißt Denken* (Tübingen: Max Niemeyer Verlag, 1954), p. 119: "Jedes anfängliche und eigentliche Nennen sagt Ungesprochenes und zwar so, daß es ungesprochen bleibt."

9. "Die Sprache im Gedicht: Eine Erörterung von Georg Trakls Gedicht," in *Unterwegs zur Sprache* (Pfullingen: Verlag Günther Neske, 1959): "versuchen wir zuerst, in den Ort des ungesprochenen Gedichtes zu weisen" (p. 39).

10. Karsten Harries, "Language and Silence: Heidegger's Dialogue with Georg Trakl," in *Martin Heidegger and the Question of Literature: Towards a Postmodern Literary Hermeneutics*, ed. William V. Spanos (Bloomington: Indiana University Press, 1979), p. 164.

struggles against and withdraws from the World, the ambit of significances and of disclosure of things in their intrinsic relatedness.

The dialogue with a Japanese, included in *On the Way to Language*, is also rich in hints about Heidegger's view on the unsayable. It brings Western thought into contact with Zen on the topic of silence. In reading this dialogue, Tetsuaki Kotoh emphasizes that silence is the place out of which language necessarily speaks in Heidegger. "The true relationship between self and language is restored when the framework of everyday language breaks down to let silence emerge and give rise to creative language. This intimate relationship between language and the ground of self (silence), which is central to Heidegger's thinking about language, . . . distinguishes Heidegger from the mainstream Western tradition, which makes *logos* central, and also brings him close to oriental thinking based on silence."[11]

Some kind of breakdown of ordinary language is necessary to free the self from the inauthentic, idle talk of *Gerede*, and it is the ensuing silence that first enables a self-disclosure of language as language. Heidegger writes, "When does language speak itself as language? Curiously enough, when we cannot find the right word for anything that concerns us, carries us away, oppresses us or encourages us. Then we leave unspoken what we have in mind and, without rightly giving it thought, undergo moments in which language itself has distantly and fleetingly touched us with its essential being."[12] This essential being of language that becomes perceptible where language breaks off Heidegger calls "the peal of silence" ("das Geläut der Stille") and "the silence of stillness" ("das Schweigen der Stille").

Although acclaimed throughout Europe and in the Orient, Heidegger preferred to live in relative seclusion in the Black Forest of southern Germany, listening for the silence of Being at the heart of language, as his essay "Language" (1950) attests. For Heidegger, language is essentially Being, the Being that is not any being but is always there in and as the Being of any being. This Being consists in any being's being bound together (λέγειν) with other beings in a world: such mutual determination is already language in its latency. Language is this bindingness of Being.[13] This is nothing that can be expressed

---

11. T. Kotoh, "Language and Silence: Self-Inquiry in Heidegger and Zen," in *Heidegger and Asian Thought*, ed. G. Parkes (Honolulu: University of Hawaii Press, 1987).

12. Heidegger, "The Nature of Language," trans. Peter D. Hertz, in *On the Way to Language*, p. 59.

13. See also Heidegger's essay "Logos (Heraklit, Fragment 50)," in *Vorträge und Aufsätze* (Pfullingen: Neske, 1954).

itself as such, but it is already there, presupposed, silently present in everything that distinctly is. It is the "peal of silence" by which language itself speaks.

The peal of silence, according to Heidegger, is the bidding of things and world into the intimacy of their dif-ference, each being called forth to presence by this dif-ference: we can perceive a thing only as part of a world and a world only as made up of things, yet as distinct from all of them. Things and world "still" each other, hold each other in the presence of Being. This silent perduring in the mutual calling of their dif-ference is the peal of stillness ("das Geläut der Stille") by which language speaks. Language, as a binding of things together in a totality of world, whereby alone they can be sustained in being, bids things into being. By calling things and world into the present of the word, language bids them into a presence and absence in and by their togetherness in articulated dif-ference. It gathers them in order to differentiate them, and it stills or conserves them in their simply, silently being-there-together. In this way, it itself "speaks" or enables them to be disclosed and thereby to disclose Being.

In order to follow out all the suggestions of Heidegger's thought, the above account of language also needs to be turned around: language is equally the *un*binding of Being. In this perspective, language lets things come to presence not by creating or constituting them as world or reality but by de-realization of itself, by its own *dis*appearance—a renunciation of its own self, a removal of its own mediation. Language in its own nature is an unbinding ("in ihr Eigentümliches entbindet"): in the weave of language we experience the unbinding bond, the untying tie ("das entbindende Band"). It is precisely in disappearing that language "happens" ("sich ereignet"). Its nature is to withdraw and conceal itself as it points away from itself to a world of reference. And yet this self-refusal of language speaks ("die Verweigerung des Sprachwesens spricht").[14] It intimates the freeing of a beyond of being that is released from language. Language, in disappearing as positive entity, or as a being, discloses Being as what witholds itself and disappears.

The implications of this line of thinking are not necessarily pursued by Heidegger to their most radically apophatic results. The disclosing of Being in and by saying is the event, the *Ereignis*, the appropriation of Being in which all comes to being and in which truth is manifest. Heidegger is mainly interested

---

14. "Der Weg zur Sprache," in *Unterwegs*, p. 231. See, further, Gerald L. Bruns, "Disappeared: Heidegger and the Emancipation of Language," in *Languages of the Unsayable: The Play of Negativity in Literature and Literary Theory*, ed. Sanford Budick and Wolfgang Iser (New York: Columbia University Press, 1989).

in language as a saying which is a showing. In the essays of *Unterwegs zur Sprache* (1959), including "Words," as elsewhere throughout his thinking, Heidegger pursues truth as disclosure. Language and even silence is primarily disclosure rather than withdrawal from disclosure. Although his researches constantly show how this phenomenon is itself beholden to what evades showing, he always emphasizes the undisclosed *in* the event of disclosure. It is not any mysterious Unmanifest but a showing that counts most for Heidegger. In this sense, the phenomenon is ultimate, and Heidegger's method remains phenomonological rather than a *via negativa*. While Heidegger constantly thought about the limits of language, he does not want to affirm the "beyond" of language: he positions himself rather as "on the way" to it. He remains committed to the truth of the world and not to any beyond-of-truth or any *other* world or "other-than-world." He saw the opening clearly, but to venture into it one can go only on faith, and that he lacked. Wittgenstein, too, saw this world beyond as being utterly beyond the pale of philosophy, yet the possibility of faith in it was very real for him and, finally, of greater importance than anything that could be articulated by philosophy.

"Words," from *On the Way to Language*

From where we are now, let us for a moment think about what Hölderlin asks in his elegy "Bread and Wine" (stanza vi):

Why are they silent, too, the theatres ancient and hallowed?
Why not now does the dance celebrate, consecrate joy?[1]

---

1. Friedrich Hölderlin, *Poems and Fragments*, trans. Michael Hamburger (Ann Arbor: University of Michigan Press, 1967), p. 249.

The word is withheld from the former place of the gods' appearance, the word as it was once word. How was it then? The approach
of the god took place in Saying itself. Saying was in itself the allowing
to appear of that which the saying ones saw because it had already
looked at them. That look brought the saying and the hearing ones
into the un-finite intimacy of the strife between men and gods. However, That which is yet above the gods and men prevailed through
this strife—as Antigone says!

> *ou gar ti moi Zeus en, ho keruxas tade,*
> (l.450)

"It was not Zeus who sent me the message" (but something
other, that directing need).

> *ou gar ti nun ge kachthes, all' aei pote*
> *ze tauta, koudeis oiden ex hotou' phane.*
> (ll.456/7)

"Not only today and tomorrow, but ever and ever it" (*ho nomos*, the
directing need) "arises and no one has looked upon that place from
which it came into radiance."

The poetic word of this kind remains an enigma. Its saying
has long since returned to silence. May we dare to think about this
enigma? We are already doing enough if we allow ourselves to be told
the enigma of the word by poetry itself—in a poem with the title:

WORDS

Wonder or dream from distant land
I carried to my country's strand

And waited till the twilit norn
Had found the name within her bourn—

Then I could grasp it close and strong
It blooms and shines now the front along . . .

Once I returned from happy sail,
I had a prize so rich and frail,

She sought for long and tidings told:
"No like of this these depths enfold."

And straight it vanished from my hand,
The treasure never graced my land . . .

So I renounced and sadly see:
Where word breaks off no thing may be.
                    [Trans. Peter Hertz (J.S.)]

The poem was first published in the 11th and 12th series of
"*Blätter für die Kunst*" in 1919. Later (1928) Stefan George included it
in the last volume of poems published in his lifetime, called *Das Neue
Reich*.

The poem is structured in seven stanzas of two lines each. The
final stanza not only concludes the poem, it opens it up at the same
time. This is already evident in the fact that only the final stanza explicitly says what is in the title: *Words*. The final stanza reads:

Where word breaks off no thing may be.

One is tempted to turn the final line into a statement with the
content: No thing is where the word breaks off. Where something
breaks off, there is a break, a breaking off. To do harm to something
means to take something away from it, to let something be lacking.
"It is lacking" means "it is missing." Where the word is missing, there
is no thing.

It is only the word at our disposal which endows the thing with
Being.

What are words, that they have such power?

What are things, that they need words in order to be?

What does Being mean here, that it appears like an endowment
which is dedicated to the thing from the word?

Questions upon questions. These questions do not immediately
arouse our contemplation in the first hearing and reading of the
poem. We are much more likely to be enchanted by the first six stanzas, for they tell of the poet's strangely veiled experiences. The final
stanza, however, speaks in a more oppressing way. It forces us to the
unrest of thought. Only this final stanza makes us hear what, according to the title, is the poetic intent of the whole poem: Words.

Is anything more exciting and more dangerous for the poet than his relation to words? Hardly. Is this relation first created by the poet, or does the word of itself and for itself need poetry, so that only through this need does the poet become who he can be? All of this and much else besides gives food for thought and makes us thoughtful. Still, we hesitate to enter upon such reflection. For it is now supported only by a single verse of the whole poem. What is more, we have changed this final verse into a statement. Of course, this act of change did not come about through sheer willfulness. Rather, we are almost forced to make the change, as soon as we notice that the first line of the final stanza ends with a colon. The colon arouses the expectation that it will be followed by a statement. This is the case in the fifth stanza, too. At the end of the first line of that stanza there is also a colon:

> She sought for long and tidings told:
> "No like of this these depths enfold."

The colon opens something up. What follows speaks, seen grammatically, in the indicative: "No like of this . . ." Furthermore, what the twilit norn says is placed between quotation marks.

The case is different in the final stanza. Here, too, there is a colon at the end of the first line. But what follows the colon neither speaks in the indicative, nor are there quotation marks around what is said. What is the difference between the fifth and the seventh stanza? In the fifth stanza, the twilit norn announces something. The announcement is a kind of statement, a revelation. In contrast, the tone of the final stanza is concentrated in the word "renounce."

Renouncing is not stating, but perhaps after all a Saying. Renouncing belongs to the verb to forgive. Accusing, charging is the same word as showing, Greek *deiknumi*, Latin *dicere*. To accuse, to show means: to allow to be seen, to bring to appearance. This, however, showing and allowing to be seen, is the meaning of the old German word *sagan*, to say. To accuse, to charge someone means: to tell him something straight to his face. Accordingly, Saying dominates in forgiving, in renouncing. How so? Renouncing means: to give up the claim to something, to deny oneself something. Because renouncing is a manner of Saying, it can be introduced in writing by a colon. Yet what follows the colon does not need to be a statement. The colon following the word "renounce" does not disclose something in the sense of a statement or an assertion. Rather, the colon discloses renunciation as Saying of that with which it is involved. With what is it involved? Presumably with that which renunciation renounces.

So I renounced and sadly see:
Where word breaks off no thing may be.

But how? Does the poet renounce the fact that no thing may be where the word breaks off? By no means. The poet is so far from renouncing this that he actually assents to what is said. Thus the direction in which the colon discloses renunciation cannot tell of that which the poet renounces. It must rather tell of that with which the poet is involved. But renouncing indisputably means: to deny oneself something. Accordingly, the final verse must, after all, tell of what the poet denies himself. Yes and no.

How are we to think this? The final verse makes us more and more thoughtful and requires us to hear it more clearly as a whole, but to hear the whole as that stanza which at the same time discloses the poem through its conclusion.

So I renounced and sadly see:
Where word breaks off no thing may be.

The poet has learned renunciation. To learn means: to become knowing. In Latin, knowing is *qui vidit*, one who has seen, has caught sight of something, and who never again loses sight of what he has caught sight of. To learn means: to attain to such seeing. To this belongs our reaching it; namely on the way, on a journey. To put oneself on a journey, to experience, means to learn.

On what journeys does the poet attain to his renunciation? Through what land do his journeys lead the traveler? How has the poet experienced renunciation? The final stanza gives the directive.

So I renounced and sadly see:

How? Just as the preceding six stanzas tell of it. Here the poet is speaking of his land. There he is speaking of his journeys. The fourth stanza begins:

Once I returned from happy sail

"Once" is used here in the old meaning which signifies "one time." In this meaning, it tells of a distinctive time, a unique experience. The telling of the experience, therefore, does not just begin abruptly with the "once." It demarcates itself sharply at the same time from all his other journeys, for the last verse of the immediately preceding third stanza terminates in three dots. The same is true of the last verse of the sixth stanza. Accordingly, the six stanzas which prepare for the seventh, the final stanza, are divided by clear signs into two groups of three stanzas, two triads.

The poet's journeys of which the first triad tells are of a different kind from the sole and unique journey to which the whole second triad is dedicated. In order to be able to contemplate the poet's journeys, particularly the unique one which allows him to experience renunciation, we must first consider the landscape to which the poet's experiencing belongs.

Twice—in the second verse of the first stanza and in the second verse of the sixth stanza, that is, at the beginning and at the end of the two triads—the poet says "my land." The land is his as the assured area of his poetry. What his poetry requires are names. Names for what?

The first verse of the poem gives the answer:

Wonder or dream from distant land

Names for what is borne to the poet from the distance as something full of wonder or for what visits him in dreams. For the poet, both of these mean in all assurance what truly concerns him, that which is. Yet he does not want to keep that which is to himself, but to portray it. In order to do this, names are necessary. They are words by which what already is and is believed to be is made so concrete and full of being that it henceforth shines and blooms and thus reigns as the beautiful everywhere in the land. The names are words that portray. They present what already is to representational thinking. By their power of portrayal the names bear witness to their decisive rule over things. The poet himself composes in virtue of the claim to the names. In order to reach them, he must first in his journeys attain to that place where his claim finds the required fulfillment. This happens at his country's strand. The strand bounds, it arrests, limits and circumscribes the poet's secure sojourn. The bourne, the well from which the twilit norn, the ancient goddess of fate, draws up the names is at the edge of the poet's land—or is the edge itself the well? With these names she gives the poet those words which he, confidently and sure of himself, awaits as the portrayal of what he believes to be that which is. The poet's claim to the rule of his Saying is fulfilled. The flourishing and shining of his poetry become presence. The poet is sure of his word, and just as fully in command of it. The last stanza of the first triad begins with the decisive "then."

Then I could grasp it full and strong
It blooms and shines now the front along . . .

Let us pay keen attention to the shift in the tenses of the verbs in the second verse of this stanza as compared with the first. The verbs now speak in the present tense. The rule of poetry is completed. It has reached its goal and is perfected. No lack, no doubt disturbs the poet's self-assurance.

Until a wholly different experience strikes him. It is told in the second triad which is formed in exact correspondence to the first. The characteristics of this correspondence are these: the last stanzas of both triads each begins with temporal indications—"Then," "And straight." A dash at the end of the second verse precedes the "Then." A sign also precedes the "And straight"—the quotation mark in the fifth stanza.

From his unique journey the poet no longer brings "wonder or dream from distant land" to his country's strand. After a good journey he arrives with a treasure at the source of the norn. The treasure's origin remains obscure. The poet simply holds it in his hand. What lies in his hand is neither a dream nor something fetched from a distance. But the strange precious jewel is both "rich and frail." Hence the goddess of fate must search long for the jewel's name and must finally take leave of the poet with the message:

"No like of this these depths enfold."

The names held in the depths of the well are taken as something slumbering which only needs to be awakened in order to be used for the portrayal of things. The names and words are like a staple supply coordinated with the things and retroactively given them for the portrayal. But this source from which until now poetic Saying took its words—words which as names portrayed that which is—this source no longer bestows anything.

What experience befalls the poet? Only this, that the name never comes for the treasure lying in his hand? Only this, that now the treasure must do without its name, but may otherwise remain in the poet's hand? No. Something else, something disturbing happens. However, neither the absence of the name nor the slipping away of the treasure is what is disturbing. What is disturbing is the fact that *with* the absence of the word, the treasure disappears. Thus, it is the word which first holds the treasure in its presence, indeed first fetches and brings it there and preserves it. Suddenly the word shows a different, a higher rule. It is no longer just a name-giving grasp reaching for what is present and already portrayed, it is not only a means of portraying what lies before us. On the contrary, the word first bestows presence, that is, Being in which things appear as beings.

This different rule of the word glances abruptly at the poet. At the same time, however, the word which thus rules remains absent. Hence the treasure slips away. But it by no means disintegrates into nothingness. It remains a treasure, although the poet may never keep it in his land.

> And straight it vanished from my hand,
> The treasure never graced my land . . .

May we go so far as to think that the poet's journeys to the norn's source have now come to an end? Presumably we may. For by this new experience the poet has caught sight of a different rule of the word, although in a veiled manner. Where does this experience take the poet and his previous poetry? The poet must relinquish the claim to the assurance that he will on demand be supplied with the name for that which he has posited as what truly is. This positing and that claim he must now deny himself. The poet must renounce having words under his control as the portraying names for what is posited. As self-denial, renunciation is a Saying which says to itself:

> Where word breaks off no thing may be.

While we were discussing the first six stanzas and considering what journey allowed the poet to experience his renunciation, the renunciation itself has also become somewhat clearer to us. Only somewhat; for much still remains obscure in this poem, above all the treasure for which the name is denied. This is also the reason why the poet cannot say what this treasure is. We have even less right to conjecture about it than he, unless the poem itself were to give us a hint. It does so. We perceive it if we listen thoughtfully enough. To do so it is enough that we ponder something which must now make us most thoughtful of all.

The insight into the poet's experience with the word, that is, the insight into the renunciation he has learned, compels us to ask the question: why could the poet not renounce Saying, once he had learned renunciation? Why does he tell precisely of renunciation? Why does he go so far as to compose a poem with the title "Words"? Answer: Because this renunciation is a genuine renunciation, not just a rejection of Saying, not a mere lapse into silence. As self-denial, renunciation remains Saying. It thus preserves the relation to the word. But because the word is shown in a different, higher rule, the relation to the word must also undergo a transformation. Saying attains to a different articulation, a different *melos*, a different tone. The poem itself, which tells of renunciation, bears witness to the fact that the poet's renunciation is experienced in this sense—by singing of renunciation. For this poem is a song. It belongs to the last part of the last volume of poems published by Stefan George himself. This last part bears the title "Song," and begins with the prologue:

What I still ponder and what I still frame,
What I still love—their features are the same.

Pondering, framing, loving is Saying: a quiet, exuberant bow, a jubilant homage, a eulogy, a praise: *laudare. Laudes* is the Latin name for songs. To recite song is: to sing. Singing is the gathering of Saying in song. If we fail to understand the lofty meaning of song as Saying, it becomes the retroactive setting to music of what is spoken and written.

With *Song*, with the last poems collected under this title, the poet definitively leaves the sphere that earlier was his own. Where does he go? To renunciation, which he has learned. This learning was

a sudden experience which he had in that instant when the wholly
different rule of the word looked at him and disturbed the self-
assurance of his earlier Saying. Something undreamed of, something
terrifying stared him in the face—that only the word lets a thing be
as thing.

From that moment on, the poet must answer to this mystery of
the word—the mystery of which he has barely an inkling, and which
he can only surmise in his pondering. He can succeed only when the
poetic word resounds in the tone of the song. We can hear this tone
with particular clarity in one of the songs which, without a title, is
published for the first time in the last part of the last book of poems
(*Das Neue Reich*, p. 137).

> In the stillest peace
> of a musing day
> Suddenly breaks a sight which
> With undreamed terror
> Troubles the secure soul
>
> As when on the heights
> The solid stem
> Towers motionless in pride
> And then late a storm
> Bends it to the ground:
>
> As when the sea
> With shrill scream
> With wild crash
> Once again thrusts
> Into the long-abandoned shell.

The rhythm of this song is as marvelous as it is clear. It is enough
to suggest it with a short remark. Rhythm, *rhusmos*, does not mean
flux and flowing, but rather form. Rhythm is what is at rest, what
forms the movement of dance and song, and thus lets it rest within
itself. Rhythm bestows rest. In the song we just heard, the structure
shows itself if we pay heed to the one fugue which sings to us, in three
forms, in the three stanzas: secure soul and sudden sight, stem and
storm, sea and shell.

But the strange thing about this song is a mark which the poet sets down, the only mark besides the final period. Even stranger is the place where he has put the mark—the colon at the end of the last line of the middle stanza. This mark, in this place, is all the more astonishing because both stanzas, the middle and the last one, begin alike with an *as* that refers back to the first stanza:

As when on the heights
The solid stem

and:

As when the sea
With shrill scream

Both stanzas appear to be arranged in the same way with regard to their sequence. But they are not. The colon at the end of the middle stanza makes the next and final stanza refer back explicitly to the first stanza, by including the second stanza with the first in its reference. The first stanza speaks of the poet disturbed in his security. But yet the "undreamed terror" does not destroy him. But it does bend him to the ground as the storm bends the tree, so that he may become open for that of which the third stanza sings after the opening colon. Once again the sea thrusts its unfathomable voice into the poet's ears which are called the "long-abandoned shell"; for until now the poet remained without the purely bestowed prevalence of the word. Instead, the names required by the norn nourished the self-assurance of his masterful proclamation.

The renunciation thus learned is no mere refusal of a claim, but rather the transformation of Saying into the echo of an inexpressible Saying whose sound is barely perceptible and songlike. Now we should be in a better position to ponder the last stanza so that it may itself speak in such a way that the whole poem is gathered up in it. If we were to succeed in this even to a small degree, we might, at favorable moments, hear more clearly the title of the poem *Words*, and understand how the final stanza not only concludes the poem, not only reveals it, but how it at the same time conceals the mystery of the word.

So I renounced and sadly see:
Where word breaks off no thing may be.

The final stanza speaks of the word in the manner of renunciation. Renunciation is in itself a Saying: self-denial . . . namely denying to oneself the claim to something. Understood in this way,
renunciation retains a negative character: "no thing," that is, not a
thing; "the word breaks off," that is, it is not available. According to
the rule, double negation produces an affirmation. Renunciation
says: a thing may be only where the word is granted. Renunciation
speaks affirmatively. The mere refusal not only does not exhaust the
essence of renunciation, it does not even contain it. Renunciation
does have a negative side, but it has a positive side as well. But to talk
about sides here is misleading. In so doing we equate what denies and
what affirms and thus obscure what truly rules in Saying. This we
must think about above all else. Still more. We need to consider what
kind of renunciation the final stanza means. It is unique in its kind,
because it isn't related to just any possession of just anything. As self-
denial, that is, as Saying, renunciation concerns the word itself. Renunciation gets the relation to the word underway toward that which
concerns every Saying as Saying. We suspect that in this self-denial
the relation to the word gains a nearly "excessive intimacy." The enigmatic quality of the final stanza grows beyond us. Nor would we
want to solve it, that enigmatic quality, but only to read, to gather our
thoughts about it.

At first we think renunciation as denying-oneself-something.
Grammatically, "oneself" is in the dative case and refers to the poet.
What the poet denies himself is in the accusative case. It is the claim
to the representational rule of the word. Meanwhile, another characteristic of this renunciation has come to light. Renunciation commits
itself to the higher rule of the word which first lets a thing be as thing.
The word makes the thing into a thing—it "bethings" the thing. We
should like to call this rule of the word "bethinging" (*die Bedingnis*).
This old word has disappeared from linguistic usage. Goethe still
knew it. In this context, however, bethinging says something different
from talking about a condition, which was still Goethe's understanding of bethinging. A condition is the existent ground for something
that is. The condition gives reasons, and it grounds. It satisfies the
principle of sufficient reason. But the word does not give reasons for
the thing. The word allows the thing to presence as thing. We shall

call this allowing bethinging. The poet does not explain what this bethinging is. But the poet commits himself, that is, his Saying to this mystery of the word. In such commitment, he who renounces denies himself to the claim which he formerly willed. The meaning of self-denial has been transformed. The "self" is no longer in the dative but the accusative case, and the claim is no longer in the accusative but the dative case. The poet's own transformation is concealed in the transformation of the grammatical meaning of the phrase "to deny the claim to oneself" into "to deny oneself to the claim." He has allowed himself—that is, such Saying as will still be possible for him in the future—to be brought face to face with the word's mystery, the be-thinging of the thing in the word.

However, even in this transformed self-denial, the negative character of renunciation still maintains the upper hand. Yet it became clearer and clearer that the poet's renunciation is in no way a negation, but rather an affirmation. Self-denial—which appears to be only refusal and self-withdrawal—is in truth nondenial of self: to the mystery of the word. This nondenial of self can speak in this way only, that it says: "may there be." From now on may the word be: the bethinging of the thing. This "may there be" lets be the relation of word and thing, what and how it really *is*. Without the word, no thing is. In the "may there be," renunciation commits itself to the "is." Hence no retroactive transformation of the final verse into a statement is needed in order to make the "is" appear. "May there be" extends to us the "is" in a veiled and therefore purer fashion.

Where word breaks off no thing may be.

In this nondenial of self, renunciation says itself as that kind of Saying which owes itself wholly to the mystery of the word. In nondenial of self, renunciation is an owing of self. Here is the abode of renunciation. Renunciation owes thanks—it is a thanking. It is not mere refusal, still less a loss.

But why, then, is the poet sad?

So I renounced and sadly see:

Is it renunciation that makes him sad? Or did sadness come over him only when he learned renunciation? In the latter case, the sadness which recently burdened his spirit could have disappeared again as soon as he had embraced renunciation as a thanks; for owing one-self as thanking is attuned to joy. The tone of joy is heard in another song. That poem, too, is without a title. But it bears such a strangely unique mark that we are compelled to listen to it in virtue of its inner kinship to the song *Words* (*Das Neue Reich*, p. 125). It reads:

> What bold-easy step
> Walks through the innermost realm
> Of grandame's fairytale garden?
>
> What rousing call does the bugler's
> Silver horn cast in the tangle
> Of the Saying's deep slumber?
>
> What secret breath
> Of melancholy just fled
> Nestles into the soul?

Stefan George is in the habit of writing all words with small initials[2] except those at the beginning of the lines. But in this poem there is a single capitalized word, almost at the center of the poem at the end of the middle stanza. The word is: Saying. The poet could have chosen this word for the poem's title, with the hidden allusion that Saying, as the tale of the fairy tale garden, tells of the origin of the word.

The first stanza sings of the *step* as the journey through the realm of Saying. The second stanza sings of the *call* that awakens Saying. The third stanza sings of the *breath* that nestles into the soul. Step (that is, way) and call and breath hover around the rule of the word. Its mystery has not only disturbed the soul that formerly was secure. It has also taken away the soul's melancholy which threatened to drag it down. Thus, sadness has vanished from the poet's relation to the word. This sadness concerned only his learning of renunciation. All this would be true if sadness were the mere opposite to joy, if melan-choly and sadness were identical.

But the more joyful the joy, the more pure the sadness slumber-ing within it. The deeper the sadness, the more summoning the joy resting within it. Sadness and joy play into each other. The play itself

---

2. In standard German, all nouns are capitalized. (Tr.)

which attunes the two by letting the remote be near and the near be remote is pain. This is why both, highest joy and deepest sadness, are painful each in its way. But pain so touches the spirit of mortals that the spirit receives its gravity from pain. That gravity keeps mortals with all their wavering at rest in their being. The spirit which answers to pain, the spirit attuned by pain and to pain, is melancholy. It can depress the spirit, but it can also lose its burdensomeness and let its "secret breath" nestle into the soul, bestow upon it the jewel which arrays it in the precious relation to the word, and with this raiment shelters it.

This, presumably, is what the third stanza of our last poem has in mind. With the secret breath of melancholy just fled, sadness permeates renunciation itself; for sadness belongs to renunciation if we think renunciation in its innermost gravity. That gravity is the non-denial of self to the mystery of the word, to the fact that the word is the bethinging of the thing.

As mystery, the word remains remote. As a mystery that is experienced, the remoteness is near. The perdurance of this remoteness of such nearness is the nondenial of self to the word's mystery. There is no word for this mystery, that is, no Saying which could bring the being of language to language.

The treasure which never graced the poet's land is the word for the being of language. The word's rule and sojourn, abruptly caught sight of, its presencing, would like to enter its own word. But the word for the being of the word is not granted.

What if this, the word for the presencing of language, were alone the treasure which, close to the poet since it lies in his hand, still vanishes and yet, having vanished, never having been captured, still remains what is most remote in the nearest nearness? In this nearness, the treasure is mysteriously familiar to the poet, otherwise he could not sing of it as "rich and frail."

Rich means: capable of bestowing, capable of offering, of allowing to attain and reach. But this is the word's essential richness that in Saying, that is, in showing, it brings the thing as thing to radiance.

Frail means according to the old verb *zarton* the same as: familiar, giving joy, saving. Saving is an offering and a releasing, but without will and force, without addiction and dominance.

The *treasure rich and frail* is the word's hidden essence (verbal) which, invisibly in its Saying and even already in what is unsaid, extends to us the thing as thing.

His renunciation having pledged itself to the word's mystery, the poet retains the treasure in remembrance by renunciation. In this way, the treasure becomes that which the poet—he who says— prefers above all else and reveres above everything else. The treasure becomes what is truly worthy of the poet's thought. For what could be more worthy of thought for the saying one than the word's being veiling itself, than the fading word for the word?

If we listen to the poem as a song in harmony with kindred songs, we then let the poet tell us, and let ourselves be told together with him, what is worthy of the thinking of poetic being.

To let ourselves be told what is worthy of thinking means—to think.

While listening to the poem, we are pondering poetry. This is how making poetry and thinking *are*.

What at first looks like the title of a thesis—making poetry and thinking—turns out to be the inscription in which our destined human existence has ever been inscribed. The inscription records that poetry and thinking belong together. Their coming together has come about long ago. As we think back to that origin, we come face to face with what is primevally worthy of thought, and which we can never ponder sufficiently. It is the same element worthy of thought that glanced abruptly at the poet and to which he did not deny himself when he said:

Where word breaks off no thing may be.

The word's rule springs to light as that which makes the thing be a thing. The word begins to shine as the gathering which first brings what presences to its presence.

The oldest word for the rule of the word thus thought, for Saying, is *logos*: Saying which, in showing, lets beings appear in their "it is."

The same word, however, the word for Saying, is also the word for *Being*, that is, for the presencing of beings. Saying and Being, word and thing, belong to each other in a veiled way, a way which has hardly been thought and is not to be thought out to the end.

All essential Saying hearkens back to this veiled mutual belonging of Saying and Being, word and thing. Both poetry and thinking are distinctive Saying in that they remain delivered over to the mystery of the word as that which is most worthy of their thinking, and thus ever structured in their kinship.

In order that we may in our thinking fittingly follow and lead this element worthy of thought as it gives itself to poetry, we abandon everything which we have now said to oblivion. We listen to the poem. We grow still more thoughtful now regarding the possibility that the more simply the poem sings in the mode of song, the more readily our hearing may err.

12. WEIL (1909–1943)

"Celui qu'il faut aimer est absent." In *La pesanteur et la grâce*, ed. Gustave Thibon (Paris: Plon, 1948), pp. 126–131.

Trans. Emma Craufurd, "He Whom We Must Love Is Absent," in *Gravity and Grace* (London: Routledge and Kegan Paul, 1952), pp. 99–102.

Simone Weil has been revered as a contemporary saint. At the same time, she is studied as one of the twentieth century's most provocative philosophers. Having entered the *École Normale Supérieure* in 1928, taking first place on the entrance exam (Simone de Beauvoir was second), she was *aggregée* in philosophy by 1931 and briefly exercised her profession as a philosophy teacher. She was, however, also a committed labor activist, and by 1933 she began subjecting herself to grueling work in factories and eventually on farms, jeopardizing her fragile health. She suffered from sinusitis and was wracked by headache pain for much of her short life. Forced to leave France in 1942 by Nazi persecutions, she worked with the French resistance in London. Refusing more nourishment than the equivalent of the war rations at home, she collapsed from physical extenuation and died a few months later.

Her life and work together testify to the erasure of the self, to a clearing away by "unsaying" that allows a divinity such as the atheist may know best to shine forth.[1] Her writings exalt suffering, humiliation, and misery, as means of negating the self and the finite world, which are nothing, so as to enable the infinite, "God," to take back what has been given in Creation, since this is all worth nothing and *is* precisely nothing—*except* in being given back to its Giver:

> God gave me being in order that I should give it back to him. It is like one of those traps whereby the characters are tested in fairy stories and tales of initiation. If I accept this gift it is bad and fatal; its virtue becomes apparent through my refusal of it. God allows me to exist outside himself. It is for me to refuse this authorization.[2]

---

1. See Weil's "L'athéisme purificateur," in *La pesanteur et la grâce*, pp. 132–133.
2. *Gravity and Grace*, p. 35.

Weil calls this self-renunciation "decreation," and under that heading in her notebooks she wrote piercing reflections such as the following:

> He emptied himself of his divinity. We should empty ourselves of the false divinity with which we were born.
> Once we have understood we are nothing, the object of all our efforts is to become nothing. It is for this that we suffer with resignation, *it is for this that we act,* it is for this that we pray.
> May God grant me to become nothing.
> In so far as I become nothing, God loves himself through me.
>
> (*Gravity and Grace*, p. 30)

There is a mystical truth to be opened up by self-surrender, though its possible descriptions are doubtful. If only the self can annihilate itself, something infinite or divine imposes itself as infusing all that is with absolute passion. In choosing not to be, and so getting ourselves out of the way, we let the miracle which is beyond being, as we know and possess it, be. Apophasis, or "not-speaking," becomes for Weil a necessary symbol for the uncompromising negation of all that is not God—which coincides with all that is something, something that can be imagined, willed, or said. Like John of the Cross, Weil makes us see that apophasis is not just a verbal technique or formal method but an existential act of silencing and stilling the self.

One particularly striking statement of the imperative of self-effacement expresses the core of Weil's thinking. Quoting Racine's Phèdre,

> "Et la mort à mes yeux ravissant la clarté
> Rend au jour qu'ils souillaient toute sa pureté . . . ."

> "And death, ravishing my eyes of their light,
> Restores to the day they sullied all its purity . . . ."

Weil echoes and reflects:

> May I disappear in order that those things that I see may become perfect in their beauty from the very fact that they are no longer things that I see.

> I do not in the least wish that this created world should fade from my view, but that it should no longer be to me personally that it shows itself. To me it cannot tell its secret which is too high. If I go, then the creator and the creature will exchange their secrets.

To see a landscape as it is when I am not there . . . .

When I am in any place, I disturb the silence of heaven and earth by my breathing and the beating of my heart.

(*Gravity and Grace*, p. 37)

Such statements may resemble Gnostic views, as some philosophers have pointed out, but more profoundly they embody an apophatic, not a dualistic, logic of negation. Negating the finite, speaking subject enables what is and cannot be said to "be" infinitely. This entails that we must accept not to exist. This renunciation is conceived as the repetition of God's act of Creation by contracting from the infinite plenitude of his own being and withdrawing into himself, in order to let others exist—an idea found in the Lurianic Kabbalah. Weil's writing imitates precisely this act of self-negation. Her aphoristic style, as is typical of apophatic authors, alludes by the use of breaks and spaces to what it renounces saying.[3] Only by rupture and tearing ("déchirement") of the discursive web of which self and world are composed does illusion dissipate, so as to allow a glimpse of the absolute Good that to us can be manifest only as absolute void.

Weil's key concepts include alterity, emptiness, and distance: "To love purely is to consent to distance, it is to adore the distance between ourselves and that which we love" (*Gravity and Grace*, p. 58). It is sometimes striking how closely her expressions resemble those of French postmodern apostles of difference and the impossible who wrote decades later: "Impossibility is the door of the supernatural. We can but knock at it. It is someone else who answers" (*Gravity and Grace*, p. 87). A crucial difference, however, is that Weil willingly configures "the impossible" with traditional mystical and religious images. Her mystical philosophy is nourished especially by the Gospels, Homer, the Upanishads, and Taoism.[4] Apophatic negation, its "purification,"

---

3. A number of contributions illuminating apophatic aspects of Weil's linguistic and aesthetic theories can be found in *The Beauty That Saves: Essays on Aesthetics and Language in Simone Weil*, ed. John M. Dunaway and Eric O. Springsted (Macon, Ga.: Mercer University Press, 1996). See in particular "Simone Weil and the Limits of Language" by J. P. Little, originally "Grandeur et misère du langage chez Simone Weil," in *Simone Weil et les langues*, ed. M. Broc-Lapeyre et al., Recherches sur la philosophie et le langage 13 (Grenoble: Département de Philosophie, Université P. Mendès-France, 1991), pp. 179–192.

4. Weil is an especially profound interpreter of the Greeks, particularly of the mystical meaning of force and war in her *L'Iliad ou le poème de la force*, published first under the pseudonym "Emile Novis" in *Cahiers du sud* XIX, 230 (December 1940–January 1941). A translation by Mary McCarthy is available in *Simone Weil: An Anthology*, ed. Siân Miles (New York: Weidenfeld & Nicolson, 1986), pp. 163–195.

is the thread drawing these diverse traditions together into the tight knot of Weil's passion.

He Whom We Must Love Is Absent

God can only be present in creation under the form of absence.

Evil is the innocence of God. We have to place God at an infinite distance in order to conceive of him as innocent of evil; reciprocally, evil implies that we have to place God at an infinite distance.

This world, in so far as it is completely empty of God, is God himself.
    Necessity, in so far as it is absolutely other than the good, is the good itself.
    That is why all consolation in affliction separates us from love and from truth.
    That is the mystery of mysteries. When we touch it we are safe.

'In the desert of the East. . . .' We have to be in a desert. For he whom we must love is absent.

He who puts his life into his faith in God can lose his faith.
    But he who puts his life in God himself will never lose it. To put our life into that which we cannot touch in any way. . . . It is impossible. It is a death. That is what is required.

Nothing which exists is absolutely worthy of love.
    We must therefore love that which does not exist.
    This non-existent object of love is not a fiction, however, for our fictions cannot be any more worthy of love than we are ourselves, and we are not worthy of it.

Consent to the good—not to any good which can be grasped or represented, but unconditional consent to the absolute good.

When we consent to something which we represent to ourselves as the good, we consent to a mixture of good and evil, and this consent produces good and evil: the proportion of good and evil in us does not change. On the other hand the unconditional consent to that good which we are not able and never will be able to represent to ourselves—such consent is pure good and produces only good, moreover, it is enough that it should continue for the whole soul to be nothing but good in the end.

Faith (when it is a question of a supernatural interpretation of the natural) is a conjecture by analogy based on supernatural experience. Thus those who have the privilege of mystical contemplation, having experienced the mercy of God, *suppose* that, God being mercy, the created world is a work of mercy. But as for obtaining evidence of this mercy directly from nature, it would be necessary to become blind, deaf and without pity in order to believe such a thing possible. Thus the Jews and Moslems, who want to find in nature the proofs of divine mercy, are pitiless. And often the Christians are as well.

That is why mysticism is the only source of virtue for humanity. Because when men do not believe that there is infinite mercy behind the curtain of the world, or when they think that this mercy is in front of the curtain, they become cruel.

There are four evidences of divine mercy here below: the favours of God to beings capable of contemplation (these states exist and form part of their experience as creatures); the radiance of these beings and their compassion, which is the divine compassion in them; the beauty of the world. The fourth evidence is the complete absence of mercy here below.[1]

1. [Weil's note:] It is precisely by this antithesis, this rending of our souls between the effects of grace within us and the beauty of the world around us, on the one hand, and the implacable necessity which rules the universe on the other, that we discern God as both present to man and as absolutely beyond all human measurement.

Incarnation. God is weak because he is impartial. He sends sunshine and rain to good and evil alike. This indifference of the Father and the weakness of Christ correspond. Absence of God. The kingdom of heaven is like a grain of mustard seed. . . . God changes nothing whatsoever. Christ was killed out of anger because he was only God.

If I thought that God sent me suffering by an act of his will and for my good, I should think that I was something, and I should miss the chief use of suffering which is to teach me that I am nothing. It is therefore essential to avoid all such thoughts, but it is necessary to love God through the suffering.

I must love being nothing. How horrible it would be if I were something! I must love my nothingness, love being a nothingness. I must love with that part of the soul which is on the other side of the curtain, for the part of the soul which is perceptible to consciousness cannot love nothingness. It has a horror of it. Though it may think it loves nothingness, what it really loves is something other than nothingness.

God sends affliction without distinction to the wicked and to the good, just as he sends the rain and the sunlight. He did not reserve the cross for Christ. He enters into contact with a human individual as such only through purely spiritual grace which responds to the gaze turned towards him, that is to say to the exact extent to which the individual ceases to be an individual. No event is a favour on the part of God—only grace is that.

Communion is good for the good and bad for the wicked. Hence, damned souls are in paradise, but for them paradise is hell.

The cry of suffering: 'Why?' This rings throughout the *Iliad*.

To explain suffering is to console it; therefore it must not be explained.

Herein lies the pre-eminent value of the suffering of those who are innocent. It bears a resemblance to the acceptance of the evil in creation by God who is innocent.

The irreducible character of suffering which makes it impossible for us not to have a horror of it at the moment when we are undergoing it is destined to bring the will to a standstill, just as absurdity brings the intelligence to a standstill, and absence love, so that man, having come to the end of his human faculties, may stretch out his arms, stop, look up and wait.

'He will laugh at the trials of the innocent.' Silence of God. The noises here below imitate this silence. They mean nothing.

It is when from the innermost depths of our being we need a sound which does mean something—when we cry out for an answer and it is not given us—it is then that we touch the silence of God.

As a rule our imagination puts words into the sounds in the same way as we idly play at making out shapes in wreaths of smoke; but when we are too exhausted, when we no longer have the courage to play, then we must have real words. We cry out for them. The cry tears our very entrails. All we get is silence.

After having gone through that, some begin to talk to themselves like madmen. Whatever they may do afterwards, we must have nothing but pity for them. The others, and they are not numerous, give their whole heart to silence.

DEPICTING, COMPOSING, REPRESENTING NOTHING

13. MALEVICH (1878–1935)

"God Is Not Cast Down." Trans. Xenia Glowacki-Prus and Arnold McMillin, in *Essays on Art, 1915–1933* (Copenhagen: Borgens Forlag, 1968), ed. Troels Andersen, vol. 1, pp. 188–223 (illustration, p. 131).

Paul Klee famously remarked that art does not render the visible but renders visible. Wassily Kandinsky's treatise *Concerning the Spiritual in Art* (1910) pursues this quest for a visible artistic expression of the invisible dimension of spirit. The Russian orthodox cult of the icon as image of an unrepresentable God strongly influenced the Russian avant-garde art that emerged at the beginning of the twentieth century with artist-theoreticians such as Kasimir Malevich. This traditional Russian orthodox spirituality, informed by the treatises of Pseudo-Dionysius the Areopagite, nourishes a rich apophatic culture, which is also reflected in philosophies such as those of Vladimir Solov'ev (1853–1900) and S. L. Frank (1877–1950).

Malevich's painting dramatizes the vocation of art, especially abstract art, to gesture toward what cannot be said or represented. Malevich expressed this essentially apophatic dimension provocatively in 1913 in a programmatic painting of a black square on a white canvas. For Malevich, this painting marked the origin of a new conception of art: "I felt only night within me and it was then that I conceived the new art, which I called Suprematism." He nevertheless recognized that this *new* art was a return to the original quest of human beings in their artistic creations: "The square of the Suprematists . . . can be compared to the symbols of primitive men. It was not their intent to produce ornaments but to express the feeling of rhythm."[1] The black square was followed in 1918 by "White on White," a painting of another square, this time white, and at an angle to the square of canvas framing it, again a minimalist evocation of the primal purity of inarticulate feeling.

A penetrating theoretician, Malevich not only painted but also delved discursively into the apophatic dimension that he called the "non-objective." He defined it in his treatise *The Non-Objective World* as "feeling," though he leaves

---

1. Malevich is quoted from L. Hilberseimer's introduction to Malevich's *The Non-Objective World*, trans. Howard Dearstyne (Chicago: Theobald, 1959), p. 8.

this term completely undefined, except to designate it as negation of all image and objectivity—"the desert." Art, as Malevich conceives it, is realized in this withdrawal from determinate form and representation—the movement of negation or apophasis.

Malevich develops his reflection on non-objective art in his essay "God Is Not Cast Down." He balances the materialist worldview of the "factory" against the spiritualist worldview of the "church" as symmetrically opposite forms of objective thinking, and suggests that art is a "third path" (sec. 27). The system "matter-body-factory" pursues its own illusion of perfection, as does the system "spirit-soul-church." Both are founded on "prejudice." Only art can free itself from objective thinking in order to investigate reality as what is nonexistent and incomprehensible (sec. 10). To see things as they really are is to see that they are not real objects or anything else that they are represented as being.

This essay, dated 1920, was evidently the text for a lecture entitled "Art, Factory and Church" given by Malevich in June 1922 at the Petrograd Museum of Artistic Culture. It was published as a book in 1922 (Vitebsk: Unovis). In its compact power and comprehensiveness, the piece as a whole illustrates the principle of an apophatic theology—God's nothingness and namelessness—together with a distinctive visionary system of philosophy that flows from it. From the first paragraph of the essay, Malevich refers to an "uncognizable stimulus," which is the "nothing" that influences and determines consciousness in all its thoughts. Echoing formulas of negative theology that have been rehearsed in orthodox theology since Pseudo-Dionysius, he describes this "nothing" as a simple, "single state without any attributes that have a name in everyday language" (sec. 1). Stimulus can be figured only metaphorically, for example, as a non-objective "cosmic flame," but usually it is considered to be objective by human practical consciousness, which attempts to "file down" its infinity (sec. 4).

The "three states of stimulus," namely, stimulus, thought, and reality, are reminiscent of the three Neoplatonic hypostases—the One, the intellect, and the world-soul—in moving from a nonexistent absolute simplicity or rest, through a mental mediation of unity and multiplicity, to the external reality of the world. Like Plotinus, Malevich denies thought to the first state: "God, as the absolute of the perfection of nature can no longer think" (sec. 13). Malevich combines these elements with a theology of the Fall of Man from perfection: "I cannot imagine how he [Man] left or excluded himself from the general absolute perfection, or why he felt it essential to think, if everything was already in the absolute. He alone began to strive for an understanding of nature, of God as perfection" (sec. 13). To seek any kind of reflective comprehension or objective definition, however, necessarily misrecognizes the infinity of stimulus. "The mistake is that a limit was established in the system" (sec. 15). Man makes limits by defining God, by making of him some kind of sense—"the most terrible thing of all" (sec. 18). For this God is the sense of Man, in other words, an idol. For Malevich, by contrast, "God is not sense, but senselessness" (sec. 18). Yet this senselessness is to be found precisely in the immediate stimulus of the senses: "Attaining God in the heavenly places is actually unnecessary for he is to be found in every one of our senses, since they are all at the same time senseless" (sec. 18).

In this highly original manner, Malevich sketches with broad strokes the lineaments of a comprehensive apophatic theology based on an infinite, incomprehensible, unnameable, and implicitly unsayable God. His term for the unsayable or inexpressible, that is, for what cannot be said, is "non-objective," since his framework is not strictly verbal so much as visual expression. God or "perfection" would be "cast down" by any objective description or demonstration.

God Is Not Cast Down

1

The basis and reason for what in society we call life I consider to be a stimulus which reveals itself in all possible forms—pure, unconscious, inexplicable; its existence has never been proved; it is without number, precision, time, space and absolute or relative condition.

I consider the second stage in life to be thought, in which stimulus accepts the visual state of what is real in itself within the bounds of the inner existence. Thought is the process or state of stimulus represented in the form of real and natural action. Thus thought is not something by means of which one can ponder some manifestation, i.e. understand, cognise, realise, know, prove or base: no, thought is simply one of the action processes of uncognisable stimulus. Therefore nothing influences me and "nothing," as an entity, determines my consciousness, for all is stimulus as a single state without any attributes that have a name in everyday language. All that through thought as a means of reflection reveals the real and is capable of dividing the real from the unreal, thus showing man this or that object in its precision and reality—all this is absurd; in actual fact we always see what we can never cognise and really see. And what man reveals or is found in the world in general despite all "graphic," "scientific" and "other" grounds, remains unproved, for all manifestations are the result of uncognisable stimulus.

2

The groundless stimulus of the universe, like that of any other manifestation down to its smallest sections, has no law, and it is only when stimulus is split into the states of the real and the natural that the first law appears, i.e. rhythm—the first and most important law of all that is manifested in life. Without it nothing can move and be created; but I do not consider rhythm to be music, for music, like everything else, is based on this law. Music, like everything else, is limited, but rhythm is unlimited. The rhythm of a machine may be alien to music; music is an attempt to link rhythms into a unity. An engineer links rhythm in a machine, but we do not consider the engineer a composer. In comparison one must grasp the fact that music is not a law of rhythm but something that is built on the rhythm of manifestation.

3

I consider stimulus and thought to be the principle bases of man's community life, and of all that is excited and has inner thoughts. I divide the whole of life into three states of stimulus; the first is stimulus; the second is thought in what is real and the third is reality in what is natural—in other words, actual fact as what is natural. These three divisions create many interrelations among themselves, and the life of the community is created. Nevertheless the facts of social life are divided into two states: the internal and the external. One should relate to the inner state those facts which are in a spiritual state or stimulus—they are called spiritualised; the facts in which stimulus exists to [a] minimum degree are called external. But this point is that of the community; in reality the pure manifestation of stimulus is never attainable in the contemplation of what is natural; and what we call inner can never be realised.

It is always within and responds to neither the real nor the natural; neither one nor the other can be comprehended as stimulus, and in order to pin down the infinite and define its limits the community has had recourse to the only law of condition. As a result life takes on an exclusively conditional appearance and reminds one of a huge nursery in which children play all sorts of games with imaginary conditions, experiencing reality—they build towers, castles, forts and towns, then destroy them, then build them again; their parents look on this as nonsense, forgetting that children's nonsense is the result of adult nonsense.

4

Man strives in his manifestations to achieve perfection through thought, i.e. to convey the reality of his stimulus but at the moment of revealing form he forgets that form is a condition and that in reality form does not exist. How, then, can he reveal stimulus when stimulus is not a form, and has no limits? Secondly, supposing that conditions were those of reality or the natural state, even at that moment the stimulus itself conditionally passes into the interior of the form, the latter, as soon as it is revealed, dies away, for it has achieved in itself a certain perfection, or, rather, a step towards perfection; thought has already passed on to stimulate another form, better able to reveal stimulus. Thus we see life in forms as a degree of stimulus, but the community sees in life objective, practical and lawful formations—consequently the essence of stimulus as non-objective is in practical consciousness considered objective.

5

Stimulus is a cosmic flame and lives on what is non-objective: only in the skull of thought does it become cool in real concepts of its immeasurableness; and thought, as a certain degree in the action of stimulus, white-hot from its flame, moves deeper and deeper into the infinite, creating in its path worlds of the universe. This stimulus gives greater value to man and places him above other things in life. To value and concern oneself with the inner life is man's true plan and he strives to convey what is inner to life, struggling with the external and trying to make all external things inner. Stimulation, as a cosmic flame, wavers in the inner man without purpose, sense or logic—in action it is non-objective. Man's striving to make his manifestations inwardly gifted is a striving to prove their stimulus, but since all his manifestations pass onto the objective, practical plane, the stimulus cannot be expressed in all its pure force.

Man, as thought and stimulus, concerns himself with perfecting his life. Does nature think about or concern itself with its perfection, or did it once think about them and now no longer does so? Everything has entered eternal movement and demands no perfection or maintenance, leaving it to man to worry about the perfection and maintenance of his life. Perhaps this is what divides him from nature: he thinks about perfection, whilst nature no longer thinks; or, perhaps, their thoughts are different. The difference is that whilst natural thought is the simple action of non-objective phenomena, his thought is practical and objective and, as a result, his life is conceived in continual maintenance and perfection; arming himself with a file, he wants to file nature down and give it a new significance, he wants to turn it into an objective, intelligent state, to make it clever with reflections on various difficult questions . . . but it has none of this, and should not be filed for it has no material unity or form. It is without limits. He strives to build all this in it, and to perfect it. Thinking of perfecting nature, his thought goes ever further and the gulf between them grows wider and wider—this gulf is his senseless culture of perfection in a concrete world. For him nature has become a mystery. The mystery stands before his pensive brow, his eyes gaze keenly and his ears are strained whilst reason exerts every effort of the intellect to think it out and traces every movement in order to understand it; but, alas, infinity has no ceiling or floor, no foundations or horizon, and, therefore, the ear cannot catch the rustle of its movement, the eye cannot see its limit and the mind cannot comprehend. Reason cannot understand anything and intelligence cannot judge anything, for there is nothing in nature that can be judged, understood, or examined; it has no unit which could be taken as a whole. All that seems to us to be separate and single is untrue; everything is at once linked and undone, but there is nothing separate, and therefore there are and can be no objects and things—hence any attempt to attain them is senseless. What can one embrace when there is neither line, plane nor volume? There is nothing that can be measured—hence geometry is the conditional visual state of non-existent figures. There is no point from which one could draw a line; even in imagination one cannot set up the point, since imagination knows that there is no empty space; nor yet can one draw the line of another figure, because everything is occupied and filled, and the point or line itself is already multitudinous, infinite in breadth, depth, height, time and space, and in infinity everything will be nothing, i.e. incomprehensible to consciousness intending to master the elucidation of the line or volume and plane. The world is like a porosity, and not a hollow one. So what will I cut out of this infinite porosity of sieves? A line or point? And can I extract from this porous sieve a line or point? Here perhaps lies reality. But we, seeing a line or volume, are convinced of their reality and existence.

6

Man is preparing to comprehend and learn "everything," but is this "everything" before him? Can he put this "everything" on a table in front of him, investigate it and describe it in books, saying "Here is a book where "everything" is described? Study it and you will know everything." It seems to me that in order to investigate, study and learn, I must be able to take out a unit that has no connection with its environment and is free from all influences and dependence: if I can do this, I shall comprehend it; if not, I shall comprehend nothing, despite the mass of extracts and conclusions obtained. Will the detective complete the investigation of a murder by finding the murderer and his motive of stealing valuables? Or must he investigate the murderer's psychology, along with his nervous and other aspects, and condemn the State for failing in its system to foresee crimes, and for being unable to distribute valuables etc.?

7

Nature is hidden in infinity and manysidedness and does not reveal itself in things; in its manifestations it has neither tongue nor form, it is infinite and boundless. The miracle of nature is that it all is contained in a small seed, and yet this 'all' cannot be embraced. Man, holding a seed, holds the universe and yet cannot examine it, regardless of all the obviousness of the latter's origin and of "scientific foundations." One must understand this small seed in order to also reveal the whole universe.

8

All things are signs of stimulus leading man into stimulus, i.e. things as signs that they contain stimulus as a non-objective state. Thing after thing, stimulus from stimulus, beginning to beginning, abstraction after abstraction—the utter senselessness of the eternal rotation fulfils its run in the vortexes of spacial rings. All human meanings also move in the vortex of objects and pursue their practical and economic consciousness, the support of all meaning and logic; but in spite of the latter they are equal to the former powerlessness, for at both ends of all objective meanings stand the poles of senselessness, like gaping abysses, in all-devouring inaccessibility, and in their vortex carry away epoch after epoch of perfection into nothingness.

9

Man's skull represents the same infinity for the movement of conceptions. It is equal to the universe, for in it is contained all that it sees in it. Likewise the sun and the whole starry sky of comets and the sun pass in it and shine and move as in nature; similarly, comets appear in it and disappear, inasmuch as they do in nature; all projects for perfection exist within it. Epoch after epoch, culture after culture appear and disappear in its infinite space.

Is not the whole universe that strange skull in which meteors, suns, comets and planets rush endlessly? And are they not simply concepts of cosmic thoughts, and are not their entire movement and space and they themselves non-objective? For if they were objective no skull would contain them. Thought moves, for stimulus moves, and in their movements they create real conceptions, or else in their creation compose what is real as actuality, and all that is created changes and passes into the eternity of non-evidence, just as it came from eternal existence. And this eternal serves as an eternal investigation for man—the investigation itself is simply the composition of conceptions, or, to be more accurate, of that which he cannot conceive, for if man could conceive anything, it would be for him finiteness. Life and infinity lie for him in the fact that he cannot conceive anything—what he does conceive is as elusive in its infinity as everything else. Thus it is difficult for him to compose and difficult to comprehend reality; he cannot establish reality, for there is nothing that does not change countless times. Its sum is unstable and its fluctuations endlessly quivering in the waves of rhythm; as a result nothing can be established in this rhythm of stimuli, the conception itself twinkles like a star and there is no possibility of establishing its reality beyond that twinkling or of establishing objects.

10

Investigating reality means investigating what does not exist and is incomprehensible; but for man what is incomprehensible is non-existent—hence it is something non-existent that is being examined. Man has defined the existence of things that were formerly incomprehensible and non-existent for him, and wants to investigate them; if we take any of the things that man has defined and try to investigate it, we see that, under pressure from our tool of investigation, it immediately disintegrates into a large number of component parts which are fully independent; further investigation will prove that the thing did not exist, that only the sum of things existed. But what is this sum of things? In what numbers can it be expressed? To answer these questions it is essential to elucidate the sum of each thing from the sum that disintegrated. One begins the investigation of the disintegrated things and under the pressure of investigation the things again disintegrate into a multitude of things, whose investigation will prove that these disintegrated things also in their turn disintegrated into independent things and bore a mass of new links and relations with new things, and so on ad infinitum. The investigation will prove that things do not exist, that at the same time there exists their infinity, "nothing" and at the same time "something." Thus the investigation has not added anything to our understanding, nor has it drawn the sum of things, for if it attempted to give a sum, it would produce a whole row of figures, whose infinity would not be read. The community treats this sum simply, dividing it up, producing a sum that it can understand, and then multiplying it endlessly according to a plan it can comprehend. I suppose that the whole of science, seeking the scientific foundations of anything, acts in the same way. Breaking up the endless string of the senseless collection of figures into separate sums, the sum of which must remain unknown, the community rejoices that it has read the sum, which is therefore clear and comprehensible; but this is only the community's delight and deception, since in reality it has understood nothing, not having read all the pages. Neither first nor last page exists, and similarly neither the first nor the last figures are known. What figures stand in a thing, and what figure of the general sum does the thing comprise? Thus one can no more build sums than one can build an object.

11

The world stands before man as an invariable fact of reality, as unshakeable reality (as people say), yet two people cannot enter this unshakeable reality, as actuality; and produce from it one sum; they cannot measure it identically. However many people enter this reality, each will bring a different reality, and some will bring nothing, for they will see nothing real—each will bring his judgement on the thing that he went to see and their judgement will be reality, proving that the object under discussion does not exist, for even the judgements themselves, in mutual exchange, create very many shades of contradiction. Therefore what we call reality is infinity without weight, measure, time or space, absolute or relative, never traced in a form. It can be neither conceived nor comprehended. There is nothing that can be comprehended, and at the same time there exists this eternal "nothing." Man is continually concerned that everything should be substantiated and reflected upon, and only then will he attempt to construct a thing, building it on a firm scientifically-based foundation, forgetting that he is building the firm foundation for the thing on something that has no foundation. So much for his unshakeable, objective logic.

12

Man is also a Cosmos or Hercules around which rotate suns and their systems; similarly there revolve around him in a whirlwind all the objects he has created, and, like the sun, he guides them and draws them after him into the unknown path of the infinite; just as the universe with all its stimuli is, perhaps, striving for unity, so do all his pulverised "objects" comprise the unity of his centre, which in its turn moves along the paths of universal passion. Thus unity after unity, joining one another, strives towards the endless path of the nonobjective.

13

Man, finding himself in the nucleus of universal stimulus, feels himself to be before the secret of perfection and fearing the darkness of mystery, hastens to find it out; but (as people say) he can only find out through perfection, for only by creating a most perfect tool can he comprehend or destroy the secret—thus speaks the logic of the community. Thus everything that is clear in nature tells him by the power of its perfection that the universe, as perfection, is God. The comprehension of God or of the universe, as perfection, became his prime objective. This comprehension is the understanding of all the manifestations of nature—simply nature, without giving it primacy or the title of perfection; but no—without this understanding of her wisdom man cannot produce any perfection, and as a result the path of his life is the path of building perfection, i.e. his life is the path of the latter. This is the viewpoint of the community as a whole. Man began to ponder all the phenomena in nature, and, on the basis of the forces of their intellectual knowledge, proposes to build his own world of concepts. Admitting the perfection of the universe, he admitted God, and at the same time admitted that nature does not think—only he thinks, for God, as the absolute of the perfection of nature can no longer think. By such an admission he has singled himself out as a thinking being and extracted himself from the perfection of God's creation. What reasons led him to effect this exit? I cannot imagine how he left or excluded himself from the general absolute perfection, or why he felt it essential to think, if everything was already in the absolute. He alone began to strive for an understanding of nature, of God as perfection; having left the state of non-thinking, which was absolute perfection, he again strives through his perfect objects to embody himself in the perfection of absolute, non-thinking action, as if some piece of carelessness had occurred and he had slipped and fallen overboard from the absolute. So it is that he, as a particle of absolute thought, having left the general orbit of the moving absolute, is now striving to join the orbit. Perhaps it is for this reason that in the earth he collects his body, in order to hurl it into infinity. First of all he freed his legs and then raised them—this was the first wrench from earth; and then, gradually, through the speed of wheels and the wings of aeroplanes, he sailed further and further to the limit of the atmosphere, and then further still to his orbits, joining the rings of movement to the absolute. In striving to overcome perfection he is forced to build his own nature—hence we can see that man is not yet embodied by universal or absolute thought as perfection; he only moves towards it: his path leads to humanity and thence to God, as perfection. His thought is strained, and the first word on his lips is "perfection" or the practicality of a thing in overcoming his life's problems, and since perfection is God, his first word will always be God. He hopes to reach God or perfection through all that he produces, and prepares to reach the throne of thought, as the absolute end, on which he will act, no longer as a man but as God, for he will incarnate himself in Him and become perfection. But what must one do for this? Not a great deal: guide the starry space of suns and the universal systems. And in the meantime our earth will carry him in its senseless fall into infinity and nothingness, to the ringing of the non-objective movement of the universe's rhythmic whirlwind.

14

Humanity by its efforts singled out thought from its environment and raises it to the throne of government: or else a new truth stimulates man and settling in him raises itself to the throne of a new path. All truths are invested in humanity and come alight within it—for this reason truth strives to rouse itself in everything in order to move everything onto a new path. This idea of truth is no longer human for it creates by means of the order "Let there be . . ." It is the highest guiding principle for people and thinks for them; they themselves do not think at all, just as they do not think about why the earth moves or whither it is bearing them. This thought is only a spark of what humanity as a whole unit must achieve in the future, and for this reason everyone strives to embody himself in universal thought—a pure thought—in order to stand on the throne of thought alone, i.e. absolute perfection (as is commonly held). Thus humanity is moving towards absolute thought through its products (even though it sees in them simple utilitarian objects). What is the ultimate significance of all this production? The only thing is its liberation from physical reality, though, in a new positive act. The achievement of acts in pure thought will make thought the means for reincarnation—an inevitable result of society's achieving perfection. Now all physical reality will rely on new organisations which will perpetuate themselves in eternity, as in nature. The liberation of man from physical labour is a condition of technology—its essence, in fact. Cannot one, then, confirm the legend, or reality, of God, as the final aim of all the community's judgements and achievements? Or, likewise, confirm the legend of the creation of paradise and man's expulsion from it—the place where he was allowed simply to contemplate the eternal self-perpetuating infallible motion of God's technology, built without the help of science, universities, literacy, engineers from the intelligentsia, workers and peasants.

15

The greatest product of all, arisen by itself, in God's triumph at being liberated from creation, was thrown into infinity. This God, the perfect thinker (as people say), created the world by his thought without a single minute's labour (except for moulding man from clay). He built the world with six repetitions of "Let there be. . . ." Six days of creation, and the universe appeared—an example of God's perfection (as people say), in which man, as a perfected creation of the earth, was offered a dominating role over all paradise. But it later turned out that man was not perfect, for he sinned. Hence sin is simply a result of the system's imperfection—crime its consequence. If God had created his system in perfection, Adam would not have sinned, and if man had built his heavenly state there would be neither courts nor crime in it. Where then does the mistake lie? The mistake is that a limit was established in the system. A system without limits is also without defects. It would seem that God set up the limit as an experiment, and that the experiment turned out to be a costly one. Paradise collapsed, and instead of its system containing perfection by means of a limit, it began to break up. Thus sinfulness and imperfections lie in prohibition. In the arrangement of man's life, all his various aspects develop by means of prohibitions, i.e. once a truth is established, it establishes prohibitions for a new one.

Even the field of technology is in the position of a prohibited truth; its field seems very straightforward in the practical sense, but many inventors have had to perish (Moller, the inventor of a stocking-knitting machine, was drowned by the people of Danzig) and in actual fact the building of a system is only brought about by means of a crime: the destruction of the previous system in order to build a new one. Every system consists of units constructed in such a way that each one moving in its appointed place cannot go beyond the limit of the system. If one unit goes beyond the system's limit, its destruction is inevitable, and there can be no system which does not bring its units within its limits. The system's perfection is marked by the fact that every unit, having free movement and not experiencing pressure, is nonetheless unable to leave the system's limits. I will call such a system generic. Generic couplings also create generic systems. For some reason the system's original sin only befell the earthly paradise and not the entire universe; even the earth itself escaped this sin, and, therefore, I perceive that the universe is without sin in its system. It, the generic system, knows neither prohibition nor limits nor bounds nor laws. There is no destruction in it, and nor can there be, since the disappearance or destruction of the planets—what the community calls a catastrophe—does not exist within it. The generic couplings will retain their power and life of movement, and since they have none of the community's perfection, their various forms are eternally equal in their couplings, and their consciousness never disappears. Adam transgressed the forbidden limit and this was enough for his entire line to be punished by banishment. Here began the history of its human suffering, sweat, callouses, bloodshed, the history of labour. This was God's terrible punishment for man. Paradise fell apart and everything scattered and grew wild. Heavenly bliss disappeared, and all that Adam had had to do was to contemplate the eternal and beautiful movement, not even thinking, since God had already thought everything out.

16

Thus God decided to build the world in order once and for all to free himself from it—to become free, to assume complete nothingness or eternal rest as a great unthinking being—for there was nothing more to think about, everything being complete. It was with this that he wanted to present man on earth. But man could not bear the system and transgressed it, leaving its plan, as a result of which the entire system collapsed and its weight fell on man. In other words, God, feeling the weight in himself, dispersed it in his system, and the weight became light and relieved him, placing man in a weightless system; and man, not feeling it, lived like an engine driver who does not feel the weight of his locomotive in motion, but has only to remove one part from the system for its weight to come down and crush him. Likewise Adam transgressed the limits of the system and its weight collapsed onto him. As a result the whole of humanity is labouring in sweat and sufferings to free itself from beneath the weight of the collapsed system, is striving to distribute the weight in systems, wishing to repair the mistake—hence his culture consists of distributing weight in systems of weightlessness. Thus each system is a fresh attempt, fresh blood for liberation.

Faster and faster, man wants to run through the systems, suffering adversity, ever faster he wishes to run through the squares of punishment and crimes; is a vengeful God really pursuing him in the form of punishments? Is man really fated, by means of the set-up of angels and the devil, to pass under their lash? Is he not running in order to run through this idea of God's set-up, a series of crimes and punishments? To run through the laws and find himself on a lawless path? To come out once and for all into a country of humanity, where he can cease his self-flagellation (as is commonly held). This is a second point for discussion. The third point or reason for his flight in the struggle is the "struggle for survival," which should be sought in weight or in the first supposition of the struggle with weight lest it crush him by its pressure. The fourth point is the striving towards God—towards the perfection in which will come bliss. One can base on these four suppositions the reasons why all the different forms of man's production arose. Accordingly, in the first instance, I suppose weight distribution or liberation in weightlessness to have been the reason for God's creation of the world and the universe. God relieved himself of weight or, as weight, dispersed himself in weightlessness but, dispersing thought in weightlessness, himself remained free. Man too in all three points strives for the same thing—to disperse weight and himself become weightless, i.e. enter God. But is it so? Is it true that man is striving towards the God with whom there has been a break? Man has become a criminal banished by him to eternal hard labour: have they parted completely or not? No, God has not abandoned him, and himself moves forward with each of man's footsteps—man cannot take a single step without God (as people say). God accompanies him today, yesterday and tomorrow, and thus they go together from day to day dispersing in labour the weight of sin. And life is created from the fact that they go along together. But where are they going? They are going home, to perfection, to eternal peace, and man goes by means of all his efforts. His efforts are the production of forms of perfection, and only insofar as they represent steps towards perfection have they a purpose and meaning. But at the same time, on his way to God, he prepared to cast Him down. But how can this be done, what must he do to cast God down when God is in every single object of creation? For each thing is built on perfection, i.e. built in God; each thing, of course, is not yet God, for it is going towards God; it is thought and thought is not yet God, as eternal, free rest. To cast down God is to cast down the perfection of things; but man stands in this perfection and at the moment his being lies in it. Thus the community has built itself God, for the non-objective universe did not say a word about his presence, nor did it show man his dwelling place. He alone concluded that nature is a pointer to the great creator of incomprehensible, infinite phenomena. And the building up of God as absolute perfection has been done firmly. Different peoples portray God in different ways, but, however they do it, all the representations have one thing in common—that God is perfection. God is defined as perfection—absolute perfection; and what is the eternal question before man, if not the question of perfection? This will be his God, expressed in different terms.

17

Each man hastens towards his perfection, strives to be nearer to God, for his perfection lies in God and accordingly each of man's steps should be directed towards God; therefore he seeks out ways and means, in other words simply seeks God's signs. Thinking of achievements he built himself two paths: the religious technical school and the state or industrial one—the church and the factory. The religious technical school strives to make man contemporary in spirit and, by means of spiritual perfection, strives to reach God. The religious technical school changes its systems, perfecting them. Hence the appearance of a multitude of religious systems claiming to be the quickest route to God. The two technical schools make for the same object, both strive to perfect technical questions, by means of which to achieve or resolve their aim. They are the same in both the deep and the superficial sense: ritual, pious attitude, worship, faith, hope for the future. Just as the church has its leaders, the discoverers of perfect religious systems, so also the industrial technical school has its own which it venerates and honours like the other. Likewise the walls of both are hung with images and portraits, martyrs and heroes in order of worth and rank, and in both cases their names are entered in calendars. Thus there is no difference. Whichever way you look at it, everything is the same: the same question, the same aim and the purpose—to seek God. If Christ said "Seek God only within yourself" any technician can say, "Seek perfection of the object only in yourself," but in neither case can one find this place, even in oneself, for where I begin there I end. (What senseless searches the community has thought up!) Nonetheless man searches for God, through his two paths. The quarrel between them takes place, or can take place only on the surface: which of the two systems will be the first to reach the place where there will be, firstly, God and, secondly, practical perfection; but not in accusations or prejudices, for both could be accused of prejudice, the former in the achievement of God and the latter in the achievement of perfection. And if the accuser is unable to accuse, then he will simply prove that both are moving towards God, as the human limit of perfection. Going deeper into the question of perfection we will find that the attainment of God or perfection as an absolute is—prejudice.

18

Man made God absolute perfection either deliberately or by accident, but, either way, in defining God in the absolute he set up a limit, for otherwise he would never have attained God. The limit of perfection lies in the absolute, and if God had no bounds, man would not have thought it possible to attain Him. But the other side has a different view; the universe, for example, has no bounds of perfection and is as limitless as God; it is therefore difficult to establish the absolute. But from the church's point of view God is without sin, and the absolute is accordingly established as the perfection of impeccability, but impeccability itself like God's perfection must be contained in the most terrible thing of all—in sense; and it is against this rock that the two paths of the factory and the church break up. God must be sense and, therefore, his perfection must have sense. What does he achieve? Can God achieve sense? No. If God achieves sense he will achieve something greater than himself, and, accordingly, he cannot himself be sense; he is only the sense of man. On the other hand, if he is not, in himself, sense, then what sense is it that man sees, and what does he hope to achieve? What senses should there be leading him to perfection? And to what perfection? God cannot be sense, for sense always begs the question "of what?"; accordingly God cannot be human sense either, for attaining it as the final sense man will not attain God, for there is a limit in God; or, to be more accurate, there stands before God the limit of all senses, but beyond the limit stands God in whom there is no sense. Thus, in the last resort, all the human senses leading to sense—God—are crowned by senselessness. Hence God is not sense, but senselessness. His senselessness should be seen in the absolute final limit as non-objective. The achievement of the finite is the achievement of the non-objective. Attaining God in the heavenly spaces is actually unnecessary for he is to be found in every one of our senses, since they are all at the same time senseless.

19

The carrying out of new religious systems has the same means as all economic, political or civil technical schools. Paganism destroyed the christian system, then the christians destroyed the heretics: thus it is in civil systems—one destroys another. Every religious system proves to the people its superiority and the bliss of attaining God, and similarly the civil system proves its bliss and its imminent achievements in perfection. Both talk about bliss, but what bliss? The first sees bliss in a spiritual existence with a spiritual God, and the view of the second comes to the same thing if one bears in mind the development of technology, which is supposed to free the body from physical labour, taking the entire labour upon itself. What, then, will the body do? Once liberated, I do not suppose it will take up the role of pure gluttony: it should have other needs—a new physical life in the spiritual. But if not, having freed the body from the physical it will prove that it built or set up a paradise, in which man will be in Adam's position. This will mean the same heaven to which religion and the church intends to lead its faithful, the only difference being that the first will bring its faithful without body, just the soul, whilst the second will leave its parish with their bodies. But if we bear in mind Christ's second coming to judge sinners we will see that all the dead will don bodies and will thus enter heaven; accordingly, the same forms of perfection lie in both systems—religion and the factory. There is one God and one bliss, and it is quite incomprehensible to me if they reproach each other with prejudices. Religion reads to its parish the holy writings on the perfection of its saints, whilst the factory reads its scientific books on perfection. The former teaches with the holy writings the way to attain religious perfection in order to become holy, whilst the factory's technical school teaches how to become a scholar. Of all those who study religion very few are found in the course of centuries or a century to be holy, just as very few of the hundreds of thousands who learn are perfect scholars—in either case, the rest remain sinners. Religion or the church proclaims as saints those who have performed miracles with man's technical ailments. The factory proclaims as scholars those who have also performed miracles with the technical failings of human life. Both have their pagans who kill the preachers of religion and the factory's technical perfection. Both types have been burnt, drowned and persecuted. Both struggle for perfection, struggle for God.

20

The striving towards unity is an obscure striving towards that which is expected to be found in the unity of God's entire management; it is unity in the Trinity governing the world, in man managing his all-human life. But human life has been divided into two concepts or notions of life. One notion sees life in the spirit as comprehension and service of God; it built itself a temple or church in which life passes in service, and for this it organises production of the means necessary for service. The second notion sees life as self-perfection and built the factory where service is carried on in the creation of purely technical means. The former creates spiritual, the latter bodily perfection. Their differences and the battle of matter and spirit lead one to think that body and soul are two hostile principles existing individually and independently, but why is there a battle between them? Is it because they were linked in pre-history and now want to break apart and live independently on their different planes? But on the other hand the spirit cannot live without matter, just as matter cannot without spirit. And there is always the third question: does matter exist? Is what we call matter simply a series of spiritual movements, and is, perhaps, what we call spirit the movement of matter? But it is for the moment unimportant which, if either, of these views is correct; what is important is the definition of life. There arises a third principle defining what life is, and on that definition depends what matter as spirit or spirit as matter turn into. One side holds that true life is only in the spirit, the other that truth is in matter, and in this way there have arisen two movements in life—the spiritual and the material. Accordingly there has never been this alleged linking of two principles, for there was one principle, examined on two planes.

What was this one principle? I by-pass the last two and place stimulus as the principle. Does it contain spirit or matter? I believe that matter does not exist, for by matter I understand an indivisible particle which, according to my earlier conclusions, does not exist in the universe; accordingly the community understands by matter certain concentrations; but a concentration is divisible and cannot, therefore, be matter. By the spiritual, too, the community understands a special state in charge of religious movement. Spirituality acts in God, but on the other hand there is a difference between the spiritual and the spirit; spirit can be everywhere—in the godly and the ungodly: we speak of raising the spirit of an army. Raising of the spirit produces the capture of a fortress and the extermination of a body of people, whereas if the spiritual state is raised the army will go from the field into the temples. Thus spirit and matter are principles which the community applies to its judgements and realises: it is a purely objective technical use and the principles are falsely divided and incorrectly understood. Having taken concentration for matter we begin to build a Weltanschauung as something real: the realism or actuality will depend on how we understand the basis, just as a building depends on its foundations. Man cannot say that he has built a single building, for the existing types of Weltanschauung are simply internal quarrels, judgements about what is unknown and may not even exist. There is no building, and I am not convinced that there will ever be one; there will not be one, because man strives to build everything on a foundation, on the law, sense, logic, practicality, i.e. on something that does not exist according to the basic conclusions he has drawn. Thus, for example, taking matter for the basis of existence he will build a material world as reality, and setting up the spiritual he will build the spiritual. But both proofs are under debate, and therefore one man says that the reality of existence is spiritual whilst another will call it material. Hence in his normal life, there exist for man two realities of the world or life; perhaps there may be even more. One man builds life or a building on the material law or reality, whilst another does so on the spiritual law, and both make observations: the materialist thinks that the man with spiritual realism is without a firm foundation and even thinks there is no foundation at all. The other sees the same being in the materialist. As a result they have no objective reality: each has his own subjective one. Men's quarreling goes on and there is still no building: both want to prove that they have an objective basis, as the only firm one, but in actual fact they both remain in the non-objective.

21

The God of perfection of the Religious and Civil technical schools is equally lofty. The perfection of the spiritual human soul is as unlimited as the production of the factories and industrial plants. Equally remote is the horizon of material perfection as bliss, and spiritual bliss is moving equally distantly towards this horizon, but they are moving by means of different kinds of fervour. The spiritual movement leads people by the path of inner suppression of the 'ego' as wisdom and will—"my will is in God and I trust myself and all my affairs to his will." Accordingly man without will and wisdom (for all this is in God) destroys himself in removing them. In other words, by destroying himself as an individually existing unit, even God, as unity, would be pulverised. If he destroys himself then what is Godly in him will be reincarnated and assembled in God; thus man's wisdom and will are Godly and as such are born to God. What then does this lead us to? Man trusting in the will of God and handing all his affairs over to Him, is left without will and wisdom and admits his own non-existence, all his affairs being the affairs of God. What is man, in such a case? The only conclusion that I can draw is that in such a position man does not exist, but God exists, as will, wisdom and perfection. Man's religious spiritual path intends only to reach heaven and to be with God, but it has no intention of incarnating itself in Him. Man is reconciled to the thought that the heights where God exists are beyond his reach—indeed, he dare not even think about them. And, in fact, where is that height, that pinnacle, reaching which we could say, "Here we are on the highest of all heights, we are perfect. I, man, have reached the frontier where I cease to be a man. I am God"? No one ever reaches this frontier, either by the Religious, spiritual path or the material, whatever systems may be invented, or however much they may be believed.

Thus there stands drawn before man a God who is unattainable despite the fact that man's imagination has limited him as the absolute.

22

The objective path simply overthrows God, seeing only prejudice in Him. It considers the people who build their life on the spiritual and the Religious simply backward in that they cannot think far enough to see that their building is built on a prejudice supporting itself on God. Placing God at the foundation of life, they reduce him to emptiness. The materialist is convinced that he builds his own life on the foundation of matter, but I wonder whether this foundation is not also built on prejudice. For what is matter? By matter I understand concentration, but what is concentration? Of what indivisible particles does it consist? No one knows. Similarly one cannot say that God consists of three parts.

Man's reasoning built God on the three principles of God, the Spirit and the Son. This is the same sort of precision as the definition of a material unit; are not, then, both foundations prejudice? The community builds a foundation convinced that it is taking a rock, nothing else; but for scientific analysis this will be not a rock, but a concentration consisting of an innumerable quantity of concentrations by no means rock-like in origin; it has been demonstrated to the community that a rock may be turned into steam like water, reduced to a liquid state like a certain concentration: thus it seems hardly possible to determine material units in the latter. So it is that the realism of the community, and in many cases that of science too, may fail in accurately determining the composition of particles. Thus man building his house on a foundation of rock, thinking it irrefutable, firm and indivisible, may be mistaken in his realism.

23

I, the factory, see only prejudice in the will of God: only my will is in everything and the sense of all perfection is in me. "I shall build the kingdom of heaven on earth and not in heaven—therefore I am God. (Again God, the "kingdom of heaven" on earth.) I hold in my hand the world of both earthly and aerial motors and cast them into space, giving a new form to matter. But it would be more to the point to say that I gave form to my reasoning. (No God, alas, is capable of giving form to matter.) Electric wires (of which I have only recently learnt) are in my hands, the earth will gain a new principle; I alone am omnipotent and powerful; I am reality; I am the clear visual force of the phenomena of matter. I am the master of the world, for labour is in my hands and I am the universe, for I possess it." Is there not a hidden motive in these words?—"The taking, possessing of all God's forces." Only God, or someone with all his features, can be "master of the world," but if man takes on all God's features will he not also take all his prejudices and will he not build a kingdom of heaven on earth on those same prejudices? Obviously a man casting God down has to build his world and his heaven on completely new principles, "real, obvious grounds" and not on God's groundless prejudices. But it turns out that all human production is built on the same bases as God's world. If each of God's worldly creations takes nourishment, then every new machine also demands nourishment. The materialist takes the latter as his starting point, and regards the fact that every-thing requires nourishment and starts from small beginnings as the most obvious basis for all materialist teaching. But for all the obvi-ousness I nonetheless have doubts. I cannot imagine that the earth and the universe were only built because at some stage something felt hungry. Had appetite not arisen in this nothingness the universe would not have existed.

Thus two men imagine the universe differently: one sees in it a spiritual, the other a material principle; one builds on the spiri-tual principle and sees something great over what the materialist sees, whilst the materialist sees the world as self-devouring matter. The "greater significance" of the spiritual consists of the fact that the spiritual does not create for the sake of devouring itself but for its non-objectivity; the materialist, on the other hand, sees the creation of that same matter as the aim of self-devourment—he creates ob-jects for his own appetite. Scientific proof, however, tells us that mat-ter does not disappear, that it can be neither burnt, baked or eaten: how, then, are we to understand the materialist conception of matter which is something that cannot eat itself? You can't boil it in a caul-dron, nor eat it up without remains. If this is so, then the action of objective consciousness is meaningless. I see no greater worth in finding some higher motive in this action or giving it priority than in giving it to the spiritual, or even Religious understanding of the world. Before both world views stands the same non-objectivity.

But if objective consciousness in objective constructions sees only a tower from which to observe the world and to achieve the pos-sibility of matter's seeing its own changes in appearance—if this is so, then it is simply female curiosity to examine oneself in a mirror. Ob-jective thinking is occupied with building a mirror—seeing the world is the reason for matter itself. But in this "if" also there is no perfec-tion, for the mirror will in any case not show all matter's aspects. The movement of objective consciousness is towards a perfection which would in any case achieve its sense, which is to build an apparatus to satiate the appetite of objective consciousness; in other words it is preparing to build matter in such a way that the latter will in any case satisfy its appetite. All this will be possible of achievement when matter is eaten without remains. The church is striving through its religion to bring man's consciousness to God, as perfection, whilst the materialist is striving to attain perfection in the machine as self-nourishment: the one intends to nourish himself with God, the other with a machine.

Striving to make itself master of the world the factory at the same time says that in order to achieve the latter one must know, learn, understand, investigate and "scientifically base" "everything"!; for you can only become master and rule the earth when you know everything. Again this "everything"! How can one collect and contain this "everything" in order to examine and study it? How can one collect it and make it the subject of our conclusive investigation? And how many apparent objects we can see around us which as soon as they are touched by our clever tools scatter—the sharper the mind, the deeper and further they go. They scatter into the heights, these objects of our study, as it were, struggling for their non-objective truth: they do not wish to be objects, and our will, wisdom, experience and visual comprehension are smashed to pieces on their non-objective truth or simply non-objectivity without any truth.

In defining God as the absolute, they defined perfection, but nonetheless this "everything" slips away, its borders cannot be grasped in the absolute and we cannot control its borders. And, in fact, with the endless worlds of the universe and the innumerable mists of rushing suns with their systems—how can any instrument measure their speed and the space they travel? All the innumerable mists of suns rush along in darkness, and we with our earth are like a speck of dust in the general dust of the worlds; we rush in a senseless vortex and up till now have been unable to establish whence and whither we are flying, or what the purpose and sense is in this endless whirlwind. And man wants to calculate all this incalculable material and make it the subject of his study and "scientific basis," a visual example for experiment. But on what, on what subject is he to carry out his experiment? Let man say when the day will come when the factory whistle will blow for the last time, when the scientific technical school will announce the last shift, that everything has been completed, "everything" learnt, and when the factory worker will cry, "Enough! Work is finished. Everything has been investigated. I am on the summit of the worlds, or I have devoured the world. I have mastered all forms of perfection. 'I am God' ".

24

Man's laborious efforts only exist because he hopes to solve a practical question by means of labour. But being unable to conclude the question, to reach the limit even in one single thing he is forced to labour, to go on reaching further, and in this way the centuries pass and the question remains unsolved. Can the moment ever come when man will be satisfied with light? The original discovery of the touchwood was of course a great achievement, but man was dissatisfied and found kerosene and later electricity; one might think that the introduction of electricity would end the question. There is enough light, but the work on light is carried further and it may be that in time our electric lights will be like mere wicklamps. Thus there is no end, no limit where man could say, "All has been exhausted." And since it is impossible to foresee and anticipate everything, a catastrophe will occur in what has been built: lack of foresight causes a sin. How strangely the world is constructed, in that man has to attain, study and build special pieces of apparatus to reveal the world's reality, to penetrate the nebula in the abyss of nonexistence. He is not yet master, since his production of things serves to overcome the unknown; his factories and industrial plants only exist because there lies hidden in nature an unknown perfection, which they are trying to collect together in their technical machine. I would consider this to be the principal basis of materialist consciousness—but not the motive of obtaining materialistic comforts, built on the motive of nourishment. And it is pure prejudice to build the world so as to produce perfection of nourishment. If material consciousness only built scaffolding in order to climb to the nebula and itself become a mist in the whirlwind of the entire cosmic vortex without entering upon any scientific or "obvious reasons," this I would consider to be points in its favour; but as soon as material consciousness becomes simply a "struggle for survival" and a struggle with nature, then I consider conquest senseless. All production as existence, as necessity is compelled to oppose production, as struggle. Man exists by production. But perhaps existence does not only lie in my creating objects, but also in the spirit of stimulus existing in man; perhaps the mere striving to comprehend the incomprehensible is also existence. Man may exist not only because he thinks, but because he is stimulated, which is the first principle of his life. Thought, after all, is only realized stimulus. Existence is action, but it is possible to act and still not be; to be means to make objects with a use and purpose—aimless action may be considered non-existence. But what existence is man striving for? He is striving for rest, i.e. inactivity, and each of his perfect machines speaks of that rest. At any rate man believes that the machine will lessen his labour and in the future will perhaps allow him to rest completely. What, then, will be liberated and given rest? His muscles and the tension of intellectual discoveries. And what action will be left to man? The thought of endless mental conquests of the unknown, for it is impossible to comprehend reality; what is grasped is one's own work, representing an imagined picture of what does not exist. But in this existence the means are not indicated by which one could understand reality, for means arise once there is an obstacle, whereas if there is no obstacle there can be no means either. Comprehension of the world as materialistic or spiritual existence is simply a fantasy of existence in which one must achieve comprehension.

25

Man on achieving perfection immediately retires into rest, i.e. the absolute; he is freed from understanding, knowledge and various proofs and cannot conceal himself from God, for God is made the absolute, free from any action.

God is rest; rest is perfection; everything has been achieved; the building of worlds is completed and movement is established in eternity. His creative thought will move, whilst he himself is liberated from madness, for he no longer creates; and the universe, like a crazy brain, moves in a whirling vortex, irresponsible as to its destination and purpose. Thus the universe is the senselessness of God liberated and concealing himself in rest. Man, likewise, achieving perfection will be liberated from his craziness and will become God. But man cannot bear rest: he is terrified by eternal rest for it signifies non-existence, and when he approaches eternal rest he approaches God: he rises up with all the strength of his craziness and cries, "No, I do not wish to exist," in other words, "I do not want to be God"!

26

My thought has arrived at God, as rest or non-existence—at the place where there are no longer any forms of perfection. What is the aim of all forms of perfection? Perfection contains the limit of the approaching nothingness, as inactive rest. This is what God should be like. If this is so, then the religious path is that of least resistance, recognising man's "nothing," leaving God's "something." Thus religion sees "nothing" or "non-existence" in man, but "existence" in God. The factory, on the other hand, sees "something" in man, but "nothing" in God, but since God is rest in perfection and since the factory also sees rest in perfection it comes in this way to God, as rest!

Religion, striving towards God, strives to turn man into "non-existence" and God into "existence." But it is unable to turn man into non-existence, for it acknowledges a soul within him, which will be "existence" in God; thus the complete rest of man's annihilation is not yet achieved by attaining God in religious perfection, for man is simply liberated from his body but remains in the soul; and the soul must still act in some way in God and in heaven.

In order to achieve complete rest or self-annihilation it is essential to free oneself from the soul too; but in the religious technical school the soul is still an indivisible atom. If religion sees God as existence, then any object in the world is also existence, for everything contains God within itself, a particle of perfection (in the common opinion) and if one examines each thing more deeply one will find it contains God with all his infinity or the absolute of what is perfect. That the thing is not turned into an object of comprehension like God himself (again in the common opinion) and, hence, the appearance of the things or man on the altars in religious festivals is logically justified, for God as perfection exists in the thing and in man. The same situation obtains in the factory, where the altar is already hung with the portraits of people in whom perfection, i.e. God, lives; there are also engineers who study their perfection, as priests do the holy writ; and just as the former teach the perfection they have learned from their teachers, so the others teach what they have learned from the perfect life of the holy teacher.

27

Man has divided his life into three paths, the spiritual or religious, the scientific or factory, and that of art. What do these paths signify? They signify perfection, and man moves along them; he moves himself as a perfected principle towards his final conception, i.e. towards the absolute; they are the three paths along which man moves towards God. In art God is conceived as beauty simply because in beauty there is God. Religion and the factory summon art to adorn them with a cloak of beauty—they are apparently not convinced of their own perfection. Like religion, so equally the factory moves solemnly in art. But despite the relationship each path considers itself of prime importance and the true path to God, an independent teaching and understanding of God. Each preaches his own path to God and links perfection (as people say) in one word.

28

The religious man in his church says, "I am standing on the true path; my church leads to the true God and all that the man outside the church says is perishable; only through me will the soul be carried to those universal heights whither no human discovery can reach. Nothing raises the soul as high as does prayer; man fears no catastrophe or death, for his soul is not subject to any catastrophe. Death exists only for the body as a technical receptacle, whilst the soul exists eternally, for it is nothing less than a particle of God. Thus all that is Godly is drawn to Him. The soul is immortal, God is immortal: all that is immortal is God. Therefore man's soul is nothing other than a particle of immortal God." Such are the church's conditions. True, like any conditions they can be overthrown or formulated differently. For example, it is very important to know whether man has a soul. If they speak of the "human soul" it is incorrect; there cannot be a human soul for the soul is immortal and all that is immortal belongs to God; hence the soul that exists in man is the soul of God: hence arises the different but quite logical conception that the soul can never be sinful. However sinful the body may be, God, being impeccable, can only leave the sinful body, and man can be without a soul, like a piece of meat. But if, against expectation, matter, or some other force composing the body exists which will not disappear under any conditions, then it is also immortal: thus the entire body, as matter, is also the body of God. Accordingly the world is without sin, for both body and soul are God. Thus I have exonerated the world from sin. What is life for the church? Man's spiritual condition. But where is spirituality to be found within Him? In the soul, for the body is sinful, and when the soul kills the sin in the body it becomes holy and turns itself into God. The body disappears and becomes soul; there is no longer any sin—there is God. God can punish neither the soul, since it is a part of himself, nor the body, since it is immortal. Hence in God there are no punishments.

29

Art recognises that it is the most important and states: "I show man beauty, and what can be higher or more perfect than beauty? He who sees me sees no sin.

He who possesses me possesses and lives by beauty; unlike other truths I contain no sin, for were there no beauty in me truths would not use me to hide their other teachings; on contact with me everything becomes filled to the brim with beauty, as perfection. The harmony of God is within me and therefore my world is perfect. Come to me: he who enters will enter harmony and hear himself in the general harmony. I crown everything with the beauty of harmony. I may be proud that God is within me, since only in me is harmony, and in harmony there is no sin. In me lies the true world of men, and I have neither prisons nor punishments: nothing can compare with me for I have already attained God. All the rest are still divided into ranks, great and small, holy and sinful; they still make war and suffer in blood and chains. Let anyone that wishes to listen to the harmony of rhythms follow my path."

30

The factory refutes the latter two and in its turn says, "I am rebuilding the world, and its body; I am changing man's consciousness and I shall make him omnipresent by the comprehension of perfection within me; by my system the world will be reincarnated in me and I shall be omniscient; I shall be God, for God merely knows the affairs of the universe. All the elements will be assembled in me and I shall be eternity. I shall make man farseeing, hearing and speaking over great distances; I shall build up the techniques of his body in a perfect pattern. I shall harmonise his will entirely within myself, and, swallowing up the will of the winds, water, fire and atmosphere, I shall make all this the simple possession of man. When all is said and done the world is simply an unsuccessful technical attempt on the part of God, which I shall build up in perfection." Who speaks so boldly through the mouth of the factory? Suddenly it is God himself shouting with its lips.

31

Thus man divided himself in three and set out along three paths to perfection, apparently not trusting any one path, not convinced that he would find by it either God or a truth leading him to perfection, as bliss or God. But having divided up each one found truth on his path and built a church, building not one, but three units of truths, which argue amongst themselves. They expect to find bliss in truth, and this is why they produce; hence each production is at once bliss and not bliss, because it has to be made. Making bliss is making truth, for truth in factory production has not yet attained the bliss achieved by Religion and art, for here everyone makes his own bliss and develops his spiritual basis. Factory workers make bliss for the enjoyment of others and therefore the new teachings of socialism are striving to make people produce their own bliss and to see that whoever does not make it does not enjoy it either. Therefore the church says: "He who does not pray and make bliss will not enter the kingdom of heaven"; the factory has produced a similar slogan "Who does not work does not eat." In either case man not making bliss does not receive it either and will not enjoy the kingdom of bliss. For both of them the making of bliss signifies attaining God's heavenly kingdom, as the final bliss. Logically it should be so for perfection is put as the aim. If any of them should say, "I want to perfect myself eternally, to be unending," it is the same as saying, "I want to be in unending God," for man has put God's infinity as his own. Religion's bliss

consists of attaining the Kingdom of heaven, which man will enter
free from all his body's various physical ailments, and, pure in soul,
will seat himself on one side of God's throne; in eternal prayer, he will
be freed from any bodily cares, for in the Kingdom of heaven perfection has been reached: there is no need to feed the body, or to overcome anything, for everything has been done and overcome—only
spiritual action remains.

What, then, does the factory or industrial plant expect to attain?
It expects by labour to attain liberation from labour. This is shown by
the anxiety and striving to liberate oneself by means of the machine—although for the time being it only lightens man's labour. If
by labour man can free himself from labour, then the church, by
prayer, ought in the Kingdom of heaven to free man or the soul from
prayer; for what prayers can one make when everything has been already attained and is in communion with God—especially if one accepts that the soul is a particle of God. Thus in future man will have
neither factories nor industrial plants: he will be relieved of this when
he attains bliss. The factories will no longer be producing bliss, for it,
the bliss, will have been attained in perfection or in God. Thus the
factory is striving to free man from all the material and physical in
the future; he will no longer need to overcome matter. Will not this
be identical to the spiritual church which is striving to free the soul
from the body, as sinful matter? But in heaven the soul will obviously
have to act in prayers. What kind of action will this be? It will be the
new composition of prayer through meditation on God. Will this not
also be identical to the factory, through which man reaches perfection of action by thought alone? His whole technical apparatus will
move; my thought moves my technical body and all the functions are
fulfilled independently of my guiding thought; all the functions have
left the power of my thought, and there is no need to guide them.
Thus I suppose that the factory—scientific perfection—is striving for
the production it has built to fulfil all man's functions, apart from the
physical, and then to leave the power of thought. It is clear that in all
these comparisons both church and factory are moving towards the
same thing (God. I am not saying the place). But there is a large difference between them in that the church frees the soul from the body,
recognising its immortality, and for the time being only souls are
rushing up to heaven. The factory takes a completely opposite line: it
seems not to know the soul, and sees man before it "obviously", with-

out any "scientific foundations"; it strives to turn this man into soul, to make him not material but spiritual, or the spirit of a new body. It prepares a new body for man as spiritual power and the result will resemble the man that the church is dividing into body and soul. An armoured tool, a car represents a small example of what I have been saying. If a man sitting in it is still separate from it, it is because this particular body that man has put on cannot fulfil all functions. The man himself, as a technical organ, can fulfil all the functions necessary for his soul, and therefore the soul lives within him and leaves him when the functions are no longer fulfilled: if a car could perfectly fulfil all man's needs he would never leave it. The features of the latter are found in a greater solution: for example, the hydroplane. Air and water are contained in it, and when everything has been provided for, man will leave his new body no more.

Thus the factory and industrial plant intend to lead man to a new mechanical kingdom, changing his body, as a soul in a new set of clothes or as a tool; in that kingdom man will be presented in the way the form of the soul is presented in the body now. The church, on the other hand, will bring the soul into the kingdom of heaven: in both states thought will soon be active, but it will no longer have power in everything—some stimuli will remain outside it. And this will be a sign that God is imminent. For thought is finishing its physical work and the kingdom of non-thinking is beginning; rest is coming, i.e. God liberated from all creation in a state of absolute rest. Nothing needs God anymore, just as God does not need anything. He no longer rules his technical kingdom. Thus everything strives towards rest or God, as a non-thinking state.

32

God did not labour—he merely created. It was human thought that in its imagination made him such a creator. In six days or by six repetitions of "Let there be . . ." he completed the creation of the world. Man's carelessness brought down God's wrath upon him, and the creator placed on him the curse of labour, birth, sweat and blood (as people say). But did man really sin, and could God punish him? This could not be, for God, having created the world retired to eternal rest; on the seventh day He entered His non-thinking kingdom, and consequently could not know what had happened to His creation, despite the fact that He was supposed to be omniscient; but perhaps He did know what would happen to Adam, and maybe this is the way it should be. In any case, entering the seventh day He entered complete rest, for He had built the world in perfection. It was an essential condition for God that He enter rest, for if He had not retired into rest He would have been forced to go on building endlessly; and creating further meant not being perfect. God would create no further for he had created perfection and there is nothing higher than that. Having created the world he retired to a state of "non-thinking" or the nothingness of rest. Whether or not the Lord banished man from paradise, I am rather inclined to think that seeing perfection, man found it imperfect and began to create afresh in the image and likeness of God. Perhaps this excessive work was the reason why he was cursed with labour, callouses and blood. Thus he naively gave himself six days of labour in which to build a new world, as a blissful paradise, intending on the seventh to enjoy eternal rest, like God. But in fact things turned out differently: weeks passed and each day of the supposed rest simply reveals more imperfections, so that on the Monday the work on perfection begins again. For God the seventh day was rest, but for man it was simply a tower from which to see all his mistakes—this is the difference between them.

33

God built perfection (as people say) but human imagination is still trying to sort out what He built it from, what His purpose and motives were, and what the aims and meaning of perfection were. It puzzles out what it has imagined, but since imagining is not reality all the imagining that it puzzles out cannot be reality; accordingly it is all nothingness, i.e. God who has entered rest; and it turned out that nothingness was God, and passing through perfection became nothingness, because this is what it was. "Nothingness" can be neither investigated nor studied, for it is "nothingness"; but in this "nothingness" appeared "something"—man; but since "something" cannot comprehend anything it automatically becomes "nothing"; hence it follows that man exists, or that God exists as "nothingness", as non-objectivity. And will not the only reality be that all the "something" that appears in the space of our imagination is simply "nothingness". Any experiment, the movement of a train or cannonball smashing walls and killing people, is no proof that the latter exists, however obvious and convincing it may be. I cannot imagine where I begin and where I end, or what part of my body the cannonball went through: after all in order to fly a cannonball must overcome space and destroy myriads of lives which we cannot see. But did it destroy them or change their movement? No, nothing was changed, for there is nothing. If there were something in the world it would not be "something". Thus there is nothing strange in God's building the universe from nothing, since man also builds everything from the nothingness of his imagination and what he imagines. He does not know that he himself is the creator of everything and that he has created God also as his imagining; but if man mistook all his imagining for God and found that his soul and body were immortal, then it would obviously follow that there is nothing in the universe apart from "he", for "he" is immortal. Man is mortal, but since nothing is mortal man does not exist. The conception of what is mortal is false, for it would destroy God. Hence, in order to destroy God one must prove the death of the soul, or the body as matter; but since the sciences and various other attempts have failed to prove the latter, it is impossible to cast God down. Thus God is not cast down.

It can be proved, as the whole of this work shows, that matter does not exist, but the sciences prove the existence of energy which comprises what we call body.

It may be taken as a mark of the perfection of universal world movement or God that man himself has discovered that nothing disappears but merely takes on a new form. Thus disappearance from view does not mean that everything has disappeared. Appearances are destroyed but not the essence, which, by man's own definition, is God; it is not destroyed by anything, and if the essence is not destroyed nor is God. Thus God is not cast down.

I spoke earlier about the fact that nothing can be proved, defined, studied or comprehended: thus all definitions remain unproved, for if anything were proved it would be for the universe and oneself. Hence any proof is simply the appearance of the indemonstrable. Man calls every appearance an object, and thus no object exists in either the demonstrable or the indemonstrable.

14. Schoenberg (1874–1951)

Moses and Aaron: Opera in Three Acts. Act II, scenes 4–5, and Act III (fragment). Trans. Allen Forte, Miniature Score (London: Decca Record Company, 1985), pp. 108–132. German original: *Moses und Aron* (Mainz: B. Schott's Söhne, ca. 1957).

Poetry often aspires to approximate the state of music—to become "pure poetry"—sound released from sense, particularly in the symbolist aesthetics that strongly influenced Richard Wagner, Arnold Schoenberg's most imposing predecessor. Yet music, too, can be construed as only striving *toward* what is inexpressible even to it. Music itself thus becomes merely one more stage on the way to the purely inexpressible. This is patently the case in relation to the revelation of a God that infinitely transcends all sensible media and their representations. The ultimately inexpressible realities (or unrealities) that music can make us feel, perhaps like no other medium, in the end transcend music, too.

This ultimate barrier to the expression of transcendence was sometimes ignored in the outlook of German Romanticism, with its exaltation of music over words, notably in the philosophy of Arthur Schopenhauer. A sensibility for the infinite and ungraspable, like that found in Novalis and other Romantics, was developed by Schopenhauer into a metaphysics of music that deeply influenced Nietzsche and Wagner. Schoenberg has sometimes been aligned with this tradition: "Schoenberg, too, reflects Schopenhauer's philosophy. Words, he thinks, are only a secondary form of expression, while music is a direct, unmediated capture of the essence of the world."[1] Yet for Schoenberg, music achieves its quintessential state precisely through its *failure* to capture what it would express. On this note, Theodor Adorno's philosophical appraisal of Schoenberg's music underscores how completely antithetical it is to the Romantic metaphysical tradition. Adorno hailed *Moses und Aron* as Schoenberg's magnum opus and as a testament to his embrace of his Jewish

---

1. Ben-Ami Scharfstein, *Ineffability: The Failure of Words in Philosophy and Religion* (Albany: SUNY Press, 1993), p. 114.

246

heritage in the face of the rise of Nazism in the early 1930s, when the opera was written.[2]

Schoenberg chooses for his magnum opus the Exodus story, the founding myth of Judaism, a story that is centrally concerned with the problem of the interdiction upon all representations of the divine: "Thou shalt not make unto thee any graven image, or any likeness of any thing . . . Thou shalt not bow down thyself to them, nor serve them" (Exodus 19:4–5). The opera stages the dramatic conflict between the human need for representation and the divine exigency of absolute transcendence. The people need tangible gods, inevitably idols, to feel secure ("Ihre leibliche Sichtbarkeit, / Gegenwart, verbürgt unsre Sicherheit," II, ii). They jeer: How can an almighty God be incapable of showing himself to us? Aaron knows how to satisfy them with images. But these are translations or idols that are equally betrayals. The true God is unrepresentable and inexpressible. He is present, Moses insists, only as pure idea or thought: "Unrepresentable God! / Inexpressible, many-sided Thought!" ("Unvorstellbarer Gott! / Unaussprechlicher, vieldeutiger Gedanke!" II, v).

Especially the episode of the Golden Calf brings to dramatic crisis the conflict between all forms of idol worship and Moses's new religion of "one eternal, omnipresent, invisible and unrepresentable God" ("Einziger, ewiger, allgegenwärtiger, / unsichtbarer und unvorstellbarer Gott!" I, i; repeated in I, iv). While music is widely believed to possess resources of expressiveness that can reach into zones where words must surrender, nevertheless, it too is an expressive medium, and it therefore cannot but betray the absolute inexpressibility of the divine vision as such. Moses is granted this unmediated vision—called his "thought" or "idea" ("Gedanke") in the opera—but, of course, he cannot express it. That is why he relies on Aaron to be his mouthpiece. Moses's inability to speak well, his lack of expressive means, according to the Exodus story (4:10–17), translates into an inability to sing in Schoenberg's opera. He has a "speaking role" ("Sprechrolle") without any musical voice, unlike Aaron, who sings with a resonant tenor. (Curiously, there is one exception where he does sing, in I, 2, bars 208–217). This is a way of signifying his renunciation of the seduction of song and, more generally, his uncompromising refusal of expression.

2. T. W. Adorno, "Sakrales Fragment: Über Schoenbergs Moses und Aron," in *Quasi una fantasia* in *Musikalische Schriften I–III, Gesammelte Schriften*, vol. 16 (Frankfurt a.M.: Suhrkamp, 1978), pp. 454–475.

Schoenberg, as a composer aiming to signify what transcends all possibilities of expression, found his own predicament mirrored in Moses's drama as recounted in Exodus. His austere and exacting art of composition makes him like Moses, but his act of writing an opera for the public makes him like Aaron. The dialectic between the two characters may thus be interpreted as a reflection of unresolved conflicts within Schoenberg himself.[3] It is not entirely clear in the opera whether Aaron's concessions to the people are unjustified or dispensable. From the dialogue they appear to be necessary and motivated by genuine love toward the people. Aaron loves the people, lives for them, and wishes to preserve them, whereas Moses loves and lives for his idea ("Ich liebe meinen Gedanken und lebe für ihn!").

The concluding scene of Act II in the excerpt here begins just as Moses comes back down from the mountain after forty days, during which the fearful people have rebelled and have induced Aaron to make the Golden Calf for them. They have surrendered themselves to unbridled orgies. At Moses's words—"Begone, you image of powerlessness to enclose the boundless in an image finite!" ("Vergeh, du Abbild des Unvermögens, / das Grenzenlose in ein Bild zu fassen")—the Golden Calf vanishes and the stage is left to the confrontation between Aaron and Moses.

Traditionally, music takes over when words fail. However, *no* music and *no* medium at all can express transcendent divinity. To convey this, Schoenberg must create the experience of silence. How can music approximate silence? Can it do this perhaps even better than words? One must listen to Schoenberg's music to judge. What can be presented in these pages is Schoenberg's libretto, which stages the conflict between expression and its impossibility as the conflict between Aaron and Moses, and thus calls attention to the silence that is enjoined by the chief protagonist. The part of the opera that was actually finished and scored by Schoenberg (the first two acts) ends with Moses's words, "O word, thou word, that I lack!" ("O Wort, du Wort, das mir fehlt!"). At the end of the third act, which Schoenberg never (and perhaps could not) set to music, Aaron dies in the desert upon Moses's bidding the soldiers to set him free. With the death of Aaron, the Mosaic revelation is left

---

3. Schoenberg wrote to his pupil, the composer Alban Berg, in August 1930, shortly after having completed Act II of *Moses und Aron* in March: "one thing must be granted me (I won't let myself be deprived of it): Everything I have written has a certain inner likeness to myself." In the text of one of the four canons he composed in 1931 while also working on the opera, he wrote, "Mirror yourself in your work." Cited by Paul Griffiths, introduction to libretto for *Moses und Aron* (London: Decca Record Company, 1985), p. 13.

without recourse to any expressive means, in a desert. Here alone, according to
Moses, can it flourish—and with it the people for whom it is destined.

The opera's unfinished state is appropriate in the end for an endeavor to
signify the inexpressible. The same fate befell Schoenberg's other major attempts on the theme of the divine transcendence and the impossible task of
expressing it: *Die Jacobsleiter* (1917–1922) and *Modern Psalms*. The latter proposes a dialogue "between the song of man and the silences of God."[4] Both
works were left incomplete by Schoenberg at his death.

---

4. George Steiner, "Schoenberg's Moses and Aaron" in *Language and Silence*,
p. 129. Steiner's essay, which is perhaps the most accessible and compelling critical account of *Moses and Aaron*, attributes to the work a decisive philosophical, religious, and
artistic significance in the history of European culture. Steiner underlines the opera's engagement with silence in music on the borders of language: "the music takes over where
the human voice is strangled or where it retreats into desperate silence" (p. 133). Another
compelling interpretation in this key is Edith Wyschogrod, "Eating the Text, Defiling the
Hands," in *God, the Gift, and Postmodernism*, ed. John D. Caputo and Michael J. Scanlon
(Bloomington: Indiana University Press, 1999), pp. 245–259.

Moses and Aaron, Act II, scenes 4–5, and Act III (fragment)

ACT TWO

Scene 4

*(In the background, as far back as possible, a man on one of the hillocks
raises himself up, peers for a time in the direction where the Mountain
of Revelation is supposed to be, there, gesticulating, he awakens several
of those lying near him and has them look in the same direction. He
cries out:)*

Man
Moses is descending from the mountain!

(After this cry, those sleeping awaken everywhere, arise, and from all sides people again stream in.)

Moses
Begone, you image of powerlessness
to enclose the boundless in an image finite!

(The Golden Calf vanishes. The crowd moves back and quickly disappears from the stage.)

Chorus
The golden rays are now quenched!
Once again our god cannot be seen.
Every joy, every pleasure, every promise is gone!
All is once more gloom and darkness!
We must now escape from his might!

(Exit all but Moses and Aron.)

Scene 5: Moses and Aron

Moses
Aron, O what have you done?

Aron
Naught different,
Just my task as it ever has been:
When your idea gave forth
no word, my word gave forth
no image for them, I worked marvels
for eyes and ears to witness.

Moses
Commanded by whom?

Aron
As always,
I heeded the voice from within.

Moses
But I did not instruct you.

Aron
Nevertheless, I still comprehended.

Moses
Cease!

Aron
Your ... mouth ...
You were far away from us ...

Moses
There with my idea.
That must have been close to you.

Aron
When you remained apart
we believed you were dead.
And since the people had long expected
both law and commandment soon
to issue from your mouth,
I was compelled to provide an image for them.

Moses
Your image faded at my word!

Aron
But your word was denied image
and marvel, which are detested by you.
And yet was the marvel an image, not more,
when your word destroyed my image.

Moses
God's eternity opposes idols' transience!
No image this, no marvel!
These are the commands!
The everlasting one spoke them,
just as these tables so temporal,
in the language you are speaking.

(He holds out the tables to Aron.)

Aron
Israel endures, thus proving the idea
of one timeless.

Moses
Grant you now the power which
idea has over both word and image?

Aron
I discern only this:
that this folk shall remain protected.
And yet, they've naught but their feeling.
I love this humble folk.
I live just for them
and want to sustain them.

Moses
If the idea wills it.
My love is for my idea. I live just for it!

Aron
You also would have loved this people,
had you only seen how they lived
when they dared to see and feel and hope.
No folk is faithful, unless it feels.

Moses
You have shaken me not!
They must comprehend the idea!
They live for that end!

Aron
What a piteous people, a folk made of
martyrs they would then be!
No folk can grasp more than just a
partial image, the perceivable part
of the whole idea.
Be understood by all the people
in their own accustomed way.

Moses
Am I to debase the idea?

Aron
Let me present it then,
describing without specifying: restrictions,
fear-inspiring yet not too harsh,
further perseverance;
the need thus will be the clearer.
Commandments stern
give rise to new hoping
and strengthen the idea.
Unbeknown, what you want will be done.
Human wavering you'll find your people
still have . . .
yet worthy of love.

Moses
I shall not live to see it!

Aron
Go on living!
Aught else is futile!
You're bounden to your idea so closely!

Moses
Bounden to my idea, as even do these
tables set it forth.

Aron
They're images also,
just part of the whole idea.

Moses
Then I smash to pieces both these tables,
and I shall also ask Him to
withdraw the task given me.

(He smashes the tables.)

Aron
Faint-hearted one!
You, who yet have God's message,
without or with the tables.
I, your mouth, do rightly guard your idea
whenever I do utter it.

Moses
In image!

Aron
Image of your idea;
they are one, as all is that emerges from it.
I simply yield before necessity;
for it is certain this folk will be sustained
to give proof of the eternal idea.
This is my mission: to speak it more simply
than I understand it.
Yet, the knowing ones surely will
ever again discover it!
Chorus *(moving past in the background, led by a pillar of fire)*
For he has chosen us before all others
as his folk, to serve the only God,
him alone to worship,
serving no one else!
Aron
Look there!

Moses
The fiery pillar!
Aron
To lead us by night—
Thus through me has God given a signal
to the people.
*(In the background day arrives quickly. The pillar of fire fades and is
transformed into the pillar of cloud. The foreground remains relatively
dark.)*
Moses
The cloudlike pillar!
Aron
It leads us by day.
Moses
Godless image!
Aron
God-sent signal, burning bush again glowing.
The infinite thus shows not himself,
but shows the way to him
and the way to the promised land!

Chorus
He will then lead us to the land
where milk and honey flow,
and we shall enjoy then
what he once did promise our fathers.

(Aron slowly exits in the background.)

Chorus
Almighty,
thou art stronger than Egyptian
gods are!

Moses
Inconceivable God!
Inexpressible, many-sided idea,
will you let it be so explained?

Shall Aron, my mouth, fashion this image?
Then I have fashioned an image too, false,
as an image must be.
Thus am I defeated!
Thus, all was but madness that
I believed before,
and can and must not be given voice.
O word, thou word, that I lack!

(Moses sinks to the ground in despair.)

ACT THREE

(Moses enters, Aron, a prisoner in chains, follows, dragged in by two soldiers who hold him fast by the shoulders and arms. Behind him come the Seventy Elders.)

Moses
Aron, now this must cease!

Aron
Will you then kill me?

Moses
It is not a matter of your life . . .

Aron
The promised land . . .

Moses
An image . . .

Aron
I was to speak in images
while you spoke in ideas;
I was to speak to the heart,
you to the mind.

Moses
You, from whom both word and image flee,
you yourself remain, you yourself live

in the images that you have provided
for the people to witness.
Having been alienated from the source, from the idea,
then neither word nor image satisfied you . . .

Aron *(interrupting)*
. . . I was to perform visible marvels
when the word and the image from the mouth
failed . . . ?

Moses
. . . but you were satisfied only by the act, the deed.
You then made of the rod a leader,
of my power a liberator.
And the waters of the Nile
attested the supreme might . . .
You then desired actually, physically,
to tread with your feet upon an unreal land
where milk and honey flowed.
You then struck the rock,
instead of speaking to it, as you were commanded to do
in order to make water flow forth from it . . .
The word alone was to have struck forth refreshment
from the naked rock . . .

Aron
Never did your word reach the people without
meaning.
And thus did I speak to the rock
in its language, which the people also understand.

Moses
You speak more simply than you understand,
for you know that the rock is, like the
wasteland and the burning bush—
three that give not to the body
what it needs with regard to spirit—
is, I say, an image of the soul,
whose very renunciation is sufficient for eternal life.
And the rock, even as all images,

obeys the word,
from whence it came to be manifested.
Thus, you won the people not for the eternal one,
but for yourself . . .

Aron
For their freedom—
so that they would become a nation.

Moses
To serve, to serve the divine idea
is the purpose of the freedom for which
this folk has been chosen.
You, however, expose them to strange gods,
to the calf
and to the pillars of fire and cloud;
for you do as the people do,
because you feel and think as they do.
And the god that you showed to them
is an image of powerlessness,
is dependent upon a power beyond itself,
must fulfil what it has promised,
must do what it is asked,
is bound by its word.
Just as men act—well
or badly—so must it;
it must punish their wickedness, reward their virtues.
But man is independent and does
what pleases him, according to free will.
Here images govern
the idea, instead of expressing it.
The almighty one (and he retains that quality forever)
is not obliged to do anything,
is bound by nothing.
He is bound neither by the transgressor's deeds,
nor by the prayers of the good,
nor by the offerings of the penitent.
Images lead and rule this folk
that you have freed,

and strange wishes are their gods,
leading them back to the slavery
of godlessness and earthly pleasures.
You have betrayed God to the gods,
the idea to images,
this chosen folk to others,
the extraordinary to the commonplace . . .

Soldiers
Shall we kill him?

Moses *(addressing all)*
Whensoever you went forth amongst the people
and employed those gifts—
which you were chosen to possess
so that you could fight for the divine idea—
whensoever you employed those gifts for false
and negative ends, that you might
rival and share the lowly pleasures
of strange peoples,
and whensoever you had abandoned
the wasteland's renunciation
and your gifts had led you
to the highest summit,
then as a result of that misuse
you were and ever shall be hurled back
into the wasteland.

(to the Soldiers)
Set him free, and if he can,
he shall live.

(Aron, free, stands up and then falls down dead.)

Moses
But in the wasteland you shall be
invincible and shall achieve the goal:
unity with God.

15. ADORNO (1903–1969)

"Fragment über Musik und Sprache." In *Quasi una fantasia* in *Musikalische Schriften I–III, Gesammelte Schriften,* vol. 16 (Frankfurt a.M.: Suhrkamp, 1978), pp. 252–256.

    Trans. Rodney Livingstone as "Music and Language: A Fragment," in *Quasi una fantasia: Essays on Modern Music* (London–New York: Verso, 1992), pp. 1–6.

    Negative Dialektik, III.iii.12 (Frankfurt a.M.: Suhrkamp, 1966), pp. 395–398.

    Trans. E. B. Ashton as *Negative Dialectics* (New York: Continuum, 1973), pp. 405–408.

Theodor Adorno is highly influential as a founding figure, together with Max Horkheimer, of the so-called Critical Theory that emanated from the Frankfurt Institute for Social Research. Adapting Hegel's historicization of Kant's critical philosophy to the critique of ideologies, this school became known for interpreting society along Marxist and psychoanalytical lines. Just as decisive for Adorno's thinking, however, was the annihilation of six million Jews, and of humanity itself, by the Nazis in the Holocaust. He famously proclaimed that to write poetry after Auschwitz is barbaric.

    Adorno's *Negative Dialectics* opens the Hegelian dialectic to a certain kind of indeterminacy. In Hegel, the dialectical process works always with and from concrete, determinate realities, moving toward the identity of subject and object, but in Adorno it is driven rather by what cannot be defined except negatively (this includes singular individuals) and leads always to non-identity ("das Nichtidentische"). Thought and history pivot on what cannot be positively delineated but can only be negatively determined, that is, the unsayable. Indeed, "saying the unsayable" is Adorno's formula for what philosophy, as negative dialectics, does. His philosophy is an attempt to say the unsayable, to think the unthinkable, by using concepts to exceed the bounds of the conceptual in a negative dialectic.[1] The concluding paragraphs of *Negative Dialektik,*

---

1. Cf. Albrecht Wellmer, "Adorno, Anwalt des Nicht-Identischen," in *Zur Dialektik von Moderne und Postmoderne: Vernunftkritik nach Adorno* (Frankfurt a.M.: Suhrkamp,

excerpted here, describe thought negating itself in order to fathom an incommensurable otherness, the Absolute or Transcendent that is not identical with it and that can be thought not in itself but only as conditioned by thinking (and thus anthropomorphized). This thinking, then, must be non-identical even with itself—it must subvert its own concepts—in order not to reduce what it thinks to identity. Such patterns of aporia are likewise familiar in the apophatic tradition.[2]

In the fragmentary piece, "Fragment über Musik und Sprache," Adorno construes music as like a language that communicates no meaning but rather presents the Name of God. He manages to sketch an entire philosophy of music as *like language* in that it is meaningful but as *unlike language* in that it always escapes from determinate meaning. Meaning is transmuted into a meaningless form, a Name, that nevertheless points to the whole. Intentions are broken and scattered and absorbed into the Name rather than being signified by a composition of discrete elements in a system. Intentional language aims to say the Absolute, but inevitably misses it, whereas music hits it immediately, but has no determinate intention by which to identify and pin it down. By evoking intention but obscuring it with indeterminacy, music expresses the inexpressible. This illuminates why Adorno was so partial to music: it makes sensuously palpable the inexpressible that is also inherent to language—as what it cannot express.

Adorno's thinking often focuses on music, understood as an indirect way of saying by the senses what cannot be said in words. Sounding like Rosenzweig, he declares, "The true language of art is speechless, its speechless moment has priority over the signifying moment in poetry, which also does not get away completely from music."[3] This residual signifying moment in music Adorno understands as the Name of God. Echoing Benjamin, he describes a language of naming that would have no meaning, no determinate content, but consist simply in the gesture of naming. This is the creative act par excellence,

---

1985): "daher auch die Forderung Adornos, die Philosophie müsse versuchen, das Undenkbare zu denken, das Unsagbare auszusprechen, also im Medium des Begriffs über den Begriff hinauszukommen" (p. 149).

2. Hent de Vries, *Theologie im Pianissimo: Zur Aktualität der Denkfiguren Adornos und Levinas* (Kampen, Netherlands: J. H. Kok, 1989), offers a searching analysis of Adorno's apophaticism. The ambiguities are also discussed by Gerrit Steunebrink, "Is Adorno's Philosophy a Negative Theology?" in *Flight of the Gods*, ed. Bulhof and ten Kate.

3. Adorno, *Ästhetische Theorie*, ed. Gretel Adorno and Rolf Tiedemann (Frankfurt a.M.: Suhrkamp, 1973), p. 171: "Die wahre Sprache der Kunst ist sprachlos, ihr sprachloses Moment hat den Vorrang vor dem signifikativen der Dichtung, das auch der Musik nicht ganz abgeht."

for it is in the image of the Creator in Genesis, who can create by his Word the very being of things, that is, unqualified being, not just their being *this* or *that*. Such naming addresses and grants the being itself of what it names. Similarly, naming God means saying nothing (God is no thing) but rather commanding the act of naming in its absolute purity. A sort of "demythologized prayer," naming the Name of God says nothing determinate, yet it bears in an inarticulable manner all the possibilities of naming and saying within itself.

Music and Language: A Fragment

Music resembles a language. Expressions such as musical idiom, musical intonation, are not simply metaphors. But music is not identical with language. The resemblance points to something essential, but vague. Anyone who takes it literally will be seriously misled.

Music resembles language in the sense that it is a temporal sequence of articulated sounds which are more than just sounds. They say something, often something human. The better the music, the more forcefully they say it. The succession of sounds is like logic: it can be right or wrong. But what has been said cannot be detached from the music. Music creates no semiotic system.

The resemblance to language extends from the whole work, the organized linking of significant sounds, right down to the single sound, the note as the threshold of merest presence, the pure vehicle of expression. The analogy goes beyond the organized connection of sounds and extends materially to the structures. The traditional theory of form employs such terms as sentence, phrase, segment, ways of punctuating—question, exclamation and parenthesis. Subordinate phrases are ubiquitous, voices rise and fall, and all these terms of musical gesture are derived from speech. When Beethoven calls for one of the bagatelles in Opus 33 to be played 'parlando' he only makes explicit something that is a universal characteristic of music.

It is customary to distinguish between language and music by asserting that concepts are foreign to music. But music does contain things that come very close to the 'primitive concepts' found in epistemology. It makes use of recurring ciphers. These were established by tonality. If tonality does not quite generate concepts, it may at least be said to create lexical items. Among these we may start by singling out those chords which constantly reappear with an identical function, well-established sequences such as cadential progressions, and in many cases even stock melodic figures which are associated with the harmony. Such universal ciphers were always capable of entering into a particular context. They provided space for musical specificity just as concepts do for a particular reality, and at the same time, as with language, their abstractness was redeemed by the context in which they were located. The only difference is that the identity of these musical concepts lay in their own nature and not in a signified outside them.

Their unchanging identity has become sedimented like a second nature. This is why consciousness finds it so hard to bid farewell to tonality. But the new music rises up in rebellion against the illusion implicit in such a second nature. It dismisses as mechanical these congealed formulae and their function. However, it does not dissociate itself entirely from the analogy with language, but only from its reified version which degrades the particular into a token, into the superannuated signifier of fossilized subjective meanings. Subjectivism and reification go together in the sphere of music as elsewhere. But their correlation does not define music's similarity to language once and for all. In our day the relationship between music and language has become critical.

The language of music is quite different from the language of intentionality. It contains a theological dimension. What it has to say is simultaneously revealed and concealed. Its Idea is the divine Name which has been given shape. It is demythologized prayer, rid of efficacious magic. It is the human attempt, doomed as ever, to name the Name, not to communicate meanings.

Music aspires to be a language without intention. But the demarcation line between itself and the language of intentions is not absolute; we are not confronted by two wholly separate realms. There is a dialectic at work. Music is permeated through and through with intentionality. This does not just date from the *stile rappresentativo*, which deployed the rationalization of music in an effort to exploit its similarity to language. Music bereft of all intentionality, the merely phenomenal linking of sounds, would be an acoustic parallel to the kaleidoscope. On the other hand, as absolute intentionality it would cease to be music and would effect a false transformation into language. Intentions are central to music, but only intermittently. Music points to true language in the sense that content is apparent in it, but it does so at the cost of unambiguous meaning, which has migrated to the languages of intentionality. And as though Music, that most eloquent of all languages, needed consoling for the curse of ambiguity—its mythic aspect, intentions are poured into it. 'Look how it constantly indicates what it means and determines it.' But its intentions also remain hidden. It is not for nothing that Kafka, like no writer before him, should have assigned a place of honour to music in a number of memorable texts. He treated the meanings of spoken, intentional language as if they were those of music, parables broken off in mid-phrase. This contrasts sharply with the 'musical' language of Swinburne or Rilke, with their imitation of musical effects and their remoteness from true musicality. To be musical means to energize incipient intentions: to harness, not indulge them. This is how music becomes structure.

This points to the question of interpretation. Interpretation is essential to both music and language, but in different ways. To interpret language means: to understand language. To interpret music means: to make music. Musical interpretation is performance, which, as synthesis, retains the similarity to language, while obliterating every specific resemblance. This is why the idea of interpretation is not an accidental attribute of music, but an integral part of it. To play music correctly means first and foremost to speak its language properly. This calls for imitation of itself, not a deciphering process. Music only discloses itself in mimetic practice, which admittedly may take place silently in the imagination, on an analogy with silent reading; it never yields to a scrutiny which would interpret it independently of fulfilment. If we were to search for a comparable act in the languages of intention, it would have to be the act of transcribing a text, rather than decoding its meaning.

In contrast to philosophy and the sciences, which impart knowledge, the elements of art which come together for the purpose of knowledge never culminate in a decision. But is music really a non-decisive language? Of its various intentions one of the most urgent seems to be the assertion 'This is how it is', the decisive, even the magisterial confirmation of something that has not been explicitly stated. In the supreme moments of great music, and they are often the most violent moments—one instance is the beginning of the recapitulation in the first movement of the Ninth Symphony—this intention becomes eloquently unambiguous by virtue of the sheer power of its context. Its echo can be heard, in a parodied form, in trivial pieces of music. Musical form, the totality in which a musical context acquires authenticity, cannot really be separated from the attempt to graft the gesture of decision on to the non-decisive medium. On occasion this succeeds so well that the art stands on the brink of yielding to assault from the dominating impulse of logic.

This means that the distinction between music and language cannot be established simply by examining their particular features. It only works by considering them as totalities. Or rather, by looking at their direction, their 'tendency', in the sense of the 'telos' of music. Intentional language wants to mediate the absolute, and the absolute escapes language for every specific intention, leaves each one behind because each is limited. Music finds the absolute immediately, but at the moment of discovery it becomes obscured, just as too powerful a light dazzles the eyes, preventing them from seeing things which are perfectly visible.

Music shows a further resemblance to language in the fact that, as a medium facing shipwreck, it is sent like intentional language on an odyssey of unending mediation in order to bring the impossible back home. But its form of mediation and the mediation of intentional language unfold according to different laws: not in a system of mutually dependent meanings, but by their lethal absorption into a system of interconnections which can alone redeem the meanings it overrides in each individual instance. With music intentions are broken and scattered out of their own force and reassembled in the configuration of the Name.

In order to distinguish music from the mere succession of sensuous stimuli it has been termed a structured or meaningful totality. These terms may be acceptable in as much as nothing in music stands alone. Everything becomes what it is in memory and in expectation through its physical contiguity with its neighbour and its mental connection with what is distant from it. But the totality is different from the totality of meaning created by intentional language. Indeed it realizes itself in opposition to intentions, integrating them by the process of negating each individual, unspecifiable one. Music as a whole incorporates intentions not by diluting them into a still higher, more abstract intention, but by setting out to proclaim the non-intentioned at the moment when all intentions converge and are fused together. Thus music is almost the opposite of a meaningful totality, even when it seems to create one in contrast to mere sensuous existence. This is the source of the temptation it feels from a sense of its own power to abstain from all meaning, to act, in short, as if it were the direct expression of the Name.

Heinrich Schenker has cut the Gordian knot in the ancient controversy and declared his opposition to both expressive and formal aesthetics. Instead he endorsed the concept of musical content. In this respect he was not unlike Schoenberg, whose achievement he failed to his shame to recognize. Expressive aesthetics focuses on polyvalent, elusive individual intentions and confuses these with the intentionless content of the totality. Wagner's theory misses the mark because it conceives of the content of music as the expression of the totality of musical moments extended into infinity, whereas the statement made by the whole is qualitatively different from that of the individual intention. A consistent aesthetics of expression ends up by succumbing to the temptation to replace the objective reality with transitory and adventitious meanings. The opposing thesis, that of music as resounding, animated form, ends up with empty stimuli or with the mere fact of organized sound devoid of every connection between the aesthetic form and that non-aesthetic other which turns it into aesthetic form. Its simple-minded and therefore ever-popular critique of intentional language is paid for by the sacrifice of art.

Music is more than intentionality, but the opposite is no less true: there is no music which is wholly devoid of expressive elements. In music even non-expressiveness becomes expression. 'Resounding' and 'animated' are more or less the same thing in music and the concept of 'form' explains nothing of what lies beneath the surface, but merely pushes the question back a stage to what is represented in the 'resounding', 'animated' totality, in short to what goes beyond form. Form can only be the form of a content. The specific necessity, the immanent logic, evaporates: it becomes a mere game in which everything could literally be something else. In reality, however, musical content is the profusion of things which obey the rules of musical grammar and syntax. Every musical phenomenon points to something beyond itself by reminding us of something, contrasting itself with something or arousing our expectations. The summation of such a transcendence of particulars constitutes the 'content'; it is what happens in music. But if musical structure or form is to be more than a set of didactic systems, it does not just embrace the content from outside; it is the thought process by which content is defined. Music becomes meaningful the more perfectly it defines itself in this sense—and not because its particular elements express something symbolically. It is by distancing itself from language that its resemblance to language finds its fulfilment.

Negative Dialectics, III.iii.12

Self-Reflection of Dialectics

The question is whether metaphysics as a knowledge of the absolute is at all possible without the construction of an absolute knowledge—without that idealism which supplied the title for the last chapter of Hegel's *Phenomenology.* Is a man who deals with the absolute not necessarily claiming to be the thinking organ with the capacity to do so, and thus the absolute himself? And on the other hand, if dialectics turned into a metaphysics that is not simply like dialectics, would it not violate its own strict concept of negativity?

Dialectics, the epitome of negative knowledge, will have nothing beside it; even a negative dialectics drags along the commandment of exclusiveness from the positive one, from the system. Such reasoning would require a nondialectical consciousness to be negated as finite and fallible. In all its historical forms, dialectics prohibited stepping out of it. Willy-nilly, it played the part of a conceptual mediator

between the unconditional spirit and the finite one; this is what intermittently kept making theology its enemy. Although dialectics allows
us to think the absolute, the absolute as transmitted by dialectics remains in bondage to conditioned thinking. If Hegel's absolute was a
secularization of the deity, it was still the deity's secularization; even
as the totality of mind and spirit, that absolute remained chained to
its finite human model.

But if our thought, fully aware of what it is doing, gropes beyond
itself—if in otherness it recognizes something which is downright incommensurable with it, but which it thinks anyway—then the only
shelter it will find lies in the dogmatic tradition. In such thoughts our
thinking is estranged from its content, unreconciled, and newly condemned to two kinds of truth, and that in turn would be incompat-
ible with the idea of truth. Metaphysics depends upon whether we
can get out of this aporia otherwise than by stealth. To this end, dialectics is obliged to make a final move: being at once the impression
and the critique of the universal delusive context, it must now turn
even against itself. The critique of every self-absolutizing particular is
a critique of the shadow which absoluteness casts upon the critique; it
is a critique of the fact that critique itself, contrary to its own tendency, must remain within the medium of the concept. It destroys the
claim of identity by testing and honoring it; therefore, it can reach no
farther than that claim. The claim is a magic circle that stamps critique with the appearance of absolute knowledge. It is up to the self-
reflection of critique to extinguish that claim, to extinguish it in the
very negation of negation that will not become a positing.

Dialectics is the self-consciousness of the objective context of
delusion; it does not mean to have escaped from that context. Its objective goal is to break out of the context from within. The strength
required from the break grows in dialectics from the context of immanence; what would apply to it once more is Hegel's dictum that in
dialectics an opponent's strength is absorbed and turned against him,
not just in the dialectical particular, but eventually in the whole. By
means of logic, dialectics grasps the coercive character of logic, hoping that it may yield—for that coercion itself is the mythical delusion,
the compulsory identity. But the absolute, as it hovers before metaphysics, would be the nonidentical that refuses to emerge until the
compulsion of identity has dissolved. Without a thesis of identity, dialectics is not the whole; but neither will it be a cardinal sin to depart
from it in a dialectical step.

It lies in the definition of negative dialectics that it will not come to rest in itself, as if it were total. This is its form of hope. Kant registered some of this in his doctrine of the transcendent thing-in-itself, beyond the mechanisms of identification. His successors, however stringently they criticized the doctrine, were reinforcing the spell, regressing like the post-revolutionary bourgeoisie as a whole: they hypostatized coercion itself as the absolute. Kant on his part, in defining the thing-in-itself as the intelligible being, had indeed conceived transcendence as nonidentical, but in equating it with the absolute subject he had bowed to the identity principle after all. The cognitive process that is supposed to bring us asymptotically close to the transcendent thing is pushing that thing ahead of it, so to speak, and removing it from our consciousness.

The identifications of the absolute transpose it upon man, the source of the identity principle. As they will admit now and then, and as enlightenment can strikingly point out to them every time, they are anthropomorphisms. This is why, at the approach of the mind, the absolute flees from the mind: its approach is a mirage. Probably, however, the successful elimination of any anthropomorphism, the elimination with which the delusive content seems removed, coincides in the end with that context, with absolute identity. Denying the mystery by identification, by ripping more and more scraps out of it, does not resolve it. Rather, as though in play, the mystery belies our control of nature by reminding us of the impotence of our power.

Enlightenment leaves practically nothing of the metaphysical content of truth—*presque rien*, to use a modern musical term. That which recedes keeps getting smaller and smaller, as Goethe describes it in the parable of New Melusine's box, designating an extremity. It grows more and more insignificant; this is why, in the critique of cognition as well as in the philosophy of history, metaphysics immigrates into micrology. Micrology is the place where metaphysics finds a haven from totality. No absolute can be expressed otherwise than in topics and categories of immanence, although neither in its conditionality nor as its totality is immanence to be deified.

According to its own concept, metaphysics cannot be a deductive context of judgments about things in being, and neither can it be conceived after the model of an absolute otherness terribly defying thought. It would be possible only as a legible constellation of things in being. From those it would get the material without which it would not be; it would not transfigure the existence of its elements, however, but would bring them into a configuration in which the elements unite to form a script. To that end, metaphysics must know how to wish. That the wish is a poor father to the thought has been one of the general theses of European enlightenment ever since Xenophanes, and the thesis applies undiminished to the attempts to restore ontology. But thinking, itself a mode of conduct, contains the need—the vital need, at the outset—in itself. The need is what we think from, even where we disdain wishful thinking. The motor of the need is the effort that involves thought as action. The object of critique is not the need in thinking, but the relationship between the two.

Yet the need in thinking is what makes us think. It asks to be negated by thinking; it must disappear in thought if it is to be really satisfied; and in this negation it survives. Represented in the inmost cell of thought is that which is unlike thought. The smallest intramundane traits would be of relevance to the absolute, for the micrological view cracks the shells of what, measured by the subsuming cover concept, is helplessly isolated and explodes its identity, the delusion that it is but a specimen. There is solidarity between such thinking and metaphysics at the time of its fall.

16. CAGE (1912–1992)

"Lecture on Nothing." In *Silence: Lectures and Writings* (Middletown, Conn.: Wesleyan University Press, 1961), pp. 109–118.

John Cage revolutionized the world of contemporary composition by his valorization of sounds divorced from any system of significance. Such sound is commonly considered "noise," but Cage accepted all audible phenomena as worthy of being musical material. He advocated compositions that would enable each sound to be heard and valued simply for its own sake, thus allowing Life back into the world of music, which had been sealed off and reserved for the controlled, intentional forms of Art. As Cage's theoretical reflections on his activity as a composer explain, "the key to this revolution is silence."[1]

What Cage means by "silence" is the whole living world of sound—everything that the art of manipulating sound, namely music, negates. A sound simply happening in the environment, during the timed pauses of conventional music, is "called silence only because it does not form part of a musical intention." Silence is the total freedom of the dimension of sound from artificial delimitations; it is sound allowed to be itself. As such, sound opens into an unconstrained, infinite dimension. This is what Cage has explored in his compositions, most provocatively in his "Silent Piece," consisting (originally) of exactly four minutes and thirty-three seconds of silence. The background noise that music attempts to cancel out is thereby discovered to be already saturated with *sounds* of "silence." These sounds—whatever sounds—are naturally there and are full of potentially intriguing musical significance, though they are usually covered over and deliberately ignored for the sake of intentional sound, which alone is allowed to count in conventional music. "Silence" in this sense is thus discovered as the richest, most all-encompassing of sounds. It is sound unintellectualized and undefined, but as such it is the

---

1. Jill Johnston, "There Is No Silence Now," *The Village Voice*, November 8, 1962, rpt. in *John Cage: An Anthology*, ed. Richard Kostelanetz (New York: Da Capo Press, 1991). Cage's theoretical writings are collected in *Silence: Lectures and Writings* (Middletown, Conn.: Wesleyan University Press, 1961) and in *A Year from Monday: New Lectures and Writings* (Middletown, Conn.: Wesleyan University Press, 1967).

undelimited source of all the energy and inspiration that sounds can communicate to us.

The delightfully entertaining "Lecture on Nothing" (1959) reflects Cage's interest in and affinities with Zen and other Eastern, apophatic traditions. It expresses a renunciation of the will to possess the sense and control even the direction and flow of one's own discourse. As a result, random phenomena suddenly become appreciable as free gifts of incalculable richness. In this key, Cage adapted methods from the ancient Chinese *Book of Changes* for his "chance operations." He advocated and implemented "indeterminacy" in the performance of music in order to enable performers to become co-creators of the music. His "Lecture" is also not without resonances of ascetic religious traditions that emphasize the value of humility and poverty of spirit. There is a surrender to the dark night of "Nothing," which thereby becomes luminous—and sonorous—day.

From "Lecture on Nothing"

This lecture was printed in Incontri Musicali, *August 1959. There are four measures in each line and twelve lines in each unit of the rhythmic structure. There are forty-eight such units, each having forty-eight measures. The whole is divided into five large parts, in the proportion 7, 6, 14, 14, 7. The forty-eight measures of each unit are likewise so divided. The text is printed in four columns to facilitate a rhythmic reading. Each line is to be read across the page from left to right, not down the columns in sequence. This should not be done in an artificial manner (which might result from an attempt to be too strictly faithful to the position of the words on the page), but with the* rubato *which one uses in everyday speech.*

I am here   ,   and there is nothing to say   .
                                                                    If among you are
those who wish to get   somewhere   ,   let them leave at
any moment   .   What we re‑quire   is
silence   ;   but what silence requires
               is   that I go on talking   .
                                                                    Give any one thought
                    a push   :   it falls down easily
;   but the pusher   and the pushed   pro‑duce   that enter‑
tainment   called   a dis‑cussion   .
                  Shall we have one later   ?

                                             ÷

Or   ,   we could simply de‑cide   not to have a dis‑
cussion   .   What ever you like   .   But
now   there are silences   and the
words   make   help make   the
silences   .

                                                          I have nothing to say
               and I am saying it   and that is
poetry   as I need it   . ·

                    This space of time   is organized
.   We need not fear these   silences, —
                                             ÷
we may love them   .

                                                                    This is a composed
talk   ,   for I am making it
               just as I make   a piece of music.   It is like a glass
                    of milk   .   We need the   glass
and we need the   milk   .   Or again   it is like an
empty glass   into which   at any
moment   anything   may be poured
.   As we go along   ,   (who knows?)
               an i‑dea may occur in this   talk   .
                                             I have no idea   whether one will
                    or not.   If one does,   let it.   Re‑
                                             ÷

gard it as something   seen   momentarily   ,   as
though   from a window   while traveling   .
If across Kansas   ,   then, of course,   Kansas
.   Arizona   is more interesting,
almost too interesting   ,   especially   for a New–Yorker   who is
being interested   in spite of himself   in everything.   Now he knows he
needs   the Kansas in him   .   Kansas is like
nothing on earth   ,   and for a New Yorker   very refreshing.
It is like an empty glass ,   nothing but wheat   ,   or
is it corn   ?   Does it matter which   ?
Kansas   has this about it: at any instant,   one may leave it,
and whenever one wishes one may return to it   .

÷

Or you may leave it   forever   and never return to it   ,
          for we pos–sess nothing   .   Our poetry now
          is the reali–zation   that we possess   nothing
.   Anything   therefore   is a delight
(since we do not   pos–sess it)   and thus   need not fear its loss
.   We need not destroy the   past: it is gone;
at any moment,   it might reappear and   seem to be   and be the present
.   Would it be a   repetition?   Only if we thought we
owned it,   but since we don't,   it is free   and so are we
.   Most anybody knows a–bout the future
          and how un–certain it is   .

÷

What I am calling   poetry   is often called   content.
I myself   have called   it form   .   It is the conti–
nuity   of a piece of music.   Continuity   today,
when it is necessary   ,   is a demonstration   of dis–
interestedness.   That is,   it is a proof   that our delight
lies in not   pos–sessing anything   .   Each moment
presents what happens .   How different
this form sense is   from that   which is bound up with
memory: themes   and secondary themes;   their struggle;
their development;   the climax;   the recapitulation   (which is the belief
that one may   own one's own home)   .   But actually,
unlike the snail   ,   we carry our homes   within us,

÷

which enables us   to fly   or to stay
, —   to enjoy   each.   But beware of
that which is   breathtakingly   beautiful,   for at any moment
                                 the telephone   may ring   or the airplane
come down in a   vacant lot   .   A piece of string
or a sunset   ,   possessing neither   ,
each acts   and the continuity   happens
.   Nothing more than   nothing   can be said.
Hearing   or making this   in music   is not different
—   only simpler—   than living this way   .
                                 Simpler, that is   ,   for me, — because it happens
                                 that I write music   .

                                           ÷ ÷

That music is   simple to make   comes from   one's willingness to ac–
cept   the limitations   of structure.   Structure is
simple   be–cause   it can be thought out,   figured out,
measured   .   It is a discipline   which,
accepted,   in return   accepts whatever   ,   even those
rare moments   of ecstasy,   which,   as sugar loaves train horses,
train us   to make what we make   .   How could I
better tell   what structure   is   than simply to
tell   about this,   this talk   which is
contained   within   a space of time   approximately
forty minutes   long   ?

                                           ÷

That forty minutes   has been divided into   five   large parts,   and
each unit   is divided   likewise.   Subdivision   in–
volving   a square root   is the only   possible subdivision which
permits   this micro–macrocosmic   rhythmic structure   ,
which I find so   acceptable   and accepting   .
As you see,   I can say anything   .
It makes very little   difference   what I say   or even how I say it.
At   this par–ticular moment,   we are passing through   the fourth
part   of a unit which is the   second unit in the second large
part of this talk   .   It is a little bit   like passing through Kansas
.   This, now, is the   end   of that second unit

.   .

                                           ÷

Now begins the   third unit   of the second part   .

                                                                    Now the

second part of that   third unit   .

                         Now its third part   .

                                                                    Now its fourth

part   (which, by the way,   is just the same

length   as the third part)   .

                         Now the fifth   and last part   .

                                        ÷

You have just   ex–perienced   the structure   of this talk   from a

microcosmic   point of view   .   From a macrocosmic

point of view   we are just passing the halfway point   in the second

large part.   The first part   was a rather rambling   discussion of

nothing   ,   of form,   and continuity

when it is the way we   now   need it.   This second

part   is about structure: how simple it is

,   what it is   and why   we should be willing   to

accept   its limitations.   Most speeches   are full   of

ideas.   This one   doesn't have to have   any

.   But at any moment   an idea   may come along

.   Then   we may enjoy it   .

                                        ÷

Structure   without life   is dead.   But Life   without

structure   is un–seen   .   Pure life

expresses itself   within   and through structure

.   Each moment   is absolute,   alive and sig–

nificant.   Blackbirds   rise   from a field making   a

sound   de–licious   be–yond   com–pare

.   I heard them

because   I ac–cepted   the limitations   of an arts

conference   in a Virginia   girls' finishing school,   which limitations

allowed me   quite by accident   to hear the blackbirds

as they flew up and   overhead   .   There was a social

calendar   and hours for breakfast   ,   but one day I saw a

                                        ÷

cardinal   ,   and the same day   heard a woodpecker.
I also met   America's youngest   college president   .
However,   she has resigned,   and people say she is   going into politics
.   Let her.   Why shouldn't she?   I also had the
pleasure   of hearing an eminent   music critic   ex–claim
that he hoped   he would live long   e–nough   to see the end
        of this craze for Bach.   A pupil once   said to me: I
understand   what you say about   Beethoven   and I think
I agree   but I have a   very serious   question   to
ask you: How do you   feel   about Bach
?   Now we have come   to the end   of the
part   about structure   .

÷ ÷

However,   it oc–curs   to me to say more   about structure
.   Specifically   this: We are
now at   the be–ginning   of the third part   and that part
is not the part   devoted   to structure.   It's the part
about material.   But I'm still talking   about structure.   It must be
clear from that   that structure   has   no point,   and,
as we have seen,   form   has no point either.   Clearly we are be–
ginning to get   nowhere   .

                    Unless some   other i–dea crops up   a–bout it that is
all I have   to say about structure   .

÷

Now about   material: is it interesting   ?
It is and it   isn't   .   But one thing is
certain.   If one is making   something   which is to be nothing
,   the one making must   love   and be patient   with
the material   he chooses.   Otherwise   he calls attention to the
material,   which is precisely something   ,   whereas it was
nothing   that was being made;   or   he calls attention to
himself,   whereas   nothing is anonymous   .
                    The technique   of handling materials   is, on the sense level
what structure as a   discipline is   on the rational level   :
                    a means   of experiencing   nothing
.

÷

I remember loving   sound   before I ever   took a music lesson
.   And so we make our   lives   by what we love
.   (Last year   when I talked here   I made a short talk.
That was because   I was talking   about something   ;   but
this year   I am talking   about nothing   and
of course will go on   talking   for a long time   .)
                                                      The other day a
pupil said,   after trying to compose   a melody   using only
three tones,   "I   felt limited   ."

          Had she   con–cerned herself   with the three tones —
her materials   —   she would not   have felt limited
                              ÷
,   and   since materials   are without feeling,
there would not have   been   any limitation.   It was all in her
mind   ,   whereas it be–longed   in the
materials   .   It became something
by not being   nothing;   it would have been   nothing by being
something   .

                                          Should one use the
materials   characteristic   of one's time   ?
Now there's a question   that ought to get us   somewhere
.   It is an intel–   lectual question
.   I shall answer it   slowly   and
autobiographically   .
                              ÷
I remember   as a child   loving   all the sounds
,   even the unprepared   ones.   I liked them
especially   when there was one at   a time   .
                     A five-finger exercise   for one hand was
full of beauty   .   Later on I
gradually liked   all the intervals   .

                                          As I look back
I realize   that I be–gan liking the octave   ;   I accepted the
major and minor   thirds.   Perhaps,   of all the intervals,
I liked these thirds   least   .   Through the music of
Grieg,   I became passionately   fond   of the fifth
.
                              ÷

Or perhaps you   could call it   puppy–dog love   ,
              for the fifth did not make me   want to write music: it made me want to de–
vote my life to   playing the works of Grieg   .
                    When later I heard   modern music,
I took, like a duck   to water, to all the   modern intervals: the sevenths,   the
seconds,   the tritone,   and the fourth   .
                    I liked Bach too   a–bout this time   ,   but I
didn't like the sound   of the thirds and sixths.   What I admired in
Bach   was the way   many things   went together
.   As I keep on   re–membering,   I see that I never
really liked the   thirds,   and this explains   why I never really
liked Brahms   .

÷

Modern music   fascinated me   with all its modern   intervals: the
sevenths,   the seconds,   the tritone,   and the fourth   and
always,   every now and then,   there was a fifth,   and that pleased me
.   Sometimes   there were single tones,   not intervals at
all,   and that was a de–   light.   There were so many in–
tervals in modern music that it fascinated   me rather than that I   loved it, and being
fascinated by it I   de–cided   to write it.   Writing it at
first   is difficult: that is,   putting the mind on it
takes the ear off it   .   However,   doing it alone,
I was free to hear   that a high sound   is different   from a
low sound even when both are called by the   same letter.   After several years of
working alone   ,   I began to feel   lonely.

÷

Studying with a   teacher,   I learned that the   intervals   have
meaning;   they are not just   sounds   but they imply
in their progressions   a sound   not actually present to the ear
.   Tonality.   I never liked tonality   .
I worked at it   .   Studied it.   But I never had any
feeling for it   :   for instance: there are some   pro–
gressions called   de–ceptive cadences.   The idea is this: progress in such a way
as to imply   the presence   of a tone not actually   present;   then
fool everyone by not   landing on it —   land somewhere else.   What is being
fooled   ?   Not the ear   but the mind
.   The whole question is   very intellectual   .
However   modern music   still fascinated me

÷

with all its modern   intervals   .   But in order to
have them   ,   the mind had fixed it   so that one had to a–
void having   pro–gressions that would   make one think of   sounds that were
not actually present   to the ear   .   Avoiding
did   not   ap–peal to me   .   I began to see
that the separation of   mind and ear   had spoiled   the sounds
, —   that a clean slate   was necessary.   This made me
not only contemporary ,   but "avant-garde."   I used noises
.   They had not been   in–tellectualized;   the ear could hear them
directly   and didn't have to go through any   abstraction   a–bout them
.   I found that I   liked noises   even more than I
liked intervals.   I liked noises   just as much as I had   liked single sounds

÷

.

                                                    Noises, too
,   had been dis–criminated against   ;   and being American,
having been trained   to be sentimental,   I fought   for noises. I liked being
on the side of the   underdog   .
I got police   per–mission   to play sirens.   The most amazing noise
I ever found   was that produced by   means of a coil of wire   attached to the
pickup arm   of a phonograph and then   amplified.   It was shocking,
really shocking,   and thunderous   .   Half intellectually   and
half sentimentally   , when the war came   a–long,   I decided to use
only   quiet sounds   .   There seemed to me
to be no truth,   no good,   in anything big   in society.

÷

But quiet sounds   were like loneliness   ,   or
love   or friendship   .   Permanent, I thought
,   values,   independent   at least from
Life, Time and   Coca-Cola   .   I must say
I still feel this way   ,   but something else is   happening
:   I begin to hear   the old sounds
—   the ones I had thought   worn out,   worn out by
intellectualization—   I begin to hear   the old sounds   as
though they are   not worn out   .   Obviously, they are
not worn out   .   They are just as   audible   as the
new sounds.   Thinking   had worn them out   .
        And if one stops thinking about   them,   suddenly they are

÷

fresh   and new.   "If you think   you are a ghost
you will become a   ghost   ."   Thinking the sounds
worn out   wore them out   .   So you see
:   this question   .   brings us back
where we were: nowhere   ,   or,
if you like   ,   where we are   .
                                               I have a story: "There was once a man
standing on a high elevation. A company of several men who happened to be walking on the road
noticed from the distance the man standing on the high place and talked among themselves about
this man. One of them said: He must have lost his favorite animal. Another man said
:   No, it must be his friend whom he is looking for. A third one said:
He is just enjoying the cool air up there. The three could not   a–gree   and the dis–

÷

cussion   (Shall we have one   later?) went on until   they reached the high
place where the man   was   .   One of the three
asked: O, friend   standing up there   ,   have you not
lost your pet animal   ?   No, sir,   I have not lost any
.   The second man asked :   Have you not lost your friend
?   No, sir   ,   I have not lost my friend
either   .   The third man asked: Are you not enjoying
the fresh breeze   up there?   No, sir   ,
I am not   .   What, then
,   are you standing up there   for   ,
             if you say no   to all our
questions   ?   The man on high said   :

÷

I just stand   ."

                                                                          If there are
no questions,   there are no answers .   If there are questions
,   then, of course,   there are answers   ,   but the
final answer   makes the   questions,   seem absurd
,   whereas the questions,   up until then,   seem more intelligent
than the answers   .   Somebody asked   De–
bussy   how he wrote   music.   He said:
I take all the tones   there are,   leave out the ones I   don't want,   and
use all the others   .   Satie said   :
When I was young,   people told me: You'll see when   you're fifty years old
.   Now I'm fifty   .   I've seen nothing   .

÷ ÷

Here we are now   at the beginning
        of the fourth large part   of this talk.
More and more   I have the feeling   that we are getting
nowhere.   Slowly   ,   as the talk goes on
,   we are getting   nowhere   and that is a pleasure

[...]

17. JANKÉLÉVITCH (1903–1985)

"Musique et Silence." In *La Musique et L'Ineffable* (Paris: Seuil, 1983; originally Paris: A. Colin, 1961), pp 161–190.

Trans. Carolyn Abbate as "Music and Silence," in *Music and the Ineffable* (Princeton: Princeton University Press, 2003), pp. 130–155.

Of Russian Jewish extraction, Vladimir Jankélévitch grew up in France and held posts as professor of philosophy in Lille and Paris. Throughout his life, his philosophical reflections, especially about time and its disjunctive, irreversible character, in the wake of Bergson and Heidegger, developed in tandem with his writings on music as a purely temporal modality of sense. His many books about music overwhelmingly privilege "contemporary" composers of Russia and France, such as Rimski-Korsakov, Rachmaninov, Moussorgski, Stravinski, Debussy, Fauré, Satie, and Ravel. Their works revealed to him the vocation of music to allude to the ineffable, which no verbal representation can express so directly.

Jankélévitch opposes the tendency of philosophy from Plato to Schopenhauer to understand music discursively as either ethical expression or the interpretation of metaphysical reality. He rejects all the rhetorical terms (exposition, theme, development) typical of music theory. He does not deny meaning to music, but he maintains that it is unlike discursive meaning in being "infinitely equivocal" and only "the sense of sense," hence inarticulable. Jankélévitch thereby undertakes to explain why music is peculiarly apt to open the horizon of the inexpressible. He conceives of music as silence interrupted or provisionally suspended ("la musique est un silence interrompu ou provisoirement suspendu," p. 167). Music breathes only in the oxygen of silence ("la musique ne respire que dans l'oxygène du silence," p. 168). Silence is conceived not as an interruption in the continuum of sound but rather, inversely, as the alpha and omega that all sound and especially music flows from and inflects, so as to render it audible.

Music does this most effectively by its own attenuation, its *pianissimo*, its virtual disappearance, its becoming *almost* nothing ("presque rien"). This attenuation is not cessation. Only the decrescendo toward extinction can signal the silence that otherwise is nothing, since it can never be present itself purely and simply as Nothing. By thus minimizing itself and its differentiated articulations of sound, music lends expression to the absolute unity and perfect order of silence that every more casual, complicated, and chaotic sound in the wide world of noise inevitably drowns out. Jankélévitch insists, therefore, on a relative notion of silence: it is not an absolute absence of sound, since such an abstract nonentity cannot be experienced, but a specific privation that renders perceptible an inexhaustible plenitude in another dimension—that of the inaudible, the supra-sensible. The topos of silence at midday, in the maximum effulgence of light, symbolizes this plenum perceived through a specific kind of absence, or a void in one sensory modality coupled with saturation in another.

Jankélévitch's writing on music is extremely poetic and evocative of the inexpressible that it theorizes. It has a contradictory way of taking back what it says so as, like music, to express nothing ("ne rien exprimer") or to achieve expressionless expression ("expression inexpressive"). In his interviews, he declared it necessary to write not *about* music but *with* music, musically.[1] His own writing by its poetry conveys this sense of rapture in the experience through music of what words cannot say.

———————————

1. V. Jankélévitch and B. Berlowitz, *Quelque part dans l'inachevé* (Paris: Gallimard, 1978), pp. 247–248.

Music and Silence

"In silence": the last words that appear in Jean Wahl's treatise on metaphysics. To apply these words to music—under the pretext that music, being born of silence, withdraws into silence—would perhaps mean confusing metaphysics with the metaphorical, and disfigure the ideas of a singular poet-philosopher. Nonetheless, the eschatological model is tempting: imagine the blank backdrop, the fabric upon which the noises of life and nature and music ultimately inscribe themselves. Just as experience (according to certain sensualist and substantialist epistemologies) carves ornamental signs into the tabula rasa, into original nonconsciousness, and just as the painter's brush deposits the picturesque wildness of color on a colorless and uniform canvas, so the unwritten page that is silence, original nothingness, gradually fills up with tumult. In this case, it is the world of noises and sounds that would constitute a parenthesis in the backdrop of silence, and that would emerge from an ocean of silence, like a ray of light that illuminates homogenous space, the black void of the χώρα (chora), for a few instants.

This is the impression made by the tolling of the discordant, arhythmic bells in Louis Vuillemin,[1] which come from a distance, and usher in the evening above the open window, among the ribbons of cloud. Noise in this case is connected to human presence, which—as loud as it may be with its cackling and shrieking and trumpets and shrill rattles—is a sigh barely audible in the eternal silence of infinite space. This presence, like civilization itself, must affirm and reaffirm itself without end, by constant vigilance and self defense, to resist the invasion of nothingness. And just as abandoned places will become overgrown, covered in wild grass little by little, from the moment we relax our vigilance, just as the most animated cities will disappear under the earth if human beings do not constantly maintain them and reclaim them from the sands, so even the most clamorous earthly reputation, sooner or later—that is to say, ultimately—will end up lost in the oceanic immensity of endless time. Oblivion, which is a kind of silence, will eventually submerge it; only a few distant memories will remain floating, and they in turn are attenuated little by little, and finally disappear completely.

If existence—which we suppose to be fragile, superficial, and provisional—tends asymptotically toward nothingness, then music, gradually exhausting all possible combinations of sounds, tends inexorably toward silence. More generally, noise accompanies change and signals mutability, the shifting of one state into another, which occurs in time. Effective movement or spatial displacement—the simplest form of change—produces an acoustic vibration in the air and is realized in consequence as disorder or chaos, acoustic agitation and cacophony. Bare time, abstract time, is silent time, but Becoming

---

1. *Soirs amoricains* op. 21, no. 1: "Au large des clochers."

is filled with events and occurrences, fitted out with concrete contents fashioned from noise. Noises succeed one another and sounds imply continuation, imply it intensely, like the notes a singer sustains and extends with vibrato: time is their natural dimension. And conversely, death is a form of stagnation, which, arresting the process of Becoming as it does all movement, forces loquacious events to fall into silence. The living, as everyone knows, have a superstitious habit of speaking softly in the presence of the dead, even though one cannot disturb a corpse and though this would actually be the proper moment to raise one's voice, loudly and vociferously. "Careful! Now we need to speak softly," says Arkel in *Pelléas* act 5, in the tongue of Michelangelo. Thus it is the living who fall in step with a lethal eternity and its quietude, where nothing will happen again, or survive, or become: history and with it the entire fracas of event has forever deserted this new eon, so perfectly void of all occurrence.

Life floats like a raft on this great volume of silence, a silence that makes all human noise a bit precarious, and makes the enchanted island that is art so precious. Poetry is a sonorous island in an ocean of prose; or (to evoke other images), the living oasis of music and poetry is as if lost in muteness, in the immense desert of prosaic existence. Just as architecture is the artifice that fills space with formal volumes, cubes and towers, just as painting populates a monochromatic surface with color—that is, with the positive polarity, the diversity inherent in multicolored splashes—so music and poetry animate time, superficially, by means of rhythm as well as mellifluous noise. Music stands out from silence and has need of silence in the same way that life has need of death, and thought—according to Plato's *Sophist*—has need of nonbeing. As something similar to a work of art, life is an animated, limited construction that stands out against lethal infinity; and music, as something similar to life—as a melodious construction, magic duration, an ephemeral adventure, and brief encounter—is isolated, between beginning and end, in the immensity of nonbeing.

Thus, one can distinguish between anterior silence and consequent silence, which are to one another as alpha to omega. The silence-before and the silence-after are no more mutually "symmetric" than beginning and end, or birth and death, within the irreversible unspooling of time.[2] Symmetry is a spatial image. A double silence

---

2. Jean Cassou, *Trois poètes*, 73, 110, silence is the "cradle of music."

bathes Debussy's music, which floats, entire, on a peaceful, silent sea. *E silentio, ad silentium, per silentium:* from silence to silence, across silence: this could be the motto of Debussy's music, since silence suffuses it, in each of its parts. If Debussy's music is thus foreshortened cosmogony, a recapitulation of the world's history, then *Pelléas et Mélisande* is in turn a foreshortening of the foreshortened. The first act begins with a mysterious noise in the lowest registers, behind which one can make out the theme associated with Golaud, dull and faraway, galloping rhythm, and soon Mélisande's theme as well: fate plots the meeting of two unknown figures in the forest, with two themes at its side. This silence is a precursor, an advance runner: silence as annunciation of the storm.

But it does not always announce a tragedy: in general, it is rather a prophetic silence, prophesying that something will appear. This is the silence that suddenly comes into being just before a concert, when the conductor's baton suppresses the cacophony of instruments and, with the first beat of the first measure, releases a harmonious symphonic torrent. And to the degree that initial silence is a promise, or a threat, terminal silence designates instead the nothingness to which life returns: music born of silence returns to silence. *Pelléas* is encompassed by the two silences. At the end of act 5, a Mélisande without substance disappears into a murmur: that which was almost nonexistent stops existing at all. "And the rest is silence."[3] There is nothing more, nothing, as at the end of Debussy's song "Colloque sentimental," where, on a frigid night, solitude and wind carry off the last words spoken by a pair of spectral lovers. Listen to the silence at the end of act 5 of *Pelléas*, silence "more silent than the soul," than death, more than all the most silent things there are. In the steppes of central Asia, an interminable ennui where a caravan, escorted by Russian soldiers, winds across the plains, some harmonious singing draws nearer, fades into distance, and finally loses itself, reabsorbed into immensity. The obstinate horizontal monotone of a dominant pedal dies out into gray uniformity; nothing remains but sand and silence.[4] The lumbering of a chariot crossing the steppe expires at the horizon.[5] The last brass bands at the festival (in Debussy's "Fêtes"), the last sighs of the bagpipe (in Bartók), the last sobs of the

3. See Aldous Huxley's essay "Music at Night."
4. Borodin: his essence.
5. Musorgsky, *Bïdlo* (from *Pictures at an Exhibition*).

mandolin (in Musorgsky) dissipate in silence.[6] *On doute—la nuit—
J'écoute—Tout fuit—Tout passe—L'espace—Efface—Le bruit.* Alain
admired these lines from Victor Hugo's *Djinns,* since it is gray desert
sand, like Siberia's solitude, that submerges all noise.[7] In all reality,
"one hears nothing more."[8]

For this reason, the works of Franz Liszt, noisy with heroism,
with epic pomp and triumphal glare, find themselves gradually in-
vaded by silence with approaching old age. A maternal silence enters
into their every pore; long pauses come to interrupt recitatives, great
voids, empty staves and measures that rarify each note, detach it from
all others. The music of the *Messe basse,* the *Valses oubliées,* the *Gon-
dole funèbre,* and the symphonic poem *Du berceau à la tombe,* becomes increasingly discontinuous. Nothingness, like the encroaching
sand, invades the melody, desiccates its verve. Could one not say that
silence exists before, after, and during? At once on both flanks and in
the interval between?

But noise's relation to silence could also be conceived in the opposite way. According to eschatology—a science that considers ins
and outs, envisages the beginning of beginnings and the end of all
ends—noise is the island in the sea, the oasis or secret garden in the
sands. If one considers the empirical fact of continuation, however,
then silence instead would constitute the interruption or the discontinuous pause within the continuity of incessant sound. Noise is
not suspended silence, but silence is noise that has ended, and the
suspension of continuity. Previously, it was change itself—living, increasing diversity—that stood out from boredom's uniform ocean-
ography and that troubled a preexisting and subterranean continu-
ousness. Silence was the backdrop suspended under Being. But now,
it is noise that constitutes a sonorous foundation, suspended under
silence. And this continuous pedal point, this obstinate fundamental
bass skewered by momentary silence is indeed more imperceptible
than the sound of the sea: it lasts our whole life and accompanies all

6. Musorgsky, *Il vecchio castello* (ibid.), Bartók, *Pro děti* (*For Children,*
no. 42); Debussy "Fêtes," from the *Nocturnes for Orchestra.*

7. "One doubts—the night—I hear—everything flees—everything
passes—in space—effacing—all noise." See Alain's commentary, *Préliminaires
à l'esthétique,* 271.

8. Ravel, *Histoires naturelles,* "Le Grillon." See also *Pelléas et Mélisande,*
act 2, scene 1.

we experience, fills our ears from the time we are born to the moment we die. As an interruption, a momentary lacuna that mars the noisy animation of Becoming, silence blossoms through voids that interrupt a perpetual din.

Now I am calling it a "din": but is it not what I called "silence" before? In the first instance, man as a creature of distractions isolated himself on his little islet of sonority to beguile away the anguish of solitude and the silence that deforms being—like a traveler lost in the night, who talks and laughs as loudly as possible to persuade himself that he is not afraid, who believes that he has put death's phantoms to flight, thanks to this noisy protective screen. Whereas now this has been inverted: the person assailed by cacophony, covering his ears, wants to protect his slip of a silent garden, shelter his little islet of silence, because henceforth it is silence that insulates, and not noise. With Debussy, music appears suddenly out of silence, where music is silence interrupted or suspended provisionally. But, being entirely *en sourdine* (muted), Fauré's music instead is itself a form of silence, the interruption of noise, a silence that breaks into noise: silence is no longer analogous to nothingness, or a source of anguish, but is a haven where contemplation co-exists with total quiet. The "Île joyeuse," to the extent that it is a sonorous island in an expanse of silence, an island of singing and laughing and crashing cymbals, is Debussy's chimera, and his alone—because it is for Debussy that jubilation is an enclave smack in the middle of nonbeing, the parenthesis delimiting nothingness.

Conversely for Fauré, the "Jardin clos," *hortus conclusus* as the Song of Songs calls it (long before Charles van Leberghe), could only be a silent garden, the garden of quietude, just as the islet whose mystery in evoked by Rachmaninoff (with Konstantin Balmont) is all silence, all somnolence.[9] This second kind of silence is no longer the limitless ocean or the unformed grayness of the ἄπειρον (infinite); rather, it delimits a well-circumscribed zone within the universal din. Rimsky-Korsakov's operas like to carve out a lake in the midst of their swarming landscapes, and this lake is a zone of solitude and silence: because a lake, which is itself closure, *hortus conclusus*—the silent island—clears a mute space at the heart of the din, just as the

9. Rachmaninoff, *Ostrovok* op. 14. Chabrier, *L'île heureuse*. Debussy, *L'île joyeuse*.

island of sonority is isolated within the immensity of silence.[10] So it is that intramusical silences or sighs—the numbered rests, subject to the chronometer, carefully timed—aerate the mass of musical discourse according to the exact rule of the metronome, since music can only breathe when it has the oxygen of silence. Conversely, ambient music filters by osmosis into the middle of an empty measure, to color and qualify silence. Just as microsilences (tiny silences within silence) will aerate endless melody, so restful shores of silence in the middle of universal noisiness constitute a safe haven for repose and reverie. No longer intoxicated with conversation as a means to fill crushing silences at all costs, a human being will now seek out the remaining slicks and shallow pools of silence, that conversation might be cut short. Her goal is no longer distraction, but contemplation.

Because silence is in itself obscure, and an object of dread, it has a function: silence is, after all, not nothingness. Absolute silence, like pure space or bare time, is an inconceivable limit. As Aristotle has already affirmed: οὐ πᾶν τὸ ἀχίνητον ἠρεμεῖ (not everything motionless is at rest).[11] What is immobile is not in repose; this fallow somnolence must conceal some deep activity. Francis Bacon says that silence is the sleep that feeds wisdom; and again, that silence is thought being fermented. Silence is one of the "negative measures" whose positive quality was affirmed by Kant, in opposition to Leibniz (the man of "reduced perceptions"). Nothingness, one might say, has no properties. One nothing cannot be distinguished from another nothing. How could they be distinguished without having qualities or a manner of being; that is, without, at least, being something? Two nothings are only a single, same nothing, a single, same zero. But silence has differential properties: and as a result, this particular nothingness is not *nothing at all*—in other words, it is not (like Parmenides' nothingness) the negation of all being; it is not a nonbeing that totally annihilates or contradicts total being. In Schelling's terms, it would be more μὴ ὄν (potential not being) than οὐχ ὄν (actual not being).

In this instance, nothingness is not the simultaneous negation of all qualities perceptible to the senses; rather, it excludes only a single

---

10. See *May Night,* act 3; *The Legend of the Invisible City of Kitezh,* act 3, scene 3; *Snegurochka,* act 4; *Mlada,* acts 2 and 4; *Sadko,* act 2.

11. Aristotle, *Physics,* 221b.

category of sensation, that of physiological hearing. Flying his true nominalist colors in denouncing the unimaginable absurdity that is "nothingness," Bergson showed that it is impossible to suppress one category of perceptions without reconstituting another in some way. Someone who closes his or her eyes to experience blindness continues to hear; someone who stops his or her ears to experience silence continues to see; and if struck blind and deaf with a single blow, still feels heat, perceives scent, and is granted coenesthesic impressions. Effacing one sense always entails the accession, even the enlivening, of another: plenitude alternates and is displaced but is never radically annihilated. Thus, silence is in turn a relative or partial nothingness and not absolute nothingness.

The most characteristic form of silence is silence brightly illuminated (though such a claim hardly entails denying that there is nocturnal silence as well). But Schelling himself observes that night favors the propagation of sounds, that night exalts sound in the same way that it draws out perfume: the composer who wrote *Les sons et les parfums tournent dans l'air du soir* dedicated the second movement of *Iberia* to the "perfumes of the night." What is true for Debussy is no less true for Albeniz: *Cordoba, La Vega,* and Loti's *Le Crépuscule* all evoke darkness made aromatic by carnations and jasmine. In the dark, our auditory perception is enhanced: and, vice versa, it is often in the full daylight that silence is most thunderous.

The silence of noon, which is the nonexistence of the auditory contrasted with a plenitude of optical existence, takes the paradox to its extreme. Noon: in the immobile suspension where all presences coexist, when the sun at its zenith reigns over a universal convocation of beings and beckons them to the siesta, when all things *are,* in actuality, and the shadow line of the virtual no longer creates any effect of contour or relief among them, no longer carves out a zone of innuendo behind them, when time, having arrived at its apogee, when time itself seems to hesitate, then the contrast between clairvoyance (which is plenitude) and silence (which is a void) reaches its point of greatest tension. This meridinal hour, quasi-indifferent, the hour of maximum clarity, the hour that Plato's *Phaedrus* calls μεσημβρία σταθερά (high noon),[12] the hour of Debussyian silence par excellence, the hour when the faun's flute begins to unfold its cantilena:

---

12. *Phaedrus* 242a.

this is the noon that is prelude to that most famous of summer after-
noons. At noon, great Pan himself (as Fyodor Ivanovich Tyuchev
says) falls asleep among a flock of nymphs, as clouds gather lazily in
the sky. Pan's son is Din, and Echo is his fiancée: and even Pan, who
made Syrinx, Pan who is the rustling of the springs and the wind's
tremors, even he becomes quiet at the exact center of day, when the
wind falls asleep. And in order not to disturb Pan's siesta, shepherds
stop blowing their rustic instruments. Schelling spoke marvelously
of the "panic silence" that suffuses a countryside that is bombarded
with light.

Things fall mute, and their muteness renders their dishearten-
ing evident-ness paradoxically enigmatic. At the opening of his collection *Impressions d'été* (*Letni dojmy*), Josef Suk allows a perfect
triad in B major to vibrate in an almost immobile state, a fascinating,
mid-day drone, as hypnotic as a lullaby. Is this not panic, static silence, in the form of sustained sound? The gentle rumor of the *silentium meridianum*? Even Debussy's first symphonic *Nocturne*,
"Nuages," is silence bathed in light.

It is not just that silence is the nothingness of a single category
of sensations within the plenitude of all others: silence itself is never
complete. The most ordinary form of silence is the silence of words.
The Ecclesiastes makes a distinction between two "occasions," χαιρὸς
τοῦ σιγᾶν χαὶ χαιρος τοῦ λαλεῖν (there is a time to be silent, and a
time to speak). Silence gives us respite from deafening verbal clamor,
just as the word gives respite from overwhelming silence. Silence is
not nonbeing, not at all, since it is simply something *other* than the
noise made by words. If the "loquela," as the preachers say, is truly the
human noise par excellence, then the muteness that suppresses
this noise will be a privileged form of silence. Music is the silence of
words, just as poetry is the silence of prose. Music, as sonorous presence, fills silence full, and yet music is itself a manner of silence: there
is a relative silence that consists in a change in the order of noise
being heard, a move from unformed, fortuitous din to sonorous
form, just as there is repose that consists in a change in one's degree
of fatigue.

To say, "We need to be quiet," one must already have made a bit
of noise. For example, to say that we do not need to speak about
music, one needs to speak, and philosophy itself, as a whole, attempts
to explain the following: that it is better not to try to say the unsayable.

Nonetheless, one must make music to obtain silence. Music, which is in itself composed of so many noises, is the silence of all other noises, because as soon as music raises its voice, it demands solitude and insists that it occupy vibrating space alone, excluding other sounds. The melodic wave never shares the place that it insists upon filling up by itself. Music is a sort of silence, and one needs silence in order to hear music; the one silence is necessary to hear the other, melodious silence. As melodious, measured noise, enchanted noise, music needs to be surrounded by silence. Music imposes silence upon words and their soft purring, that is, upon the most facile and voluble noise of all, the noise of idle chatter. Noise is left speechless, the better to hear the incantation. Presences can coexist in space, but in the sounding succession of noises, simultaneity is mutually disturbing and uncoordinated voices will mutually disturb one another. Those voices require either polyphonic synchronization or the precaution of silence, which isolates music from cackling conversation.

And yet music, forcing human beings to be quiet, is also imposing something on their voices: the sustained, faintly solemn intonations of singing. Singing does away with telling, or saying. Singing is a way of being quiet. Federico Mompou gave the name *Musica callada* to a suite of nine small "pieces" that I would have called nine "silences," in which the *soledad sonora* of St. John of the Cross is given a chance to sing. Music rises up out of silence, divine music. With Ravel, when the crickets' chirping stops ("one hears nothing more"), vast chords ascend in the night sky; when pointless conversations cease, music (like supplication) will populate the empty space. With this, music buoys up the heavy weight of logos, loosens the devastating hegemony of the word, and prevents the human genus from becoming overidentified with the spoken alone. In Ravel, the "musician of silence" described by Mallarmé assumed earthly form.[13]

Furthermore, music is not just discourse fallen silent. The "silence of music" is itself a constituent part of audible music. It is not just that music needs words to fall silent so that it might sing: silence also inhabits and dampens audible music. Laconic tendencies, reticence, and the pianissimo are like silences within silence. In effect, brachylogy—brevity, concision of diction—is a form of silence in the music of Satie or Mompou. The *pièce brève* is a silence not in that it

13. In "Sainte," set to music by Ravel.

emerges from silence, but indirectly, in that it expresses a desire to retighten the grip, a will to concentration. Concision harbors the wish to disturb silence as little as possible. Thus *reticence* must be considered a privileged form of silence: for the silence that is no longer "tacit" or simply "taciturn," but "reticent," is a special form of silence, the one that arises quite suddenly, at the brink of mystery, at the threshold of the ineffable, where the vanity and impotence of words have become all too obvious. Reticence is a refusal to go on and on, resistance to the practice of inertia, to the ease of oratorical automatism. It says "No!" to the temptations of verbosity and to loquacious puffery, and in this is a costly and wholly astonishing choice: for freedom. Just as "will"—a semantic negative, in the sense of something imposed upon others, or as desire—can in fact be more positive than "consent," so *not saying* is often more persuasive than *saying everything*. There is a sort of mental reserve in the face of the inexpressible, which goes beyond anger suppressing its threat, beyond innuendo (which prefers to insinuate or imply), and this reserve flows not so much from a sense of discouragement as from an intimation of poetry, from the glimpse of the mystery.

According to Plotinus, this is the mystic ecstasy of the sage, who, having rejected all forms of discourse, πάντα λόγον ἀφείς, "putting away all reasoning,"[14] no longer dares to offer a single word, οὐδ᾽ ἂν ὅλως φθέγξασθαι δύναιτο, "nor is he able to utter a word."[15] Music in its entirety—in that it causes words to be quiet, commands the cessation of noise—could thus be the silence of discourse. And music itself, as we have seen, sometimes expresses itself allusively, half-speaking, not at all exhaustively. Plotinus's suspension of logos and Debussy's interrupted serenade are two ways to strangle eloquence, two forms of human propriety in the face of the untellable. What do they tell us, these moments where implications are left hanging? They are saying, Finish this yourselves because I have said too much. Like Arkel, they whisper that the human soul is very, very silent; "she needs silence, now."[16] In opposition to logos with its surfeit of eloquence, which wants to say everything and claims to speak of everything, they elect to suggest, to advise us gently that we should leave

---

14. *Enneads* VI.8, 19.
15. *Enneads* VI.8, 19.
16. *Pelléas*, act 5, scene 2.

Louis Aubert, *Crépuscules d'Automne* no. 3, "Silence"

in silence, σιωπή σαντας δεῖ ἀπελθεῖν, "we must go away in si-lence."[17]

I would claim that musical silence is not the void; and in effect it is also not only "cessation." Instead, it is "attenuation." Like reticence, or interrupted development, it expresses the wish to return to silence as soon as possible; an attenuation of intensity, it is at the threshold of the inaudible, a game played with almost-nothing.

So listen more closely! The pianissimo, though still audible, is the almost imperceptible form of the supersensory: it is *hardly* percep-tible. On the border of the material and immaterial, of the physical and transphysical, the almost-nothing designates minimal existence, beyond which would be nonexistence, nothing pure and simple.[18] The great masters of the pianissimo, Fauré, Debussy, and Albeniz, op-erate at the limits of noise and silence, in the border zone where those with particularly sharp ears will perceive an infinitesimal sound, mi-cromusic. No hand is light enough, or so imponderable, that it could

---

17. *Enneads* VI.8, 11.

18. Almost-nothings: Debussy, the end of *Pelléas*, act 1; "Les Cloches à travers les feuilles" from the *Images* for piano; *Mouvement* for piano; the end of *Jeux;* the end of "Brouillards." Nothing more: Debussy, the end of *Lindaraja* for two pianos; the end of "Le Faune" (*Fêtes galantes* II); the end of "Colloque sen-timental"; "De grève" from *Proses lyriques.*

extricate from the piano every infratone and ultratone taken prisoner by Albeniz's divine *Jerez*. Archangelic hands would be needed, and they would still be too heavy for this art of brushing lightly, for an immaterial contact even more imperceptible than the phantom touch of the asymptote. At the end of *Fête-Dieu à Seville*, music itself becomes a supernatural silence, a mysterious silence. Gabriel Fauré, the poet of half-light and the penumbra (like Michelangelo or Maeterlinck) invites us to speak softly, "very softly" (the last words of Verlaine's poem "C'est l'extase" and the last words—almost—of *Pelléas et Mélisande*). "Let us delve into our love for deep silence," says "En sourdine," one of Verlaine's *Fêtes galantes* in its whispering, rustling night. Just as human beings keep watch for the "indistinct threshold where night becomes dawn"[19] and the moment when day begins to darken, that they might witness the messages borne by dawn and twilight, so they listen, passionately, for the birth and extinguishing of sound, that they might overhear the secrets harbored by life, and death. If the first and last verses of Victor Hugo's *Djinns* correspond to the silences that are anterior and ulterior limits of music, the second and penultimate verses represent two pianissimos, two minimal musics, and not two nothings. They are the two almost-nothings, a passage that represents nothing passing into something:

> In the plain,
> A sound is born;
> This is the breath
> Exhaled by night.

And then, something into nothing:

> This vague noise
> Lulled to its own sleep,
> It is the lament,
> (Almost extinguished)
> Of a saint
> For one who is dead.

---

19. Fauré, *Le Jardin clos*, op. 106, no. 3: "La Messagère."

Debussy for his part seeks to grasp the liminal moment when silence becomes music. This is the "antecedent pianissimo," music that is hardly audible, emerging from the "antecedent silence." In the opening of *La mer*, a clamor arises from the enigmatic depths where music is improvising itself into being. For the sea's silence is no more empty than the desert's: "Immense murmur, nonetheless silent," are the words of Charles van Leberghe, Fauré's favorite poet, from the "very first words" of the *Chanson d'Ève*.[20] All sorts of possible musics shudder within this undifferentiated rumor, the vibrating nebulousness that is inhabited by air's voice and water's voice, intermingled.

The other threshold gives access to terminal nothingness. Making infinite gradations in the nuances of imperceptibility, Debussy deliberately attenuates his decrescendos to the point where almost-nothing and nothing become indistinguishable. "Hardly," *estinto, perdendosi*. Music asymptotically approaches the extreme limit beyond which silence reigns: instrumental vibrations, dying away gradually, end by dying out into nothingness, like the lethal pianissimo that expires at the end of Gabriel Dupont's "La mort rôde," one of his "Lifeless Hours."[21] The beginning and end of Debussy's *Nocturne* for orchestra, "Nuages," is an immaterial tremor, sliding silence and shuddering plumes: archangel wings brushing featherbed clouds would make more noise than the violins' shivering bows, and threefold pianissimo "*ppp*," fourfold, a thousand-fold "*p*" or a hundred-thousand-fold "*p*" would convey no more than the faintest idea of such an infinitesimal "piano." Mélisande, at the end of act 5, dissolves into silence like the clouds of this first *Nocturne*—cloud herself, a faint wind as she is the "breath of night," impalpable, imponderable Mélisande is losing herself, and, thinned to nothingness, self-annihilating, she will return to non-being.

The almost-nonexistent dies out at last as the whisper of its own disappearance, *perdendosi*. The prelude Debussy called "Brouillards" also annihilates itself as this same *perdendosi*, as does the pointless gyration called "Mouvement"; in the same way the piano prelude "Les fées sont des exquises danseuses" fades away. The dying woman in act 5, no "exquisite dancer," is nonetheless veritable cloud

---

20. Gabriel Fauré, *La chanson d'Ève* op. 95, 1: "Paradise" (the title was invented by Fauré).
21. *Heures dolentes* XI.

and vapor: like the bubble that bursts at the faintest touch, the "small, silent creature" disappears, conjured away by death. At the end of the second movement of the *Faust Symphony*, the enthusiastic Faustian theme, transfigured by Marguerite's passion, dies out in A-flat major as a hyper-natural sonority, so sublime it seems to have issued directly from the Beyond. Marguerite and Mélisande, sisters in innocence. A simple sigh or (as Ivan Bunin says of Olga Meshchorskaya, untimely dead) "a slight respiration":[22] this is all that remains of Chaikovsky's *Berceuse* op. 72 once sleep has ravished consciousness, and overwhelms it. The last lines of Bunin's admirable story could surely be applied to translucent Mélisande, "that slight hint of breath has now dissipated into the All, in this cloud-covered sky, in the spring's cold wind."

If silence smooths the way for the transmission of a "message," this is because the negation that is silence suppresses or attenuates those aspects of experience that are most showy or ostentatious. To seek silence is to seek a meta-empirical Beyond, a supersensory realm more essential by far than the realm occupied by existence, which roars at high volume, with a booming voice. This quest gets us ready—if not to recognize truth, then at least to receive it. The chimera of the Beyond will survive all disappointments. For the ancient Greeks, who were a visually oriented people, optical phenomenality was by far the more exuberant and attractive principle: thus, for them, the search for intelligible knowledge entailed the idea of converting the invisible into that which could be seen. For Heraclites, even the idea of super-sensible harmony involves the notion of an "invisible" harmony. Certainly the sixth book of the *Republic* insists upon the parallelism between vision and intuition: the myth of the cave beckons us to choose the path of light.

But this is allegory, and that is the point. Here and there within the visible thing—the sunlight—Plato begins to see the truth of the Good, a thing that can be known and that is more luminous than light itself. And if Platonic "contemplation" is always connected to the spectacular—that which can be envisaged—then ideas themselves are "forms" in a merely figural sense. In the *Banquet*, this no-

---

22. In his *Un légère respiration* (1916). And "Wie ein Hauch" (Schoenberg, *Sechs kleine Klavierstücke* op. 19, no. 6 [end]); Debussy, "Colloque sentimental," (end); Liszt, *Faust Symphony* movement 2.

tion explains the paradox of beauty as something beyond sensory and visual perception, supersensible and supervisible. Plotinus (in this, systematizing the "hyperbole") would envisage an "amorphous" and "nonplastic" hyperessence, existing beyond Appearance with its gaudy colors. Nevertheless, it would be an exaggeration to claim that the Greeks were not (in their own way) on the lookout for the inaudible mystery that lurks beyond acoustic appearances. Plato already senses the futility of rhetoric and flees the clamor of the agora. Is the dialectic of the dialogue—which cuts off discursive eloquence and fragments an orator's long tirade—not analogous to the "interrupted serenade," and in this, is it not one of the forms assumed by silence? Dialogue: is it not continuous discourse chopped off, and interrupted and fragmented? Irony, in turn, is a question asked in expectation of an answer, interrogation suspended in silence. Gorgias makes a peroration, but Socrates simply listens. This is perhaps the proper moment to recall that Satie, himself the author of a *Socrate,* gave his cadences the allure of an "un-insistent request,"[23] and that Federico Mompou—whose laconic style, whose reticence with regard to prolixity and excess develops into a phobia—also nurtured a preference for the interrogative mode.

Walter Pater has reflected at some length upon Plato's admiration for the "apophthegma" and the ῥήματα βραχέα (terse sentences) of the Lacedemonians.[24] Plato (master of the dialogue, if not of aphorism) recognizes his own sobriety, his own aversion toward verbal excess in these brief phrases; after his fashion, he is applauding the repression of idle Athenian conversation. In the works of the Neoplatonists, there is a profound distrust of logos. Plotinus's *Of Contemplation* pushes the paradox to its extreme in its search for the "word that is mute," λόγος σιωπῶν.[25] From this point on, one no longer even need ask a question; it is sufficient to be silent and understand: ἐχρῆν μὲν μὴ ἐρωτᾶν, ἀλλὰ συνιέναι χαὶ αὐτὸν σιωπῇ, ὥσπερ ἐγὼ σιωπῶ χαὶ οὐχ εἴθισμαι λέγειν, "you ought not to ask, but to understand in silence, you, too, just as I am silent and not in the habit of

---

23. See *Le Fils des Étoiles,* the first *Gnossienne.* Also, Mompou, *1er Dialogue, Scènes d'enfants* ("Jeu").

24. See Plato, *Protagoras* 342e, 343a. See Pater, *Platon et le Platonisme,* trans. Samuel Jankélévitch (Paris: Payot, 1923), 235–36; 264.

25. *Enneads* III.8, 6; "silent rational form" in Armstrong's translation.

asking."²⁶ Not daring to offer even a single word, the wise man will soar into God's presence once he has abandoned logos.²⁷ Pseudo-Dionysius the Areopagite, who identifies invisible mystery and inaudible mystery, thus points out a "shadow more luminous than silence"²⁸ set apart from visible rays of light, for black darkness is the origin of resplendent "light." Fyodor Ivanovich Tyuchev writes, "thought becomes falsehood, once it is expressed."²⁹ This sense of the inexpressible, does it not seal the lips of those who have felt it? The Bergsonian distrust of language will thus merge with the philosophy of the apophatic.

And hence it is not just that acoustic din—as an opaque screen—puts obstacles in the way of truth and intercepts communication. This din can be, in itself, a seductive, diabolically deceptive principle, one that not only diverts but also *perverts.* Odysseus, the allegorical personification of mystery, covers his ears in order not to hear the Sirens, the principle of Error—that is, to render himself deaf to suasive music as to treacherous temptation.

For the Sirens' music is more than distracting noise, more than noise that diverts or dissipates, preventing reflective thought: it is a fraudulent art of pleasing. All that is really needed to stifle and obscure our silent dialogue with reason is the gaudy racket of the public market, ὁ ἐντὸς τῆς ψυχῆς πρὸς αὐτὴν διάλογος ἄνευ φωνῆς γιγόμενος, λόγος εἰρημένος . . . σιγῇ πρὸς αὐτόν, "what we call thought is speech that occurs without the voice, inside the soul in conversation with itself . . . in silence to oneself."³⁰ But the Siren concert is not (just) gaudy racket. The enchantresses posted along the way to Ithaca—which is the road toward Truth—want to lead us astray, send us on a detour, and make us deviate from the narrow path. And just as light illuminates all presences, makes manifest the coexistence of existing things, and communicates being, yet can turn into deceptive

26. *Enneads* III.8, 4; see also VI.8, 11.

27. *Enneads* IV.8, 19.

28. *Mystical Theology,* 997b.

29. "Silentium" (1830). See Fyodor Stepun, *La tragédie de la création* (Paris: Logos russe, 1910); *La tragédie de la conscience mystique* (Paris: Logos russe, 1911–12). Also S. L. Frank, *Zivoye znaniye* (Berlin: Obelisk, 1923).

30. Plato, *The Sophist* 263e, trans. N. P. White, in J. Cooper, ed., Plato: Complete Works (Hackett, London: 1997); Plato, *Theaetetus* 190a; see also *Philebus* 38e.

shimmer in a mirage, thus the word, which can bring human beings together, can also isolate them from one another once it turns into a lie. The word, a double-edged sword, is a vehicle for intellectual activity yet also derails it, signifies and disfigures, bears meaning and prevents one from thinking at all.

But there is still more: of all forms of appearance, the form of appearance assumed by sound is the most futile: more so than space stirred by air, the Harlequin cape of our multicolored existence, emptier than any hodgepodge of blaring, violently ostentatious color. Much (audible) ado about nothing! Optical appearance creates volume—though specious and inconsistent, appearing to be other and more than it is: yet at least the great bluff of existence will survive the instant, even if it deflates sooner or later. Even a ripple in the water extends beyond the instant. But acoustic furor's particular hollowness is futile twice over, demanding as it does continual renewal in order to endure. Failing that, it will fall flat and revert to silence. Thus, acoustic furor is actually the hollowness of hollowness, *vanitas vanitatis,* futility to the second power. An ephemeral mode, it demands constant maintenance. Sound resounds in time, and collapses instantly if one does not ceaselessly reanimate it, like the trumpet call that is broken off when one no longer blows into the instrument. Must we shout ourselves hoarse, till the end of time, that music might endure?

Grandiloquent music, resembling angry shrieks, is a form of emphatic stupidity: it sounds empty and it contains nothing but wind. If a frivolous definition of "emphasis" naively mistakes sheer volume for reality, or takes appearance for essence, then appreciating understatement means coming to terms with disproportion and makes us recognize that existence, with distracting irony, assumes paradoxical form, as a chiasmus: there is no simple proportional relationship between a given being's true importance and the volume of sound it emits, between its ontological weight and its phenomenological acoustic volume. Any being's degree of Being is not always in direct consequence to its phenomenal glare. No, the most important thing is not necessarily that which conveys the impression of importance. "His strength is astonishing to little children. He shifts an enormous stone (made of pumice)."[31] Satie's humor, does it not serve to deflate

---

31. Satie, *Le porteur de grosses pierres* (*Chapitres tournés en tous sens,* 2).

the megalomania inherent in glorious surface appearances? The re-
dundancy that wants to appear big as an ox is reduced to the shady
maneuver it always was.

More specifically, noise (which encumbers all space with its presence) will have existence without a guarantee of consistency or density. Truly important things make less noise than loud, insolent ex-
istences, with all their fanfares. Understatement (not taken in by any
of it) is thus the opposite of emphasis, just as seriousness is to futility.
God, according to scripture, does not come with the noise of wrath-
fulness but as imperceptibly as a breeze. Or (not according to scripture, but as I prefer to put it, to evoke *Pelléas et Mélisande* one more
time): God arrives on tiptoe, furtively, pianissimo, just like Death in
act 5: an almost-nothing, an imperceptible sigh, softer, if possible,
than Olga Meshchorskaya's breaths. Or, as Arkel says:

> I saw nothing. Are you sure? . . . I heard nothing at all . . . so
> quickly, so quickly . . . she departed without saying anything . . .
> she needs silence, now.

Many radical events and changes will resemble the deep, weary
labor of Death in that they take place silently, in the clandestine realm
of the almost-nothing. The work of thought makes no noise, nor
more do lovers; they make no noise while absorbed in their mysterious, silent colloquy, and François de Sales pays homage to their taciturnity: "Even though lovers have nothing secret to say, they like
nonetheless to say it secretly."[32]

Viewed in its positive aspects, silence provides a favorable condition for concentrated attention; as the *Phaedo* says, silence is the necessary condition for "contemplation." Not just blackness, but silence
as well, is necessary for hearing the "interior voices" of reflection,
which Malebranche dubbed "the Word of human intelligence." The
author of *Méditations chrétiennes et metaphysiques* compared attention to a "natural prayer" that solicits grace from a super-sensory
Truth. Human beings in a contemplative state can hear in silence, just
as animals with night vision can see in the dark. Plotinus himself,
who otherwise dismisses the noise made by logos, Plotinus seeks silence not to put a stethoscope to its chest and divine some inaudible

---

32. *Traité de l'amour de Dieu* VI: 6.

language, supernatural speech, a secret voice, but to contemplate a great spectacle, θέαμα, θεώρημα.[33] It is in the Bible every so often that hearing trumps vision, and that God at certain moments reveals himself to man in the form of the spoken Word. Hear, O Israel! For while no one has ever seen God, some have been able to hear Him.[34] Σχότος, γνόφος, φωνὴ μεγάλη, "gloom, darkness, a loud voice," as Deuteronomy V.22 puts it. Is it not from the midst of a cloud that God proclaims the Law?

It is silence that allows us to hear *another voice*, a voice speaking *another language*, a voice that comes *from elsewhere*. This unknown tongue spoken by an unknown voice, this *vox ignota*, hides behind silence just as silence itself lurks behind the superficial noise of daily existence. Knowledge deepened by dialectics enables an individual who listens attentively to burrow through thick layers of noise to discover transparent strata of silence. And then, he or she will delve into the infinite within the depths of silence, to discover therein the most secret of all musics. Silence is beyond noise, but the "invisible harmony" of the Greeks, the great cryptic or esoteric harmony, is beyond even silence itself. Imagine the look on the face of a man who had captured a barely perceptible message from some distant sphere: heart pounding, he would hold his breath, that all his senses might drink in the cryptogram, the unknown sign, the sigh that has come to him across infinite space.

In truth the "musical message" is no metaphysical message: or, at least, it is only metaphysical by virtue of a metaphor and, in some sense, spiritually. Music, this voice from another order, does *not* come from another world, and even less from the otherworldly. This distant voice is not in reality sent to us from far-off lands. Where does it come from, then, the unknown voice? From the conditions inside us, yet from nature exterior to us. Silence brings into being the latent counterpoint between past and future voices, a counterpoint that jams the noisy tumult of the present; and on the other hand, silence reveals the inaudible voice of absence, a voice that is concealing the

---

33. *Enneads* III.8, 4; and VI.8, 19 θεάσεται (he will see); ιδ' ων (seeing).

34. Θεόν οὐδεὶς ἑώρακεν πώποτε (John I.18, no one has ever seen God); θεὸν οὐδεὶς πώποτε τεθέαται (I Ep. John IV.12, no one has even seen God); οὔτε φωνὴν αὐτοῦ πώποτε ἀκηκόατε οὔτε εἶδος αὐτοῦ ἑωράκατε (John V.37, you have never heard his voice, nor have you seen his form); see also Exodus XXXIII.20; Deuteronomy V.22.

deafening racket made by presences. Whereas music, audible silence, by nature seeks the pianissimo rustling of memory, heard like the voice of a distant friend who whispers at our mind's ear. I have shown how music, as the language of Becoming, will also be the language of memories, and how memory renders all expression evasive. Ricordanza, the spell of memory: furrowed by long silences, Franz Liszt's *Valses oubliées* appear out of the mists of memory. Debussy's prelude "Des pas sur la neige," a long meditation on the vestiges of departed presence, speaks (in a low voice) of the nostalgia of absence, of remorse and its melancholia. "Colloque sentimentale" evokes old things—things that are past, distant, irrevocable, things that will never again be—right before being collapsed into the nothingness of a frigid night. Confidences about things past are whispered into our mental ear.

But more than this: we also receive forecasts of things to come as well, and more still, things promised, hoped for, and things whose coming is passionately awaited. Rimsky-Korsakov's *Legend of the Invisible City of Kitezh* is telling us about the future: in that deep silence, in the midst of boundless solitude of the banks of the Volga, the soul's ear and the corporeal ear hear the distant bells; the distant sound takes shape not in the depths of reminiscence—in some mysterious past—but at the horizon of an undefined future. This is Celestial Kitezh: our hope. Lesser Kitezh is the real and perceptible city, as noisy as Musorgsky's open-air market in Limoges; and when its deafening racket falls silent, then and then alone do we hear the carillons of the invisible city. The city is invisible but not inaudible.

It is not just that silence allows memories of the past to be invoked, or the bells of Easters yet to come to be heard; silence also develops the infinitesimal sounds of a universal multipresence. Fyodor Tyuchev said it beautifully: just as night makes stars appear in the sky, so when the tumult that is vigilance withdraws, the sounds that are interior, the magical singing, the dream-like images of fantasy can appear. But night also unveils the secret noises of cosmic existence, and not just those of subjectively perceptible music. For night, as much as silence, discloses the infrasensory noise of nature to human consciousness. The innumerable voices that people midnight's silence will echo against the thunderous silence of noon. The susurrations of a nocturnal animal,[35] a falling dewdrop, the sigh of a blade of grass. It is late; from faraway a bell tolls the hours of the night; a fountain chatters beneath its breath in the darkness at the heart of the garden; the wind blows dead leaves and makes them crackle. "You could hear the water as it slept."[36] You could hear the grass as it grew. Just as you can hear something prowling somewhere at the edge of the moonlight, in act 4, scene 4 of *Pelléas et Mélisande*. Lend an ear to the vast rustlings of coleopteran wings, at the end of *L'Enfant et les Sortilèges*. In "The Night's Music," Bela Bartók listens to automatic insect chirping, even to the bird that taps its beak, repeatedly, on a hollow wooden tree trunk. And then—interrupting animal and vegetable sound—comes human singing, rising from faraway in the darkness.

Supersensory voices and infrasensory voices are something else entirely, of an entirely other sonic order than the noises of day. Just as clairvoyants, or those endowed with superhuman sight, see in the darkness—with second sight (which is intuition)—and see invisible essences hidden behind that which exists visibly, so silence allows a kind of "second hearing" to develop, aural finesse, which allows human beings to perceive the least murmur of wind and night. Silence is a good conductor: it transmits implications hidden within what we can and do hear and allows a universal mystery and its voices to approach human beings.

Music renews its strength at the fountain of silence. But in what sense? To appreciate this suitably, we must first learn to distrust optical metaphors and the specious symmetries of synaesthesia. For there is an entire rhetoric of silence that shares nothing with metaphysics, except its conceits. Is silence the night of words? Is night the silence of light? These are (self-evidently) manners of speaking. One easily attributes the quality of sound to silence since by means of contrasts silence makes sound appear, and sound divides silence, and disturbs silence. The "immense murmur" mentioned in the *Chanson d'Ève* is indistinguishable from the silence that has made it perceptible to begin with, and Gabriel Dupont writes a song about "the silence of water." Night noises, transcribed by Bartók: are they not the *noise of*

35. Bartók, *Microcosmos* II: 63 "Susurration."
36. *Pelléas et Mélisande,* act 2, scene 1.

silence?[37] And I myself: have I not talked about dialogue as a form of silence, the silence inherent in brachylogy? The idea of a deafening silence: would this not appear to be as perfectly aligned with the Areopagites' negative philosophy, as much as the paradox of a blinding darkness?

Above all, however, we need to resist a Manichaean urge to hypostatize silence. Not some least-of-Beings, not merely noise that is degraded or rarefied, not the primitive, negative state of a normally sonorous milieu (as is, for instance, the curse of losing one's voice)— silence is no longer the obverse of a positive. In its own way, it is a form of plenitude, in its own way, a vehicle that conveys other things: underneath the banal, busy plenitude of daily life, silence reveals a more dense, more inspiring plenitude, otherwise populated, inhabited by other voices: and thus, silence inverts the usual relationship between fullness and emptiness, just as understatement is not inexpressive, but allusive. In other words, just as the "inexpressive Espressivo" is not a lesser form of expressiveness, but a kind of eloquence, so silence is not Nonbeing, but, rather, something other than Being.

The other voice, the voice that silence allows us to hear, is named Music. Without being pointlessly metaphorical, one could nonetheless say that silence is the desert where music blossoms and that music, a desert flower, is itself a sort of enigmatic silence. Whether reminiscence or prophecy, music and the silence that envelops it are *of this world*. Yet if this enigmatic voice is not disclosing the secrets of the Beyond, it may nonetheless remind us of the mystery that *we* bear within ourselves. And if no one possesses physiological hearing acute enough to overhear messages from an otherworldly realm, everyone can hear this "romance" without words and without specific signifying powers, which is called music. Everyone understands the voice that takes us prisoner, and does so, moreover, where there is nothing to understand, no conclusion to be drawn—and yet the voice tells us of our fate. Isaiah said of solitude: it will flower like a lily, sprouting and growing everywhere; it will be in effusions of joy and praise; the glory of Lebanon will be granted it, the radiance of Mount Carmel and of Sharon. And what the prophet Isaiah says about solitude, I will in turn repeat about silence. Silence, too, will exult, and the roses

---

37. *Pelléas et Mélisande*, act 2, scene 3.

of Sharon will blossom in its bare soil. The sands of silence will cover
the tumultuous waters; the arid desert of silence will be peopled with
murmurs and the sound of wings, with ineffable music. In solitude,
where Fevronia once dwelled, as in the joyous din of daily life, we can
sometimes hear the bells—the babble of bells from the City of Silence, which resound almost imperceptibly, in the depths of night.

18. Beckett (1906–1989)

L'innommable (Paris: Minuit, 1953), pp. 201–213. Trans. by author as *The Unnamable* (New York: Grove Press, 1958), pp. 169–179.

Nouvelles et Textes Pour Rien (Paris: Minuit, 1958), *Text #8*, pp. 167–174. Trans. by author as "Texts for Nothing," #8, in *Stories and Texts for Nothing* (New York: Grove, 1967), pp. 111–115.

Throughout his *oeuvre*, Samuel Beckett takes on the issue of the unsayable specifically in terms of the problem of ending, that is, of bringing any action—or utterance—to an end. Meaning articulated in time always shifts or slips and is never definitively said. The dramatic impossibility of ending the wait for Godot or the game of the play *Endgame* is mirrored and focused by a parallel narrative impossibility in the novel. Beckett's novels concentrate on the more interior problem of ending the speech of the speaking subject. Ending is impossible so long as one is a finite voice and consciousness, for ending embraces the whole and totalizes one's life and world, which nevertheless escape one's grasp as inexhaustible. The *all* can never be completely said by any *me*. The end of this *me* would be my death, and this is what I cannot say, and cannot finally grasp and conclusively express, as long as I am still speaking and so still *am*. Any saying of one's own death is fictitious and mendacious, as long as one lives and speaks. Beckett represents the longing for this end as a caressing of peace and silence, but, of course, as long as writing goes on this silence eludes him—and his reader.

Beckett's experiments with the logic and limits of language are often consciously theologized. Specifically, they resemble, though often in the mode of parody, negative theology. Shira Wolosky observes that "the premises and practices of negative theology act as a generative condition of Beckett's books," yet she maintains that "he should not be mistaken for a negative theologian," but should be seen rather as a "counter-mystic."[1] For Beckett does not reject language as inadequate to any essence or super-essence but instead exposes language as the origin of identity and essence. Wolosky argues that for Beckett

---

1. Shira Wolosky, *Language Mysticism: The Negative Way of Language in Eliot, Beckett, and Celan* (Stanford: Stanford University Press, 1995), p. 93.

there is no inner self that would be left if language were to be stripped away. Beckett relentlessly demonstrates that the self is inextricable from the language in which it projects and quests after itself. Wolosky presents this as a rather unprecedented reversal, one which previous critics have missed. Yet the idea of the purely verbal status of the subject or object of negative theology is not new to the apophatic tradition. As Michel de Certeau emphasizes, it is especially characteristic of seventeenth-century mysticism.[2]

Beckett's novels *Murphy* (1938) and *Watt* (1953) adumbrate a quest to free oneself—by withdrawal from the body into pure mind—for the culminating experience of Nothing. This is suggested by passages such as the following:

> Murphy began to see nothing . . . the accidentless One-and-Only, conveniently called Nothing. . . . His other senses also found themselves at peace, an unexpected pleasure. Not the numb peace of their own suspension, but the positive peace that comes when the somethings give way, or perhaps simply add up, to the Nothing.[3]

Watt's quest is even more obviously modeled on that of negative theology. It revolves around a "Mr. Knott," who, being purely negative ("not") and aporetic (like a "knot") in character, is analogous to an inaccessible God. The difficulty of defining *what* this God is is signalled by the very title "Watt," which sounds like an Irish vernacular pronunciation of the term "what," as in the colloquial expression "what-not." Yet language, as definition and description, hinges on this concept of whatness or quiddity. The result of this frustrated quest is that all verbalization proves fallacious and must be abandoned—if only that were possible. But this is not possible within Beckett's opus, so long as it goes on. And the texts themselves self-consciously turn and re-turn their attention precisely to this fate of continuation, of having fatally, irrevocably begun. The problem, as already demonstrated pathetically and hilariously in Beckett's theater, is how to end, or how to reach the silence that is caressingly envisaged and longingly sought. It is still being sought in vain at the end of the meditation of *The Unnamable* with its final, stridently self-contradictory words, "I can't go on, I'll go on."

---

2. See, for example, Michel de Certeau, *L'absent de l'histoire* (Tours: Mame, 1973), p. 153. See also de Certeau's "L'énonciation mystique," *Recherches des sciences religieuses* 54/2 (1976): 183–215.

3. *Murphy* (New York: Grove Press, 1957 [1938]), p. 246.

Beckett's novels seek to establish on a foundation of self-certainty the Cartesian self of the narrating voice, but all the figurations of voice that they invent actually defeat this endeavor because they represent the self in terms of others, never just in itself. Beckett's persona in *L'Innommable* seeks desperately to escape from *langue*, that is, from others speaking in him ("Ils m'ont gonflé de leurs voix, tel un ballon, j'ai beau me vider, c'est encore eux que j'entends," p. 64). It is a voice that listens to itself, interrupts itself, interrogates itself, but it can find no identity for itself: ". . . I, who cannot be I, of whom I can't speak, of whom I must speak, that's all hypotheses, I said nothing, someone said nothing. . . ." (p. 165).

The Unnamable is filled with a longing for silence, for its own end ("I'll find silence, and peace at last"). Thus its very discourse is by definition self-defeating: "this futile discourse which is not credited to me and brings me not a syllable nearer silence" (*The Unnamable*, p. 26). The true self would, presumably, be attained in silence. As the culminating volume of Beckett's trilogy announces from its title, this true self would be "the Unnamable." It is beyond representation. Therefore every representation actually betrays it, and so Beckett's texts deploy endless strategies for their own undoing, techniques of taking to pieces the representations they offer—*as if* the true self could emerge then as beyond representation, in silence.

The narrator is happy for his linguistic projects to fail, but he wants to achieve silence thereby, silence without afterthoughts: "I don't mind failing, it's a pleasure, but I want to go silent. Not as just now, the better to listen, but peacefully, victorious, without ulterior object [sans arrière-pensée]. Then it would be a life worth having, a life at last. My speech-parched voice at rest would fill with spittle, I'd let it flow over and over, happy at last, dribbling with life, my pensum ended, in the silence" (p. 30). This voice persistently seeks to void itself—it pursues by this means its own complete perfection and release. It will then be free of its blather, free to be silent ("libre, libre de ma bave, libre de me taire").

Bruce F. Kawain explains the self-destructing rhetoric of *The Unnamable* in terms of the narrating self and the never exhaustively sayable self-reflexivity that underlies so much modern fiction:

> In Beckett's *The Unnamable*, which is one long attempt to explain the situation of the narrating/narrated self, the foregone conclusion that the explanations will never be adequate to their subject becomes a demonstration in itself; the more the explanations fail, the more the reader is forced to intuit why they fail. Beckett's reader confronts a system whose

limits are analogous to those of his or her own verbal consciousness. These limited systems engage each other dialectically, and any synthesis that emerges in the reader's intuitive consciousness suggests that we are more than we can name, that we have resources that transcend the verbal.[4]

Another form taken by Beckett's deep mistrust of language, which conditions all he writes, is his determined effort to eliminate all figuration. By means of austere descriptions of literal physical movement reduced to such terms as "right-left, high-low, turn-straight, go-stop," for example, in *Fizzles*, he attempts to strip language of all but its positive, denotative sense.[5]

The selection here from *The Unnamable* consists in the concluding pages of Beckett's novel and thereby of his magnum opus, the trilogy, made up of the novels *Molloy, Malone Dies,* and *The Unnamable.* It is a rhapsody on the unnameable, which constitutes a leitmotif of his output as a whole. The narrator relentlessly denounces language as betrayal and distortion of truth. Silence is the "only chance . . . of saying something at last that is not false." His motto or epitaph, he suggests earlier, should be "we are silent about ourselves (De nobis ipsis silemus)" (p. 58).

In "Texts for Nothing," Beckett's meditations attempt characteristically to evade the figural propensities of language so as to say nothing and, above all, to end and eliminate themselves in silence. Text 2 counsels, "Better be silent, it's the only method, if you want to end" (p. 83). Yet the discourse that results is another descant on the empty source of saying, of this "I," which is not one, on itself. This is the continuation of the project of *The Unnamable.* But it again proves to be impossible to realize. Impossible though it be to end, naming and speaking prove equally to be impossible: "Name, no, nothing is namable, tell,

    4. Bruce F. Kawain, *The Mind of the Novel: Reflexive Fiction and the Ineffable* (Princeton: Princeton University Press, 1982), p. 7.
    5. See Stanley Cavell, "Ending the Waiting Game," in *Must We Mean What We Say?* (Cambridge: Cambridge University Press, 1976). Other critics who have studied specific aspects of Beckett's mistrust of language include Paul Foster, *Beckett and Zen: A Study of Dilemma in the Novels of Samuel Beckett* (London: Wisdom Publication, 1989); Niklaus Gessner, *Die Unzulänglichkeit der Sprache: Eine Untersuchung über Formzerfall und Beziehungslosigkeit bei Samuel Beckett* (Zürich: Juris, 1957); and Carla Locatelli, *Unwording the Word: Samuel Beckett's Prose Works After the Nobel Prize* (Philadelphia: University of Philadelphia Press, 1990). Wolfgang Iser, "The Pattern of Negativity in Beckett's Prose," *The Georgia Review* 29/3 (1975): 706–719, describes Beckett's prose as a "relentless process of negation . . . a ceaseless rejection and denial of what has just been said" (p. 2).

no, nothing can be told, what then, I don't know, I shouldn't have begun" (Text 11, p. 127).

The ineffable is in many ways the central obsession of Beckett throughout his work. Yet there is also in him an impulse to parody all this intolerably pious talk of the Ineffable. This very word and concept can function dogmatically and mindlessly, in the a-critical fashion of a religious dogma. In *Watt*, Beckett pays homage, mockingly, to "what we know partakes in no small measure of the nature of what has so happily been called the unutterable or ineffable, so that any attempt to utter or eff it is doomed to fail, doomed, doomed to fail" (p. 62). The thinly veiled obscenity of an "f" word, I would suggest, blasphemes this unspeakably holy (hole-y?) Nothing that is not so much as a word that can be said. It is a pungent irony that "the ineffable," as one more way of conceptualizing and verbalizing what cannot be said, becomes itself an object of mockery in Beckett's writings. For, taken as a name and a concept, not for its intent to gesture beyond all names and concepts, "The Ineffable" is just one more lying, linguistic idol: "For the only way one can speak of nothing is to speak of it as though it were something, just as the only way one can speak of God is to speak of him as though he were a man."[6]

The fact that the impossible quest for the unnameable is tightly interwoven with the impossible quest for the authentic "I" is the more ironic when we consider that the texts we read here are Beckett translating himself from French into his own native language, English—itself, however, already a foreign imposition upon him as an Irishman. This double loss of his "own" voice is peculiarly appropriate as a metaphor for Beckett's entire literary enterprise as an extravagant artifice of self-disappropriation through language.

---

6. *Watt* (New York: Grove, 1959 [1953]), p. 77.

From *The Unnamable* (conclusion)

The silence, speak of the silence before going into it, was I there already, I don't know, at every instant I'm there, listen to me speaking

of it, I knew it would come, I emerge from it to speak of it, I stay in
it to speak of it, if it's I who speak, and it's not, I act as if it were,
sometimes I act as if it were, but at length, was I ever there at length, a
long stay, I understand nothing about duration, I can't speak of it, oh
I know I speak of it, I say never and ever, I speak of the four seasons
and the different parts of the day and night, the night has no parts,
that's because you are asleep, the seasons must be very similar, perhaps it's springtime now, that's all words they taught me, without
making their meaning clear to me, that's how I learnt to reason, I use
them all, all the words they showed me, there were columns of them,
oh the strange glow all of a sudden, they were on lists, with images
opposite, I must have forgotten them, I must have mixed them up,
these nameless images I have, these imageless names, these windows I should perhaps rather call doors, at least by some other name,
and this word man which is perhaps not the right one for the thing
I see when I hear it, but an instant, an hour, and so on, how can they
be represented, a life, how could that be made clear to me, here, in
the dark, I call that the dark, perhaps it's azure, blank words, but I use
them, they keep coming back, all those they showed me, all those I remember, I need them all, to be able to go on, it's a lie, a score would
be plenty, tried and trusty, unforgettable, nicely varied, that would
be palette enough, I'd mix them, I'd vary them, that would be gamut
enough, all the things I'd do if I could, if I wished, if I could wish, no
need to wish, that's how it will end, in heart-rending cries, inarticulate murmurs, to be invented, as I go along, improvised, as I groan
along, I'll laugh, that's how it will end, in a chuckle, chuck chuck,
ow, ha, pa, I'll practise, nyum, hoo, plop, psss, nothing but emotion,
bing bang, that's blows, ugh, pooh, what else, oooh, aaah, that's love,
enough, it's tiring, hee hee, that's the Abderite, no, the other, in the
end, it's the end, the ending end, it's the silence, a few gurgles on
the silence, the real silence, not the one where I macerate up to the
mouth, up to the ear, that covers me, uncovers me, breathes with me,
like a cat with a mouse, that of the drowned, I've drowned, more than
once, it wasn't I, suffocated, set fire to me, thumped on my head with
wood and iron, it wasn't I, there was no head, no wood, no iron, I
didn't do anything to me, I didn't do anything to anyone, no one did
anything to me, there is no one, I've looked, no one but me, no, not
me either, I've looked everywhere, there must be someone, the voice
must belong to someone, I've no objection, what it wants I want, I am

it, I've said so, it says so, from time to time it says so, then it says not, I've no objection, I want it to go silent, it wants to go silent, it can't, it does for a second, then it starts again, that's not the real silence, it says that's not the real silence, what can be said of the real silence, I don't know, that I don't know what it is, that there is no such thing, that perhaps there is such a thing, yes, that perhaps there is, somewhere, I'll never know. But when it falters and when it stops, but it falters every instant, it stops every instant, yes, but when it stops for a good few moments, a good few moments, what are a good few moments, what then, murmurs, then it must be murmurs, and listening, some-one listening, no need of an ear, no need of a mouth, the voice listens, as when it speaks, listens to its silence, that makes a murmur, that makes a voice, a small voice, the same voice only small, it sticks in the throat, there's the throat again, there's the mouth again, it fills the ear, there's the ear again, then I vomit, someone vomits, someone starts vomiting again, that must be how it happens, I have no explanations to offer, none to demand, the comma will come where I'll drown for good, then the silence, I believe it this evening, still this evening, how it drags on, I've no objection, perhaps it's springtime, violets, no, that's autumn, there's a time for everything, for the things that pass, the things that end, they could never get me to understand that, the things that stir, depart, return, a light changing, they could never get me to see that, and death into the bargain, a voice dying, that's a good one, silence at last, not a murmur, no air, no one listening, not for the likes of me, amen, on we go. Enormous prison, like a hundred thou-sand cathedrals, never anything else any more, from this time forth, and in it, somewhere, perhaps, riveted, tiny, the prisoner, how can he be found, how false this space is, what falseness instantly, to want to draw that round you, to want to put a being there, a cell would be plenty, if I gave up, if only I could give up, before beginning, be-fore beginning again, what breathlessness, that's right, ejaculations, that helps you on, that puts off the fatal hour, no, the reverse, I don't know, start again, in this immensity, this obscurity, go through the motions of starting again, you who can't stir, you who never started, you the who, go through the motions, what motions, you can't stir, you launch your voice, it dies away in the vault, it calls that a vault, perhaps it's the abyss, those are words, it speaks of a prison, I've no objection, vast enough for a whole people, for me alone, or wait-ing for me, I'll go there now, I'll try and go there now, I can't stir, I'm there already, I must be there already, perhaps I'm not alone, perhaps a whole people is here, and the voice its voice, coming to me fitfully, we would have lived, been free a moment, now we talk about it, each one to himself, each one out loud for himself, and we listen, a whole people, talking and listening, all together, that would ex, no, I'm alone, perhaps the first, or perhaps the last, talking alone, listening alone, alone alone, the others are gone, they have been stilled, their voices stilled, their listening stilled, one by one, at each new-coming, another will come, I won't be the last, I'll be with the others, I'll be as gone, in the silence, it won't be I, it's not I, I'm not there yet, I'll go there now, I'll try and go there now, no use trying, I wait for my turn, my turn to go there, my turn to talk there, my turn to listen there, my turn to wait there for my turn to go, to be as gone, it's unending, it will be unending, gone where, where do you go from there, you must go somewhere else, wait somewhere else, for your turn to go again, and so on, a whole people, or I alone, and come back, and begin again, no, go on, go on again, it's a circuit, a long circuit, I know it well, I must know it well, it's a lie, I can't stir, I haven't stirred, I launch the voice, I hear a voice, there is nowhere but here, there are not two places, there are not two prisons, it's my parlour, it's a parlour, where I wait for nothing, I don't know where it is, I don't know what it's like, that's no business of mine, I don't know if it's big, or if it's small, or if it's closed, or if it's open, that's right, reiterate, that helps you on, open on what, there is nothing else, only it, open on the void, open on the nothing, I've no objection, those are words, open on the silence, look-ing out on the silence, straight out, why not, all this time on the brink of silence, I knew it, on a rock, lashed to a rock, in the midst of si-lence, its great swell rears towards me, I'm streaming with it, it's an image, those are words, it's a body, it's not I, I knew it wouldn't be I, I'm not outside, I'm inside, I'm in something, I'm shut up, the silence is outside, outside, inside, there is nothing but here, and the silence outside, nothing but this voice and the silence all round, no need of walls, yes, we must have walls, I need walls, good and thick, I need a prison, I was right, for me alone, I'll go there now, I'll put me in it, I'm there already, I'll start looking for me now, I'm there somewhere, it won't be I, no matter, I'll say it's I, perhaps it will be I, perhaps that's all they're waiting for, there they are again, to give me quittance, wait-ing for me to say I'm someone, to say I'm somewhere, to put me out, into the silence. I see nothing, it's because there is nothing, or it's because I have no eyes, or both, that makes three possibilities, to choose from, but do I really see nothing, it's not the moment to tell a lie, but how can you not tell a lie, what an idea, a voice like this, who can check it, it tries everything, it's blind, it seeks me blindly, in the dark, it seeks a mouth, to enter into, who can query it, there is no other, you'd need a head, you'd need things, I don't know, I look too often as if I knew, it's the voice does that, it goes all knowing, to make me think I know, to make me think it's mine, it has no interest in eyes, it says I have none, or that they are no use to me, then it speaks of tears, then it speaks of gleams, it is truly at a loss, gleams, yes, far, or near, distances, you know, measurements, enough said, gleams, as at dawn, then dying, as at evening, or flaring up, they do that too, blaze up more dazzling than snow, for a second, that's short, then fizzle out, that's true enough, if you like, one forgets, I forget, I say I see nothing, or I say it's all in my head, as if I felt a head on me, that's all hypotheses, lies, these gleams too, they were to save me, they were to devour me, that came to nothing, I see nothing, either because of this or else on account of that, and these images at which they watered me, like a camel, before the desert, I don't know, more lies, just for the fun of it, fun, what fun we've had, what fun of it, all lies, that's soon said, you must say soon, it's the regulations. The place, I'll make it all the same, I'll make it in my head, I'll draw it out of my memory, I'll gather it all about me, I'll make myself a head, I'll make myself a memory, I have only to listen, the voice will tell me everything, tell it to me again, everything I need, in dribs and drabs, breathless, it's like a confession, a last confession, you think it's finished, then it starts off again, there were so many sins, the memory is so bad, the words don't come, the words fail, the breath fails, no, it's something else, it's an indictment, a dying voice accusing, accusing me, you must accuse someone, a culprit is indispensable, it speaks of my sins, it speaks of my head, it says it's mine, it says that I repent, that I want to be punished, better than I am, that I want to go, give myself up, a victim is essential, I have only to listen, it will show me my hiding-place, what it's like, where the door is, if there's a door, and whereabouts I am in it, and what lies between us, how the land lies, what kind of country, whether it's sea, or whether it's mountain, and the way to take, so that I may go, make my escape, give myself up, come to the place where the axe falls, without further ceremony, on all who come from here, I'm not the first, I won't be the first, it will best me in the end, it has bested better than me, it will tell me what to do, in order to rise, move, act like a body endowed with despair, that's how I reason, that's how I hear myself reasoning, all lies, it's not me they're calling, not me they're talking about, it's not yet my turn, it's someone else's turn, that's why I can't stir, that's why I don't feel a body on me, I'm not suffering enough yet, it's not yet my turn, not suffering enough to be able to stir, to have a body, complete with head, to be able to understand, to have eyes to light the way, I merely hear, without understanding, without being able to profit by it, by what I hear, to do what, to rise and go and be done with hearing, I don't hear everything, that must be it, the important things escape me, it's not my turn, the topographical and anatomical information in particular is lost on me, no, I hear every-thing, what difference does it make, the moment it's not my turn, my turn to understand, my turn to live, my turn of the lifescrew, it calls that living, the space of the way from here to the door, it's all there, in what I hear, somewhere, if all has been said, all this long time, all must have been said, but it's not my turn to know what, to know what I am, where I am, and what I should do to stop being it, to stop being there, that's coherent, so as to be another, no, the same, I don't know, depart into life, travel the road, find the door, find the axe, perhaps it's a cord, for the neck, for the throat, for the cords, or fingers, I'll have eyes, I'll see fingers, it will be the silence, perhaps it's a drop, find the door, open the door, drop, into the silence, it won't be I, I'll stay here, or there, more likely there, it will never be I, that's all I know, it's all been done already, said and said again, the departure, the body that rises, the way, in colour, the arrival, the door that opens, closes again, it was never I, I've never stirred, I've listened, I must have spoken, why deny it, why not admit it, after all, I deny nothing, I admit noth-ing, I say what I hear, I hear what I say, I don't know, one or the other, or both, that makes three possibilities, pick your fancy, all these sto-ries about travellers, these stories about paralytics, all are mine, I must be extremely old, or it's memory playing tricks, if only I knew if I've lived, if I live, if I'll live, that would simplify everything, impos-sible to find out, that's where you're buggered, I haven't stirred, that's all I know, no, I know something else, it's not I, I always forget that, I resume, you must resume, never stirred from here, never stopped telling stories, to myself, hardly hearing them, hearing something else, listening for something else, wondering now and then where I got them from, was I in the land of the living, were they in mine, and where, where do I store them, in my head, I don't feel a head on me, and what do I tell them with, with my mouth, same remark, and what do I hear them with, and so on, the old rigmarole, it can't be I, or it's because I pay no heed, it's such an old habit, I do it without heeding, or as if I were somewhere else, there I am far again, there I am the absentee again, it's his turn again now, he who neither speaks nor listens, who has neither body nor soul, it's something else he has, he must have something, he must be somewhere, he is made of silence, there's a pretty analysis, he's in the silence, he's the one to be sought, the one to be, the one to be spoken of, the one to speak, but he can't speak, then I could stop, I'd be he, I'd be the silence, I'd be back in the silence, we'd be reunited, his story the story to be told, but he has no story, he hasn't been in story, it's not certain, he's in his own story, unimaginable, unspeakable, that doesn't matter, the attempt must be made, in the old stories incomprehensibly mine, to find his, it must be there somewhere, it must have been mine, before being his, I'll recognize it, in the end I'll recognize it, the story of the silence that he never left, that I should never have left, that I may never find again, that I may find again, then it will be he, it will be I, it will be the place, the silence, the end, the beginning, the beginning again, how can I say it, that's all words, they're all I have, and not many of them, the words fail, the voice fails, so be it, I know that well, it will be the silence, full of murmurs, distant cries, the usual silence, spent listening, spent waiting, waiting for the voice, the cries abate, like all cries, that is to say they stop, the murmurs cease, they give up, the voice begins again, it begins trying again, quick now before there is none left, no voice left, nothing left but the core of murmurs, distant cries, quick now and try again, with the words that remain, try what, I don't know, I've forgotten, it doesn't matter, I never knew, to have them carry me into my story, the words that remain, my old story, which I've forgotten, far from here, through the noise, through the door, into the silence, that must be it, it's too late, perhaps it's too late, perhaps they have, how would I know, in the silence you don't know, perhaps it's the door, perhaps I'm at the door, that would surprise me, perhaps it's I, perhaps somewhere or other it was I, I can depart, all this time I've journeyed without knowing it, it's I now at the door, what door, what's a door doing here, it's the last words, the true last, or it's the murmurs, the murmurs are coming, I know that well, no, not even that, you talk of murmurs, distant cries, as long as you can talk, you talk of them before and you talk of them after, more lies, it will be the silence, the one that doesn't last, spent listening, spent waiting, for it to be broken, for the voice to break it, perhaps there's no other, I don't know, it's not worth having, that's all I know, it's not I, that's all I know, it's not mine, it's the only one I ever had, that's a lie, I must have had the other, the one that lasts, but it didn't last, I don't understand, that is to say it did, it still lasts, I'm still in it, I left myself behind in it, I'm waiting for me there, no, there you don't wait, you don't listen, I don't know, perhaps it's a dream, all a dream, that would surprise me, I'll wake, in the silence, and never sleep again, it will be I, or dream, dream again, dream of a silence, a dream silence, full of murmurs, I don't know, that's all words, never wake, all words, there's nothing else, you must go on, that's all I know, they're going to stop, I know that well, I can feel it, they're going to abandon me, it will be the silence, for a moment, a good few moments, or it will be mine, the lasting one, that didn't last, that still lasts, it will be I, you must go on, I can't go on, you must go on, I'll go on, you must say words, as long as there are any, until they find me, until they say me, strange pain, strange sin, you must go on, perhaps it's done already, perhaps they have said me already, perhaps they have carried me to the threshold of my story, before the door that opens on my story, that would surprise me, if it opens, it will be I, it will be the silence, where I am, I don't know, I'll never know, in the silence you don't know, you must go on, I can't go on, I'll go on.

Texts for Nothing, #8

Only the words break the silence, all other sounds have ceased. If I were silent I'd hear nothing. But if I were silent the other sounds would start again, those to which the words have made me deaf, or which have really ceased. But I am silent, it sometimes happens, no, never, not one second. I weep too without interruption. It's an unbroken flow of words and tears. With no pause for reflection. But I speak softer, every year a little softer. Perhaps. Slower too, every year a little slower. Perhaps. It is hard for me to judge. If so the pauses would be longer, between the words, the sentences, the syllables, the tears, I confuse them, words and tears, my words are my tears, my eyes my mouth. And I should hear, at every little pause, if it's the silence I say when I say that only the words break it. But nothing of the kind, that's not how it is, it's for ever the same murmur, flowing unbroken, like a single endless word and therefore meaningless, for it's the end gives the meaning to words. What right have you then, no, this time I see what I'm up to and put a stop to it, saying, None, none. But get on with the stupid old threne and ask, ask until you answer, a new question, the most ancient of all, the question were things always so. Well I'm going to tell myself something (if I'm able), pregnant I hope with promise for the future, namely that I begin to have no very clear recollection of how things were before (I was!), and by before I mean elsewhere, time has turned into space and there will be no more time, till I get out of here. Yes, my past has thrown me out, its gates have slammed behind me, or I burrowed my way out alone, to linger a moment free in a dream of days and nights, dreaming of me moving, season after season, towards the last, like the living, till suddenly I was here, all memory gone. Ever since nothing but fantasies and hope of a story for me somehow, of having come from somewhere and of being able to go back, or on, somehow, some day, or without hope. Without what hope, haven't I just said, of seeing me alive, not merely inside an imaginary head, but a pebble sand to be, under a restless sky, restless on its shore, faint stirs day and night, as if to grow less could help, ever less and less and never quite be gone. No truly, no matter what, I say no matter what, hoping to wear out a voice, to wear out a head, or without hope, without reason, no matter what, without reason. But it will end, a desinence will come, or the breath fail better still, I'll be silence, I'll know I'm silence, no, in the silence you can't know, I'll never know anything. But at least get out of here, at least that, no? I don't know. And time begin again, the steps on the earth, the night the fool implores at morning and the morning he begs at evening not to dawn. I don't know, I don't know what all that means, day and night, earth and sky, begging and imploring. And I can desire them? Who says I desire them, the voice, and that I can't desire anything, that looks like a contradiction, it may be for all I know. Me, here, if they could open, those little words, open and swallow me up, perhaps that is what has happened. If so let them open again and let me out, in the tumult of light that sealed my eyes, and of men, to try and be one again. Or if I'm guilty let me be forgiven and graciously authorized to expiate, coming and going in passing time, every day a little purer, a little deader. The mistake I make is to try and think, even the way I do, such as I am I shouldn't be able, even the way I do. But whom can I have offended so grievously, to be punished in this inexplicable way, all is inexplicable, space and time, false and inexplicable, suffering and tears, and even the old convulsive cry, It's not me, it can't be me. But am I in pain, whether it's me or not, frankly now, is there pain? Now is here and here there is no frankness, all I say will be false and to begin with not said by me, here I'm a mere ventriloquist's dummy, I feel nothing, say nothing, he holds me in his arms and moves my lips with a string, with a fish-hook, no, no need of lips, all is dark, there is no one, what's the matter with my head, I must have left it in Ireland, in a saloon, it must be there still, lying on the bar, it's all it deserved. But that other who is me, blind and deaf and mute, because of whom I'm here, in this black silence, helpless to move or accept this voice as mine, it's as him I must disguise myself till I die, for him in the meantime do my best not to live, in this pseudo-sepulture claiming to be his. Whereas to my certain knowledge I'm dead and kicking above, somewhere in Europe probably, with every plunge and suck of the sky a little more overripe, as yesterday in the pump of the womb. No, to have said so convinces me of the contrary, I never saw the light of day, any more than he, ah if no were content to cut yes's throat and never cut its own. Watch out for the right moment, then not another word, is that the only way to have being and habitat? But I'm here, that much at least is certain, it's in vain I keep on saying it, it remains true. Does it? It's hard for me to judge. Less true and less certain in any case than when I say I'm on earth, come into the world and assured of getting out, that's why I say it, patiently, variously, trying to vary, for you never know, it's perhaps all a question of hitting on the right aggregate. So as to be here no more at last, to have never been here, but all this time above, with a name like a dog to be called up with and distinctive marks to be had up with, the chest expanding and contracting unaided, panting towards the grand apnoea. The right aggregate, but there are four million possible, nay probable, according to Aristotle, who knew everything. But what is this I see, and how, a white stick and an ear-trumpet, where, Place de la République, at pernod time, let me look closer at this, it's perhaps me at last. The trumpet, sailing at ear level, suddenly resembles a steam-whistle, of the kind thanks to which my steamers forge fearfully through the fog. That should fix the period, to the nearest half-century or so. The stick gains ground, tapping with its ferrule the noble bassamento of the United Stores, it must be winter, at least not summer. I can also just discern, with a final effort of will, a bowler hat which seems to my sorrow a sardonic synthesis of all those that never fitted me and, at the other extremity, similarly suspicious, a complete pair of brown boots lacerated and gaping. These insignia, if I may so describe them, advance in concert, as though connected by the traditional human excipient, halt, move on again, confirmed by the vast show windows. The level of the hat, and consequently of the trumpet, hold out some hope for me as a dying dwarf or at least hunchback. The vacancy is tempting, shall I en-throne my infirmities, give them this chance again, my dream infir-mities, that they may take flesh and move, deteriorating, round and round this grandiose square which I hope I don't confuse with the Bastille, until they are deemed worthy of the adjacent Père Lachaise or, better still, prematurely relieved trying to cross over, at the hour of night's young thoughts. No, the answer is no. For even as I moved, or when the moment came, affecting beyond all others, to hold out my hand, or hat, without previous song, or any other form of concession to self-respect, at the terrace of a café, or in the mouth of the under-ground, I would know it was not me, I would know I was here, beg-ging in another dark, another silence, for another alm, that of being or of ceasing, better still, before having been. And the hand old in vain would drop the mite and the old feet shuffle on, towards an even vainer death than no matter whose.

19. STEINER

"Silence and the Poet." In *Language and Silence: Essays on Language, Literature, and the Inhuman* (New York: Atheneum, 1967; original edition 1958), pp. 36–54.

George Steiner's essay "Silence and the Poet" recapitulates admirably much of the itinerary covered by this anthology and history. It is an eloquent, though rather pessimistic, statement about the role of silence in poetry. Despite his acute attention to classic authors such as Dante and John of the Cross, Steiner represents the encroachment of silence as a characteristically modern predicament. An inhuman age of barbarism has caused silence to become the inevitable mode of writers today. The essay witnesses to a postwar climate of desolation and shame over the silence in which Nazi extermination camps had carried out their deathly work. This has provoked the "crisis of language" that Adorno likewise registered in declaring that after Auschwitz, to write poetry is barbaric. Certainly, there is nothing exclusively modern in a preoccupation with silence and the unsayable. Nevertheless, it *does* say something about our contemporary culture that it can produce the synthesis represented by the book in hand and gather into some semblance of a coherent heritage the many voices from disparate traditions and provenances that converge within these covers.

In another essay in *Language and Silence,* "The Retreat from the Word," again Steiner's sympathy for apophatic currents is somewhat curbed by his apocalyptic perception of the eclipse of language in modern times, which he sees as marred by a degradation of the word. However, if we take into account the word's cyclical need to extricate itself from formalized systems, clearly evidenced at each historical juncture where apophasis returns to ascendancy, we can understand that the limit-experiences in which the word defaults and decomposes are also the necessary condition for its regeneration.

"Silence and the Poet" suggestively fits into this group of selections also because it exemplarily embodies the potential of literary criticism to become creative work in its own right. Such commentary, through its synoptic vision, can open perspectives that reach in many ways beyond the individual works it considers. Among the arts, criticism alone has the ability to comment

explicitly and synthetically on silence and apophasis at work in all other domains of culture. Harold Bloom's writings on Gnostic traditions offer another
eminent witness to this formidable capacity of literary and cultural criticism.[1]

---

1. See in particular Harold Bloom, *Omens of Millenneum: The Gnosis of Angels,
Dreams, and Resurrection* (New York: G. P. Putnam, 1996).

Silence and the Poet

Both Hebraic and Classical mythology have in them the traces of an
ancient fear. The tower broken in Babel and Orpheus torn, the
prophet blinded so that sight is yielded for insight, Tamyris killed,
Marsyas flayed, his voice turning to the cry of blood in the wind—
these tell of a sense, deeper rooted than historical memory, of the
miraculous outrage of human speech.

That articulate speech should be the line dividing man from the
myriad forms of animate being, that speech should define man's singular eminence above the silence of the plant and the grunt of the
beast—stronger, more cunning, longer of life than he—is classic doctrine well before Aristotle. We find it in Hesiod's *Theogony* (584).
Man is, to Aristotle, a being of the word (ζῷον λόγον ἔχον). How the
word came to him is, as Socrates admonishes in the *Cratylus*, a riddle,
a question worth asking so as to goad the mind into play, so as to
wake it to the wonder of its communicative genius, but it is not a
question to which a certain answer lies in human reach.

Possessed of speech, possessed by it, the word having chosen the
grossness and infirmity of man's condition for its own compelling
life, the human person has broken free from the great silence of matter. Or, to use Ibsen's image: struck with the hammer, the insensate
ore has begun to sing.

But this breaking free, the human voice harvesting echo where
there was silence before, is both miracle and outrage, sacrament and

blasphemy. It is a sharp severance from the world of the animal, man's begetter and sometime neighbor, the animal who, if we rightly grasp the myths of centaur, satyr, and sphinx, has been inwoven with the very substance of man, and whose instinctive immediacies and shapes of physical being have receded only partially from our own form. This harsh weaning, of which antique mythology is so uneasily conscious, has left its scars. Our own new mythologies take up the theme: in Freud's grim intimation of man's backward longing, of his covert wish for re-immersion in an earlier, inarticulate state of organic existence; in Claude Lévi-Strauss's speculations on man's self-banishment, by his Promethean theft of fire (the choice of cooked over raw food), and by his mastery of speech, from the natural rhythms and anonymities of the animal world.

If speaking man has made of the animal his mute servant or enemy—the beasts of the field and forest no longer understand our words when we cry for help—man's control of the word has also hammered at the door of the gods. More than fire, whose power to illumine or to consume, to spread and to draw inward, it so strangely resembles, speech is the core of man's mutinous relations to the gods. Through it he apes or challenges their prerogatives. Nimrud's tower was built of words; Tantalus gossiped, bringing to earth in a vessel of words the secrets of the gods. According to the Neo-Platonic and Johannine metaphor, in the beginning was the Word; but if this *Logos*, this act and essence of God is, in the last analysis, total communication, the word that creates its own content and truth of being— then what of *zoon phonanta*, man the speaking animal? He too creates words and creates with words. Can there be a coexistence other than charged with mutual torment and rebellion between the totality of the *Logos* and the living, world-creating fragments of our own speech? Does the act of speech, which defines man, not also go beyond him in rivalry to God?

In the poet this ambiguity is most pronounced. It is he who guards and multiplies the vital force of speech. In him the old words are kept resonant, and the new are lifted to the common light out of the active dark of individual consciousness. The poet makes in dangerous similitude to the gods. His song is builder of cities; his words have that power which, above all others, the gods would deny to man, the power to bestow enduring life. As Montaigne recognizes of Homer:

Et, à la vérité, je m'estonne souvent que luy, qui a produit et mis en credit au monde plusieurs deitez par son auctorité, n'a gaigné rang de Dieu luy mesme. . . .

The poet is maker of new gods and preserver of men: thus Achilles and Agamemnon live, Ajax's great shade is burning still, because the poet has made of speech a dam against oblivion, and death blunts its sharp teeth upon his word. And because our languages have a future tense, which fact is of itself a radiant scandal, a subversion of mortality, the seer, the prophet, men in whom language is in a condition of extreme vitality, are able to look beyond, to make of the word a reaching out past death. For which presumption—to presume means to *anticipate* but also to *usurp*—they are grimly taxed.

Homer, the master-builder and rebel against time, in whom the conviction that the "winged word" shall outlast death speaks out in constant jubilation, goes blind. Orpheus is torn to bleeding shreds. Yet the word will not be quenched; it sings in the dead mouth:

> *membra iacent diversa locis, caput, Hebre, lyramque*
> *excipis: et (mirum!) medio dum labitur amne,*
> *flebile nescio quid queritur lyra, flebile lingua*
> *murmurat exanimis, respondent flebile ripae.*

Mirum! says Ovid: a marvel, a wonder, but also a scandal and defiance to the gods. Out of the gates of death man pours the living stream of words. And how may we read the torment of Marsyas, Apollo's challenger, that cruel fable of lyre against pipe which haunts the Renaissance to the time of Spenser, if not as a warning of the bitter intimacies and necessary vengeances between God and the poet? Poets are not, as officious mythology would have it, sons of Apollo, but of Marsyas. In his death cry they hear their own name:

> this is already beyond the endurance
> of the god with nerves of artificial fiber
>
> along a gravel path
> between box espaliers
> the victor departs

wondering
whether out of Marsyas' howling
there will some day arise
a new brand
of art—let us say—concrete

suddenly
at his feet
falls a petrified nightingale
he looks back
and sees
that the tree to which Marsyas was fastened
has gone white-haired

completely
   (from the Polish of Zbigniew Herbert,
    translated by Czesław Miłosz)

To speak, to assume the privileged singularity and solitude of man in the silence of creation, is dangerous. To speak with the utmost strength of the word, which is the poet's, supremely so. Thus even to the writer, perhaps to him more than to others, silence is a temptation, a refuge when Apollo is near.

Gradually this ambivalence in the genius of language, this notion of the god-rivaling, therefore potentially sacrilegious character of the act of the poet, becomes one of the recurrent tropes in Western literature. From Medieval Latin poetry to Mallarmé and Russian Symbolist verse, the motif of the necessary limitations of the human word is a frequent one. It carries with it a crucial intimation of that which lies outside language, of what it is that awaits the poet if he were to transgress the bounds of human discourse. Being, in the nature of his craft, a reacher, the poet must guard against becoming, in the Faustian term, an overreacher. The daemonic creativity of his instrument probes the outworks of the City of God; he must know when to draw back lest he be consumed, Icarus-like, by the terrible nearness of a greater making, of a *Logos* incommensurable with his own (in the garden of fallen pleasures, Hieronymus Bosch's poet is racked on his own harp).

But it is decisively the fact that language does have its frontiers, that it borders on three other modes of statement—light, music, and silence—which gives proof of a transcendent presence in the fabric of the world. It is just because we can go no further, because speech so marvelously fails us, that we experience the certitude of a divine meaning surpassing and enfolding ours. What lies beyond man's word is eloquent of God. That is the joyously defeated recognition expressed in the poems of St. John of the Cross and of the mystic tradition.

Where the word of the poet ceases, a great light begins. This *topos*, with its historical antecedents in neo-Platonic and Gnostic doctrine, gives to Dante's *Paradiso* its principal motion of spirit. We may understand the *Paradiso* as an exercise, supremely controlled yet full of extreme moral and poetic risk, in the calculus of linguistic possibility. Language is deliberately extended to the limit case. With each act of ascent, from sphere to radiant sphere, Dante's language is submitted to more intense and exact pressure of vision; divine revelation stretches the human idiom more and more out of the bounds of daily, indiscriminate usage. By exhaustive metaphor, by the use of similes increasingly audacious and precise—we hear the prayer in the syntax—Dante is able to make verbally intelligible the forms and meanings of his transcendent experience.

The characteristic rhetorical movement is one of initial retreat from the luminous, hermetic challenge, followed by an ingathering of utmost concentration, and a thrust forward into language unprecedented, into analogies and turns of statement which the poet himself discovers, which he had not known previously to lie within his grasp. First there is defeat. Words cannot convey what the pilgrim sees:

> *Perch' io lo ingegno, l'arte e l'uso chiami*
> *sì nol direi che mai s'imaginasse. . . .*
> (x)

> *e il canto di quei lumi era di quelle;*
> *chi non s'impenna sìche lassù voli,*
> *dal muto aspetti quindi le novelle.*
> (x)

The poet seeks refuge in muteness. Whereupon the upward surge, the verbalization of the hitherto incommunicable occurs through some miracle of simplicity, by way of a simile invoking a ball-game, hot wax flowing from the impress of a seal-ring, the shoemaker hammering at his nails. As if the grace of divine meaning were such that it can, under the poet's persuasion, enter the most natural, straightforward of our imaginings.

But as the poet draws near the Divine presence, the heart of the rose of fire, the labor of translation into speech grows ever more exacting. Words grow less and less adequate to the task of translating immediate revelation. Light passes to a diminishing degree into speech; instead of making syntax translucent with meaning, it seems to spill over in unrecapturable splendor or burn the word to ash. This is the drama of the final Cantos. As the poet moves upward his words fall behind. Until, in verse 55 of Canto xxxiii *il parlar nostro*, our human discourse, fails utterly:

> *Da quinci innanzi il mio veder fu maggio*
> *che il parlar nostro ch' a tal vista cede,*
> *e cede la memoria a tanto oltraggio.*

Words failing, memory, which is their confine, breaks also. This is an outrage (*oltraggio*); but it is a sacred, affirmative outrage, a manifest proof of being of that which surpasses all human speech. From that literally unspeakable light and glory, the tongue of the poet strives to bring back to us one single spark:

> *e fa la lingua mia tanto possente*
> *ch'une favilla sol della tua gloria*
> *possa lasciare alla futura gente. . . .*

After which speech yields entirely to the inexpressible language of light, and the poet, at the absolute summit of his powers, compares his art unfavorably with the inarticulate babblings of an unweaned child:

> *Omai sarà più corta mia favella,*
> *pure a quel ch' io ricordo, che di un fante*
> *che bagni ancor la lingua alla mammella.*

The circle is complete: at its furthest reach, where it borders on light, the language of men becomes inarticulate as is that of the infant before he masters words. Those who would press language beyond its divinely ordained sphere, who would contract the *Logos* into the word, mistake both the genius of speech and the untranslatable immediacy of revelation. They thrust their hands into fire instead of gathering light. That directed light beams (lasers) would one day become carriers of the word might have seemed to Dante a wondrous but not irrational adjunct to his vision.

One tradition finds light at the limits of language. Another, no less ancient or active in our poetry and poetics, finds music.

The interpenetration of poetry and music is so close that their origin is indivisible and usually rooted in a common myth. Still today the vocabulary of prosody and poetic form, of linguistic tonality and cadence, overlaps deliberately with that of music. From Arion and Orpheus to Ezra Pound and John Berryman, the poet is maker of songs and singer of words. There are many and intricate strains (itself a musical term) in the concept of the musical character of poetic speech. The fortunes of Orpheus, as we follow them in Pindar and Ovid, in Spenser, Rilke, and Cocteau, are almost synonymous with the nature and functions of poetry. Because he is part Orpheus, the poet in Western literature is architect of myth, magician over savagery, and pilgrim toward death. The notion that the structure of the universe is ordered by harmony, that there is a music whose modes are the elements, the concord of the planetary orbits, the chime of water and blood, is ancient as Pythagoras and has never lost its metaphoric life. Until the seventeenth century and the "untuning of the sky," a belief in the music of the spheres, in Pythagorean or Keplerian accords and temperance between star and planet, between harmonious functions in mathematics and the vibrant lute string, underlies much of the poet's realization of his own action. The music of the spheres is guarantor and counterpoint to his own use of ordering, harmonious "numbers" (the terminology of rhetoric is consistently musical).

Hearkening to this music, as does Lorenzo in the garden at Belmont, he receives not only echo but that assurance of a transcendent presence, of a convention of statement and communication reaching beyond and concentric to his own which Dante receives from exceeding light:

> Look how the floor of heaven
> Is thick inlaid with patens of bright gold.
> There's not the smallest orb which thou behold'st

But in his motion like an angel sings,
Still quiring to the young-eyed cherubins;
Such harmony is in immortal souls!

Patens are the small flat dishes used in Holy Communion—by which choice of word Shakespeare would have us note that communion and communication through transcendent harmony are vitally akin.

From this vast topic of the interactions of music with language, I want to abstract only one theme: the notion that poetry leads *toward* music, that it passes into music when it attains the maximal intensity of its being. This idea has the evident, powerful implication that music is, in the final analysis, superior to language, that it says more or more immediately. The thought of rivalry between poet and musician is antithetical to the origins and full realization of both; it rends Orpheus more decisively than did the women of Thrace. Yet it too has its long, though often subterranean history. We find evidence of it in Plato's arguments on the respective functions of poetry and music in education, and in Patristic beliefs, which are at once related to Platonism but different in stress and conclusion, on the irrational, perhaps daemonic powers of music as contrasted with the rationality and verifiability of the word. In the Johannine beginning is the Word; in the Pythagorean, the accord. The rival claims of singer and speaker, moreover, are a Renaissance *topos* long before they find comic echo in Molière's *Bourgeois Gentilhomme* and in Richard Strauss's uses of Molière and of the music-language quarrel in *Ariadne*. The possible blackness of that quarrel, the way in which it may search out and articulate the soul's relationship to God, is at the heart of Mann's *Doctor Faustus*.

But it is not the contest I want to draw attention to: it is the recurrent acknowledgment by poets, by masters of language, that music *is* the deeper, more numinous code, that language, when truly apprehended, aspires to the condition of music and is brought, by the genius of the poet, to the threshold of that condition. By a gradual loosening or transcendence of its own forms, the poem strives to escape from the linear, denotative, logically determined bonds of linguistic syntax into what the poet takes to be the simultaneities, immediacies, and free play of musical form. It is in music that the poet hopes to find the paradox resolved of an act of creation singular to the creator, bearing the shape of his own spirit, yet infinitely renewed in each listener.

The fullest statement of this hope, of this submission of the word to the musical ideal, can be found in German Romanticism. It is in the writings and indeed personal lives of Tieck, Novalis, Wackenroder, E. T. A. Hoffmann, that the theory of music as the supreme, quintessential art, and of the word as its prelude and servant, is carried to the highest pitch of technical and philosophic implication. Novalis' *Hymns to the Night* turn on a metaphor of cosmic musicality; they image the spirit of man as a lyre played upon by elemental harmonies, and seek to exalt language to that state of rhapsodic obscurity, of nocturnal dissolution from which it may most naturally pass into song. From Hoffmann to Mann's Adrian Leverkühn, the artist is, archetypally, a musician; for it is in music, far more than in speech or the plastic arts, that aesthetic conventions are brought near to the source of pure creative energy, that their roots in the subconscious and in the Faustian core of life itself are most nearly touched.

These writers were not necessarily of the first rank; but it would be difficult to exaggerate their influence on the European sensibility. Through them the idea of "correspondence"—all sensory stimuli are interchangeable and interwoven dialects in a universal language of perception—the belief in the uniquely generative character of musical composition, in its "privileged daemonism," and the key idea that verbal language is in some manner a lesser thing than music but a road toward it, pass into the repertoire of romantic, symbolist, and modern feeling. These writers prepared Wagner, and their premonitions found in him, and partially in Nietzsche, an extraordinary fulfillment.

Wagner pertains to language and the history of ideas as richly as he does to music (in the very long run perhaps more so). He made of the relationships between language and music the crux of his vision. In the *Gesamtkunstwerk* the upward aspiration of word toward musical tone and the latent antagonism between the two modes of statement were to be conjoined in a synthesis of total expression. In the love-duet of Act II of *Tristan* the words dim to outcry, to a stutter of swooning consciousness (deliberately infantile as is the stutter of the poet at the summit of the *Paradiso*), and pass through virtuosity of sonorous appropriation into something that is no longer speech. Music reaches out into this twilight zone to enclose the word in its own more comprehensive syntax. What is not entirely manifest in Wagner's theory becomes so in fact: music is master of the bargain. Aspiring to synthesis, or more exactly to organic coexistence, language loses the authority of rational statement, of designation through governed structure, which are its proper genius.

The Wagnerian influence on literary aesthetics from Baudelaire to Proust, and on the philosophy of language from Nietzsche to the early Valéry was immense. It brings with it two distinct yet related motifs: the exultation of the poet at being *almost* musician (a vision of self at work no less in Mallarmé than in Auden); but also a sad condescension to the verbal medium, a despair at being restricted to a form of expression thinner, narrower, much nearer the surface of the creative mind than is music. Thus Valéry to Gide in April 1891:

> *Je suis dans* Lohengrin *jusqu' aux yeux. . . . Cette musique m'amènera, cela se prépare, à ne plus écrire. Déjà trop de difficultés m'arrêtent.* Narcisse a *parlé dans le désert . . . être si loin de son rêve. . . . Et puis quelle page écrite arrive à la hauteur des quelques notes qui sont le motif du Graal?*

Something of this haughty exasperation certainly survives in Valéry's later view of poetry as a mere "exercise" or "game" akin to mathematics and by no means superior to it.

"What written page can attain the heights of the few notes of the Grail motif?" The question and the implicit ordering of linguistic and musical means is current in the whole Symbolist movement. It is most carefully worked out in the poetry of Rilke, in Rilke's determination to guard both the genius of language and its rights of kinship to music. Rilke celebrates the power of language to rise toward music; the poet is the chosen instrument of that upward transmutation. But the metamorphosis can be achieved only if language preserves the identity of its striving, if it remains itself in the very act of change. In the *Sonnets to Orpheus* language meditates with delicate precision on its own limits; the word is poised for the transforming rush of music. Yet Rilke, who always works on the frontier between both, recognizes that something is dissolved, perhaps lost, in the crowning change:

> *Gesang, wie du ihn lehrst, ist nicht Begehr,*
> *nicht Werbung um ein endlich noch Erreichtes;*
> *Gesang ist Dasein. Für den Gott ein Leichtes.*

Wann aber sind *wir? Und wann wendet* er
an unser Sein die Erde und die Sterne?
Dies ists *nicht, Jüngling, dass du liebst, wenn auch*
die Stimme dann den Mund dir aufstösst,—lerne
vergessen, dass du aufsangst. Das verrinnt.
In Wahrheit singen, ist ein andrer Hauch.
Ein Hauch um nichts. Ein Wehn im Gott. Ein Wind.

The principal moods and energies of Symbolism and of the Wagnerian dialectic of musical totality now lie behind us. But the idea that music *is* deeper, more comprehensive than language, that it rises with immediacy from the sources of our being, has not lost its relevance and fascination. As has often been observed, the attempt to deepen or reinforce a literary structure by means of musical analogy is frequent in modern poetry and fiction (in the *Four Quartets*, in Proust, in Broch's *Death of Virgil*). But the impulse toward a musical ideal is more far-reaching.

There is a widespread intimation, though as yet only vaguely defined, of a certain exhaustion of verbal resources in modern civilization, of a brutalization and devaluation of the word in the mass-cultures and mass-politics of the age. What more is there to say? How can that which is novel and discriminating enough to be worth saying get a hearing amid the clamor of verbal inflation? The word, especially in its sequential, typographic forms, may have been an imperfect, perhaps transitory code. Music alone can fulfill the two requirements of a truly rigorous communicative or semiological system: to be unique to itself (untranslatable) yet immediately comprehensible. Thus (in defiance, I think, of the specialized conventions of different musical "languages") argues Lévi-Strauss. He characterizes the composer, the inventor of melody, as *un être pareil aux dieux* even as Homer was characterized by Montaigne. Lévi-Strauss sees in music *le suprême mystère des sciences de l'homme, celui contre lequel elles butent, et qui garde la clé de leur progrès.* In music our deafened lives may regain a sense of the inward motion and temperance of individual being, and our societies something of a lost vision of human accord. Through music the arts and exact sciences may reach a common syntax.

We are back with Pythagoras or, more humbly, we live in rooms in which the record-cabinet has replaced the bookshelf.

Although they go beyond language, leaving verbal communication behind, both the translation into light and the metamorphosis into music are positive spiritual acts. Where it ceases or suffers radical mutation, the word bears witness to an inexpressible reality or to a syntax more supple, more penetrating than its own.

But there is a third mode of transcendence: in it language simply ceases, and the motion of spirit gives no further outward manifestation of its being. The poet enters into silence. Here the word borders not on radiance or music, but on night.

This election of silence by the most articulate is, I believe, historically recent. The strategic myth of the philosopher who chooses silence because of the ineffable purity of his vision or because of the unreadiness of his audience has antique precedent. It contributes to the motif of Empedocles on Aetna and to the gnomic aloofness of Heraclitus. But the poet's choice of silence, the writer relinquishing his articulate enactment of identity in mid-course, is something new. It occurs, as an experience obviously singular but formidable in general implication, in two of the principal masters, shapers, heraldic presences if you will, of the modern spirit: in Hölderlin and Rimbaud.

Each is among the foremost poets of his language. Each carried the written word to the far places of syntactic and perceptual possibility. In Hölderlin German verse attains an unsurpassed concentration, purity, and wholeness of realized form. There is no European poetry more mature, more inevitable in the sense of excluding from itself any looser, more prosaic order. A poem by Hölderlin fills a gap in the idiom of human experience with abrupt, complete necessity, though we had not previously known such a gap to exist. With Rimbaud poetry demands and is accorded the freedom of the modern city—those privileges of indirection, of technical autonomy, of inward reference and sub-surface rhetoric which almost define the twentieth-century style. Rimbaud left his thumbprint on language, on the name and nature of the modern poet, as Cézanne did on apples.

Yet as important as the work itself is the intense after-life of Hölderlin and Rimbaud in the mythology, in the active metaphors of the modern literary condition. Beyond the poems, almost stronger than they, is the fact of renunciation, the chosen silence.

By the age of thirty Hölderlin had accomplished nearly his whole work; a few years later he entered on a quiet madness which lasted thirty-six years, but during which there were a few sparks of the old lucid power (the famous quatrain written down, apparently impromptu, in April 1812). At eighteen Rimbaud completed the *Saison en enfer*, and embarked on the other hell of Sudanese commerce and Ethiopian gun-running. From it he poured out a deluge of exasperated letters; they bear the marks of his temper and harsh concision, but contain no line of poetry or reference to the work of genius left behind. In both cases, the precise motives and genesis of silence remain obscure. But the myths of language and poetic function that spring from the silence are clear and constitute a shaping legacy.

Hölderlin's silence has been read not as a negation of his poetry but as, in some sense, its unfolding and its sovereign logic. The gathering strength of stillness within and between the lines of the poems have been felt as a primary element of their genius. As empty space is so expressly a part of modern painting and sculpture, as the silent intervals are so integral to a composition by Webern, so the void places in Hölderlin's poems, particularly in the late fragments, seem indispensable to the completion of the poetic act. His posthumous life in a shell of quiet, similar to that of Nietzsche, stands for the word's surpassing of itself, for its realization not in another medium but in that which is its echoing antithesis and defining negation, silence.

Rimbaud's abdication is seen to have a very different sense. It signifies the elevation of action over word. "Speech that leads not to action," wrote Carlyle, "still more that hinders it, is a nuisance on the Earth." Having mastered and exhausted the resources of language as only a supreme poet can, Rimbaud turns to that nobler language which is the deed. The child dreams and babbles; the man does.

Both gestures of sensibility, both theoretic models, have exercised tremendous influence. This revaluation of silence—in the epistemology of Wittgenstein, in the aesthetics of Webern and Cage, in the poetics of Beckett—is one of the most original, characteristic acts of the modern spirit. The conceit of the word unspoken, of the music unheard and *therefore* richer is, in Keats, a local paradox, a neo-Platonic ornament. In much modern poetry silence represents the claims of the ideal; to speak is to say less. To Rilke the temptations of silence were inseparable from the hazard of the poetic act:

> *Was spielst du, Knabe? Durch die Gärten gings*
> *wie viele Schritte, flüsternde Befehle.*

Was spielst du, Knabe? Siehe deine Seele
verfing sich in den Stäben der Syrinx.

Was lockst du sie? Der Klang ist wie ein Kerker,
darin sie sich versaümt und sich versehnt;
stark ist dein Leben, doch dein Lied ist stärker,
an deine Sehnsucht schluchzend angelehnt.

Gieb ihr ein Schweigen, dass die Seele leise
heimkehre in das Flutende und Viele,
darin sie lebte, wachsend, weit und weise,
eh du sie zwangst in deine zarten Spiele.

Wie sie schon matter mit den Flügeln schlägt:
so wirst du, Traümer, ihren Flug vergeuden,
dass ihre Schwinge, vom Gesang zersägt,
sie nicht mehr über meine Mauern trägt,
wenn ich sie rufen werde zu den Freuden.

This sense of the work of art as entrapped, diminished when it is given articulate form and thus enters into a condition where it is both static and public, is not mystical, though it borrows some of the traditional tones of mysticism. It is grounded in historical circumstance, in a late stage of linguistic and formal civilization in which the expressive achievements of the past seem to weigh exhaustively on the possibilities of the present, in which word and genre seem tarnished, flattened to the touch, like coin too long in circulation. It is also part of a recognition, developed during the Romantic movement and given new metaphors of rationality by Freud, that art, so far as it is public communication, must share in a common code of surface meaning, that it necessarily impoverishes and generalizes the unique, individual life-force of unconscious creation. Ideally each poet should have his own language, singular to his expressive need; given the social, conventionalized nature of human speech, such language can only be silence.

But neither the paradox of silence as the final logic of poetic speech nor the exaltation of action over verbal statement, which is so strong a current in romantic existentialism, accounts for what is probably the most honest temptation to silence in contemporary feeling. There is a third and more powerful impulse, dating from circa 1914. As Mrs. Bickle expresses it in the closing sentence of that black comedy of novelist and recalcitrant subject, James Purdy's *Cabot Wright Begins*, "I won't be a writer in a place and time like the present."

The possibility that the political inhumanity of the twentieth century and certain elements in the technological mass-society which has followed on the erosion of European bourgeois values have done injury to language is the underlying theme of this book. In different essays I have discussed specific aspects of linguistic devaluation and dehumanization.

To a writer who feels that the condition of language is in question, that the word may be losing something of its humane genius, two essential courses are available: he may seek to render his own idiom representative of the general crisis, to convey through it the precariousness and vulnerability of the communicative act; or he may choose the suicidal rhetoric of silence. The sources and development of both attitudes can be seen most clearly in modern German literature, written as it is in the language which has most fully embodied and undergone the grammar of the inhuman.

To Kafka—and this is the core of his representative role in modern letters—the act of writing was a miraculous scandal. The live nakedness of his style takes no syllable for granted. Kafka names all things anew in a second Garden full of ash and doubt. Hence the tormented scruple of his every linguistic proposal. The *Letters to Milena* (they are the finest of modern love letters, the least dispensable) come back and back to the impossibility of adequate statement, to the hopelessness of the writer's task which is to find language as yet unsullied, worn to cliché, made empty by unmeditated waste. Arrested, in his own life and background, between conflicting idioms (Czech, German, Hebrew), Kafka was able to approach the very act of speech from outside. Listening to the mystery of language with more acute humility than ordinary men, he heard the jargon of death growing loud inside the European vulgate. Not in any vague, allegoric sense, but with exact prophecy. From the literal nightmare of *The Metamorphosis* came the knowledge that *Ungeziefer* ("vermin") was to be the designation of millions of men. The bureaucratic parlance of *The Trial* and *The Castle* have become commonplace in our herded lives. The instrument of torture in "In the Penal Colony" is also a printing press. In short, Kafka heard the name Buchenwald in the word *birchwood*. He understood, as if the bush had burned for him again, that a great inhumanity was lying in wait for European man, and that parts of language would serve it and be made base in the process (one thinks of the modulations from "central intelligence" in the fiction of Henry James to Central Intelligence in Washington). In such a time the act of writing might be either frivolous—the cry in the poem smothering or beautifying the cry in the street—or altogether impossible. Kafka found metaphoric expression for both alternatives.

So did Hofmannsthal in the most mature, elusive of his comedies, *Der Schwierige*. Momentarily buried alive in the trenches, Hans Karl Bühl returns from the wars profoundly distrustful of language. To use words as if they could truly convey the pulse and bewilderments of human feeling, to entrust the quick of the human spirit to the inflated currency of social conversation, is to commit self-deception and "indecency" (the key word in the play). "I understand myself much less well when I speak than when I am silent," says Bühl. Asked to orate in the Upper House on the high theme of the "reconciliation of nations," Kari draws back with fastidious, pessimistic insight. To open one's mouth on such a topic is to "wreak unholy confusion." The very fact that one sees to *say* certain things "is an indecency." The close contemporaneity between Wittgenstein's *Tractatus* and the parables of silence in Hofmannsthal and other German and Austrian writers of the 1920's needs study. An estrangement from language was, presumably, a part of a more general abandonment of confidence in the stabilities and expressive authority of central European civilization.

Nine years after Kafka's death, on the eve of actual barbarism, Schoenberg concluded *Moses und Aron* with the cry "O word, thou word that I lack." At almost the same time, the incompatibility between eloquence, the poet's primary delight in speech, and the inhuman nature of political reality, became the theme of the art of Hermann Broch.

Because their language had served at Belsen, because words could be found for all those things and men were not struck dumb for using them, a number of German writers who had gone into exile or survived Nazism, despaired of their instrument. In his *Song of*

Exile, Karl Wolfskehl proclaimed that the true word, the tongue of the living spirit, was dead:

> *Und ob ihr tausend Worte habt:*
> *Das Wort, das Wort ist tot.*

Elisabeth Borcher said: "I break open stars and find nothing, and again nothing, and then a word in a foreign tongue." A conclusion to an exercise in linguistic-logical analysis, which Wittgenstein carefully stripped of all emotive reference, though he stated it in a mode strangely poetic, strangely reminiscent of the atmosphere of Hölderlin's notes on Sophocles, of Lichtenberg's aphorisms, had turned to a grim truth, to a precept of self-destructive humanity for the poet. "Whereof one cannot speak, thereof one must be silent."

But this sense of a death in language, of the failure of the word in the face of the inhuman, is by no means limited to German.

During the political crisis of 1938, Adamov asked himself whether the thought of being a writer was not an untimely joke, whether the writer would ever again, in European civilization, have a living, humane idiom with which to work:

> *Le nom de Dieu ne devrait plus jaillir de la bouche de l'homme. Ce*
> *mot dégradé par l'usage, depuis si longtemps, ne signifie plus rien.*
> *Il est vidé de tout sens, de tout sang. . . . Les mots, ces gardiens du*
> *sens ne sont pas immortels, invulnérables. . . . Comme les hommes,*
> *les mots souffrent. . . . Certains peuvent survivre, d'autres sont in-*
> *curables. . . . Dans la nuit tout se confond, il n'y a plus de noms, plus*
> *de formes.*

When war came, he wrote: "Worn, threadbare, filed down, words have become the carcass of words, phantom words; everyone drearily chews and regurgitates the sound of them between their jaws."

More recently, Ionesco has published the following from his *Journal:*

> It is as if, through becoming involved in literature, I had used up all possible symbols without really penetrating their meaning. They no longer have any vital significance for me. Words have

killed images or are concealing them. A civilization of words is a civilization distraught. Words create confusion. Words are not the word [*les mots ne sont pas la parole*]. . . . The fact is that words say nothing, if I may put it that way. . . . There are no words for the deepest experience. The more I try to explain myself, the less I understand myself. Of course, not everything is unsayable in words, only the living truth.

These two last sentences echo, almost exactly, Hofmannsthal's Kari Bühl. The writer, who is by definition master and servant of language, states that the living truth is no longer sayable. The theater of Beckett is haunted by this insight. Developing Chekhov's notion of the near-impossibility of effective verbal interchange, it strains toward silence, toward an *Act Without Words*. Soon there will be plays in which absolutely nothing is said, in which each personage will struggle to achieve the outrage or futility of speech only to have the sound turn to gibberish or die in their grimacing mouths. The first articulate word spoken will bring down the curtain.

Under the influence, perhaps, of Heidegger and of Heidegger's gloss on Hölderlin, recent French linguistic philosophy also assigns a special function and prestigious authority to silence. For Brice Parain, "language is the threshold of silence." Henri Lefebvre finds that silence "is at once inside language, and on its near and far sides." Much of his theory of speech depends on the organized patterns of silence in the otherwise continuous and consequently indecipherable linguistic code. Silence has "another speech than ordinary saying" (*un autre Dire que le dire ordinaire*), but it is meaningful speech nevertheless.

These are not macabre fantasies or paradoxes for logicians. The question of whether the poet should speak or be silent, of whether language is in a condition to accord with his needs, is a real one. "No poetry after Auschwitz," said Adorno, and Sylvia Plath enacted the underlying meaning of his statement in a manner both histrionic and profoundly sincere. Has our civilization, by virtue of the inhumanity it has carried out and condoned—we are accomplices to that which leaves us indifferent—forfeited its claims to that indispensable luxury which we call literature? Not for ever, not everywhere, but simply in this time and place, as a city besieged forfeits its claims to the freedom of the winds and the cool of evening outside its walls.

I am not saying that writers should stop writing. This would be fatuous. I am asking whether they are not writing too much, whether the deluge of print in which we seek our deafened way is not itself a subversion of meaning. "A civilization of words is a civilization distraught." It is one in which the constant inflation of verbal counters has so devalued the once numinous act of written communication that there is almost no way for the valid and the genuinely new to make themselves heard. Each month must produce its masterpiece and so the press hounds mediocrity into momentary, fake splendor. The scientists tell us that the acceleration of specialized, monographic publication is such that libraries will soon have to be placed in orbit, circling the earth and subject to electronic scanning as needed. The proliferation of verbiage in humanistic scholarship, the trivia decked out as erudition or critical re-assessment, threatens to obliterate the work of art itself and the exacting freshness of personal encounter on which true criticism depends. We also speak far too much, far too easily, making common what was private, arresting into the clichés of false certitude that which was provisional, personal, and therefore alive on the shadow-side of speech. We live in a culture which is, increasingly, a wind-tunnel of gossip; gossip that reaches from theology and politics to an unprecedented noising of private concerns (the psychoanalytic process is the high rhetoric of gossip). This world will end neither with a bang nor a whimper, but with a headline, a slogan, a pulp novel larger than the cedars of Lebanon. In how much of what is now pouring forth do words become word—and where is the silence needed if we are to hear that metamorphosis?

The second point is one of politics, in the fundamental sense. It is better for the poet to mutilate his own tongue than to dignify the inhuman either with his gift or his uncaring. If totalitarian rule is so effective as to break all chances of denunciation, of satire, then let the poet cease—and let the scholar cease from editing the classics a few miles down the road from the death camp. Precisely because it is the signature of his humanity, because it is that which makes of man a being of striving unrest, the word should have no natural life, no neutral sanctuary, in the places and season of bestiality. Silence *is* an alternative. When the words in the city are full of savagery and lies, nothing speaks louder than the unwritten poem.

"Now the Sirens have a still more fatal weapon than their song," wrote Kafka in his *Parables*, "namely their silence. And though admittedly such a thing has never happened, still it is conceivable that someone might possibly have escaped from their singing; but from their silence certainly never."

How silent must that sea have been; how ready for the wonder of the word.

20. PHILIP

Looking for Livingstone: An Odyssey of Silence (Stratford, Ontario: Mercury Press, 1991), pp. 30–31, 60–75.

Marlene Nourbese Philip blends mythological and historical imagination, in poetry and prose, in her tale of pursuing Dr. David Livingstone, widely acclaimed as the "discoverer" of the "silent continent." The black, female, first-person narrator travels back through untold eons of time to encounter "Livingstone-I-presume" and settle some accounts with him, but also to surrender to the seductive intercourse of word and silence that blemishes purity and yet, after all, is our common heritage. Word and silence—here identified as male and female, discoverer and discovered, colonizer and colonized—are roles that can be reversed, but in the end the two come back together and, in some sense, need each other and belong together.

The protagonist is passionately interested in "the possible independence of that Silence—independent of the Word." Sometimes she is not sure she needs words at all. Nevertheless, this "stubborness" finally yields, and her autistic fantasy of a silent femininity with no need of masculinity and its words proves untenable, for it is merely the hurt inversion of Livingstone's stubborn subjugation of Africa's supposed silence to his own presumptuous pronouncements. An alternative is to transform this hierarchy, and to reinvent silence as no longer the repressed female but rather the fine flower of a femininity that delivers masculinity in its conquering, yet withering verbalness from sterility: "I want to make the desert of words bloom—with Silence!"

Philip's fresh, original meditation on and exaltation of silence contemplates its productivity, its fecundity, in an age of the desertification of discourse. At the extreme limits of colonial, patriarchal discourse, the rejuvenating voice of suppressed silence restores life and color and sex to the formal language of literature and history. This mission is not without precedent in the apophatic movements of the past that likewise were engendered as reactions against the stagnation of languages long since rigidly codified, and as such no longer able to evoke a "something" that shelters in silences and shies away from saying, something that without a certain violation cannot be said. This "some-

344

thing," elicited by delicate attentiveness, and not perhaps without reverent violence, is the irrepressible source of spontaneity and flow in language and life alike.

From *Looking for Livingstone: An Odyssey of Silence*

In the beginning was—
nothing
      could
      would
be
  without Silence
          culture
nurturing the paradise
      the parasite in word
with the upon of
        hang
        wait
        depend
Word and Silence feed
        the share
in need
    wed
content
    with the conspire
in symbiosis—
      embryo word

clasped
        clings to the surround in
Silence
        divided by the Fall
in word into
                silence minus word
wanting Silence
                cleft
                        one
into two
        halved into twin
                into split
                        severed
by the Lord in word
                        whole
original

In the beginning was
the ravage
        in
word inside time
                inside
History
        Silence seeks the balance
in revenge
the cut in precise
                cleaves to the ever in Word
seeking to silence
Silence

THE FIRST AND LAST DAY OF THE MONTH OF NEW MOONS
(OTHERWISE KNOWN AS THE FIRST AND LAST MONTH) IN THE
EIGHTEEN BILLIONTH YEAR OF OUR WORD, WHICH IS THE
SAME AS THE END OF TIME, WHICH IS THE SAME AS THE FIF-

TEENTH DAY OF JUNE, NINETEEN HUNDRED AND EIGHTY SEVEN
IN THE YEAR OF OUR LORD

SOMEWHERE, AFRICA
0000 HOURS

1st – 15th June—have lost tracks yet again, but believe him to be
in the area—I must—will find him soon—somewhere—What is it
going to be like, meeting him? Have been trying to imagine it—have
even been practising my opening words: "Hello there, Mr. Livingstone"; "Good day to you, Sir"; "Well, fancy meeting you here";
"Good to see you, you old bugger,"—they all sounded forced. Would
I be cool enough to give him a first rate black hand shake and say, "Yo
there, Livi baby, my man, my main man!"?

20TH – 30TH JUNE
0600 HOURS

Have picked up his tracks again—he is close—so close I can
smell him!—checked my Polaroid camera again. (I had been lucky to
get it cheap from a group I met a hundred and fifty years earlier.) I
want to record for posterity my first sighting of him.

31ST DAY OF JUNE
2800 HOURS

Finally (silence) Dr. Livingstone, I presume? (silence) we meet
(silence) he and I (silence) in a clearing (silence) in a forest (silence)
somewhere (silence) in time (silence) it doesn't matter (silence) This
man of God (silence) and medicine—an unbeatable combination
(silence) "foe of darkness" (silence) Shaman (silence) Witch-doctor
(silence) Holy Man (silence) Prophet (silence) Charlatan (silence) He
(silence) and I (silence) and my silence (silence)—his discovery (silence)
  I had been searching for him for an eternity, it seemed—eighteen
billion years—the age of the universe; advancing deeper and deeper
into Silence, my silence, picking up the odd rumour about him here
and there, following tracks—some of them old and stale long before

I got to them; I had been locked up, tested, challenged—even be-trayed—in my search for Livingstone. He would open "a path to the interior or perish." I followed him, opening a path to my interior, or I would, as surely as he did, perish.

And now here he was—here we were—nothing that had hap-pened to me along the way prepared me for this—he and I . . . and Si-lence . . . my silence. We looked at each other . . . across a distance of some three feet—the infinite in time—my silence. I looked at my cheap, digital watch—I had picked it up somewhere along the way—it was 2800 hours exactly. I looked at him standing there with his guides, Susi, Chuma and Gardener.

"You're new here, aren't you?" I said, and didn't raise my hat—I didn't have one to raise, and even if I did I wouldn't have—raised it. Which of us reached out first, I don't know—it didn't matter—I took his hand and he mine. This old white man—tall, gaunt—my neme-sis—half-blind, bronzed by the African sun, the indiscriminate African sun—malarial, sick or crazy—it was all the same.

(silence) Dr. Livingstone, I presume? (silence) I presume (si-lence) Dr. Livingstone (silence) I presume—he and I . . . Livingstone, the discoverer, riding on the adventure in the word that hacks and cuts and thrusts its way through the wet and moist climate of Silence, plunging ever deeper into the heart of a continent . . . and Silence—the discovered silence—my silence. Or was it the other way around? I, the discoverer—he, the discovered. I had nothing to say to him; after eighteen billion years of travel, what was there to say—what could I say? That I had found what I had started out with? Silence?

How cocky he was—Livingstone—and proud of his discoveries. His face brightened and his eyes shone with excitement as he boasted about his exploits: "You must have heard of my journeys across Africa," he said, "bringing Christianity and civilization to the natives. The Queen honoured me for that, you know, and for my work against the slave trade—a terrible thing, that, terrible!" I let him go on and said nothing for a while. Then I spoke, "You're nothing but a cheat and a liar, Livingstone-I-presume. Without the African, you couldn't have done anything—nothing—and what I did, I did all by myself—no guides, no artificial horizons, no compasses—nothing—not even the 'good book'—just me, me and more me. *That* is true discovery, Livingstone-I-presume. No one, but no one had been there before me to visit—to discover my Silence. And furthermore, while

you thought you were discovering Africa, it was Africa that was discovering you." At these words, he bit hard on his bottom lip (I
thought he would draw blood) but said nothing. I could tell he was
very upset. "By the way," I continued, "did you know those bloody
South Africans bombed your town, the one named after you—
Livingstone, foe of darkness—let's see, it was in nineteen hundred
and eighty seven, I believe, in April to be exact—by the old calendar."

"Did they bomb it because it was named after me?" I had caught
his interest again. "They never did like me preaching against their en-
slavement of the African—those Boers—" he shook his head for emphasis—"a nasty lot they were back then—very nasty lot."

"They still are, Livingstone-I-presume, they still are a nasty lot,
but why do you always think you are the reason for everything—you
really aren't that important. No, they didn't bomb it because of you,
but let's put it this way—they would still be mad at you today." He
sulked for a long time after this—just like a little boy—while his
helpers made us coffee and a meal. He did know how to travel in
style, that Livingstone.

Over coffee I gave him credit for discovering my silence, and
bringing it out for all the world to see and cherish and love; I told him
how indispensable he had been to this, that were it not for him, I
would never have set out on my travels to find my interior—the
source of my silence—which was he perhaps. This cheered him up,
and he grew visibly happier; he puffed himself up—if he didn't have
Africa, at least he had my silence.

After the meal we sat down outside his tent to an excellent
cognac—Christian man though he was; and while his helpers stoked
up the fire, we began talking—exchanging stories, maps and curios—
each trying to best the other for the most outrageous, most out-
landish tale. I told him all about the ECNELIS, the CLEENIS and the
NEECLIS and many of the other peoples I had "visited" on my travels. The Museum of Silence really had him beat, though—he had
nothing, absolutely nothing, to compare with that. We laughed a lot,
he and I, and I got Susi, one of his helpers, to take a picture of us
both—Livingstone-I-presume and I, side by side on my quilt of Silence, smiling at the camera. We both said nothing for a while.

"I want to tell you about a dream I had, Livingstone-I-presume,
while on my travels. Being a man of God you might find it interesting."

"Hmm," was all he said. He seemed sunk in his own thoughts.

"In the dream I stood on top of a very high hill, Livingstone, just outside a city. It was just before the end of the day, and the sky-scrapers glistened and shone in that last blaze of light you get with sunsets."

"What's a skyscraper?" I looked at him—of course, he wouldn't know what I was talking about.

"A very very tall building, Livingstone-I-presume, which scrapes the sky—literally. Anyway, it was a wonderful sunset, the sky all smudged and streaked with red and orange, the best ever sunset I've seen. You must have seen some glorious ones on this continent, haven't you?" He nodded. "Suddenly I heard a voice behind me telling me that everything before me was mine. I turned to see who had spoken: a tall white man in a pith helmet and freshly pressed white ducks stood there smiling at me. Now that I think about it, Liv-ingstone-I-presume, he looked a lot like you. Anyway, in the dream I asked him what he meant, and waving his arms at the scene spread out below us, he told me again that it was mine—all mine." Liv-ingstone was listening attentively; before going on I reached for the coffee pot and refilled my tin mug. "So, I asked 'pith helmet' what the catch was—I was suspicious as hell and my voice and attitude showed this. The old bugger just stood there looking at me slyly, pretending not to know what I meant. I asked him why he wanted to give me 'all this' and waved my arms just as he had done at the scene below us. He still didn't answer me, but took off his helmet and mopped his balding head with a white handkerchief. Finally I got re-ally impatient with him, told him to go to hell, and said I was leaving.

"What do you think he wanted, Livingstone-I-presume?"

"Hmm, what's that?"

"You haven't been listening, have you?"

"Oh, yes, it was reminding me of the temptation of Christ in the desert."

"I thought you would say that—but I didn't tell him to 'Get thee behind me, Satan.' I wanted him right up front where I could keep my eyes on him. But you still haven't told me what you think the man in my dream—'pith helmet'—wanted."

"I don't know—was he offering to make you queen of the city?"

I laughed—"Nothing so simple as that, Livingstone. He wanted my—" I leant over and whispered in his ear. He looked puzzled.

"Silence?" he said. I nodded. "Why did he want that?"

"He was offering me words, Livingstone—if I had words, he said, I could be a witness to all that had gone wrong. I could speak out, condemn—I could even blame them. I couldn't do that with silence, he told me. I was just silent with silence. At that point in my dream, I came awake, and I remember thinking that if he wanted my silence so much, there had to be some value in it—don't you think so, Livingstone-I-presume?" I didn't wait for an answer, and continued. "It is the only thing I have that is not contaminated. My Silence—my very own Silence." Livingstone said nothing. "Well, what do you think?" I asked.

"I don't know what to make of it, although I do agree with what he said to you."

"You would."

"But you're so much more powerful with words, aren't you—"

"Are you, Livingstone? And whose words are you—am I—powerful with?" He and I stared at each other, then he looked away, still not saying anything. "By the way, was it you in that dream, or the devil offering me the keys to the city?" He merely shook his head—which of the questions was he saying no to?—I still don't know.

"You know, Livingstone-I-presume, I'm tired—really tired of these travels. I have found what I came for—have you?"

"Have I what? and why do you keep calling me Livingstone-I-presume?"

"Found what you came for—and I don't know why I call you Livingstone-I-presume—you look like Livingstone-I-presume, I suppose."

"Hmm . . . well, I found fame—a name—made history, helped establish civilization—they called me the 'foe of darkness,' you know."

"And what a foe you were." He understood my tone, and gave me a funny look. "Little did you know how close the darkness was, eh, Livingstone-I-presume? I myself prefer 'thin edge of the wedge' as a title to describe you."

"What do you mean by the darkness being close?"

"It would take too long to explain, Livingstone, but let's say the darkness wasn't all out there—in the 'dark continent.' You and your kind carried their own dark continents within them." I was getting to him—I noticed he hadn't said anything about discovering any lakes or rivers. "And what about Victoria Falls," I needled him, "didn't you *discover* that?"

He smiled modestly, "Well, I suppose you could say that—although the Africans did know of it—but I was the first—the first European to—"

"You lie, Livingstone-I-presume. The Portuguese were there before you—"

"Half-castes—not Europeans!"

"Bull-shit!—you made that up so you could capture the glory yourself, and long before you, or any Portuguese for that matter, crossed Africa coast to coast—from Loanda to Quilimane—long before that, Africans had done it—so put that in your metaphorical pipe and smoke it." He shut up after that. For a while.

"Well, what did you discover?" he asked finally. "And by the way, what did you say your name was?"

I laughed. "I didn't, Livingstone-I-presume. Just call me The Traveller—that'll do for now." I looked at him, took a sip of my cognac—"As to your first question—thought you'd never ask. You really want to know?"

"Well, I thought since we were sharing confidences—"

"Confidences shit—I'm sharing nothing with you, but I will *tell* you—Silence—"

"Silence?"

"Silence."

"You discovered silence."

"I did—you want to quarrel with that?"

"No, but—"

"But you're curious—you want to know whether I have written any books about my discoveries, or my exploits—whether I've won any awards, was given the keys to any cities—European, of course—made any money, received any honorary degrees—right, Livingstone-I-presume?"

"Well, that would be proof—"

"Proof of what—you ask for proof that I discovered my Silence—my very own Silence—when you're sitting right there in front of me? You want facts, dates and years—the time down to the last millisecond—don't you? and titles of books like TRAVELS WITH MY SILENCE; or MY LIFE WITH THE CLEENIS, or HOW I BROUGHT THE WORD TO THE CESLIENS—what about MY MEETING WITH LIVINGSTONE-I-PRESUME?"

"That would help."

"Do you know what a fact is, Livingstone-I-presume?"

"Yes—of course."

"No you don't—a fact is whatever anyone, having the power to enforce it, says is a fact. Power—that is the distinguishing mark of a fact. Fact—Livingstone discovered Victoria Falls."

"*That* is a fact."

"*That,* Livingstone-I-presume, is a lie, *and* a fact, because you and your supporters, your nation of liars, had the power to change a lie into a fact. Those falls had a name long before you got to them— you remember what it was—the name?"

"No."

"Of course you wouldn't—I'll tell you—Mo-si-o-a-tun-ya— Mosioatunya or The Smoke That Thunders—remember now? And who first named the falls? The Africans, yet the 'fact' we have lived with, is that you, Livingstone-I-presume, 'discovered' Victoria Falls. Now if *I* had the power, I could make 'Livingstone is a liar and a cheat' into a fact—I could say Sekeletu, chief of the Makololo, discovered the Falls, and *that* would be a fact, Livingstone-I-presume. *If* I had the power."

"All right, all right, I see your point," he said sullenly.

"Livingstone, since we're dealing with facts, I want to ask you two questions. Promise me you'll answer honestly?"

"I am a man of my word." His tone rebuked me and he pulled himself up even taller.

"And how, Livingstone—and how. Now—how many converts did you actually make in your entire time in Africa?" For several minutes there was nothing but silence. Eventually his answer came—

"One, I believe." He seemed to shrink into his tall, gaunt frame.

"Sechele, Chief of the Bakwains?" I added. He nodded. "And he afterwards reverted to his African religion, didn't he?" He nodded again and said nothing. "Second question." He looked at me, his face tight with a mixture of anger and shame. He seemed fearful of what the next question would be, and for one brief moment I let myself feel sorry for him, but it was a cheap emotion—he didn't need pity. "Remember your promise now." I cautioned him. "Didn't you advocate the destruction of African society and religious customs so you could bring European commerce more easily to the Africans, and then Christianity?" The silence between us stretched on for an eternity.

"I am waiting, Livingstone-I-presume," I said finally.

"Yes, I did, but I had to, don't you see, I had to—my work—"
I raised my hand and he fell silent. "You're not on trial before me,
Livingstone—but how I wish you were."

"But I had a lot of respect and admiration for Africans—"

"I'm sure you did, Livingstone," I said, pouring myself another
drink.

"Read my journals, you'll see what I thought of them, I even—"
He fell silent once again before my gaze. I smiled at him and he
dropped his eyes. We sat like that for a while, every now and again
one of us stoking the fire, until he broke the silence.

"You said you discovered silence—I don't understand how you
can do that—discover silence, I mean. It's not a thing like a river, or a
waterfall, or a country."

"Oh, Livingstone-I-presume, how very, very stupid you are." He
looked all crestfallen again—"Come on, come on, cheer up—have
another cognac." I held out the bottle. "It's damn good, isn't it—and
don't take it to heart—you're one stubborn son of a bitch and I respect you for it." His face brightened. "You know what they say about
you?" He shook his head. "That where there was a blank before you
filled in—charted and mapped—"

"And so I did, so I did!—" his eagerness to claim his discoveries
was both child-like and overwhelming.

"No, Livingstone-I-presume, you did not. Shall I tell you what
you did?" He was all huffy again at my interruption and merely
shrugged. "You captured and seized the Silence you found—
possessed it like the true discoverer you were—dissected and analysed
it; labelled it—you took their Silence—the Silence of the African—
and replaced it with your own—the silence of your word."

"No, no—I insist—" I had not seen him so adamant before—
"I broke the silence that was there before and *that* was a good thing—
silence is never a good thing . . ."

"Isn't it now, Livingstone-I-presume? Isn't it? Is that the gospel
according to Livingstone?" He made a rude sound under his breath,
and shifted his body restlessly.

"You say Silence is not a thing like a waterfall, or a river that can
be discovered, but I assure you I have mapped and measured my own
Silence to the last millimetre, and it exists, Livingstone-I-presume, let
me tell you, it exists—so tangible I can even touch it at times—like

this—" I reached out and lay my hand on his. He looked down—my black hand resting on his—scrawny, knobbly and white. We looked at each other.

"I have two riddles for you, Livingstone-I-presume—a riddle, a riddle, a riddle ma ree: what is both noun and verb as well as sentence?"

"Noun, verb and sentence?" he repeated to himself under his breath.

Around us it had now become quite dark—the fire lit up his gaunt face, leaving his thin, raddled body in darkness. As he puzzled over the question his face seemed to float—

"Give up?" I asked.

"Yes."

"Silence."

"Silence?"

"Yes, Silence. Silence is a noun, yes?" He nodded. "To silence is a verb, and silence is a sentence."

"How sentence?"

"As in punishment—Livingstone-I-presume—or sanction—you know, I silence *you*."

He laughed, "Clever—very clever."

"Another one?"

"Yes."

"What kind of sentence can only be broken, not appealed?" The sound of crickets was now loud around us—I put some more wood on the fire.

"Well, I know now it has to do with silence . . . and you said that silence was a sentence—one breaks silence, doesn't one?"

"One? *I*, *me*, Livingstone-I-presume, *I* break *my* silence—the sentence of my silence."

"Oh, yes, I see now."

"But that wasn't bad, Livingstone-I-presume, wasn't bad at all."

We were silent for a while, listening to the sounds of the forest—my silence between us. "Tell me, Livingstone, do you think Silence has an inherent meaning—beyond what words impose . . . in their absence?"

"I don't believe I understand what you mean."

"Oh dear, oh dear, you are slow—well, we have words, don't we?" He nodded. "But there had to have been Silence before there were words, right?" He nodded again. "Well, that's what I'm interested in—the possible independence of that Silence—independent of word. Is there a philosophy, a history, an epistemology of Silence—or is it merely an absence of word?"

"Oh yes, I see, I see—"

He didn't—I could tell. He was just an old man—tired like me, like me obsessed with discovery—for the sake of discovery, perhaps. We were both silent—

"If I could just draw it, give it a shape, Livingstone-I-presume, make it tangible—would I pattern it like words—could there be a grammar of Silence that I could parse and analyse? What *is* the logic of Silence?"

"But, my child, you need the word for all that, and there's the rub."

I looked at the tired, pale face, ghostly in the firelight, saw the dying fire, the outline of the tent, the cognac in my shot glass—"I am *not* your child, Livingstone-I-presume," I said very, *very* softly, my tone almost threatening, "and I'm not sure I need words. I'm like you, you see, stubborn. You refused to believe the Zambesi was unnavigable, remember?—from the coast up to the highlands of Shire. I want to make the desert of words bloom—with Silence!"

"Surely you mean the desert of silence bloom with words—"

"You are a hard nut to crack, Livingstone-I-presume, real hard—but crack you will. You remind me of my father—all word, word, and more word—no Silence. It *is* the coarsest of currencies, you know—the word—crass and clumsy as a way of communication; a second cousin, and a poor one at that, of Silence." He looked at me as if I was crazy and went off into one of his sulks again. I let him be while I poured some more cognac and put some wood on the fire. "Now that I have found you—or rather, we have found each other," I said, "I want to ask one thing of you."

"What is that?"

"A kiss—"

He sat up straight—I poked at the fire—"You heard me, Livingstone-I-presume—a kiss—one, small kiss—on the lips—to seal this unholy pact of ours: your Word, my Silence."

All his native, ramrod, Scottish Calvinism, honed in the cold kirks of the highlands, rose like bile in his throat, and he was outraged.

"Relax, Livingstone-I-presume, I have done worse things—a lot worse things—or better, depending on how you look at it—with you . . . in my dreams." I smiled at him.

He blanched even more, betraying the African sun.

"There *is* no law against dreaming, is there?" I asked him.

"There should be," he muttered, "in cases like this." This coming from the man who had as much as abandoned his wife for his adventures in the "dark continent." Was that a lesser sin than my request for one, small kiss? But his Christian piety was deeply offended.

"Oh, bugger of, Livingstone-I-presume, bugger off." He didn't say anything more for a while. Then he asked, "What is it you want of me?" His words came slowly, almost as if he didn't want to ask them or feared the answer. Or both.

I sighed. I was weary. "Nothing of *you*, Livingstone-I-presume. But often over the centuries while I searched for you, I would see myself as a shadow, a dark ghost—a memory almost—haunting you in your sleepless nights down throughout the ages—refusing to let you rest in the silence of your lies. Now that I've met you, I don't know—" My voice faded away; then I continued. "What do you know of elephants, Livingstone? You must have seen a few in Africa in your time."

"Nothing," he replied. I could hear the "what now" in his reply.

"Did you know that female elephants send out mating calls to the males at frequencies so low humans can't hear?" I sensed him getting tense again. "Relax, Livingstone—this is not about sex, but just think, your Word, my Silence—matching frequencies so low, so precise only we could hear. Word and Silence—which of the two sent out the mating call, Livingstone, *your* Word or *my* Silence? Have you thought of that? Maybe this *is* about sex after all, Livingstone-I-presume—what do you think?"

He said nothing, his only reply a sound, part sigh and part grunt.

(silence) It grew dark (silence) in the forest (silence) we sat on (silence) he, Livingstone-I-presume (silence) and I (silence) before the dying (silence) embers and my Silence (silence) and all around us was Silence (silence)

One hundred thousand years later, there we were—still sitting before the fire—Livingstone and I and Silence. I stretched out my hand and touched him—he seemed asleep; I shook him gently by the shoulder,

"David, David—are you awake?"

"Hmm, what is it?"

"I want to ask you something—"

"Yes, yes, go ahead."

"When you lay dying . . . in the swamps of Bangweolo—in your hut—do you remember?"

"Yes, I do."

"What was the last thing you embraced . . . before you died—your word or your silence . . . what was it, David, Word or Silence?" And all around us was Silence . . . and yet more Silence . . .

How long was it before I prompted him again? "Did you hear me, David?" Perhaps one, maybe two hundred years. "What was the last thing—Word or Silence?"

"Why, I believe it was . . ."

"Yes, yes," I urged him. "What was it?"

"It was neither word nor silence . . . but . . ."

"But what, David?"

"God! . . . yes, now I see . . . that is what it was . . . God! until you asked I never would have . . ."

"Oh, Livingstone-I-presume, you would have to go and complicate matters further with God, wouldn't you?" And all around was Silence . . . waiting   patient   content   willing to enfold   embrace everything   the Word, even.

I couldn't see Livingstone now—so black had it grown   I reached out   my hand   felt the evidence   of SILENCE all around   around me   original primal   alpha *and* omega   and forever through its blackness   I touched something   warm familiar like my own   hand   human   something I could not   see in the SILENCE   reaching out   through the SILENCE of space   the SILENCE of time   through the silence of SILENCE   I touched it his hand   held it   his hand   *and* the SILENCE

I surrendered   to the SILENCE   within

THE
UNUTTERABLY OTHER

21. BATAILLE (1897–1962)

L'expérience intérieure (Paris: Gallimard, 1954), pp. 49, 24–29, 130–136.
Trans. Leslie Anne Boldt, *Inner Experience* (Albany: SUNY Press, 1988), pp. 36–37, 12–16, 112–116.

Georges Bataille rejects all discourses and their "projects" in order to adhere to the sole, unconditional authority of "inner experience." The movement of inner experience is inaccessible to words, and Bataille violently rejects them in his journey to the limits of the possible. "And I know that I have but to break discourse in me and then ecstasy is there, from which discourse alone distances me, the ecstasy that discursive thought betrays . . ."[1] Bataille explores the terrifying territory of silence in a dialectical reversal of traditional forms of Christian mysticism, which he attacks with vehement rhetoric in a savagely Nietzschean spirit.

Words are the narcotic of an intoxication—our "normal" state—from which Bataille's "method" seeks to cure us. He would liberate us from their spell, under which we wander "lost among babblers in a night" ("perdus entre des bavards, dans une nuit"). As he writes in the preface to *L'expérience intérieure*: "The self-avowed suffering of the disintoxicated is the subject of this book" ("La souffrance s'avouant du désintoxiqué est l'objet de ce livre," p. 10). By withdrawal of the drug of discourse, we are forced to sober up to the unendurable pain and torment of the consciousness that we are not All. We wake up then to the pain of our finitude and mortality. We have immediate, "inner" experience of the limits of our existence, and this is unspeakable torment and despair. Discourse only mollifies this wound, which is the cut and bleeding of existence as a separate individual. So Bataille's method strives to eradicate discourse from within us and thereby to make us face the Unspeakable. This is not an abstract Ineffable that would serve to close and secure a system of discourse—quite the contrary.

---

1. *Inner Experience*, p. 59. "Et je sais qu'il suffit de briser le discours en moi, dès lors l'extase est là, dont seul m'éloigne le discours, l'extase que la pensée discursive trahit la donnant comme issue et trahit la donnant comme absence d'issue" (*L'expérience intérieure*, p. 73).

The section "The Torment" ("Le supplice") recounts a new approach to inner experience, one for the first time not aimed at salvation. It is rather anguish and despair, the state of being torn asunder ("déchirement"), suffered to the limit of the possible. This is necessary to completely break down the essentially linguistic structures and defenses of the ego that shield it from existence. Discourse is the form taken by our evasions, our "projects." Consequently, inner experience is achieved by silencing discourse. Bataille continually launches aggressive attacks against words, even poetry. Like Levinas, he seeks escape from "verbal servilities" that reduce every Other to commensurability by the systematization and homogenization of language. Instead, he exalts the "sovereignty" of inner experience as a sole authority unto itself. In the section on method, Bataille repeatedly underlines the imperative of ending all discourse, since discourse postpones *existence*—facing the inarticulate and incommensurable—and distracts us from the experience of sheer torment and ecstasy. Until we arrest and eradicate them, words are always busy in us, like ants, burying the exposure of naked vulnerability by construction of projects. In addition to silence, the laugh is a key method for tearing discourse apart. Likewise the "interior cry."

To attain inner experience, Bataille recommends a "plenitude of means" rather than asceticism, a method of excess rather than a negative way of privations. "One attains the extreme limit in the fullness of means: it demands fulfilled beings, ignoring no audacity. My principle against ascesis is that the extreme limit is accessible through excess, not through deficiency."[2] Nevertheless, sacrifice and a certain renunciation are still necessary: one has to renounce something, namely, the desire to be All ("cesser de vouloir être tout," p. 34).

Accordingly, the unsayable of Bataille is not an emptiness due to transcendence of all finite content. It is filled with preverbal, inarticulate expression and sensation. Sensory and emotional intensity to the limit of the possible for a mortal being in the pain and anguish of fragmentariness and finitude are what cannot be said; they are that for the sake of which speaking in all forms must be renounced. For Bataille, a "holocaust of words" is necessary in which all words are offered up in sacrifice to what they cannot say.[3]

---

2. "On atteint l'extrême dans la plenitude des moyens: il y faut des êtres comblés, n'ignorant aucune audace. Mon principe contre l'ascèse est que l'extrême est accessible par excès, non par défaut" (p. 34).

3. Crucial for tracing Bataille's apophatic critique of discourse is his essay "Hegel, la mort et le sacrifice," in *Oeuvres complètes* (Paris: Gallimard, 1971–88), vol. 12, pp. 326–345.

Hence Bataille's rejection of all evasions through discourse, since "True silence takes place in the absence of words" ("Le vrai silence a lieu dans l'absence des mots," *L'expérience intérieure*, p. 30). Of course, Bataille's "contestation" is itself articulated in discourse and as a "method." The dialectical reversal of discourse seems essential to this radically non-discursive method. If the method could simply be practiced without being articulated, then why this book and so many others by Bataille expressing and articulating the necessity of silence? Bataille seems to be in exactly the same dilemma that he ascribes to Saint Ignatius: completely abhoring discourse, yet trying to remedy its defects by creating a struggle within discourse against itself. Hence "silence" denies its status as a word. This inner tension and striving against its very existence as language marks Bataille's discourse as quintessentially apophatic.

L'expérience intérieure was first published in 1943 and reissued later as volume 1 of Bataille's *La somme athéologique*, which also comprises three other works (*Le coupable*, *Sur Nietzsche: Volonté de chance*, and *Méthode de méditation*) written during the torment of the war years, from 1939 to 1945. Collected in volumes 5 and 6 of Bataille's *Oeuvres complètes*, these works join the *Conférences sur le non-savoir* in volume 8 in articulating Bataille's relation to negative theology.

Laurens ten Kate has assessed this relation in terms of a continuity with Nietzsche's diagnosis and prescriptions for a modernity that has killed God.[4] Bataille attempts to give a positive turn to God's death or disappearance by proposing a "sacred philosophy" of God's absence. The sacred is the relation to the outer limit or exterior that is obliterated by the instrumentalization of all beings and values in modern society and culture. In modern times, after the death of God announced by Nietzsche, this limit can be given no name or description, for it is no longer inhabited by the gods, nor does it any longer represent an other world. The exterior has become empty. Yet modernity still needs to communicate with this empty space, according to Bataille. Only by transgression of the immanence of total instrumentality can the experience of the extreme be preserved. The word "God" remains sacred as the denial of total instrumentality of all that is. It is received as a "gift of loss" precisely through the experience of God's absence. This is the basis for a new way to speak about and *to* God (as in the blasphemous prayer to God at the end of

---

4. Laurens ten Kate, "The Gift of Loss: A Study of the Fugitive God in Bataille's Atheology, with References to Jean-Luc Nancy," in *Flight of the Gods*, ed. Bulhof and ten Kate, especially pp. 263–265.

Inner Experience) that is located between atheism and belief—and refuses the refuge of either—in order to remain open to the extreme, to the experience of the outer limit.

From *Inner Experience*

The Torment

Forgetting of everything. Deep descent into the night of existence. Infinite ignorant pleading, to drown oneself in anguish. To slip over the abyss and in the completed darkness experience the horror of it. To tremble, to despair, in the cold of solitude, in the eternal silence of man (foolishness of all sentences, illusory answers for sentences, only the insane silence of night answers). The word *God*, to have used it in order to reach the depth of solitude, but to no longer know, hear his voice. To know nothing of him. God final word meaning that all words will fail further on: to perceive its own eloquence (it is not avoidable), to laugh at it to the point of unknowing stupor (laughter no longer needs to laugh, nor crying to cry, nor sobbing to sob). Further on one's head bursts: man is not contemplation (he only has peace by fleeing); he is supplication, war, anguish, madness.

Principles of a Method and a Community

I come to the most important point: *it is necessary to reject external means.* The dramatic is not being in these or those conditions, all of which are positive conditions (like being half-lost, being able to be saved). It is simply to be. To perceive this is, without anything else, to contest with enough persistance the evasions by which we usually escape. It is no longer a question of salvation: this is the most odious of evasions. The difficulty—that contestation must be done in the name of an authority—is resolved thus: I contest in the name of contestation what experience itself is (the will to proceed to the end of the possible). Experience, its authority, its method, do not distinguish themselves from the contestation.[1]

I could have told myself: value, authority—this is ecstasy; inner experience is ecstasy; ecstasy is, it seems, communication, which is opposed to the "turning in on oneself" of which I have spoken. I would have in this way *known* and *found* (there was a time when I thought myself to know, to have found). But we reach ecstasy by a contestation of knowledge. Were I to stop at ecstasy and grasp it, in the end I would define it. But nothing resists the contestation of knowledge and I have seen at the end that the idea of communication itself leaves naked—not knowing anything. Whatever it may be—failing a positive revelation within me, present at the extreme—I can provide it with neither a justification nor an end. I remain in intolerable non-knowledge, which has no other way out than ecstasy itself.

State of nudity, of supplication without response, wherein I nevertheless perceive this: that it depends on the flight from excuses. So that—precise knowledge remaining as such, with only the ground, its foundation, giving way—I grasp while sinking that the sole truth of man, glimpsed at last, is to be a supplication without response.

Taken with belated simplicity, the ostrich, in the end, leaves an eye, free from the sand, bizarrely open . . . But that one should come to read me—should one have the good will, the greatest attention, should one arrive at the ultimate degree of conviction—one will not be laid bare for all that. For nudity, to sink, supplication are at first notions added to others. Although linked to the flight from evasions, in that they themselves extend the realm of knowledge, they are themselves reduced to the state of evasions; such is the work of discourse in us. And this difficulty is expressed in this way: *the word silence is still a sound*, to speak is in itself to imagine knowing; and to no longer know, it would be necessary to no longer speak. Were the

---

1. As I write in Part 4 [of *Inner Experience*], the principle of contestation is one of those upon which Maurice Blanchot insists as on a foundation.

sand to permit my eyes to open—I have spoken: the words *which serve only to flee*, when I have ceased to flee, bring me back to flight. My eyes are open, it is true, but it would have been necessary not to say it, to remain frozen like an animal. I wanted to speak, and, as if the words bore the weight of a thousand slumbers, gently, as if appearing not to see, my eyes closed.

It is through an "intimate cessation of all intellectual operations" that the mind is laid bare. If not, *discourse* maintains it in its little complacency. Discourse, if it wishes to, can blow like a gale wind—whatever effort I make, the wind cannot chill by the fireside. The difference between inner experience and philosophy resides principally in this: that in experience, what is stated is nothing, if not a means and even, as much as a means, an obstacle; what counts is no longer the statement of wind, but the wind.

At this point we see the second meaning of the word dramatize: it is the will, adding itself to discourse, not to be content with what is stated, to oblige one to feel the chill of the wind, to be laid bare. Hence we have dramatic art, using non-discursive sensation, making every effort to strike, for that reason imitating the sound of the wind and attempting to chill—as by contagion: it makes a character tremble on stage (rather than resorting to these coarse means, the philosopher surrounds himself with narcotic signs). With respect to this, it is a classic error to assign St. Ignacious' *Exercises* to discursive method: they rely on discourse which regulates everything, but in the dramatic mode. Discourse exhorts: imagine the place, the characters of the drama, and remain there as one among them; dissipate—extend for that reason your will—the absence, the dazed state, to which words are inclined. The truth is that the *Exercises*, in absolute horror of discourse (of absence), try to cope with it through the tension of discourse, and this artifice often fails. (On the other hand, the object of contemplation which they propose is no doubt drama, but engaged in the historical categories of discourse—far from the God without form and without mode of the Carmelites, more eager than the Jesuits for inner experience.)

The weakness of the dramatic method is that it forces one to always go beyond what is naturally felt. But the weakness is less that of the method than it is ours. And it is the powerlessness, not the voluntary side of the process which stops me (to which here is added sarcasm: the comical appearing to be not authority, but one who, though desiring it, does not manage in his efforts to submit to it).

As a matter of fact, contestation would remain powerless within us if it limited itself to discourse and to dramatic exhortation. That sand into which we bury ourselves in order not to see, is formed of words, and contestation, having to make use of them, causes one to think—if I pass from one image to another different one—of the stuck, struggling man whose efforts sink him for certain: and it is true that words, their labyrinths, the exhausting immensity of their "possibles", in short their treachery, have something of quicksand about them.

We would not get out of this sand, without some sort of cord which is extended to us. Although words drain almost all life from within us—there is almost not a single sprig of this life which the bustling host of these ants (words) hasn't seized, dragged, accumulated without respite—there subsists in us a silent, elusive, ungraspable part. In the region of words, of discourse, this part is neglected. Thus it usually escapes us. We can only attain it or have it at our disposal on certain terms. They are the vague inner movements, which depend on no object and have no intent—states which, similar to others linked to the purety of the sky, to the fragrance of a room, are not warranted by anything definable, so that language which, with respect to the others, has the sky, the room, to which it can refer— and which directs attention towards what it grasps—is dispossessed, can say nothing, is limited to stealing these states from attention (profiting from their lack of precision, it right away draws attention elsewhere).

If we live under the law of language without contesting it, these states are within us as if they didn't exist. But if we run up against this law, we can in passing fix our awareness upon one of them and, quieting discourse within us, linger over the surprise which it provides us. It is better then to shut oneself in, make as if it were night, remain in this suspended silence wherein we come unexpectedly upon the sleep of a child. With a bit of chance, we perceive from such a state what favors the return, increases the intensity. And no doubt the slumber of the child is not the main reason why a mother is passionately retained, for a long spell, next to a cradle.

But the difficulty is that one manages neither easily nor completely to silence oneself, that one must fight against oneself, with precisely a mother's patience: we seek to grasp within us what subsists safe from verbal servilities and what we grasp is ourselves fighting the battle, stringing sentences together—perhaps about our effort (then about its failure)—but sentences all the same, powerless to grasp anything else. It is necessary to persist—making ourselves familiar, cruelly so, with a helpless foolishness, usually concealed, but falling under full light: the intensity of the states builds quite quickly and from that moment they absorb—they even enrapture. The moment comes when we can reflect, link words together, once again no longer silence ourselves: this time it is off in the wings (in the background) and, without worrying any longer, we let their sound fade away.

This mastery of our innermost movements, which in the long run we can acquire, is well known: it is *yoga*. But *yoga* is given in the form of coarse recipes, embellished with pedantism and with bizarre statements. And *yoga*, practiced for its own sake, advances no further than an aesthetics or a hygiene, whereas I have recourse to the same means (laid bare), *in despair*.

Christians dispensed with these means, but experience was for them only the last stage of a long ascesis (Hindus give themselves up to aesceticism, which procures for their experience an equivalent of religious drama which they are lacking). But not being able and not wanting to resort to aescesis, I must link contestation to the *liberation from the power of words* which is mastery. And if, as opposed to the Hindus, I have reduced these means to what they are, then affirmed that one must take into consideration the inspiration which resides in them, I can also not fail to say that one cannot reinvent them. Their practice heavy with tradition is the counterpart of common culture, which the freest of the poets have not been able to do without (no great poet who hasn't had a secondary education).

What I have taken on is as far removed as I can make it from the scholastic atmosphere of *yoga*. The means of which it is a question are double; one must find *words* which serve as sustenance for practice, but which turn us away from those objects the whole group of which keeps us hemmed in; *objects* which cause us to slip from the external (objective) plane to the interiority of the subject.

I will give only one example of a "slipping" *word*. I say *word*: it could just as well be the sentence into which one inserts the word, but I limit myself to the word *silence*. It is already, as I have said, the abolition of the sound which the word is; among all words it is the most perverse, or the most poetic: it is the token of its own death.

Silence is given in the sick delectation of the heart. When the fragrance of a flower is charged with reminiscences, we linger alone over breathing it in, questioning it, in the anguish of the secret which its sweetness will in an instant deliver up to us: this secret is only the inner presence, silent, unfathomable and naked, which an attention forever given to words (to objects) steals from us, and which it ultimately gives back if we give it to those most transparent among objects. But this attention does not fully give it up unless we know how to detach it, in the end, even from its discontinuous objects, which we can do by choosing for them as a sort of resting place where they will finally disappear, the silence which is no longer anything.

The resting place which the Hindus chose is no less inner: it is breath. And just as a "slipping" word has the property of capturing the attention given in advance to words, so breath captures the attention which gestures have at their command, the movements directed towards objects: but of these movements breath alone leads to interiority. So that Hindus, breathing gently, deliberately—and perhaps in silence—have not wrongly given to breath a power which is not the one which they had thought, but which opens no less the secrets of the heart.

Silence is a word which is not a word and breath an object which is not an object . . .

Ecstasy
Tale of a Partly-Failed Experience

At the moment when daylight fades, when silence invades an increasingly pure sky, I found myself alone, seated on a narrow white veranda, not seeing anything of where I was but the roof of a house, the foliage of a tree and the sky. Before getting up in order to go to bed, I felt the extent to which the sweetness of things had penetrated me. I had just had the desire for a violent alteration of spirit and, in this sense, I saw that the felicitous state into which I had fallen did not differ entirely from "mystical" states. At the very least, as I had passed suddenly from inattention to surprise, I felt this state with more intensity than one normally does and as if another and not I had experienced it. I could not deny that, with the exception of attention, which was lacking only at first, this banal felicity was an authentic inner experience, obviously distinct from project, from discourse. Without giving these words more than an evocative value, I thought that the "sweetness of the sky" communicated itself to me and I could feel precisely the state within me which responded to it. I felt it to be present inside my head like a vaporous streaming, subtly graspable, but participating in the sweetness of the outside, putting me in possession of it, making me take pleasure in it.

I remembered vividly having known a similar sort of felicity in a car while it rained and while hedges and trees, barely covered with tenuous foliage, emerged from the spring mist and came slowly towards me. I entered into possession of each damp tree and only left it sadly for another. At that moment, I thought that this dreamy pleasure would not cease belonging to me, that I would live from that moment on, endowed with the power to enjoy things in a melancholy way and breathe in their delights. I must admit today that these states of communication were only rarely accessible to me.

I was far from knowing what I see clearly today, that anguish is linked to them. I couldn't understand at the time that a trip which I had been greatly looking forward to had only brought me uneasiness, that everything had been hostile for me, beings and things, but above all men, whose empty lives in remote villages I was obliged to see—empty to the point of diminishing him who perceives them—at the same time that I saw a self-assured and malevolent reality. It is from having escaped for a moment, by means of a precarious solitude, from so much poverty, that I perceived the tenderness of the damp trees, the heartrending strangeness of their passing: I remember that, in the back of the car, I had abandoned myself, I was absent, sweetly elated; I was gentle, I gently absorbed things.

I remember having made a comparison of my enjoyment and those which the first volumes of *Remembrance of Things Past* describe. But at that time, I had only an incomplete, superficial idea of Marcel Proust (*The Past Recaptured* had not yet appeared) and young, I dreamed only of naive possibilities of triumph.

Upon leaving the veranda to go to my room, I began to contest within myself the unique value which I had attributed earlier to ecstasy before the empty unknown. The state into which I had just entered without thinking of it—was I to have contempt for it? But why? What gave me the right to classify, to place such an ecstasy above slightly different possibilities, less strange but more human and, it seemed to me, as profound?

But whereas ecstasy before the void is always fleeting, furtive and has only little concern to "persevere in being", the felicity in which I was immersed wished only to last. I should have, by this fact, been alerted: on the contrary, I took pleasure in it and, in the peacefulness of my room, I practiced running through the possible depth of it. The streaming of which I have spoken right away became more intense: I dissolved into a more solemn felicity in which I captured a diffuse sweetness by enveloping it. It suffices to arouse in oneself an intense state in order to be liberated from the agitating obtrusiveness of discourse: attention passes then from "projects" to the being which one is, which, little by little, is put into motion, emerges from the shadows; it passes from effects on the outside, possible or real (from projected, or reflected, or realized action) to this inner presence which we cannot apprehend without a startled jump of our entire being, detesting the servility of discourse.

This plenitude of inner movement, distinguishing itself from the attention normally paid to objects of discourse, is necessary to the arresting of the latter. This is why the mastery of this movement, which the Hindus strive to obtain in *yoga*, increases the little chance which we have of getting out of prison. But this plenitude is itself only a chance. It is true that in it, I lose myself, I gain access to the "un-known" in being, but *my* attention being necessary to plenitude, this self attentive to the presence of this "unknown" only loses itself in part—it can also be distinguished from it: its durable presence still requires a contestation of the known appearances of the subject which have remained, and of the object, which it still is. For *I* remain: everything escapes if I have not been able to lose myself in Nothing-ness; what I have glimpsed is brought back to the level of objects known to me.

If I only gain access to the simple intensity of inner movement, it goes without saying that discourse is only rejected for a time, that it remains at bottom the master. I can drop off into a quickly accessible felicity. At the very most: I am not abandoned in the same way to the arbitrary power of action; the rhythm of projects which is dis-course slows down; the value of action remains contested within me to the benefit of a different "possible" whose direction I see. But the mind attentive to inner movement only gains access to the unknow-able depth of things: by turning to an entire forgetting of self—not satisfying itself with anything, going always further to the impossible. I knew this, however I lingered that day over the movement which a chance felicity had awakened within me: it was a prolonged plea-sure, a pleasant possession of a slightly insipid sweetness. I by no means forgot myself in this way, I tried to capture the fixed upon ob-ject, to envelope its sweetness in my own sweetness. At the end of a very short period of time, I refused the reduction of experience to the poverty which I am. Even my "poverty", in its own interest, de-manded that I emerge from it. Revolt often has humble beginnings, but once begun doesn't stop: I first wanted to return from a contem-plation which brought the object back to me (as usually happens when we enjoy scenery) to the vision of this object in which I lose myself at other times, which I call the unknown and which is distinct from Nothingness by nothing which discourse can enunciate.

First Digression on Ecstasy before an Object: The Point

If I describe the "experience" which I had on that day, it is because it had a partly-failed character: the bitterness, the humiliating bewilderment that I found in it, the breathless efforts to which I was reduced "in order to emerge" illuminate better the region in which experience takes place than less breathless movements, reaching their goal without error.

However, I will put off to a later point this tale (which, for other reasons, exhausts me, as much as the failed experience exhausted me). I would like, if possible, to leave nothing in the shadows.

If dozing beatitude is linked, as one might expect, to the faculty which the mind assumes in order to provoke its inner movements, it is time for us to emerge from it—even if this means making ourselves the prey of disorder. Experience would only be an enticement, if it weren't revolt: in the first place against the attachment of the mind to action (to project, to discourse—against the verbal servitude of reasonable being, of the servant); in the second place against the reassurances, the submissiveness which experience itself introduces.

The "I" embodies currish docility—not to the extent that it is absurd, unknowable *ipse*, but an equivocation between the particularity of this *ipse* and the universality of reason. The "I" is in fact the expression of the universal. It loses the wildness of *ipse* in order to give a domesticated appearance to the universal; owing to this ambiguous and submissive position, we represent to ourselves the universal itself in the likeness of the one who expresses it, like a domesticated being, in opposition to wildness. The "I" is neither the irrationality of *ipse*, neither that of the whole, and that shows the foolishness which the absence of wildness (common intelligence) is.

In Christian experience, rebellious anger opposed to the "I" is still ambiguous. But the terms of equivocation are not the same solely from the point of view of reason. It is often the wild *ipse* (the proud master) who is humiliated; but sometimes it is the servile "I". And in the humiliation of the servile "I", the universal (God) is restored to pride. Hence the difference between a mystic (negative) theology and the positive one (but in the end the mystic is subordinated, the Christian attitude is servile; in common piety, God himself is a completed servant).

Ipse and the whole together slip away from the clutches of discursive intelligence (which enslaves); the middle terms alone are assimilable. But in its irrationality, proud *ipse*, without having to humiliate itself, can, casting the middle terms into darkness, in a single and abrupt renunciation of itself (as *ipse*), attain the irrationality of the whole (in this case knowledge is still mediation—between me and the world—but negative: it is the rejection of knowledge, night, the annihilation of all middle terms, which constitute this negative mediation). But the whole, in this case, is only called the whole temporarily; *ipse*, losing itself in it, moves toward it as towards an opposite (a contrary thing) but it in no less way moves from the unknown to the unknown, and, no doubt, there is still knowledge, strictly speaking, as long as *ipse* can be distinguished from the whole, but in *ipse's* renunciation of itself, there is fusion: in fusion neither *ipse* nor the whole subsist. It is the annihilation of everything which is not the ultimate "unknown", the abyss into which one has sunk.

Understood in this way, the full communication which is experience leading to the extreme limit is accessible to the extent that existence successively strips itself of its middle terms: of that which originates in discourse, then—if the mind enters into a nondiscursive inwardness—of all that returns to discourse given that one can have distinct awareness of it—in other words, that an ambiguous "I" can make of it a "servile possession".

In these conditions this still appears: the dialogue from person to person, from soul to God, is a voluntary and temporary mystification (of oneself). Existence ordinarily communicates itself; it leaves its ipseity to meet fellow beings. There is communication, from one being to another (erotic communication) or from one to several others (sacred or comic communication). But *ipse* encountering in a final step, instead of a fellow being, its opposite, tries nevertheless to find again the terms of situations in which it was accustomed to communicating, of losing itself. Its frailty demands that it be available for a fellow being and that it not be able to make from the first step the leap into the impossible (for *ipse* and the whole are opposites, while the "I" and God are like beings).

For one who is a stranger to experience, that which precedes is obscure—but it is not destined for him (I write for one, who, entering into my book, would fall into it as into a hole, who would never again get out). One can choose between two things: either the "I" speaks in me (and most will read what I write as if "I", vulgarly, had written it) or *ipse*. *Ipse* having to communicate—with others who resemble it—has recourse to degrading sentences. It would sink into the insignificance of the "I" (the ambiguous), if it didn't try to communicate. In this way, poetic existence in me addresses itself to poetic existence in others, and it is a paradox, no doubt, if I expect of fellow creatures drunk with poetry that which I wouldn't expect knowing them to be lucid. Now I cannot myself be *ipse* without having cast this cry to them. Only by this cry do I have the power to annihilate in me the "I" as they will annihilate it in them if they hear me.

22. JABÈS (1912–1991)

El, ou le Dernier Livre (Paris: Gallimard, 1973), pp. 47–48, 72, 89, 91–92, 99, 113, 115, 118–119. Trans. Rosmarie Waldrop, *The Book of Questions: El, or the Last Book* (Middleton, Conn.: Wesleyan University Press, 1984), pp. 39–40, 62, 72, 75, 77, 85, 97, 101–102.

    Le Livre des Ressemblances (Paris: Gallimard, 1976), pp. 67–68. Trans. Rosmarie Waldrop, *The Book of Resemblances* (Middleton, Conn.: Wesleyan University Press, 1990), pp. 48–49.

Edmond Jabès, a Francophone Egyptian Jew, interprets the diaspora of the Jews as paradigmatic of the condition of exile of the modern writer. The "word" is perpetually involved in a nomadic movement inscribed into the very name of the name ("nom-ade"); it is perpetually exiled from the reality it intends but in fact can present only as absent, for language can never make present what it represents. This separation of language and the reality it projects is indeed infinite, and the proliferation of words is always merely a further deferral and dispersion of meaning. This description of the human predicament in language reflects—or deflects—an eminently and expressly Jewish sense of distance and difference from a transcendent deity. Language in general, like the unpronounceable Name of God, is dependent on a silent instance within it that it cannot grasp or say.

    The genesis of this condition of exile in and into language isolated by silence is symbolized by Moses's breaking of the tablets of the Law. Subsequently, all human speech and writing is fallen and fragmentary and attempts vainly to reconstruct the original tablets written with the finger of God. Human writing, in this perspective, is the exile from original, full meaning and order; it is, in Blanchot's terms, a "writing of disaster," an "absence of the book." Writing henceforth delivers no Law but can only generate endless commentary on the irremediably lost and absent Word, which has become silence: indeed, commentary ("comment taire," literally, "how to be silent") is essentially a silencing of the original. Language, exiled from its own essential meaning, is in movement through history and only by its shifts and slips allows a glimpse of the utopia of pure and full meaning that has been forever lost. Only this endless exile enables humans to live, giving them room to breathe. Without this distance, they would be simply smothered by the absolute. Moses's breaking of the Book was in this sense necessary to open up a space of relative autonomy for the finite and human.

According to the sixteenth century Spanish Kabbalist Isaac Luria, this human space of exilic movement is made by God's own self-exile, his withdrawal into himself (*zimzum*). It is by contracting into himself that the absolute Being, who was all in all, first created a space of nothing, a space emptied of his own infinite presence. This is the space of the universe, of Creation, a space emptied of absolute plenum, cleared for difference and for the nondivine. Such is the sphere in which human existence and history unfold.

The uncompromising transcendence of the Jewish God renders him absent from the world, and especially from the *word* in which he is revealed but, at the same time, concealed. The word remains as a trace of God's withdrawal from the world. The withdrawing of God is the precondition for the existence of anything else. Otherwise, God is all in all, and existence is saturated by His being alone. The word makes a beginning, interrupts eternity, and in so doing marks an absence of God by opening up a gap in His eternal presence. This trace of divinity in the word is the trace of eternity in time, as Saint Augustine also taught.[1] That there be meaning articulated in language requires an obliteration of the absolute presence of God, a forgetting. Forgetfulness is the condition and the "beginning" (*El*, p. 69) of any articulable meaning. So only by remembering this forgetting can we hope to regain any inkling of the eternity that reigned before time began.

All *our* meanings, as reductions to definite terms of the Boundless—*Ein Sof*, of Kabbalistic tradition—are necessarily tinged with silence and absence. They are constitutively bereft of the infinite that they have broken up into pieces of finite meaning. However, *questioning* is a mode of keeping our language open as a broken fragment addressed ultimately to the infinite and unsayable, the "divine": "All questions are first of all questions put to God."[2] Indeed, God is a question ("Dieu est une question") for us who are nothing ("pour nous qui ne sommes rien").[3] For us who are nothing, the truth is the void, and God as our truth and our void is revealed in the open question.

All our words are images of an unspeakable Word, but ideally, Jabès would eliminate all terms and images. His language, though vividly imaged,

---

1. Cf. Karmen MacKendrick, *Immemorial Silence* (New York: SUNY Press, 2001), pp. 49ff.

2. Jabès, "The Question of Displacement into the Lawfulness of the Book," in *The Sin of the Book: Edmond Jabès*, ed. Eric Gould (Lincoln: University of Nebraska Press, 1985), p. 234.

3. *Le Livre des Questions* (Paris: Gallimard, 1963), p. 126.

negates its own images and strives after a neutrality without image and without name. Rather than suppressing or negating imagery, he neutralizes it and thus opens it up to an imageless abyss within its midst, the abyss of what cannot be imagined or figured or said. Moses asks God his name, hardly suspecting that God cannot be expressed except by the absence of any name. Yet this absence to which all names belong is figured as the Book; hence Jabès's works are imbued with the sense of silence as the alpha and omega of a Book into which everything that is anything finite or determinate falls and disappears.

Jabès breaks down even the arch-figure of the Book in order to let out the silence and emptiness at its center. By removing the central, open-ended letter V of this word LI(V)RE (book), he turns it into LIRE (read). A homologous excision is performed upon the word LI(B)RE (free) in order to liberate the freedom hidden in the midst of the activity of reading (LIRE). Further elimination of the letters left at the center in each case (L[IR]E) yields LE, the definite article in French signifying a noun or name in general. It is also the Hebrew Name of God, EL, in reverse. Doubled into a chiasmus, it even becomes the feminine third-person pronoun, ELLE. By such means, the Name of God is shown over and over again to be dwelling silently in the core of language. It is an infinity and abyss into which every manifest, finite form of speech collapses. Nothingness, the empty, unpronounceable silence of the divine Name, opens as a void within the core of every word that in turn opens into a desert miraculously fertile in uncontainable meanings.

From the early stages of Jabès's project, silence is thus foregrounded as the background and unique ground of all language and expression. His literary achievement consists primarily of the seven-volume *Le Livre des Questions*, followed by the three-volume *Le Livre des Ressemblances* and the four-volume *Le Livre des Limites*. In the first volume of *The Book of Questions*, which bears the same name as the series, Jabès questions imaginary rabbi-poets, ostensibly to interrogate silence for its answers to his questions: "Interrogate me, you for whom I speak. I draw answers to your questions from silence, where they are mounted" ("Interroge-moi, toi pour qui je parle. Du silence où elles sont enchâssées, je tire les réponses à tes questions"). True human dialogue is a silent dialogue, such as transpires between hands and eyes or, more precisely, "pupils" ("*Le vrai dialogue humain, celui des mains, des prunelles est un dialogue silencieux,*" *Le Livre des Questions*, p. 68).

El, ou le Dernier Livre (1973), the final book or "period" in the seven volumes making up the *Livre des Questions* (1963–1973), begins by citing the Kabbalah and its use of the image of the point as a figure for God: God reveals and makes Himself manifest as a point ("Dieu, *El*, pour se révéler, Se manifesta par un point. *La Kabbale*"). This image is developed throughout the book and by the end becomes an image for the last book itself (*"Ce point / El / Le dernier livre?"* p. 111). This point, in fact, opens as a hole into which all disappears as into the Absolute, that is, into the absolute, imperceptible unity of the One, which coincides with Nothing, as suggested by the palindrome: "L'UN = NUL" ("ONE = NONE").

Central to Jabès's discourse is the idea of God as "the silence of all words." God's Word is "an unfathomable abyss beyond words toward which all words tend, as toward an unutterable obsession beset by fever and revolt." God is "what is unattainable within all that we attain," and we experience His Word always and only in its brokenness in our words: "only through its infinite fracture can we approach the Totality which, in itself would be neither more nor less than a flight of our fancy . . . ."[4] Our words are thus oriented toward the infinity of his Word, which, as broken into mortal finitude, can only convey emptiness, exile, and silence.

The space of human history is linguistic throughout its whole extent. Yet it is also nothing but a relation and a reference to what remains outside it, to the unspeakable divine Name. This Name is the unbroken wholeness of the Law that the intact tablets *would* have revealed, as if immediately in its oneness, and hence without the mediation of finite, broken, human words. This utopic language of the impossible Name is what Benjamin, too, in "Die Aufgabe des Übersetzers," envisages as glimpsed in and through the act of translation. It is the originary, imaginary whole vase of which all the languages of the world are but the shards.

---

4. Jabès, "The Question of Displacement into the Lawfulness of the Book." Citations, pp. 228–229, 237.

From *El, or the Last Book*

(*"We read the word in the sunburst of its limits, as we read the Law through Moses' angry gesture, through the breaking of the divine Tables,"* he said.

In the exploded word, God collides with the hostility of the letters.

Even outside the Name, God is a prisoner of the Name.

"I have worked an unforgivable breach in the lives of human beings. This I regret. Thus," he said, "God speaks to God."

The reach of the book depends on its violence which the margins hawk.

God's rape is from the Prophet's innate conviction that the Book can be read without mediation. Basic error.

By turning their back on the Tables, the chosen people gave Moses a master-lesson in reading. From instinct—for is the Book not prior to man?—they raised the rape of God to the level of original death. And, rising up against the letter, their independence consecrated the fracture in which God writes Himself against God.

The destroyed book allows us to read the book.

"People of the Book, the Jews have been called. This would imply that God is the only writer, and every book a privileged moment in the reading of the Book," he said.

"O my brothers with your red and tired eyes, when writing and reading are part of the same act, which of you can accept without bristling that his reading has been prompted?

"The Jew of the Book is not the faithful, but the unbeliever, the rebel, the exile, the one for whom the book is each time different at the risk of not existing at all."

"But all these recorded readings," he added, "all these piles of works will waste away. Did not God, before man, expose His word and, in spite of Himself, reduce it to dust?

"And to dust thou shalt return, like your name.

"Dust is watered by blood.")

———

("God spoke, and what He said became our symbols. The shape of a letter is perhaps the shape of His face. God has as many faces as there are letters in an alphabet. God is written in all languages.

"You will be able to contemplate God once you have learned to listen to words, to look at them carefully, that is, once you have learned to read," he had noted.

"His voice is inaudible, but it is the supporting silence which allows our sounds to be discrete," he had added.

"You will shatter the image of words. You will take away their sound. You will divert them from their meaning. You will turn them into holes.
"Then reading and writing will throw you into the vortex of a voice absorbed into the void," he had also noted.)

———

Dieu = Vide = Vie d'yeux.
God = Emptiness = Life of the eyes.
He said: "God is empty of emptiness. God is the life of emptiness. He is empty of any life of the eyes. Death cries her eyes out, mourning."

Cieux, 'the heavens,' a plural composed of *ciel* and *yeux,* 'heaven' and 'eyes.'

Dieu is also in the word *Cieux,* as a unique silence: in the mirror of the page, *D* turns *C* at the first touch of the eraser.

Thus 'heavens' is the silent plural of 'God.'

Dieu. Di eu. Dis (à) eux. The empty space between two syllables turns God into 'tell them.' God lets us tell our grief, our mourning.

You use 'God' and 'Gods,' 'Place' and 'Places' interchangeably. Because God is many Gods within God, many Places within the Place.

All mourning mourns, above all, God.

To dominate the space between words, to make sure its silence is neutral.

Let the fire be the sword of fire, and the well the water that quenches your thirst.

To fall silent, we must have talked a great deal.
. . . to fall silent, that is, finally not to fail.

In the desert, breasts are dunes.

He was fed with sand.

————

We must protect our words from contagion by the winged, the airy word.
The airy, *aérien,* word is threatened from within by the word *rien,* by airy 'nothing.'

"Mysterious epidemic," she said. "Words were dying of their absence."

Take the *l* out of *voile,* 'veil,' and you get *voie,* the 'way.'
A wing was unveiling the day.

"*Aérien* can be read *A et Rien* or *A est rien.*
"In the first case, 'A and Nothing,' we have the letter *A,* which is known to contain all others, and then *Nothing.*
"In the second case, '*A is Nothing.*'
"From this we can only conclude that *A* is *All* and *Nothing* at the same time," he said.
"Likewise the point."

"The blank page is this sky never blue, which is everywhere," you said.

————

I must warn you: writing leads to suicide. Is it only one human life that is at stake in the act of writing? And what is a human life compared to the life of a word? Perhaps nothing. Or all. Or All of a Nothing or again Nothing of an All.

Thus they died. Thus he again picked up his pen, and this natu-ral, almost automatic gesture suddenly seemed so loaded with un-known forces that he shivered.

(*The unsayable settles us in those desert regions which are the home of dead languages. Here, every grain of sand stifled by the mute word offers the dreary spectacle of a root of eternity ground to dust before it could sprout. In the old days, the ocean would have cradled it. Does the void torment the universe, and the universe in turn vex the void? Roots buried in sand keep longing for their trees. The deepest weep for their fruit. They are reborn of their tears.*

Fish can only evolve in water. Man can only grow on earth. The word can only live within death.

So it seemed that, once death had blasted him with his own pen, the writer would finally be able to speak, on the far side of the night. But to whom? And for what purpose? Perhaps, by renounc-ing speech, he could come to inhabit the inaudible word which God holds in His own keeping to sound the silence.)

———

I build a book on our sacrificed lives. Could there be a life at the borders of life where we repeat once more—but for which impenetrable purpose?—our characteristic gestures, our most intimate, most weighty words?

Could it be that writing is this other life stuck in the fens of the page? Here, any life devoted to its disconcerting duration gets bogged down.

A decoy, I tell you, the open wounds of a decoy which the meaning given to our words—and woes—keeps us and others from contemplating.

From these wounds we shall have drawn milk.

———

Today was my place.

Four times God fell silent in His Name. Four times, on the way up and down each slope of the mountain, have we faced the silence of the letter.

"Pride is the hope to conquer the four divine letters of the unpronounceable Name, and our fall, to be inevitably engulfed in each one," she had said.

———

(*Who writes? And why this intermediary between you and me? Probably to allow us to turn away from an utterance whose shards we have unearthed in all good faith.*

"What is Your Name?" Moses had asked God, in despair. What is Your Name, that is, what is Your glory? Whereas divine truth, unlike man who expects to be named, can only make itself felt in the absence of any name.

God is the high calling to this presumptuous and harrowing departure towards a totality eager to absorb us in its own annihilation.

God knew that a name wears away even as it forms and that the invisible—which we cannot circumscribe—is His Omnipotence. Where there is nothing, All is intact: only fragments can be grasped.

God did not say: "The world I created, but the world I am creating." As if any act of creation were only the initial focus of its permanent challenge.

We have prepared for a word which will be dead on arrival. All our attempts to approach it will have failed.

Our experiment of writing will, in the final analysis, have been only one more step towards death.

How far, O how far will we venture into the dark of darks, the blank of blanks of a colorless universe?)

From *The Book of Resemblances*

God: an endless word.

Any end insults the question.

The question of the infinite is the feverish question a closed world puts to a world flaunting its openness.

Miracles are beyond question.

———

"The word *God* interests me," he said, "because it defies understanding and, being incomprehensible as a word, escapes sense, which it transcends and annuls. So that it is always a word before or after words, a word without words, past or future, a futile word whose use shocks the mind.

"Questioning God means questioning the void. Pure questioning without object, questioning the question.

"How could we understand God? God cannot be closed in on. God's closure is God: non-closure or after-closure.

"We must question the ungraspable, unthinkable, grasped and thought in their arbitrary absence, their jealously protected not-knowing, in failure, pain and blood.

"To question God means hurling Him to His death, making the place of death into the locus of all indeterminable places of anxious questioning of God."

And he added: "I write at the feet of a word which cannot be explained to the words I live with. A word that invades and troubles, that defies the human order which other words try to respect."

"Is the unpronounceable name of God not also," he said elsewhere, "the erased name of the unthought on which all thinking crashes and breaks?"

(*"God is a word too many, which troubles our peace like desire weighing on desire—an undesired, irresistible desire,"* wrote Reb Gabri.)

———

The first book and the last share an unbiddable silence.

Any page of writing is a knot of silence unraveled.

Quiet abyss.

23. CELAN (1920–1970)

Selected poems. Trans. Michael Hamburger, *Poems of Paul Celan*
(New York: Persea Books, 1995), pp. 112–113, 136–137, 170–171, 174–175,
178–179, 188–189, 192–193, 238–239, 278–279, 350–351, 352–353.

Paul Celan was born Paul Antschel, a German-speaking Jew in Czernowitz,
Romania, on the eastern outskirts of the Austro-Hungarian Empire, which
was occupied successively in his lifetime by Germans and Russians. Both of his
parents perished in Nazi concentration camps. He described himself as "one of
the last who must live out to the end the destiny of the Jewish spirit in Europe."[1] After a brief period in Vienna, he established himself in 1948 in Paris,
where he married the artist Gisèle de Lestrange and taught German literature
at the *École Normale Supérieur*, before ending his life in the river Seine.

Celan has become ever more widely acclaimed as the creator of an original poetry and poetics in which words verge upon silence. In his book on
Celan, Blanchot, commenting especially on the lyric "Sprich auch du," has
provocatively expressed the negative poetics of silence and absence at the heart
of Celan's poetry. He suggests that blanks, stops, and pauses are constitutive of
a "non-verbal rigor" which substitutes a void for meaning, "as if the void were
less a lack than a saturation, a void saturated with the void" ("comme si le vide
était moins un manque qu'une saturation, un vide saturé de vide").[2] As Theodor Adorno had already influentially written, "Celan's poems attempt to express the most extreme horror (das äußerste Entsetzen) through remaining
silent (durch Verschweigen) . . . ."[3]

However, widely divergent ways of interpreting the silence generated by
Celan's language have emerged in the critical literature. On the one hand, his
poems are said to evoke a utopic, pure language born from silence ("die reine,

---

1. Cited by John Felstiner, *Paul Celan: Poet, Survivor, Jew* (New Haven: Yale University Press, 1995), p. 80.

2. Maurice Blanchot, *Le dernier à parler* (Saint Clément: fata morgana, 1984).

3. Adorno, *Ästhetische Theorie*. Other highly influential philosophical interpretations of Celan include Jacques Derrida, *Schibboleth* (Paris: Galilée, 1986), and Hans-
Georg Gadamer, *Wer bin Ich und wer bist Du? Ein Kommentar zu Paul Celans Gedichte-
folge 'Atemkristal'* (Frankfurt a.M.: Suhrkamp, 1973).

aus dem Schweigen heraus geborene Sprache"), which does not exist except as an unheard claim ("unerhörten Anspruch") in every poem.[4] And they are read, accordingly, for their "intentionality focused on language."[5] On the other hand, the silences of his poems can also be read as *deixis*, as pointing dumbly in the manner of an index to contextual circumstances unsayable in their concreteness.[6] Consequently, some have devoted enormous effort to searching out historical and biographical keys to what Celan cryptically leaves unsaid.[7] So, while Celan has become more and more widely recognized as the poet of unspeakability par excellence, the bases and thrust of this poetic of silence remain in the highest degree controversial. Is Celan's language mystic or antimystic? Is it a dissolving of reference or an absolute intensifying of reference in relation to history and specifically the Holocaust?

The Holocaust experience around which his poetry revolves stands as the incomparable "that which happened" ("das, was geschah") that it is impossible to say or name. But this historical catastrophe is not really accessible as history, and it is not only an event in the past. In its very uniqueness and incomparability it becomes for Celan the key to interpreting the situation of human beings at all times—that is, simply as in time, in time which is always catastrophic by its very nature. It is the nature of time to isolate moments of "encounter" ("Begegnung") of the wholly Other into their strange, uncanny, incomprehensible singularity. This singular reality can be touched on only in a unique, incomprehensible encounter. Celan speaks of encountering himself by writing from or to a specific date: *his* 20th of January—the day on which the Nazi party met at Wansee and formally decided on "the final solution," that is, liquidation of the Jewish race. This time, an emblem of annihilation, is the reality Celan approaches over and over again in his poems.

---

4. Hermann Burger, *Paul Celan: Auf der Suche nach der verlorenen Sprache* (Zürich and Munich: Artemis, 1974), p. 9, echoing phrases from Celan's "Büchner-Preis-Rede."

5. Winfried Menninghaus, *Paul Celan: Magie der Form* (Frankfurt a.M.: Suhrkamp, 1980), reads Celan's poetry for its "Intention auf die Sprache," a phrase borrowed from Benjamin's "Die Aufgabe des Übersetzers." This focus is concentrated especially in the name, as in the language mysticism of the Kabbalah. See also Dietlind Meinecke, *Wort und Name bei Paul Celan* (Berlin: Gehlen, 1970).

6. See Lorenz, *Schweigen in der Dichtung: Hölderlin – Rilke – Celan.*

7. See Marlies Janz, *Vom Engagement absoluter Poesie: Zur Lyrik und Ästhetik Paul Celans* (Frankfurt a.M.: Suhrkamp, 1976). These questions are pursued in criticism in English in *Argumentum e Silentio: International Paul Celan Symposium*, ed. Amy D. Colin (Berlin: Walter de Gruyter, 1987), and *Word Tracings: Readings of Paul Celan*, ed. Aris Fioretos (Baltimore: Johns Hopkins University Press, 1994).

Language itself must enact annihilation, if reality is to be realized uniquely, "once," as in "Einmal." Articulation in language enacts annihilation of the One and Infinite ("Eins und Unendlich, / vernichtet"). The world is thereby washed of generalization, and what things really are ("wirklich") behind the masks that words place in front of them can show through. This unveiling is experienced as light and salvation ("Licht war. Rettung").

By breaking out of all constructions that identify us by words, we enter into real time, which is a breaking, an abolishing of every continuous, settled narrative that encloses time between the set meanings of a beginning and an end. Celan parallels (and perhaps depends on) Benjamin's theory of Messianic time as a discontinuous, eruptive "now" or *Jetztzeit*. The poem, as a breaking open of language, first enables this open time of the break to transpire. In this sense, poems are "underway" ("unterwegs"). "Toward what? Toward something open, inhabitable, an approachable you, perhaps, an approachable reality."[8]

This "you," however, is radically unknowable and can be designated only as "other": "The poem intends another, needs this other, needs an 'over-against.' It goes toward it, bespeaks it. For the poem, everything and everybody is a figure of this other toward which it is heading" (p. 49). Indeed, the poem and everything in it is to be understood only in terms of this intention moving towards an Other that no word can name but that every word intends and adumbrates. Hence what the poem approaches is described as the "altogether Other" ("ganz Andere"). Vis-à-vis this wholly Other, language is reduced to silence. This happens in amazing ways in virtually every poem Celan writes. As he himself observes, the poem today exhibits a "strong tendency toward growing dumb" ("eine starke Neigung zum Verstummen," p. 48).

The poem can only approach and bespeak—not say or express—this altogether Other. For this, there can be no words. Only the failing and foundering of words—accentuated or seconded by their artfully deliberate dissection and destruction—can express this intention directed toward the wholly Other. Language vis-à-vis this wholly Other can grasp and express nothing properly in name and concept, but rather passes "through terrifying silence, through the thousand darknesses of murderous speech." The language Celan writes of, and himself writes, "went through. It gave me no words for what was happening, but went through it. Went through and could resurface, 'enriched' by

8. *Paul Celan: Collected Prose*, trans. Rosmarie Waldrop (Manchester: Carcanet, 1986), p. 34. German quotations are from Celan's poetological addresses at Bremen and Darmstadt ("Der Meridian"), printed in *Gesammelte Werke*, ed. Beda Allemann and Stefan Reichert (Frankfurt a.M.: Suhrkamp, 1983).

it all" (p. 34). Even growing dumb in relation to unspeakable happenings can enrich language by its brush with a historical reality that it cannot represent or name. This is language that goes mad, like Hölderlin, remembering not by representation but by its very blindness.

In "Stumme Herbstgerüche" ("Dumb Autumn Smells"), the past present in memory is evoked by dumb sensations. An inarticulable otherness or foreignness is made present in strangely familiar smells of a certain season— smells apt to send us back to childhood experiences that we cannot voluntarily remember. These sensations are after the fact, hence odors of "autumn." In them, something preverbal becomes palpable. Such sensory rememoration is the unspeakable residue of what is actually experienced *before* it is bent and broken ("ungeknickt") by verbal articulation. Such past lostness is *almost* made present and lived—but not quite, since in being recovered by memory and language it loses this very lostness, and thereby its only chance to truly live: in language live sensory impulses are appropriated by lifeless abstractions.

As Celan adumbrates it, an encounter with the Other demands total abandon and relinquishment of identity. The encounter is essentially destructive of self and world as we know them. Only thus can we perhaps be "we without us" ("wir ohne uns," "Die Pole"). In this free, open dimension beyond the poles of objective consciousness instituted by language and the oppositions necessary to all verbal meaning—a region we may cross over into during sleep—it is possible to "say that Jerusalem *is*." Of course, this depends on you and me giving up all articulable definition, all identity, and becoming only one another's indeterminacy, one another's "whiteness." In this indefinable region, where words lose conceptual grip, you and I actually encounter each other and coincide in an openness that is engendered by prayer ("betest") or, ambiguously, by love in a more profane sense of bedding ("bettest").

Celan's poems are about human communication and its necessary condition—total loss of identity. Only in becoming No One can we become open to encountering the wholly Other. And only thus are we able to encounter our own authentic selves rather than some superficial *persona* we fancy ourselves to be. The poems reach toward an impossible communication in which I and you, self and other, are encountered not as represented in any world and thus by language but more nakedly as beyond language. Free of the inevitable lies of language, we encounter each other as neither you nor I but as No One. In poems such as "Psalm" and "Mandorla," Nothing and No One cancel the possibility of reference to any definable realities, but thereby open reference to the unnameable, indefinable beyond of language that is more riveting and compelling, more real, than any reality we can name or say.

The metamorphosis of the Addressee of the poem into a nameless, non-descript Other, which nevertheless in this very indeterminacy mysteriously coincides with the "we" speaking the poems, finds expression in "Es ist nicht mehr," which hints that perhaps you and I are (not even) the nameless weight that holds back the void that accompanies us in every hour. This emptiness, rather than what is proper to either of us, this "other" with regard to all heaviness experienced in time, is perhaps really you—and me, too. We both have—or will have—no name, when the heaviness of the hour is no more, when we have broken out of time and been freed from all weight or content of identity.

Death to any verbalizable self and the breaking of communication by word or even glance between subjects becomes the awakening to an apparently mystic sunrise in silence in "Mit allen Gedanken" ("With All My Thoughts"). Not unlike sexual opening ("your lap opened," "tat sich dein Schoß auf"), what transpires in mists and vapors of unknowing is "as good as a name" ("so gut wie ein Name"). Naming is a sort of presencing of the named, but here the encounter has taken place without naming, indeed, precisely because of the avoidance of naming. It is the deeper reality of the self that cannot be named for which Celan's poetry indefatigably searches—with stunning verbal resourcefulness. It is experienced only in silence charged "with all my thoughts."

In "Unten" ("Below"), Celan hints that below the level of speech and consciousness, a silent nearness in communication with eyes takes place as a "Gast-Gespräch," a "guest-conversation," which can be at home only in forgetfulness. This communication between would-be aliens is led home, syllable by syllable, through the dismemberment of language in Celan's poem. The poem wagers chaos in the "dayblind dice," the contingent, chance happenings that occur sheltered from day or blinded from the wakefulness of consciousness that then intervenes in events to order them with its "gross hand." Conscious talk is simply "too much," for with it the subtle, communicative silence of the eyes, in which the other appears, is hardened, "thingified," crystallized, killed into "style," imagined as a conventional dress, or a costume covering over and muffling silence ("Tracht deines Schweigens").

In "Weggebeizt" ("Etched Away"), poetic language is represented as a language that is effaced. It is literally corroded or "bitten away" to such an extent that the "poem" ("Gedicht") becomes "no poem" ("Genicht"). In being appropriated in different ways, according to how different experiences of readers rub off onto it and etch away at it, the poem's determinate, possessive, falsifying character as a "my-poem" ("Mein-gedicht") dissolves into the hundred-tongued polysemy and disappropriation that causes it to be divested of all proper character and to converge upon the "be-nothinged" no-poem ("das

Genicht"). This, however, sets it free ("frei"), whirls it out ("aus-") from all contraints and all enclosures of semantic structures, as it makes its way through the frozen formations of others' (its readers') experiences. Sedimented in their own temporalities and personal histories, and structured like breath turned to crystal—the "Atemkristall"—it then witnesses to that most intimate moment of the turning of breath, where speech is suspended and the outside of time and language takes place invisibly, leaving only the formal structure, the crystal deposit of words, behind. This "conversion" experience of life and breath, this "Atemwende"or "turning of breath" is the suspension of language and the rupturing of time that the poem, leaving behind all its verbal deposits, miraculously provokes.

Sometimes it seems that the silencing of language makes the Inexpressible appear to the eye. For example, in "Ein auge, offen" ("An Eye, Open"), the eye totally, defenselessly, and painfully open, brings in all images with a tear, as broken or at least not whole ("halb"). But in this total openness of the break, what is perceived is the no-more-to-be-named ("Das nicht mehr zu Nennende"). It is no one's voice ("Niemandes Stimme"); it is not even received as an object from without but is already "audible in the mouth" ("hörbar im Mund") —that is, as indistinct from the physical organ of the emitting voice.

In Celan's poetic lexicon, the series Eye—Image—blind (Auge-Bildblind) parallels the series Mouth—Word—dumb (Mund-Wort-stumm).[9] Both are dead ends. For that reason, however, they force open a way into a different dimension, one of encounter with an Other. A poem is "essentially dialogue," the openness of an encounter without hermeneutic closure—hence its putative difficulty and darkness. This means that what the poem intends cannot as such appear but can only be signaled by flagging the language that *does* appear in the poem as inadequate and inauthentic. It is "art" in spite of itself, but as marking an attention toward something "altogether other" than what it makes manifest and expresses. This wholly other must be encountered in the darkness of a blind "step" into silence ("Der Meridian"). For this otherness is encountered precisely where language in the poem is made to stop and where a step is taken beyond what language can say, where something may be "seen," though this too is a blind seeing. It is rather a "going," as in "Engführung," into fields where concentration camps witness to the inexpressible, and an encountering of what cannot be any object of representation or consciously reflective "experience."

---

9. See Gerhard Neumann, "Die 'absolute' Metapher: Ein Abgrenzungsversuch am Beispiel Stéphane Mallarmés und Paul Celans," *Poetica* (Munich) 3/1–2: 188–223.

These examples illustrate some crucial apophatic aspects and features of Celan's poetics. The withdrawal of reality before language, the consequent isolation of language from reality (the "loneliness" of the poem) paradoxically leads to the meeting with oneself and with the Other. Only outside the linguistic fabric of the world is the encounter with the wholly Other, who alone is real, possible. Only encountering this unknowable Other can I encounter my own self as singularity. In "Die Pole," this is an unrestricted, infinite, eternal ("für immer") reality ("Wirklichkeit"), which cannot appear as real in ordinary language, and which is betrayed by any representation or manifestation. Such reality is won only by language giving itself up in helplessness.

"Die Pole" belongs to those poems which Celan wrote at the end of his life in conjunction with his trip to Jerusalem. They are particularly charged with the tension of apocalypse, but it is the empty spaces of the text that become revelatory, as again in "Die Posaunenstelle." Here the trumpets of apocalypse are found in the incandescent empty-text ("glühenden / Leertext"), in the hole in time ("im Zeitloch") into which we literally "hear" ourselves. They sound in the unrepresentable immediacy of the word before it even leaves the mouth: "hear yourself in with the mouth" ("hör dich ein / mit dem Mund").

Selected Poems

Unten

Heimgeführt ins Vergessen
das Gast-Gespräch unsrer
langsamen Augen.

Heimgeführt Silbe um Silbe, verteilt
auf die tagblinden Würfel, nach denen
die spielende Hand greift, groß,
im Erwachen.

Und das Zuviel meiner Rede:
angelagert dem kleinen
Kristall in der Tracht deines Schweigens.

Below

Led home into oblivion
the sociable talk of
our slow eyes.

Led home, syllable after syllable, shared
out among the dayblind dice, for which
the playing hand reaches out, large,
awakening.

And the too much of my speaking:
heaped up round the little
crystal dressed in the style of your silence.

Ein Auge, Offen

Stunden, maifarben, kühl.
Das nicht mehr zu Nennende, heiß,
hörbar im Mund.

Niemandes Stimme, wieder.

Schmerzende Augapfeltiefe:
das Lid
steht nicht im Wege, die Wimper
zählt nicht, was eintritt.

Die Träne, halb,
die schärfere Linse, beweglich,
holt dir die Bilder.

An Eye, Open

Hours, May-coloured, cool.
The no more to be named, hot,
audible in the mouth.

No one's voice, again.

Aching depth of the eyeball:
the lid
does not stand in its way, the lash
does not count what goes in.

The tear, half,
the sharper lens, movable,
brings the images home to you.

Mit allen Gedanken

Mit allen Gedanken ging ich
hinaus aus der Welt: da warst du,
du meine Leise, du meine Offne, und—
du empfingst uns.

Wer
sagt, daß uns alles erstarb,
da uns das Aug brach?
Alles erwachte, alles hob an.

Groß kam eine Sonne geschwommen, hell
standen ihr Seele und Seele entgegen, klar,
gebieterisch schwiegen sie ihr
ihre Bahn vor.

Leicht
tat sich dein Schoß auf, still
stieg ein Hauch in den Äther,
und was sich wölkte, wars nicht,
wars nicht Gestalt und von uns her,
wars nicht
so gut wie ein Name?

With All My Thoughts

With all my thoughts I
went out of the world: and there you were,
you my quiet, my open one, and—
you received us.

Who
says that everything died for us
when our eyes broke?
Everything awakened, everything began.

Great, a sun came drifting, bright
a soul and a soul confronted it, clear,
masterfully their silence mapped out
an orbit for the sun.

Easily
your lap opened, tranquilly
a breath rose up to the aether
and that which made clouds, was it not,
was it not a shape come from us,
was it not
as good as a name?

Stumme Herbstgerüche

Stumme Herbstgerüche. Die
Sternblume, ungeknickt, ging
zwischen Heimat und Abgrund durch
dein Gedächtnis.

Eine fremde Verlorenheit war
gestalthaft zugegen, du hättest
beinah
gelebt.

Dumb Autumn Smells

Dumb autumn smells. The
marguerite, unbroken, passed
between home and chasm through
your memory.

A strange lostness was
palpably present, almost
you would
have lived.

Psalm

Niemand knetet uns wieder aus Erde und Lehm,
niemand bespricht unsern Staub.
Niemand.

Gelobt seist du, Niemand.
Dir zulieb wollen
wir blühn.
Dir
entgegen.

Ein Nichts
waren wir, sind wir, werden
wir bleiben, blühend:
die Nichts-, die
Niemandsrose.

Mit
dem Griffel seelenhell,
dem Staubfaden himmelswüst,
der Krone rot
vom Purpurwort, das wir sangen
über, o über
dem Dorn.

Psalm

No one moulds us again out of earth and clay,
no one conjures our dust.
No one.

Praised be your name, no one.
For your sake
we shall flower.
Towards
you.

A nothing
we were, are, shall
remain, flowering:
the nothing-, the
no one's rose.

With
our pistil soul-bright,
with our stamen heaven-ravaged,
our corolla red
with the crimson word which we sang
over, O over
the thorn.

Es ist nicht mehr

Es ist nicht mehr
diese
zuweilen mit dir
in die Stunde gesenkte
Schwere. Es ist
eine andre.

Es ist das Gewicht, das die Leere zurückhält,
die mit-
ginge mit dir.
Es hat, wie du, keinen Namen. Vielleicht
seid ihr dasselbe. Vielleicht
nennst auch du mich einst
so.

It Is No Longer

It is no longer
this
heaviness
lowered at times together with you
into the hour. It is
another.

It is the weight holding back the void
that would
accompany you.
Like you, it has no name. Perhaps
you two are one and the same. Perhaps
one day you also will call
me so.

Mandorla

In der Mandel—was steht in der Mandel?
Das Nichts.
Es steht das Nichts in der Mandel.
Da steht es und steht.

Im Nichts—wer steht da? Der König.
Da steht der König, der König.
Da steht er und steht.

      Judenlocke, wirst nicht grau.

Und dein Aug—wohin steht dein Auge?
Dein Aug steht der Mandel entgegen.
Dein Aug, dem Nichts stehts entgegen.
Es steht zum König.
So steht es und steht.

      Menschenlocke, wirst nicht grau.
      Leere Mandel, königsblau.

Mandorla

In the almond—what dwells in the almond?
Nothing.
What dwells in the almond is Nothing.
There it dwells and dwells.

In Nothing—what dwells there? The King.
There the King dwells, the King.
There he dwells and dwells.

      Jew's curl, you'll not turn grey.

And your eye—on what does your eye dwell?
On the almond your eye dwells.
Your eye, on Nothing it dwells.
Dwells on the King, to him remains loyal, true.
So it dwells and dwells.

Human curl, you'll not turn grey.
Empty almond, royal-blue.

Weggebeizt

Weggebeizt vom
Strahlenwind deiner Sprache
das bunte Gerede des An-
erlebten—das hundert-
züngige Mein-
gedicht, das Genicht.

Aus-
gewirbelt,
frei
der Weg durch den menschen-
gestaltigen Schnee,
den Büßerschnee, zu
den gastlichen
Gletscherstuben und -tischen.

Tief
in der Zeitenschrunde,
beim
Wabeneis
wartet, ein Atemkristall,
dein unumstößliches
Zeugnis.

Etched Away

Etched away from
the ray-shot wind of your language
the garish talk of rubbed-
off experience—the hundred-
tongued pseudo-
poem, the noem.

Whirled
clear,
free
your way through the human-
shaped snow,
the penitents' snow, to
the hospitable
glacier rooms and tables.

Deep
in Time's crevasse
by
the alveolate ice
waits, a crystal of breath,
your irreversible
witness.

Einmal

Einmal,
da hörte ich ihn,
da wusch er die Welt,
ungesehn, nachtlang,
wirklich.

Eins und Unendlich,
vernichtet,
ichten.

Licht war. Rettung.

Once

Once
I heard him,
he was washing the world,
unseen, nightlong,
real.

One and Infinite,
annihilated,
ied.

Light was. Salvation.

Die Posaunenstelle

Die Posaunenstelle
tief im glühenden
Leertext,
in Fackelhöhe,
im Zeitloch:

hör dich ein
mit dem Mund.

The Trumpet Part

The trumpet part
deep in the glowing
lacuna
at lamp height
in the time hole:

listen your way in
with your mouth.

Die Pole

Die Pole
sind in uns,
unübersteigbar
im Wachen,
wir schlafen hinüber, vors Tor
des Erbarmens,

ich verliere dich an dich, das
ist mein Schneetrost,

sag, daß Jerusalem *ist*,

sags, als wäre ich dieses
dein Weiß,
als wärst du
meins,

als könnten wir ohne uns wir sein,

ich blättre dich auf, für immer,

du betest, du bettest
uns frei.

The Poles

The Poles
are inside us,
insurmountable
when we're awake,
we sleep across, up to the Gate
of Mercy,

I lose you to you, that
is my snowy comfort,

say that Jerusalem *is*,

say it, as though I were this
your whiteness,
as though you
were mine,

as though without us we could be we,

I open your leaves, for ever,

you pray, you bed
us free.

24. LEVINAS (1906–1995)

Autrement qu'être et au-delà de l'essence (Paris: Livre de Poche, 1990), pp. 13–30, 242–244, 251–253.

Trans. Alphonso Lingis as Otherwise than Being or Beyond Essence (Dordrecht: Kluwer, 1991), pp. 3–14, 155–156, 161–162.

Emmanuel Levinas makes a radical break with philosophical tradition since the Greeks by beginning his thought not from essences and identities of beings but from the other person to whom we are ethically responsible, even before we realize what or who we are. Our knowledge of beings, including our own, is secondary and derivative with respect to our moral responsibilities as humans. Levinas makes ethics "first philosophy," disputing the right to this title with metaphysics and, withal, asserting the ethical relation to the other as bearing a significance more originary than that disclosed by any science of beings. Being human is about being good before it is about knowing anything. For humans, sense is prior to essence, and the sense and significance of human things derives always from our relatedness to others.

Levinas's thinking focuses on how the proffering of language entails going out from oneself toward the Other. Language, as communicative address, is per se an exiting of the order of being and essence so as to recognize what is radically other than being—the other person in his or her singularity, which is not reducible to categories of being and not an identity to be grasped in knowing, but rather a naked appeal of the Other that claims and obligates one infinitely. The word used to address, or simply to communicate contact with another person, signifies by transcending the realm of beings and their identities (the order of the Same). It opens a space for subjectivity that is other than all that objectively is, a space for recognizing the other person facing me as sovereign subject with an ethical claim upon me rather than as an object at my disposal.

Language per se has the significance of proximity and responsibility to the Other. It betokens unconditional obligation in proximity and availability to the Other. Language in this sense is not an articulable language that can be said. Nevertheless, Levinas understands it precisely as a Saying before language ("dire d'avant le langage"). At the origin of language, this Saying is what cannot be said, though it is the significance of language per se, beyond any of the

significances assigned it by its users. As such, language is respect for and exposure to radical alterity—the other person—that trumps every positive object
or interest an individual might conceive. Though Saying is irreducibly linguistic in a deep sense—precisely a "Saying"—it is also what language cannot say:
it presents itself in a Face, the Face of the Other. It is the silent speaking of this
Face that commands everything that, humanly, we can do and be.

Thus the principal characteristic of this Other—and of the entire sphere
of ethical relation that Levinas would open up—is its unsayability. Anything
that is *said* is ipso facto translated into the language of being and thereby betrays the significance of the "otherwise than being." The central problem of
Levinas's thought becomes that of finding a language to convey this significance of naked relation, beyond being and essence, to the unsayable otherness
of the Other.

What language could possibly express this unconceptualizable, inarticulate sensibility to the Other? How can the Other, who is "other" to every comprehension in terms of the self and the same, possibly enter into or be conveyed by language without being stripped of its absolute alterity? The alterity
of the Other is infinite and cannot be contained in any closed system of meanings and references. This leaves Levinas, in effect, without a language, without
any language: the Infinite that approaches in the Other is per se unsayable.
This was pointed out in an acute analysis of Levinas's thinking, particularly of
his first major philosophical work, *Totality and Infinity* (*Totalité et infini*, 1961),
by Jacques Derrida:

> If one thinks, like Levinas, that the positive Infinite tolerates or even re-
> quires infinite alterity, then it is necessary to renounce every language, be-
> ginning with the word *infinite* and the word *other*. The infinite is not un-
> derstood as Other except in the form of the in-finite. As soon as one wants
> to think Infinity as positive plenitude (pole of the non-negative tran-
> scendence of Levinas), the Other becomes unthinkable, impossible, un-
> sayable. It is perhaps towards this unthinkable-impossible-unsayable that
> Levinas calls us beyond Being and Logos (of the tradition). But this appeal
> ought not to be able to be either thought or said. In any case, the fact that
> the positive plenitude of the classic infinite cannot be translated into lan-
> guage except in being betrayed by a negative word (in-finite) locates per-
> haps the point where, most profoundly, thought breaks from language.[1]

1. Derrida, "Violence et métaphysique: Essai sur la pensée d'Emmanuel Levinas,"
L'écriture et la différence (Paris: Seuil, 1967), p. 168.

The negative way would be the only way for Levinas to intimate his key notions, as Derrida argues: "To say that the infinite exteriority of the Other is *not* spatial, is *non*-exteriority and *non*-interiority, not to be able to designate it otherwise than by a negative way, is this not to recognize that the infinite (designated itself also in its actual positivity by a negative way: in-finite) simply is not said?"[2]

Derrida is fundamentally right that Levinas has no proper language for his philosophy. Derrida's critique is based on the fact that Levinas must, nevertheless, (mis)use the language of being and totality. His terms (transcendence, exteriority, infinite, other) all derive from the language of ontology, that is, from the discourse of being and its modes and negations.

The inadequacy of any language Levinas can use for the purposes he defines belongs to the predicament of intending . . . what cannot be said, and Levinas's philosophy can very well be presented as a philosophy of the unsayable-impossible-unthinkable. The incomparable thinking and saying that takes place so remarkably in Levinas's texts describe rather what happens at the level of a *witness* to the Other that these texts can neither state nor say, nor directly reveal, since this is what cannot be said or thought.

Levinas's Infinite is, indeed, strictly speaking unsayable. Especially pursuant to Derrida's critique this becomes a dominant axis of Levinas's own exposition of his thought. To think the ways of saying the unsayable in language becomes Levinas's principal task in his second main philosophical work, *Otherwise than Being or Beyond Essence* (*Autrement qu'être et au-delà de l'essence*, 1974). He fissions language into a *Dire* and a *Dit*, a Saying and a Said, and it is this ambiguity, or "amphibole," that enables something that is by rights unsayable to be, in a manner, expressed. He adopts the technique of phenomenological reduction for moving back from the Said to the Saying that it has translated and thereby betrayed. To return to the signification of the *Dire* requires a "phenomenological reduction" that in effect "describes the indescribable" ("La remontée vers le Dire est la Réduction phénoménologique où l'indescriptible se décrit," p. 91). This reduction enables us to interpret the *Dit* as a trace of something radically other, a *Dire*. Levinas expounds this view in an important passage on the Reduction (pp. 75–77).

The *Dire* (Saying) is expounded by Levinas as responsibility for the Other ("*dire, c'est répondre d'autrui*," p. 80). This responsibility exposes and isolates

---

2. "Dire que l'extériorité infinie de l'Autre *n*'est *pas* spatiale, est *non*-extériorité et *non*-intériorité, ne pouvoir la désigner autrement que par voie négative, n'est-ce pas reconnaître que l'infini (désigné lui aussi dans sa positivité actuelle par voie négative: in-fini) ne se dit pas?" (p. 167).

the subject and makes it *one* and beyond being in the sense of the *Parmenides*: "The subject will describe itself as nude and naked, as *one* or as *someone*, expelled to a before of being, vulnerable, which is to say precisely sensible, and to which, as to the *one* of Plato's *Parmenides*, being cannot be attributed."[3] The unsayable Saying or *Dire* of the subject is a *one* or uniqueness without identity ("Unicité sans identité," p. 95). In its exposure to the Other, the subject is nothing in and for itself; it is *only* for the Other, and this responsibility alone makes it one ("l'un-dans-la-responsabilité," p. 94). *Dire*—Saying—is a denuding by the self of all identity and an exposing of self to the Other (p. 85). It is therefore nameless, though it can be addressed in a pre-nominative form, a pure pronoun that is not properly a name: "By way of exception, and by an abuse of language, one can name it Me or I. But the denomination, here, is only a pro-nomination: there is *nothing* which names itself *I*; I is said by he who speaks."[4]

Naming and designating this oneness beyond Being escapes Being and its logic. It belongs rather to the ethics of naming God: "But the Name outside essence or beyond essence, the individual anterior to individuality is called God. It precedes all divinity, that is, the divine essence that the false gods, as individuals sheltering in their concept, claim."[5] Although Derrida's critique makes Levinas anxious to deny the identification of his thinking with negative theology, in fact Plato, Plotinus, and the One beyond Being consistently turn up as starting points for his own effort to think beyond being that can be said. All of Levinas's thinking of transcendence in an ethical sense falls under the rubric of the Platonic pointing toward a Good beyond Being. Levinas thereby places himself in the company of an apophatic tradition of Neoplatonic thinkers who seek the ultimate principle of reality beyond Being (and so also typically beyond speech, the Logos).

However, for Levinas, going beyond being is not going beyond language. Language itself already comes from beyond being; it is prophetic and revelatory in the Bible, which provides a certain context for all Levinas's thinking—however rigorously philosophical, and to that extent Greek, this thinking

---

3. "Le sujet se décrira dénudé et dénué, comme *un* ou comme *quelqu'un*, expulsé en deça de l'être, vulnérable c'est-à-dire précisément sensible et auquel, comme à l'*un* du *Parménide* platonicien, l'être ne saurait s'attribuer" (p. 91).

4. "A titre exceptionnel, et par abus du langage, on peut le nommer Moi ou Je. Mais la dénomination, ici, n'est que pro-nomination: il n'y a rien qui se nomme *je*; je se dit par celui qui parle" (pp. 94–95).

5. "Mais le Nom hors l'essence ou au-delà de l'essence, l'individu antérieur à l'individualité se nomme Dieu. Il précède toute divinité, c'est-à-dire l'essence divine que revendiquent comme les individus s'abritant dans leur concept—les faux dieux" (p. 85n).

remains in its articulation.[6] Language calls us to responsibility for an Other beyond all determinations of my being or of any being. Indeed, Levinas understands the relation with the Other fundamentally in terms of language. Yet it is language before the beginning of articulation and understanding that is ethically potent; such "language" is unsayable in its very Saying.

The following excerpts are from a book dedicated to the victims of the Holocaust. As such, it undertakes to let their silence speak. Levinas's philosophy, though formed in the phenomenological school of Husserl and Heidegger, constantly witnesses to his life as a Lithuanian Jew displaced to France by the convulsions of European history in the first half of the twentieth century. His thought seeks to convey the state of trauma, of suffering the insurgency of the Other to which, deeply and defenselessly, it is beholden—and to be transfigured and "glorified" thereby.

---

6. This crucial aspect of Levinas is only thinly disguised even in his most rigorously philosophical writing and is openly avowed in *L'au-delà du verset: Lectures et discours Talmadiques* (Paris: Minuit, 1982).

From *Otherwise Than Being or Beyond Essence,* chapter 1

Essence and Disinterest

There is something to be said, Novalis wrote, in favor of passivity. It is significant that one of Novalis' contemporaries, Maine de Brain, who wished to be the philosopher of activity, will remain essentially

the philosopher of two passivities, the lower and the higher. But is
the lower lower than the higher?

Jean Wahl, *Traité de métaphysique,*

1953, p. 562

1. Being's "Other"

If transcendence has meaning, it can only signify the fact that the
event of being, the *esse,* the *essence,* passes over to what is other than
being. But what is *Being's other?* Among the five "genera" of the *Sophist* a genus opposed to being is lacking, even though since the *Republic* there had been question of what is beyond essence. And what
can the *fact* of passing over mean here, where the passing over, ending at being's other, can only undo its facticity during such a passage?

Transcendence is passing over to being's *other,* otherwise than
being. Not *to be otherwise,* but *otherwise than being.* And not to not-
be; passing over is not here equivalent to dying. Being and not-being
illuminate one another, and unfold a speculative dialectic which is a
determination of being. Or else the negativity which attempts to
repel being is immediately submerged by being. The void that hollows out is immediately filled with the mute and anonymous rustling
of the *there is,* as the place left vacant by one who died is filled with
the murmur of the attendants. Being's essence dominates not-being
itself. My death is insignificant—unless I drag into my death the
totality of being, as Macbeth wished, at the hour of his last combat.
But then mortal being, or life, would be insignificant and ridiculous
even in the "irony with regard to oneself" to which it could in fact be
likened.

To be or not to be is not the question where transcendence is
concerned. The statement of being's *other,* of the otherwise than
being, claims to state a difference over and beyond that which separates being from nothingness—the very difference of the *beyond,* the
difference of transcendence. But one immediately wonders if in the
formula "otherwise than being" the adverb "otherwise" does not inevitably refer to the verb to be, which simply has been avoided by an
artificially elliptical turn of phrase. Then what is signified by the verb
to be would be ineluctable in everything said, thought and felt. Our
languages woven about the verb to be would not only reflect this

undethronable royalty, stronger than that of the gods; they would
be the very purple of this royalty. But then no transcendence other
than the factitious transcendence of worlds behind the scenes, of the
Heavenly City gravitating in the skies over the terrestrial city, would
have meaning. The Being of beings and of worlds, however different
among themselves they may be, weaves among incomparables a common fate; it puts them in conjunction, even if the unity of Being that
assembles them is but an analogical unity. Every attempt to disjoin
the conjunction and the conjuncture but emphasizes them. The *there
is* fills the void left by the negation of Being.

2. Being and Interest

The essence thus works as an invincible persistance in essence, filling
up every interval of nothingness which would interrupt its exercise.
Esse is *interesse;* essence is interest. This being interested does not appear only to the mind surprised by the relativity of its negation, and
to the man resigned to the meaninglessness of his death; it is not reducible to just this refutation of negativity. It is confirmed positively
to be the *conatus* of beings. And what else can positivity mean but
this *conatus?* Being's interest takes dramatic form in egoisms struggling with one another, each against all, in the multiplicity of allergic
egoisms which are at war with one another and are thus together.
War is the deed or the drama of the essence's interest. No entity can
await its hour. They all clash, despite the difference of the regions to
which the terms in conflict may belong. Essence thus is the extreme
synchronism of war. Determination is formed, and is already undone, by the clash. It takes form and breaks up in a swarming. Here is
extreme contemporaneousness or immanence.

   Does not essence revert into its other by peace, in which reason,
which suspends the immediate clash of beings, reigns? Beings become patient, and renounce the allergic intolerance of their persistence in being; do they not then dramatize the *otherwise than being?*
But this rational peace, a patience and length of time, is calculation,
mediation and politics. The struggle of each against all becomes exchange and commerce. The clash of each against all in which each
comes to be with all, becomes reciprocal limitation and determination, like that of matter. But the persisting in being, interest, is maintained by the future compensation which will have to equilibriate the

concessions patiently and politically consented to in the immediate. The beings remain always assembled, present, in a present that is extended, by memory and history, to the totality determined like matter, a present without fissures or surprises, from which becoming is expelled, a present largely made up of re-presentations, due to memory and history. Nothing is gratuitous. The mass remains permanent and interest remains. Transcendence is factitious and peace unstable. It does not resist interest. And the ill-kept commitment to recompense virtue and chastise vices, despite the assurances of those who claim it was made for a term more distant than the distance that separates the heavens from the earth, will accredit strange rumors about the death of God or the emptiness of the heavens. No one will believe in their silence.

Commerce is better than war, for in peace the Good has already reigned. And yet we must now ask if even the difference that separates essence in war from essence in peace does not presuppose that *breathlessness of the spirit*, or the spirit holding its breath, in which since Plato what is beyond the essence is conceived and expressed? And ask if this breathlessness or holding back is not the extreme possibility of the Spirit, bearing a sense of what is beyond the essence?

3. The Said and the Saying

Is not the inescapable fate in which being immediately includes the statement of being's *other* not due to the hold the *said* has over the *saying*, to the *oracle* in which the said is immobilized? Then would not the bankruptcy of transcendence be but that of a theology that thematizes the *transcending* in the logos, assigns a term to the passing of transcendence, congeals it into a "world behind the scenes," and installs what it says in war and in matter, which are the inevitable modalities of the fate woven by being in its interest?

It is not that the essence qua persistence in essence, qua *conatus* and interest, would be reducible to a word-play. Saying is not a game. Antecedent to the verbal signs it conjugates, to the linguistic systems and the semantic glimmerings, a foreword preceding languages, it is the proximity of one to the other, the commitment of an approach, the one for the other, the very signifyingness of signification. (But is approach to be defined by commitment, and not rather commitment by approach? Perhaps because of current moral maxims in which the word *neighbor* occurs, we have ceased to be surprised by all that is involved in proximity and approach.) The original or pre-original saying, what is put forth in the foreword, weaves an intrigue of responsibility. It sets forth an order more grave than being and antecedent to being. By comparison being appears like a game. Being is play or detente, without responsibility, where everything possible is permitted. But is play free of interest? Right off a stakes, money or honor, is attached to it. Does not disinterestedness, without compensation, without eternal life, without the pleasingness of happiness, complete gratuity, indicate an extreme gravity and not the fallacious frivolity of play? By anticipation let us ask: does not this gravity, where being's *esse* is inverted, refer to this pre-original language, the responsibility of one for the other, the substitution of one for the other, and the condition (or the uncondition) of being hostage which thus takes form?

But this pre-original saying does move into a language, in which saying and said are correlative of one another, and the saying is subordinated to its theme. It can be shown that even the distinction between Being and entities is borne by the amphibology of the said, though this distinction and this amphibology are not thereby reducible to verbal artifices. The correlation of the saying and the said, that is, the subordination of the saying to the said, to the linguistic system and to ontology, is the price that manifestation demands. In language qua said everything is conveyed before us, be it at the price of a betrayal. Language is ancillary and thus indispensable. At this moment language is serving a research conducted in view of disengaging the *otherwise than being* or *being's other* outside of the themes in which they already show themselves, unfaithfully, as being's *essence*—but in which they do show themselves. Language permits us to utter, be it by betrayal, this *outside of being*, this *ex-ception* to being, as though being's other were an event of being. Being, its cognition and the said in which it shows itself signify in a saying which, relative to being, forms an exception; but it is in the said that both this exception and the birth of cognition [la naissance de la connaissance] show themselves. But the fact that the ex-ception shows itself and becomes truth in the *said* can not serve as a pretext to take as an absolute the apophantic variant of the saying, which is ancillary or angelic.

An ancillary or angelic variant, however sublime it be, the apophantic form of the saying is only mediating. For thematization, in which being's essence is conveyed before us, and theory and thought, its contemporaries, do not attest to some fall of the saying. They are motivated by the pre-original vocation of the saying, by responsibility itself. We will see more of this further.

But apophansis does not exhaust what there is in saying. The apophansis presupposes the language that answers with responsibility, and the gravity of this response is beyond the measure of being. The impossibility of declining responsibility is reflected only in the scruple or remorse which precedes or follows this refusal. The reality of the real ignores scruples. But, though naturally superficial, essence does not exclude the retreats of responsibility in the way that being excludes nothingness. And the gravity of the responsible saying retains a reference to being, whose nature will have to be made clear. Moral impossibility is not of lesser gravity; it does not situate responsibility in some low tension zone, at the confines of being and non-being. This gravity of the *otherwise than being* shows now, in a still confused way, its affinity with ethics. We have been seeking the *otherwise than being* from the beginning, and as soon as it is conveyed before us it is betrayed in the said that dominates the saying which states it. A methodological problem arises here, whether the pre-original element of saying (the anarchical, the non-original, as we designate it) can be led to betray itself by showing itself in a theme (if an an-archeology is possible) and whether this betrayal can be reduced; whether one can at the same time know and free the known of the marks which thematization leaves on it by subordinating it to ontology. Everything shows itself at the price of this betrayal, even the unsayable. In this betrayal the indiscretion with regard to the unsayable, which is probably the very task of philosophy, becomes possible.

When stated in propositions, the unsayable (or the an-archical) espouses the forms of formal logic; the beyond being is posited in doxic theses, and glimmers in the amphibology of *being* and *beings*—in which beings dissimulate being. The *otherwise than being* is stated in a saying that must also be unsaid in order to thus extract the *otherwise than being* from the said in which it already comes to signify but a *being otherwise*. Does the beyond being which philosophy states, and states by reason of the very transcendence of the *beyond*, fall unavoidably into the forms of the ancillary statement?

Can this *saying* and this *being unsaid* be assembled, can they be at the same time? In fact to require this simultaneity is already to reduce being's *other* to *being* and *not being*. We must stay with the extreme situation of a diachronic thought. Skepticism, at the dawn of philosophy, set forth and betrayed the diachrony of this very convey-ing and betraying. To conceive the *otherwise than being* requires, per-haps, as much audacity as skepticism shows, when it does not hesitate to affirm the impossibility of statement while venturing to *realize* this impossibility by the very statement of this impossibility. If, after the innumerable "irrefutable" refutations which logical thought sets against it, skepticism has the gall to return (and it always returns as philosophy's illegitimate child), it is because in the contradiction which logic sees in it the "at the same time" of the contradictories is missing, because a secret diachrony commands this ambiguous or enigmatic way of speaking, and because in general signification signi-fies beyond synchrony, beyond essence.

4. Subjectivity

To conceive the otherwise than being we must try to articulate the breakup of a fate that reigns in essence, in that its fragments and mo-dalities, despite their diversity, belong to one another, that is, do not escape the same order, do not escape Order, as though the bits of the thread cut by the Parque were then knotted together again. This effort will look beyond freedom. Freedom, an interruption of the de-terminism of war and matter, does not escape the fate in essence and takes place in time and in the history which assembles events into an *epos* and synchronizes them, revealing their immanence and their order.

The task is to conceive of the possibility of a break out of es-sence. To go where? Toward what region? To stay on what ontological plane? But the extraction from essence contests the unconditional privilege of the question "where?"; it signifies a null-site [non-lieu]. The essence claims to recover and cover over every ex-ception— negativity, nihilation, and, already since Plato, non-being, which "in a certain sense is." It will then be necessary to show that the exception of the "other than being," beyond not-being, signifies subjectivity or humanity, the *oneself* which repels the annexations by essence. The ego is an incomparable unicity; it is outside of the community of genus and form, and does not find any rest in itself either, unquiet, not coinciding with itself. The outside of itself, the difference from oneself of this unicity is non-indifference itself, and the extraordi-

nary recurrence of the pronominal or the reflexive, the *self (se)*—
which no longer surprises us because it enters into the current flow of
language in which things show *themselves,* suitcases fold and ideas are
understood (les choses *se* montrent, les bagages *se* plient et les idées *se*
comprennent). A unicity that has no site, without the ideal identity a
being derives from the kerygma that identifies the innumerable aspects of its manifestation, without the identity of the ego that coincides with itself, a unicity withdrawing from essence—such is man.

The history of philosophy, during some flashes, has known this
subjectivity that, as in an extreme youth, breaks with essence. From
Plato's One without being to Husserl's pure Ego, transcendent in
immanence, it has known the metaphysical extraction from being,
even if, betrayed by the said, as by the effect of an oracle, the exception restored to the essence and to fate immediately fell back into the
rules and led only to worlds behind the scenes. The Nietzschean man
above all was such a moment. For Husserl's transcendental reduction will a putting between parentheses suffice—a type of writing, of
commiting oneself with the world, which sticks like ink to the hands
that push it off? One should have to go all the way to the nihilism of
Nietzsche's poetic writing, reversing irreversible time in vortices, to
the laughter which refuses language.

The philosopher finds language again in the abuses of language
of the history of philosophy, in which the unsayable and what is beyond being are conveyed before us. But negativity, still correlative
with being, will not be enough to signify the *other than being.*

5. Responsibility for the Other

But how, at the still temporal breaking point where being *comes to
pass,* would being and time fall into ruins so as to disengage subjectivity from its essence? Do not the falling into ruins and the dis-
engagement last; do they not occur in being? The *otherwise than being*
cannot be situated in any eternal order extracted from time that
would somehow command the temporal series. Kant has shown the
impossibility of that in the antithesis of the fourth Antinomy. It is
then the temporalization of time, in the way it signifies being and
nothingness, life and death, that must also signify the *beyond being
and not being;* it must signify a difference with respect to the couple
being and nothingness. Time is essence and monstration of essence.
In the temporalization of time the light comes about by the instant

falling out of phase with itself—which is the temporal flow, the differing of the identical. The differing of the identical is also its manifestation. But time is also a recuperation of all divergencies, through retention, memory and history. In its temporalization, in which, thanks to retention, memory and history, nothing is lost, everything is presented or represented, everything is consigned and lends itself to inscription, or is synthetized or, as Heidegger would say, assembled, in which everything is crystallized or sclerosized into substance—in the recuperating temporalization, without time lost, without time to lose, and where the being of substance comes to pass—there must be signaled a lapse of time that does not return, a diachrony refractory to all synchronization, a transcending diachrony.

The meaning of this signalling will have to be clarified. Can it preserve a relationship across the break of the diachrony, without, however, restoring to representation this "deep formerly" as a past that had flowed on, without signifying a "modification" of the present and thus a commencement, a principle that would be thematizable, and therefore would be the origin of every historical or recallable past? Can it, on the contrary, remain foreign to every present, every representation, and thus signify a past more ancient than every representable origin, a pre-original and anarchical *passed*? The signalling of this pre-original past in the present would not again be an ontological relation.

But if time is to show an ambiguity of being and the otherwise than being, its temporalization is to be conceived not as essence, but as saying. Essence fills the said, or the epos, of the saying, but the saying, in its power of equivocation, that is, in the enigma whose secret it keeps, escapes the epos of essence that includes it and signifies beyond in a signification that hesitates between this beyond and the return to the epos of essence. This equivocation or enigma is an inalienable power in saying and a modality of transcendence. Subjectivity is a node and a denouement—of essence and essence's other.

But how is the saying, in its primordial enigma, said? How is time temporalized such that the dia-chrony of transcendence, of the other than being, is signalled? How can transcendence withdraw from *esse* while being signalled in it? In what concrete case is the singular relationship with a past produced, which does not reduce this past to the immanence in which it is signalled and leaves it be past, not returning as a present nor a representation, leaves it be past without reference to some present it would have "modified," leaves it be a past, then, which can not have been an origin, a pre-original past, an-archical past?

A linear regressive movement, a retrospective back along the temporal series toward a very remote past, would never be able to reach the absolutely diachronous pre-original which cannot be recuperated by memory and history. But it may be that we have to unravel other intrigues of time than that of the simple succession of presents. Men have been able to be thankful for the very fact of finding themselves able to thank; the present gratitude is grafted onto itself as onto an already antecedent gratitude. In a prayer in which the worshipper asks that his prayer be heard, the prayer as it were precedes or follows itself.

But the relationship with a past that is on the hither side of every present and every re-presentable, for not belonging to the order of presence, is included in the extraordinary and everyday event of my responsibility for the faults or the misfortune of others, in my responsibility that answers for the freedom of another, in the astonishing human fraternity in which fraternity, conceived with Cain's sober coldness, would not by itself explain the responsibility between separated beings it calls for. The freedom of another could never begin in my freedom, that is, abide in the same present, be contemporary, be representable to me. The responsibility for the other can not have begun in my commitment, in my decision. The unlimited responsibility in which I find myself comes from the hither side of my freedom, from a "prior to every memory," an "ulterior to every accomplishment," from the non-present par excellence, the non-original, the an-archical, prior to or beyond essence. The responsibility for the other is the locus in which is situated the null-site of subjectivity, where the privilege of the question "Where?" no longer holds. The time of the *said* and of *essence* there lets the pre-original saying be heard, answers to transcendence, to a dia-chrony, to the irreducible divergency that opens here between the non-present and every representable divergency, which in its own way—a way to be clarified—makes a sign to the responsible one.

6. Essence and Signification

But is not the relationship with this pre-original a recuperation? Let us look into this more closely. The response of the responsible one does not thematize the diachronical as though it were retained, remembered or historically reconstructed. It can not thematize or comprehend. Not out of weakness; to what could not be contained there corresponds no capacity. The non-present is in-comprehend-able by reason of its immensity or its "superlative" humility or, for example, its goodness, which is the superlative itself. The non-present here is invisible, separated (or sacred) and thus a non-origin, an-archical. The Good cannot become present or enter into a representation. The present is a beginning in my freedom, whereas the Good is not presented to freedom; it has chosen me before I have chosen it. No one is good voluntarily. We can see the formal structure of nonfreedom in a subjectivity which does not have time to choose the Good and thus is penetrated with its rays unbeknownst to itself. But subjectivity sees this nonfreedom redeemed, exceptionally, by the goodness of the Good. The exception is unique. And if no one is good voluntarily, no one is enslaved to the Good.

Immemorial, unrepresentable, invisible, the past that bypasses the present, the pluperfect past, falls into a past that is a gratuitous lapse. It cannot be recuperated by reminiscence not because of its remoteness, but because of its incommensurability with the present. The present is essence that begins and ends, beginning and end assembled in a thematizable conjunction; it is the finite in correlation with a freedom. Diachrony is the refusal of conjunction, the non-totalizable, and in this sense, infinite. But in the responsibility for the Other, for another freedom, the negativity of this anarchy, this refusal of the present, of appearing, of the immemorial commands me and ordains me to the other, to the first one on the scene and makes me approach him, makes me his neighbor. It thus diverges from nothingness as well as from being. It provokes this responsibility against my will, that is, by substituting me for the other as a hostage. All my inwardness is invested in the form of a despite-me, for-another. Despite-me, for-another, is signification par excellence. And it is the sense of the "oneself," that accusative that derives from no nominative; it is the very fact of finding oneself while losing oneself.

What is exceptional in this way of being signalled is that I am ordered toward the face of the other. In this order which is an ordination the non-presence of the infinite is not only a figure of negative theology. All the negative attributes which state what is beyond the essence become positive in responsibility, a response answering to a non-thematizable provocation and thus a non-vocation, a trauma.

This response answers, before any understanding, for a debt contracted before any freedom and before any consciousness and any present, but it does answer, as though the invisible that bypasses the present left a trace by the very fact of bypassing the present. That trace lights up as the face of a neighbor, ambiguously him *before whom* (or *to whom*, without any paternalism) and him *for whom* I answer. For such is the enigma or ex-ception of a face, judge and accused.

What is positive in responsibility, outside of essence, conveys the infinite. It inverses relationships and principles, reverses the order of interest: in the measure that responsibilities are taken on they multiply. This is not a *Sollen* commanding the infinite pursuit of an ideal. The infinity of the infinite lives in going backwards. The debt increases in the measures that it is paid. This divergency perhaps deserves the name glory. The positivity of the infinite is the conversion of the response to the infinite into responsibility, into approach of the other. The Infinite is non-thematizable, gloriously exceeds every capacity, and manifests, as it were in reverse, its exorbitance in the approach of a neighbor, obedient to its measure. Subjectivity, prior to or beyond the free and the non-free, obliged with regard to the neighbor, is the breaking point where essence is exceeded by the infinite.

It is the breaking-point, but also the binding place; the glow of a trace is enigmatic, equivocal. It is so in still another sense, which distinguishes it from the appearing of phenomena. It cannot serve as the point of departure for a demonstration, which inexorably would bring it into immanence and essence. A trace is sketched out and effaced in a face in the equivocation of a saying. In this way it modulates the modality of the transcendent.

The infinite then cannot be tracked down like game by a hunter. The trace left by the infinite is not the residue of a presence; its very glow is ambiguous. Otherwise, its positivity would not preserve the infinity of the infinite any more than negativity would.

The infinite wipes out its traces not in order to trick him who obeys, but because it transcends the present in which it commands me, and because I cannot deduce it from this command. The infinite who orders me is neither a cause acting straight on, nor a theme, already dominated, if only retrospectively, by freedom. This detour at a face and this detour from this detour in the enigma of a trace we have called illeity.

Illeity lies outside the "thou" and the thematization of objects. A neologism formed with *il* (he) or *ille*, it indicates a way of concerning me without entering into conjunction with me. To be sure, we have to indicate the element in which this *concerning* occurs. If the relationship with illeity were a relationship of consciousness, "he" would designate a theme, as the "thou" in Buber's I-thou relation does, probably—for Buber has never brought out in a positive way the spiritual element in which the I-thou relationship is produced. The illeity in the beyond-being is the fact that its coming toward me is a departure which lets me accomplish a movement toward a neighbor. The positive element of this departure, that which makes this departure, this diachrony, be more than a term of negative theology, is my responsibility for the others. Or, one may say, it is the fact that the others show themselves in their face. There is a paradox in responsibility, in that I am obliged without this obligation having begun in me, as though an order slipped into my consciousness like a thief, smuggled itself in, like an effect of one of Plato's wandering causes. But this is impossible in a consciousness, and clearly indicates that we are no longer in the element of consciousness. In consciousness this "who knows where" is translated into an anachronical overwhelming, the antecedence of responsibility and obedience with respect to the order received or the contract. It is as though the first movement of responsibility could not consist in awaiting nor even in welcoming the order (which would still be a quasi-activity), but consists in obeying this order before it is formulated. Or as though it were formulated before every possible present, in a past that shows itself in the present of obedience without being recalled, without coming from memory, being formulated by him who obeys in his very obedience.

But this is still perhaps a quite narrative, epic, way of speaking. Am I the interlocutor of an infinity lacking in straightforwardness, giving its commands indirectly in the very face to which it ordains me? Illeity, which does not simply designate an oblique presentation to a squinting look, may indeed first signify such a disposition of personages. But we must go all the way. The infinite does not signal itself to a subjectivity, a unity already formed, by its order to turn toward the neighbor. In its *being* subjectivity undoes *essence* by substituting itself for another. Qua one-for-another, it is absorbed in signification, in saying or the verb form of the infinite. Signification precedes essence. It is not a stage of cognition calling for the intuition that would fulfill it, nor the absurdity of nonidentity or of impossible identity. It is the glory of transcendence.

Substitution is signification. Not a reference from one term to another, as it appears thematized in the said, but substitution as the very subjectivity of a subject, interruption of the irreversible identity of the essence. It occurs in the taking charge of, which is incumbent on me without any escape possible. Here the unicity of the ego first acquires a meaning—where it is no longer a question of the ego, but of me. The subject which is not an ego, but which I am, cannot be generalized, is not a subject in general; we have moved from the ego to me who am me and no one else. Here the identity of the subject comes from the impossibility of escaping responsibility, from the taking charge of the other. Signification, saying—my expressivity, my own signifyingness qua sign, my own verbality qua verb—cannot be understood as a modality of being; the disinterestedness suspends essence. As a substitution of one for another, as me, a man, I am not a transubstantiation, a changing from one substance into another, I do not shut myself up in another identity, I do not rest in a new avatar. As signification, proximity, saying, separation, I do not fuse with anything. Have we to give a name to this relationship of signification grasped as subjectivity? Must we pronounce the word expiation, and conceive the subjectivity of the subject, the otherwise than being, as an expiation? That would perhaps be bold and premature. At least we can ask if subjectivity qua signification, qua one-for-another, is not traceable back to the vulnerability of the ego, to the incommunicable, non-conceptualizable, sensibility. . . .

From *Otherwise than Being or Beyond Essence,* chapter 5 (section 3)

The very discussion which we are at this moment elaborating about signification, diachrony and the transcendence of the approach beyond being, a discussion that means to be philosophy, is a thematizing, a synchronizing of terms, a recourse to systematic language, a constant use of the verb being, a bringing back into the bosom of being all signification allegedly conceived beyond being. But are we being duped by this subreption? The objections are facile, like those that, since the birth of philosophy, are thrown at skepticism. What about our discussion, narrating, as though they were fixed in themes, the anarchy and the non-finality of the subject in which the Infinite would pass? They are thus found to answer in the end not with responsibility, but in the form of theoretical propositions, to the question "What about . . . ?" They do not answer the proximity of the neighbor. The discussion thus remains ontological, as though the comprehension of being ordered all thought and thinking itself. By the very fact of formulating statements, is not the universality of the thematized, that is, of being, confirmed by the project of the present discussion, which ventures to question this universality? Does this discourse remain then coherent and philosophical? These are familiar objections!

But does the coherence that would be lacking in this discussion consist in the immobility of the instant of truth, in its possibility of synchrony? The objection would then presuppose what is in question: the reference of all signification to essence. But our whole purpose was to ask if subjectivity, despite its foreignness to the said, is not stated by an abuse of language through which in the indiscretion of the said everything is shown. Everything is shown by indeed betraying its meaning, but philosophy is called upon to reduce that betrayal, by an abuse that justifies proximity itself in which the Infinite comes to pass. But this remains to be shown.

That the ontological form of the said could not alter the signification of the beyond being which shows itself in this said devolves from the very contestation of this signification. How would the contestation of the pretension beyond being have meaning if this pretention were not heard? Is there a negation in which the sense of which the negation is a negation is not conserved? The contradiction which the signification of the beyond being—which evidently is not—should compromise is inoperative without a second time, without *reflection* on the condition of the statement that states this signification. In this reflection, that is, only after the event, contradiction appears: it does not break out between two simultaneous statements, but between a statement and its conditions, as though they were in the same time. The statement of the beyond being, of the name of God, does not allow itself to be walled up in the conditions of its enunciation. It benefits from an ambiguity or an enigma, which is not the effect of an inattention, a relaxation of thought, but of an extreme proximity of the neighbor, where the Infinite comes to pass. The Infinite does not enter into a theme like a being to be given in it, and thus belie its beyond being. Its transcendence, an exteriority, more exterior, more other than any exteriority of being, does not come to pass save through the subject that confesses or contests it. Here there is an inversion of order: the revelation is made by him that receives it, by the inspired subject whose inspiration, alterity in the same, is the subjectivity or psyche of the subject. The revelation of the beyond being is perhaps indeed but a word, but this "perhaps" belongs to an ambiguity in which the anarchy of the Infinite resists the univocity of an originary or a principle. It belongs to an ambiguity or an ambivalence and an inversion which is stated in the word God, the *apex* of vocabulary, admission of the stronger than me in me and of the "less than nothing," nothing but an abusive word, a beyond themes in a thought that does not yet think or thinks more than it thinks. . . .

It is through its ambivalence which always remains an enigma that infinity or the transcendent does not let itself be assembled. Removing itself from every memorable present, a past that was never present, it leaves a trace of its impossible incarnation and its inordinateness in my proximity with the neighbor, where I state, in the autonomy of the voice of conscience, a responsibility, which could not have begun in me, for freedom, which is not my freedom. The fleeting trace effacing itself and reappearing is like a question mark put before the scintillation of the ambiguity: an infinite responsibility of the one for the other, or the signification of the Infinite in responsibility. There is an ambiguity of the order that orders to me the neighbor who obsesses me, for whom and before whom I answer by my ego, in which being is inverted into a substitution, into the very possibility of gift—and of an infinite illeity, glorious in the human plot hatched in proximity, the subversion of essence into substitution. In it I could not arise soon enough to be there on time, nor approach without the extraordinary distance to be crossed augmenting before every effort to assemble it into an itinerary. Illeity overflows both cognition and the enigma through which the Infinite leaves a trace in cognition. Its distance from a theme, its reclusion, its holiness, is not its way to effect its being (since its past is anachronous and anarchic, leaving a trace which is not the trace of any presence), but is its glory, quite different from being and knowing. It makes the word God be pronounced, without letting "divinity" be said. That would have been absurd, as though God were an essence (that is, as though he admitted the amphibology of being and entities), as though he were a process, or as though he admitted a plurality in the unity of a genus. Does God, a proper and unique noun not entering into any grammatical category, enter without difficulties into the vocative? It is non-thematizable, and even here is a theme only because in a said everything is conveyed before us, even the ineffable, at the price of a betrayal which philosophy is called upon to reduce. Philosophy is called upon to conceive ambivalence, to conceive it in several times. Even if it is called to thought by justice, it still synchronizes in the said the diachrony of the difference between the one and the other, and remains the servant of the saying that signifies the difference between the one and the other as the one for the other, as non-indifference to the other. Philosophy is the wisdom of love at the service of love.

25. BLANCHOT (1907–2003)

"Comment Découvrir l'Obscur?" in *L'Entretien infini* (Paris: Galli-mard, 1969), pp. 57–69.

Trans. Susan Hanson as "How to Discover the Obscure?" in *The Infinite Conversation* (Minneapolis: University of Minnesota Press, 1993), pp. 40–48.

A prolific writer of narratives, critical essays, and aphoristic reflections and fragments, Maurice Blanchot has experimented with many different forms of the written word (typically allowing them to invade and interrupt each other), but he has brought to all of them his tenacious pursuit of evasion and efface-ment of all that would name or define him and what he writes. Language, as Blanchot reinvents and presents it in his uncannily polished, peculiarly per-fect prose, emulates a condition of blankness or whiteness ("blancheur," it is tempting to say). It is language that remembers, or is in search of, something that it cannot say, something which escapes all efforts to re-present it. Recalci-trant to presence, this unmentionable "before" resists being brought to light and rather inhabits the shadows of past and future cast by language itself.

Language, in failing to make present, nevertheless intimates something that haunts the various modes of pseudo-presence such as past perfect and fu-ture anterior. Language, moreover, has the capacity of unselfing, of losing identity, and so of suffering what is other than it to be received into it, undo-ing and, in effect, "othering" it. It is just that this Other to language cannot be detected except as an effect—or rather defect—of language.

Writing in particular works this undoing of language—by *un*working ("désoeuvrement"). In writing, one can step outside time and outside reality altogether. Not, of course, in the *activity* of writing, but in the passivity from which writing unconsciously comes when it cuts all ties with what is in any way already given in the world, and so erases the present. Writing thereby places itself outside the very alternative of the linguistically fabricated con-cepts of inside and outside. The One and the Other, being and non-being, form wholes that writing can withdraw from and interrupt, being bound by no logic and being part of no whole, but rather a cut from nowhere into nothing. Writing cuts into the present of every presence in order to repeat it

427

eternally, but as *in*actual and as *not* happening, and thus as opening up a gap in reality. By voiding the present, writing delivers all it touches from the dictatorship of the One (one word, one world, one reality), but also deprives it of the unity necessary to being said or sayable.

Blanchot found an apt mythological emblem for what cannot be said in the song of the Sirens.[1] The Sirens' mysterious power to draw humans to their death and to awaken self-destructive desire resides not so much in a particular quality of their song as in what it lacks ("ce chant énigmatique qui est puissant par son défaut," p. 11). As Kafka well understood, the Sirens' song attracts by its silence; its very disappearing is the secret of its success. Their song is "a place of aridity and drought, where silence, like noise, was burning in the one who had had at his disposal all ways of access to the song" ("un lieu d'aridité et de sécheresse où le silence, comme le bruit, brûlait, en celui qui en avait eu la disposition, toute voie d'accès au chant," p. 10).

Our speaking, deeply considered, is a silence: "it says in silence the speaking that silence is" (ibid.). And yet this silence of language needs to be thought of as outside language and even as without relation to language. It is only in the loss of relation to it through language that this unsayable can be detected at all. What cannot be said is not a state but a becoming, or rather an unbecoming, a losing of whatever it is (not), even the possibility of being designated as "what cannot be said." Blanchot thinks in and around the paradoxical il-logic of what cannot be said, for it is nevertheless "what must be said," which he follows unflinchingly to some of its most excruciatingly difficult, indigestible implications. All the ways of unsaying are never nearly enough to unsay our language sufficiently so as to liberate what it oppresses. The necessary passivity can never be passive enough, and this drives the passion for it to an absolute intensity.

Blanchot's later work refines upon the apophatic a/logic or rather il/logic (illness of the Logos) discovered especially in writing. Not negation, as in (a certain) negative theology, but the *neutre* is its open secret. For negation posits a definite something that is negated, whereas the "neutre" is only an indeterminate "not-quite-nothing" that is left by the indefinite, open series of retractions: neither . . . nor . . . nor, etc., that is the mark of the "neutre." Blanchot strains to negate even all the negative aspects of the "neutre," since they nevertheless posit a certain something to be negated and thus make an attribution

---

1. "Le chant des sirèns," in Blanchot, *Le livre à venir* (Paris: Gallimard, 1959), pp. 9–17. Trans. Lydia Davis as "The Song of the Sirens," in *The Gaze of Orpheus* (Barrytown, N.Y.: Station Hill, 1981), pp. 105–113.

to "what" shirks every name and attribute. The "neutre" lets an indefinite series of negations accumulate ("une série non définitive de négations"). This is an extension of the apophatic way that raises it to a higher power of recursive self-abnegation.

Like Blanchot's own name, curiously a purely white ("blanche"), a blank appellative, the "neutre" endeavors to neutralize all determinate namings and to remain the name for nothing nameable and for namelessness itself. It hints that at the heart of every name is a neutral namelessness, neither this nor that, yet not quite nothing either. The "neutre" is a name continuously in process of its own infinite effacement as name. It does not negate naming; it is after all a name, a common noun, but it names nothing and is in a constant movement neutralizing every affirmation or negation that a name can make. For Blanchot, just such an un-working ("désoeuvrement") of naming is at work in the empty core of every name and is even grafted on to every word ("Greffé sur toute parole: le neutre").[2]

Blanchot's thought developed in close dialogue over many decades with Levinas, his onetime fellow philosophy student at Strasbourg. Particularly in his collections of (a)philosophical fragments, he seeks to give Levinas's notion of the unsayable transcendence of the Other a turn away from the theological and to think it in purely secular terms of political community. "Whereas for Levinas, the Name of God designates the radical alterity that transcends every system of language and all possibility of comprehension, Blanchot refuses this Name in the name of the radical namelessness of the Other, the other man." Blanchot thus voices "the infinite demand of refusal, of refusal maintained in the name—without name—of the Other."[3]

Blanchot's seminal insight is into the lie of language inherent in the unity of the name that belies the discontinuity and disaster of things just below and before and outside the ordered constructions made by words. Destructuration of language leads to madness and ultimately death, but it also releases the most secret, unsoundable, unsayable reserves of our desire. Blanchot's language studies the ways of letting itself go, of slipping into oblivion, in order to "remember" what was lost by the advent of language and its ordered unity. This brings back a relation to what cannot and never could be said, what is

---

2. Blanchot, *Le pas au-delà* (Paris: Gallimard, 1973), p. 117.

3. Leslie Hill, *Blanchot: Extreme Contemporary* (New York: Routledge, 1997), p. 178. See also Gerald Bruns, *Maurice Blanchot: The Refusal of Philosophy* (Baltimore: Johns Hopkins University Press, 1997).

radically without relation to language.[4] Paradoxically, the "relation" to what cannot be said can only "be" at all in becoming a non-relation or relationless relation.

Blanchot emphasizes that "the neutre changes the relation into non-relation" ("le neutre change le rapport en non-rapport," *Le pas au-delà*, p. 102). The "neutre" is rather an indetermination of language underlying all its determinations, what Blanchot describes as a "dispersed silence." It is as if language itself were, in general, neuter ("comme si était neutre le langage 'en général,'" p. 103), and in relation to language everything "else" turns elusively indefinite, precisely "neutre."

Many of the most incisive later forays into this elusive, apophatic terrain are found in Blanchot's fragmentary writings, comprising *L'entretien infini*, *Le pas au-delà*, and *L'écriture du désastre*. His particular use of the fragment owes much to the Jena Romantics, especially Friedrich Schlegel and Novalis (Schelling also was among them), who began discovering and exploiting the resources of this form for the purpose of obliquely expressing what proved inexpressible in prose statements.

Fragments from Blanchot's *The Step Not Beyond* (1973) exhibit the anonymous and the "neutre" as it escapes from every linguistic formulation, and Blanchot's writing of or around them exposes language as a loss of itself. The reflections on the anonymous belong to Blanchot's general attack on naming and its mendacious unities and violations of the nameless. They illustrate how the "neutre" slips in between the twin pitfalls of affirmation and of negation—the latter of which posits affirmation in order to negate it. In these reflections, Blanchot delivers his analysis of how the structurings of language are a falsification of a more primal disorder which cannot be named or said, affirmed or articulated, because all these linguistic operations are inevitably ordering functions. It is only in language's ceding to a chaos in its midst that it can re-member, by forgetting all that its saying as such conspires to deny and belie.[5]

---

4. Cf. Karmen MacKendrick, *Immemorial Silence*, pp. 17ff., as well as Kevin Hart, *The Dark Gaze* (Chicago: University of Chicago Press, 2004). Hart's most sustained commentary on the piece here anthologized is "The Impossible," in *Religion, Modernity and Postmodernity*, ed. Paul Heelas (Oxford: Blackwell, 1998).

5. For intensely apophatic fragments in *The Step Not Beyond* (Albany: SUNY Press, 1992), trans. Lycette Nelson, see pp. 34–39 ("The anonymous after the name is not the nameless anonymous"), p. 48 ("The name of God"), p. 81 ("Distancing oneself appears"), p. 83 ("The power to name the neutre" and "The neutre can be named"), pp. 118–119 ("The fragility of what already breaks"), p. 121 ("It is not that the anonymous"). Originals in *Le pas au-delà*, pp. 52–57, 69–70, 101–106, 113, 115, 116, 117, 162–163, 165.

Fragments from *The Writing of the Disaster* (1980) emphasize that the disaster cannot be said or thought. It cannot even happen or come to be as an event. It is always outside whatever happens, ungraspably impinging from a distance. It is the event of what cannot arrive, of what is always coming without ever arriving. This is another vocabulary for the apophatic. It is characterized not only by contradiction and self-erasure and retraction, but also by its orientation to what is outside it, and this is what makes it more than linguistic nihilism. Blanchot's writing turns passionately toward what is irrecoverably outside it.[6]

The exposition that best illustrates how Blanchot comes to his notion of the neuter is "How to Discover the Obscure?" in *The Infinite Conversation*. This piece takes as its point of departure Yves Bonnefoy's "poétique de l'espoir," a "poetics of hope" which is against hope in anything that could actually be realized and is rather hope that is *only* hope, alien to any present of possession, hope in what is *always* yet to come. This, then, is hope in the impossible. It is hope more exactly in what is beyond the reach of language, for language defines and dominates the realm of the possible.

Beyond circumscribing all that is conceivable, language harbors a higher mode of possibility than that of the "merely possible." Conceivability, according to Blanchot, claims to ground a priori all that actually is. Possibility in this sense is the power to articulate and thereby to dictate. Language as power is a form of violence: it annihilates the real. For possibility appropriates all that is, projecting it into its conception of what *could* be. The realm of possibility and power imposes its powerful unifying order on what *actually* is irreducibly multiple and diverse and as such recalcitrant to any general order. Is there, then, a language which can escape this tyranny, a thought and language of the *im*possible, of what no general order of things can comprehend within its

---

6. See especially *The Writing of the Disaster*, new ed. (Lincoln: University of Nebraska, 1995), trans. Ann Smock, pp. 10–11 ("Wittgenstein's mysticism" and "Not to write"), p. 14 ("From the moment"), p. 16 ("The discourse on passivity necessarily betrays passivity"), p. 21 ("It is upon losing what we have to say that we speak"), pp. 33–34 ("The passive need not take place"), pp. 38–39 ("Trust in language is the opposite . . ."), p. 51 ("Silence is perhaps a word"), p. 52 ("A word that is almost deprived of meaning"), p. 53 ("May what is written resound in the stillness"), p. 57 ("In the silent outside" and "These names"), p. 59 ("The language of awaiting—perhaps it is silent"), p. 72 ("A Primal Scene?"), p. 87 ("Words to avoid because of their excessive theoretical freight," "There remains the unnamed" and "There remains the unnamed"), p. 114 ("In 'indiscretion with respect to the *in*effable'"), p. 122 ("To keep still"), p. 137 ("To keep a secret"), pp. 139–140 ("Why one God?"). Originals in *L'écriture du désastre* (Paris: Gallimard, 1980), pp. 14, 23, 39, 58, 66, 86, 87, 88, 94–96, 98, 138, 139, 176, 187, 211–212.

scheme of possibilities a priori? Such a language would be relation to an Other through passion for the Outside of the whole structure of possibility that language erects.

What Blanchot proposes, in effect, is that there is, free from all structures of possibility, a non-empirical experience of unmediated being such as the Neoplatonists once envisaged. However, it should be characterized as an experience not of the transcendent One but of the Outside. Impossibility is then the passion for the Outside, before every act and initiative and consciousness. Like the Neoplatonists, Blanchot identifies this Impossibility with being itself—with that which is. But this being at the same time precedes being in any determinate, articulated form. It is thus also the Other of being, more originary than any being that can be named. For Blanchot, therefore, it is without name, "neutre."

The "neutre" denies nothing. One is tempted to say it "includes," if only by way of a "relationless relation," everything, but *as* neutral and anonymous, as nothing sayable or assertable or nameable. One is tempted also to say that Blanchot denies at least one thing: that theology can be any kind of basis or matrix for the writing of the disaster presented in his works. As a denial, however, this would betray the fundamental thrust of that writing. The juxtaposition of the writing of the disaster with theology is not effaced so long as it is still in process of being effaced. In this sense, the distancing from theology and ontology in Blanchot is "infinite" and thereby becomes an "infinite conversation" ("entretien infini").

How to Discover the Obscure?

This hope is not just any hope. Just as there are two poetries, "the one chimerical, deceiving and fatal," "there are two hopes." Poetic hope is to be reinvented, or to put this another way: it is up to poetry to "found a new hope." Even as hope is all but identified with poetry—so that the reality of poetry would be that of hope—hope appears, coming after it, as the gift that poetry would offer us. Poetry would be the medium of this new hope. Hence the affirmation: poetry is a means and not an end.

Hope is to be reinvented. Would this mean that what this hope aims at is to be obtained through invention, a beautiful utopian future, or through the splendor of the imaginary that certain romantics are said to have had as their horizon? Not at all. The hope that passes by way of the ideal—the lofty heavens of the idea, the beauty of names, the abstract salvation of the concept—is a weak hope. Hope is true hope insofar as it aspires to give us, in the future of a promise, what is. What is is presence. But hope is only hope. There is hope when, far from any present grasp, far from any immediate possession, it relates to what is always yet to come, and perhaps will never come; hope says the hoped-for coming of what exists as yet only in hope. The more distant or difficult the object of hope is, the more profound and close to its destiny as hope is the hope that affirms it: I hope little when what I hope for is almost at hand. Hope bespeaks the possibility of what escapes the realm of the possible; at the limit, it is relation recaptured where relation is lost. Hope is most profound when it withdraws from and deprives itself of all manifest hope. But at the same time we must not hope, as in a dream, for a chimerical fiction. It is against this that the new hope appoints itself. Hoping not for the probable, which cannot be the measure of what there is to be hoped for, and hoping not for the fiction of the unreal, true hope— the unhoped for of all hope—is an affirmation of the improbable and a wait for what is.

On the first page of his book, one of the most beautiful, Yves Bonnefoy has written: "*I dedicate this book to the improbable, that is to say, to what is. To a spirit of vigil. To the negative theologies. To a poetry longed for, of rains, of waiting and of wind. To a great realism that aggravates instead of resolving, that designates the obscure, that takes clarity for clouds that can always be parted. That has concern for a clarity high and impracticable.*"

Why the improbable? And how would what is be the improbable? The improbable escapes proof, not because it cannot be demonstrated for the time being but because it never arises in the region where proof is required. The improbable is what arises in a way other than through the approbation of proof. The improbable is not simply that which, remaining within the horizon of probability and its calculations, would be defined by a greater or a lesser probability. The improbable is not what is only very slightly probable. It is infinitely more than the most probable: "*that is to say, what is.*" And yet what is remains the improbable.

What does such a word seek to tell us? I would like to clarify it by translating it in this way: were there a meeting point between possibility and impossibility, the improbable would be this point. But what do these two new names indicate to us?

Possibility: language as power

They belong to our everyday vocabulary. We say something is possible when a conceivable event does not run up against any categorical impediment within a given horizon. It is possible: logic does not prohibit it, nor does science or custom object. The possible, then, is an empty frame; it is what is not at variance with the real, or what is not yet real, or, for that matter, necessary. But for a long time we have been alert to another sense. Possibility is not what is merely possible and should be regarded as less than real. Possibility, in this new sense, is more than reality: it is to be, plus the power to be. Possibility establishes and founds reality: one is what one is only if one has the power to be it. Here we see immediately that man not only has possibilities, but is his possibility. Never are we purely and simply, we are only on the basis of and with regard to the possibilities that we are; this is one of our essential dimensions. The word possible becomes clear, then, when it is placed in relation with the word power [*pouvoir*], first in the sense of capacity, then in the sense of a power that is commanded or a force [*puissance*]. (I am simplifying a great deal.) To what extent is power as a force an alteration, to what extent a definition of possibility? With this latter, at least, power [*puissance*] comes to be, and the appropriation that is accomplished by possession receives its determination. Even death is a power, a capacity. It is not a simple event that will happen to me, an objective and observable fact; here my power to be will cease, here I will no longer be able to be here. But death, insofar as it belongs to me and belongs to me alone, since no one can die my death in my stead or in my place, makes of this non-possibility, this impending future of mine, this relation to myself always open until my end, yet another power [*pouvoir*]. Dying, I can still die, this is our sign as man. Retaining a relation to death, I appropriate it as a power: this is the utmost limit of my solitary resolution. And we have seen that death seized again as a power, as the beginning of the mind, is at the center of the universe where truth is the labor of truth.

From this perspective, our relations in the world and with the world are always, finally, relations of power [*puissance*], insofar as power is latent in possibility. Let us restrict ourselves to the most apparent characteristics of our language. When I speak I always exercise a relation of force [*puissance*]. I belong, whether or not I know it, to a network of powers of which I make use, struggling against the force that asserts itself against me. All speech is violence, a violence all the more formidable for being secret and the secret center of violence; a violence that is already exerted upon what the word names and that it can name only by withdrawing presence from it—a sign, as we have seen, that death speaks (the death that is power) when I speak. At the same time, we well know that when we are having words we are not fighting. Language is the undertaking through which violence agrees not to be open, but secret, agrees to forgo spending itself in a brutal action in order to reserve itself for a more powerful mastery, henceforth no longer affirming itself, but nonetheless at the heart of all affirmation.

Thus begins that astonishing future of discourse wherein secret violence, disarming open violence, ends by becoming the hope and the guarantee of a world freed from violence (and all the same constituted by it). This is why (I say this in passing, and these things can only be said in passing) we are so profoundly offended by the use of force that we call torture. Torture is the recourse to violence—always in the form of a technique—with a view to making speak. This violence, perfected or camouflaged by technique, wants one to speak, wants speech. Which speech? Not the speech of violence—unspeaking, false through and through, logically the only one it can hope to obtain—but a true speech, free and pure of all violence. This contradiction offends us, but also unsettles us. Because in the equality it establishes, and in the contact it reestablishes between violence and speech, it revives and provokes the terrible violence that is the silent intimacy of all speaking words; and thus it calls again into question the truth of our language understood as dialogue, and of dialogue understood as a space of force exercised without violence and struggling against force. (The expression "We will make him see reason" that is found in the mouth of every master of violence makes clear the complicity that torture affirms, as its ideal, between itself and reason.)

The thought (of) the impossible: the *other* relation

As soon as we are in relation within a field open to possibility, and opened by possibility, force threatens. Even comprehension, an essential mode of possibility, is a grasp that gathers the diverse into a unity, identifies the different, and brings the other back to the same through a reduction that dialectical movement, after a long trajectory, makes coincide with an overcoming. All these words—grasp, identification, reduction—conceal within themselves the rendering of accounts that exists in knowledge as its measure: reason must be given. What is to be known—the unknown—must surrender to the known. But then comes this apparently innocent question: might there not exist relations, that is to say a language, escaping this movement of force through which the world does not cease to accomplish itself? In this case, such relations, such a language, would also escape possibility. An innocent question, but one that is already questioning at the margins of possibility and that, in order to guard its dignity as a question, must avoid disintegrating in the ecstasy of a response without thought, to which it may well lead.

We sense, of course, that impossibility—now employing this word as though by chance—could not be an easy movement, since we would see ourselves drawn by it away from the space in which we exercise power, if only in a negative manner, by the simple fact of living and dying. Likewise, if the thought of the impossible were entertained, it would be a kind of reserve in thought itself, a thought not allowing itself to be thought in the mode of appropriative comprehension. This is a dangerous direction, and a strange thought. It must be added, however, that the impossible is not there in order to make thought capitulate, but in order to allow it to announce itself according to a measure other than that of power. What would this other measure be? Perhaps precisely the measure of the *other*, of the other as other, and no longer ordered according to the clarity of that which adapts it to the same. We believe that we think the strange and the foreign, but in reality we never think anything but the familiar; we think not the distant, but the close that measures it. And so again, when we speak of impossibility, it is possibility alone that, providing it with a reference, already sarcastically brings impossibility under its rule. Will we ever, then, come to pose a question such as: what is impossibility, *this non-power that would not be the simple negation of power?* Or will we ask ourselves: how can we discover the obscure?; how can it be brought out into the open? What would this experience of the obscure be, whereby the obscure would give itself in its obscurity?

And, continuing to question, will we ask ourselves further: if there is possibility—because, always being able, we are the being that is fixed toward the future, always ahead of itself and even in the delay it also is, forewarning and anticipating itself—would we not be fortunate to be drawn into an entirely other experience, if it happened that this experience were that of a time out of synchrony and as though deprived of the dimension of passing beyond, henceforth neither passing nor ever having had to pass?

This is an experience we do not have to go very far to find, if it is offered in the most common suffering, and first of all in physical suffering. No doubt, where it is a matter of a measured suffering, it is still endured, still, of course, suffered, but also brought back into our grasp and assumed, recaptured and even comprehended in the patience we become in the face of it. But it can lose this measure; it is even of its essence to be always already beyond measure. Suffering is suffering when one can no longer suffer it, and when, because of this non-power, one cannot cease suffering it. A singular situation. Time is as though arrested, merged with its interval. There, the present is without end, separated from every other present by an inexhaustible and empty infinite, the very infinite of suffering, and thus dispossessed of any future: a present without end and yet impossible as a present. The present of suffering is the abyss of the present, indefinitely hollowed out and in this hollowing indefinitely distended, radically alien to the possibility that one might be present to it through the mastery of presence. What has happened? Suffering has simply lost its hold on time, and has made us lose time. Would we then be freed in this state from any temporal perspective and redeemed, saved from time as it passes? Not at all: we are delivered over to another time—to time as other, as absence and neutrality; precisely to a time that can no longer redeem us, that constitutes no recourse. A time without event, without project, without possibility; not that pure immobile instant, the spark of the mystics, but an unstable perpetuity in which we are arrested and incapable of permanence, a time neither abiding nor granting the simplicity of a dwelling place.

We must admit that, considered in this light, this experience has a pathetic appearance, but on condition that one also give the word pathos its non-pathetic sense. It is a question not of that paroxysmic state where the self cries out and is torn apart, but rather of a suffering that is almost indifferent, not suffered, but neutral (a phantom of suffering) insofar as the one who is exposed to it, precisely through this suffering, is deprived of the "I" that would make him suffer it. So now we see it: the mark of such a movement is that, by the fact that we experience it, it escapes our power to undergo it; thus it is not beyond the trial of experience, but rather that trial from which we can no longer escape. An experience that one will represent to oneself as being strange and even as the experience of strangeness. But if it is so, let us recognize that it is this not because it is too removed. On the contrary, it is so close that we are prohibited from taking any distance from it—it is foreign in its very proximity.

But we have a word that designates what is so close that it destroys all proximity—a word before which we once again find ourselves. I am referring to the immediate: the immediate that allows no mediation, the absence of separation that is absence of relation as well as infinite separation because this separation does not reserve for us the distance and the future we need in order to be able to relate ourselves to it, to come about in it.

Thus we can begin to surmise that "impossibility"—that which escapes, without there being any means of escaping it—would be not the privilege of some exceptional experience, but behind each one and as though its other dimension. And we can surmise as well that if possibility has its source in our very end—which it brings to light as the power most proper to us, according to Hölderlin's demand: "For what I want is to die, and it is for man a right"—it is from this same source that "impossibility" originates, though now sealed originarily and refusing itself to all our resources: there where dying means losing the time in which one can still come to an end and entering into the infinite "present" of a death impossible to die; a present toward which the experience of suffering is manifestly oriented, the suffering that no longer allows us the time to put a limit to it—even by dying—since we will also have lost death as a limit.

The passion of the outside

Here we will have to ask ourselves whether we have reached a point from which we might become attentive to what until now has offered itself to us merely as the other side of possibility. This is hardly certain. Nevertheless, we have arrived at a few characteristics. First this one: in impossibility time changes direction, no longer offering itself out of the future as what gathers by going beyond; time, here, is rather the dispersion of a present that, even while being only passage does not pass, never fixes itself in a present, refers to no past and goes toward no future: *the incessant.* A second trait: in impossibility, the immediate is a presence to which one cannot be present, but from which one cannot separate; or, again, it is what escapes by the very fact that there is no escaping it: the *ungraspable that one cannot let go of.* Third trait: what reigns in the experience of impossibility is not the unique's immobile collecting unto itself, but the infinite shifting of dispersal, a non-dialectical movement where contrariety has nothing to do with opposition or with reconciliation, and where the *other* never comes back to the same. Shall we call it becoming, the secret of becoming? A secret that stands apart from every secret and that gives itself as the diverging of difference.

If we hold these traits together—the present that does not pass, while being only passage; that which cannot be let go of, while offering nothing to hold onto; the too-present to which access is denied because it is always closer than any approach, reversing itself to become absence and thus being the too-present that does not present itself, yet without leaving anything in which one might absent oneself from it—we perceive that in impossibility it is not only the negative character of the experience that would make it perilous, but also "the excess of its affirmation" (what in this excess is irreducible to the power to affirm). And we perceive that what comes into play in impossibility does not withdraw from experience, but is the experience of what no longer allows itself to be withdrawn; what accords neither distance nor retreat, and without ceasing to be radically different. Thus we could say (very approximately and provisionally) that what is obscure in this movement is what it discloses: what is always disclosed without having had to disclose itself, and has always in advance reduced all movement of concealing or self-concealing to a mode of the manifest. A present in which all things present, including the self that is there present, are suspended, and yet a present exterior to itself, the very exteriority of presence. Finally, we perceive here the point at which time and space would rejoin in an originary disjunction: "presence" is as much the intimacy of instancy as the dispersal of the Outside. More precisely, it is intimacy as the Outside, the exterior become an intrusion that stifles, and the reversal of both the one and the other; what we have called "the vertigo of spacing."

But all of these traits tend to delimit, in its limitlessness, the fact that impossibility is nothing other than the mark of what we so readily call experience, for there is experience in the strict sense only where something radically *other* is in play. And here is the unexpected response: radical non-empirical experience is not at all that of a transcendent Being; it is "immediate" presence or presence as Outside. The other response is this: impossibility, which escapes every negativity, does not cease to exceed, in ruining it, every positivity; impossibility being that in which one is always already engaged through an experience more initial than any initiative, forestalling all beginning and excluding any movement of action to disengage from it. But we know, perhaps, how to name such a relation, which is the hold over which there is no longer any hold, since it is again what we have tried to designate (confusedly) by the term *passion*. So we shall be tempted to say provisionally: impossibility is relation with the Outside; and since this relation without relation is the passion that does not allow itself to be mastered through patience, impossibility is the passion of the Outside itself.

These remarks once again assembled, we see that the situation with regard to our questioning at the beginning has reversed itself. It is no longer impossibility that would be the non-power: it is the possible that is merely the power of the no. Should we then say: impossibility is being itself? Certainly, we must! Which amounts to recognizing in possibility the sovereign power to negate being: man, each time that he is on the basis of possibility, is the being *without* being. The struggle for possibility is this struggle against being.

But must we not also say: impossibility, neither negation nor affirmation, indicates what in being has always already *preceded* being and yields to no ontology? Certainly, we must! Which amounts to the presentiment that it is again being that awaits in possibility, and that if it negates itself in possibility, it is in order better to preserve itself from this *other* experience that always precedes it and is always more initial than the affirmation that names being. This would be the experience that the Ancients no doubt revered under the title of Destiny: that which diverts from every destination and that we are seeking to name more directly in speaking of the *neutral.*

But what does such a whirlwind of rarefied notions, this abstract storm, signify? That we have just been toyed with by the indefinite overturning that is the "attraction" of the impossible relation, a relation to which those extraordinary Ancients had also become attentive in their encounter with Proteus. As men of measure through knowledge of the lack of measure that was close to them, did they not recommend that Proteus be held firmly and bound in order that he should agree to declare himself truthfully in the most simple form? Simplicity is, in fact, what alone answers to the duplicity of the enigma. When, for example, Simone Weil says simply, "Human life is *impossible.* But misfortune alone makes this felt," we understand very well that it is not a question of denouncing the unbearable or the absurd character of life—negative determinations that belong to the realm of possibility—but of recognizing in impossibility our most human belonging to immediate human life, the life that it falls to us to sustain each time that, stripped through misfortune of the clothed forms of power, we reach the nakedness of every relation: that is to say, the relation to naked presence, the presence of the other, and in the infinite passion that comes from it. In the same way, Simone Weil writes: "Desire is impossible." And now we understand that desire is precisely this relation to impossibility, that it is impossibility become relation—*separation* itself, in its absolute—that becomes alluring and takes form. And we will begin also to understand why, in inspired words, René Char has said: "*The poem is the realized love of desire that has remained desire.*" And finally, if ever we were to declare imprudently that communication is impossible, we should understand that such a sentence, so clearly rash, is not meant to negate scandalously the possibility of communication, but to alert us to that other speech that speaks only when it begins to respond to the other region that is not governed by the time of possibility. In this sense, yes, we must for an instant say it, if only to forget it just as immediately:

"communication" (to take up again a term that is here out of place since there is no longer any common measure) exists only when it escapes power and when impossibility, our ultimate dimension, announces itself in it.

Naming the possible, responding to the impossible

Let us leave this path of reflection. We ought not count on a simple confrontation of words to prove that poetry might orient us toward another relation—a relation with the obscure and the unknown that would be a relation neither of force [*puissance*], nor of comprehension, nor even of revelation. We sense even that it is not the role of language, be it literary or that of poetry, even true poetry, to bring to light or to the firmness of a name what would affirm itself, unformulated, in this relation without relation. Poetry is not there in order to say impossibility: it simply answers to it, saying in responding. Such is the secret lot, the secret decision of every essential speech in us: *naming* the possible, *responding* to the impossible. A lot that nevertheless must not lead to a kind of allotment, as though we were free to choose between a speech for naming and a speech for responding; as though, finally, between possibility and impossibility there were a frontier, perhaps moving, but always determinable according to the "essence" of the one and the other.

Naming the possible, responding to the impossible. Responding does not consist in formulating an answer, in such a way as to appease the question that would obscurely come from such a region; even less in transmitting, in the manner of an oracle, a few truth contents of which the daytime world would not yet have knowledge. It is poetry's existence, each time it is poetry, that in itself forms a response and, in this response, attends to what is addressed to us in impossibility (by turning itself away). Poetry does not express this, does not say it, does not draw it under the attraction of language. But it responds. Every beginning speech begins by responding; a response to what is not yet heard, an attentive response in which the impatient waiting for the unknown and the desiring hope for presence are affirmed.

26. DERRIDA (1930–2004)

Sauf le nom (Paris: Galilée, 1993), pp. 15–21, 38–65.
 Trans. John P. Leavey, Jr., as "Sauf le nom (Post-Scriptum)," in Jacques Derrida, *On the Name* (Stanford: Stanford University Press, 1995), ed. Thomas Dutoit, pp. 35–38, 46–56.

Jacques Derrida's writing highlights the ways that virtually all language undoes or "deconstructs" itself. Not surprisingly, then, the question of his relation to negative theology has pursued him throughout his career. Many have pointed out the analogies between his thought and negative theologies, and various critics have interpreted Derrida precisely as some brand of negative theologian. Derrida was already concerned to deny this identification of his thought with negative theology in "La différance," his 1968 manifesto address to the *Société française de philosophie*. Still, the suspicion has persisted. A number of Derrida's essays from the late 1980s and early 1990s concentrate on this issue, in particular "How to Avoid Speaking: Denials" ("Comment ne pas parler: dénégations"), which Derrida composed for a colloquium in Jerusalem in 1986. The essay treats this venue as a symbolic place of apocalypse, a place where the author will finally have to reveal himself and his true relationship with negative theology. Of course, just such a final revelation is impossible for Derrida. The gathering in Jerusalem nevertheless provided him with an occasion for a teasing meditation upon the question and upon these theological traditions emphasizing the limits of language and its status as what he calls "the trace."

Derrida calls this essay the most autobiographical discourse he has ever ventured upon.[1] He is speaking of himself, or of what is closest to him by his birth in Algeria, with a heritage at once Jewish and Arab, even while speaking of the "other," namely, Greek and Christian philosophy and theology. He suggests that his reluctance or even inability to speak of negative theology—a promise that he acknowledges he has continually deferred—is linked with his inability to speak of himself. The inner void or "internal desert" he describes

---

1. "Comment ne pas parler: dénégations," in *Psyche: Inventions de l'autre* (Paris: Galilée, 1987), p. 562, n. 1.

443

in this essay is mysteriously linked to God, *his* God, about whom he cannot speak, even though he "quite rightly passes for an atheist."[2]

In this essay "on what cannot be said," Derrida discusses Neoplatonism, Pseudo-Dionysius, Meister Eckhart, Heidegger, and others. He undertakes to differentiate his own thinking from various traditions and authors of so-called negative theology, whether ancient, medieval, or modern. His attempt perhaps cannot be conclusive but must, by its nature, be ongoing. As David Klemm, in a "hermeneutical" reading of Derrida's relation to negative theology, suggests, it is impossible to identify deconstruction with negative theology; but then it is impossible, by Derrida's own account, for negative theology to have any identity whatsoever. Nevertheless, the relation between deconstruction and negative theology as a theological hermeneutic proves to be reciprocal. Just as every negative theology, to the extent that it makes predications and claims, is vulnerable to being deconstructed, so deconstruction can always be hermeneutically appropriated: its denial of continuity and its rupture of sense make a sense of their own and, when articulated, take on relatively stable meaning in words passing for currency in a certain community. It is this reciprocal interplay between moments of disruption and of re-connection, each continually overturning the other, that is the manifestation of God as both coming to and eluding language, that is, a "God who is God as the double overturning of the drift of signifiers by stable meaning and of stable meaning by the drift of signifiers."[3]

A few years later, in "Post-Scriptum" (*Sauf le nom*), Derrida again engages directly with apophatic tradition in a reading of Silesius Angelus's *Cherubinischer Wandersmann*. Yet, since it is characteristic of negative theologies to negate all positive specifications of their object and of themselves, this particular historical site translates itself into something much more universal.

---

2. This confession runs as a refrain throughout John D. Caputo's *The Prayers and Tears of Jacques Derrida* (Bloomington: Indiana University Press, 1997). Yet in his essay "Circumfession," in Jacques Derrida and Geoffrey Bennington, *Jacques Derrida* (Chicago: University of Chicago Press, 1993), Derrida avows that he prays all the time and is a man of prayers and tears. On Derrida's "religion," see, further, *Derrida and Religion: Other Testaments*, ed. Yvonne Sherwood and Kevin Hart (New York: Routledge, 2005), where Derrida says in the opening interview: "When I pray, I am thinking about negative theology, about the unnamable, the possibility that I might be totally deceived by my belief, and so on" (p. 30).

3. David E. Klemm, "Open Secrets: Derrida and Negative Theology," in *Negation and Theology*, ed. Robert P. Scharlemann (Charlottesville: University Press of Virginia, 1992), p. 21. See also the approaches of Hent de Vries, Ilse N. Bulhof, and Rico Sneller in *Flight of the Gods*, ed. Bulhof and ten Kate.

Derrida sees in negative theology a movement of universalizing translation ("un mouvement de traduction universalisante," p. 71) that nevertheless avoids imposing any sort of hegemonic universal. It is a universality that remains open and always futural, to come ("à venir"). Indeed, Derrida suggests that the openness and indeterminacy of negative theology may be necessary for any tenable idea of contemporary Europe and for any possible political democracy or universal, law-governed community today ("Mais il n'y aurait plus de 'politique', de 'droit' ou de 'moral' *sans* cette possibilité [de théologie négative] . . . ," p. 106).[4]

Any morality or politics or juridical institution requires recognition of otherness, and this means a capability of negating or suspending all determinations emanating from the self and same, so as to be able to receive the other on its own terms. This Other must be any and every other—as well as being "wholly other" ("Tout autre est tout autre"). By relativizing and negating all determinate content of its own, Derrida argues, negative theology proffers the only possibility of universal translatability able to receive and transmit otherness. And precisely this is necessary to unrestrictive political community. The very transgressiveness of boundaries characteristic of negative theology, as a theology that is equivocally atheistic, is also necessary to a community that is open and democratic.

In the opening section of the essay, Derrida points out that negative theology testifies to the desire of God, where the subject and object of this desire are ambiguous: there are no givens, no defined interlocuters prior to this discourse that could establish its bearings. It moves to and beyond all such boundaries and limits. The question of who is speaking to whom must be left open. In fact, the essay is written in dialogue form, thereby breaking the discourse of (or on) negative theology into more than one unidentified voice.

In this indefiniteness, desire for God becomes desire for universal community (*Sauf le nom*, p. 102). This is a community that is not exclusive but rather infinitely open, a democracy that is always "to come." Yet, at the same time, negative theology turns out to be possible only as a deposit of the past, a tradition defined by a body of canonical texts. Though without any proper content or characteristic, paradoxically this discourse called negative theology becomes a canon and a corpus. Perhaps that is all it is, since it can have no definition or essence. Negative theology is a pure formality: it "consists" purely

---

4. The mutual implication of democracy and deconstruction is explored from numerous angles in *La démocratie à venir: Autour de Jacques Derrida*, ed. Marie-Louise Mallet (Paris: Galilée, 2004).

of certain recognizable forms of discourse, negative forms. It is manifest in language that constantly challenges and negates language at its limit. As the experience of the essence of language and of what this leaves out, namely, everything that is not merely *some*thing, negative theology is *itself* nothing, yet it leaves a remainder on the corpus of language, like a scar. Language remains always broken open to what exceeds it, thanks to its dependence on something radically other and unsayable, which can only be apprehended negatively, in the inability of language by itself to achieve closure.

Since negative theology cannot exist as such, it can only register its effects—in language. It is a kind of universal language, or rather the unlimited translatability of language which refuses all definitive content. It is both more and less than a language. It exceeds every language and interrogates the very possibility of language, particularly of propositional language, such as the statement: "what one calls Negative Theology . . . is a language." This language without content is the inexhaustible self-depletion of language ("son inépuisable épuisement . . ."). It is the *kenosis* or self-emptying, the "desertification" of language translated and transferred through tradition, and emptied of intrinsic, intentional content. Apophatic discourse—understood as a writing after the fact, after this death and voiding of meaning, or as "post-script"— testifies to what it cannot convey. It remains as a nameless name, a name without name, to the extent that it is the name for what it exposes as unnameable.

Saving the name without the name—literally, "sauf le nom" in both these senses—is the highly paradoxical stance of negative theology, in which it rhymes with deconstruction. Negative theology is taken by Derrida as a model for the movement of twisting away from systems that deconstruction also enacts. This movement beyond every name and every manifest form of being, or beyond being itself, initiates the process of universalization of negative theology. It is unrestricted translatability by virtue of negating and moving beyond every determinate form of language. It goes beyond and outside itself, hence its spurning of identity to the point that it cannot even be said to be (*Sauf le nom*, p. 84). Negative theology is a discourse, nothing but a discourse, yet it is also the absolute denial of discourse. It refers beyond itself to what it cannot say, and is in fact nothing but this reference. As such, it is the model for language in general: all language is an irreducible reference to its own borders, the borders of language into which language disappears ("Il n'y a que du bord dans le langage," p. 64).

The name is thus "saved" only by being lost in order to save what bears the name. This silent bearer of the name has no name. It is everything *save for* ("sauf") the name—which, however, is nothing, or only an artifice, and in any case not the thing it names ("le nom n'est rien, en tout cas n'est pas la 'chose' qu'il nomme," p. 112). Traditionally, the purpose of negative theology is to keep God safe ("sauf") from idolatry and sacrilege by giving us nothing of him to know and say—except the name, even while, and precisely in, declaring him unnameable. Negative theology is language sacrificing itself in order to save and keep safe ("sauf") what it can only fail to name. Despite its specific historical site as a Christian theological appropriation of Greek philosophy, and as embodied in Western civilization and ultimately in the ideal of an unrestricted democracy that would involve no exclusions and thus have no set definition, negative theology enacts itself as a movement of universalization and at the same time of self-effacement. Derrida's work suggests that negative theology epitomizes the West's inveterate penchant for world domination and at the same time, inseparably, for self-deconstruction.

From "Sauf le nom (Post-Scriptum)"

— . . .

—Sorry, but more than one, it is always necessary to be more than one in order to speak, several voices are necessary for that . . .

—Yes, granted, and par excellence, let us say exemplarily, when it's a matter of God . . .

—Still more, if this is possible, when one claims to speak about God according to what they call apophasis [*l'apophase*], in other words, according to the voiceless voice [*la voix blanche*], the way of theology called or so-called negative. This voice multiplies itself, dividing within itself: it says one thing and its contrary, God that is without being or God that (is) beyond being. The *apophasis* is a declaration, an explanation, a response that, taking on the subject of God a negative or interrogative form (for that is also what *apophasis* means), at times so resembles a profession of atheism as to be mistaken for it. All the more because the modality of *apophasis*, despite its negative or interrogative value, often recalls that of the sentence, verdict, or decision, of the *statement* [in English in the original— Ed.]. I would like to speak to you, don't hesitate to interrupt me, of this multiplicity of voices, of this quite initial, but interminable as well, end of monologism—and of what follows . . .

—Like a certain mysticism, apophatic discourse has always been suspected of atheism. Nothing seems at once more merited and more insignificant, more displaced, more blind than such a trial [*procès*]. Leibniz himself was inclined to this. Heidegger recalls what he said of Angelus Silesius: "With every mystic there are some places that are extraordinarily bold, full of difficult metaphors and inclining almost to Godlessness, just as I have seen in the German poems of a certain Angelus Silesius, poems beautiful besides."
  Inclining, but not going beyond incline or inclination, not even or almost (*beinahe zur Gottlosigkeit hinneigend*), and the oblique slope [*penchant*] of this *clinamen* does not seem separable from a certain boldness of language [*langue*], from a poetic or metaphoric tongue . . .

—And beautiful besides, don't forget, Leibniz notes this as if it were a matter of an addition or an accessory (*im übrigen schönen Gedichten*), but I wonder if it isn't a matter there, beauty or sublimity, of an essential trait of negative theology. As for the example of Angelus Silesius . . .

—Let's leave this question aside for the moment: does the *heritage* of Angelus Silesius (Johannes Scheffler) belong to the tradition of negative theology in the strict sense or not? Can one speak here of a "strict sense"? You couldn't deny, I think, that Angelus Silesius keeps an evident kinship with apophatic theology. His example signifies for us, at this moment, only this affinity between the atheism suspected by Leibniz and a certain apophatic boldness. This apophatic boldness always consists in going further than is reasonably permitted. That is one of the essential traits of all negative theology: passing to the limit, then crossing a frontier, including that of a community, thus of a sociopolitical, institutional, ecclesial reason or raison d'être.

—If on the one hand apophasis inclines almost toward atheism, can't one say that, on the other hand or thereby, the extreme and most consequent forms of declared atheism will have always testified [*témoigné*] to the most intense desire of God? Isn't that from then on a program or a matrix? A typical and identifiable recurrence?

—Yes and no. There is one apophasis that can in effect respond to, correspond to, correspond with the most insatiable *desire of God*, according to the history and the event of its manifestation or the secret of its nonmanifestation. The other apophasis, the other voice, can remain readily foreign to all desire, in any case to every anthropotheomorphic form of desire.

—But isn't it proper to desire to carry with it its own proper suspension, the death or the phantom of desire? To go toward the absolute other, isn't that the extreme tension of a desire that tries thereby to renounce its own proper momentum, its own movement of appropriation?

—To testify, you were saying, to testify to the desire *of* God. The phrase is not only equivocal, of an equivocity essential, signifying, decisive in its very undecidability, to wit, the equivocity that the double genitive marks ("objective" and "subjective," even before the grammatical or ontological upsurge of a subject or an object), in other words, the equivocity of the origin and of the end of such a desire: does it come from God in us, from God for us, from us for God? And as we do not determine *ourselves before* this desire, as no relation to self can be sure of preceding it, to wit, of preceding a relation to the other, even were this to be through mourning, all reflection is caught in the genealogy of this genitive. I understand by that a reflection on self, an autobiographical reflection, for example, as well as a reflection on the idea or on the name of God. But your phrase is otherwise equivocal: when it names *testimony*. For if atheism, like aphophatic theology, testifies to the desire of God, if it avows, confesses, or indirectly signifies, as in a symptom, the desire of God, in the presence of whom does it do this? Who speaks to whom? Let us stay a little while with this question and feign to know what a discourse of negative theology is, with its determined traits and its own proper inclination. To whom is this discourse addressed? Who is its addressee? Does it exist before this interlocutor, before the discourse, before its actualization [*son passage à l'acte*], before its performative accomplishment? Dionysius the Areopagite, for example, articulates a certain prayer, turned toward God; he links it with an address to the disciple, more precisely to the becoming-disciple of him who is thus called to hear. An apostrophe (to God) is turned toward another apostrophe in the direction of him . . .

—Never of her . . .

How, today, can one speak—that is, speak together, address someone, testify—on the subject of and in the name of negative theology? How can that take place today, today still, so long after the inaugural openings of the *via negativa*? Is negative theology a "topic" [English in original—Ed.]? How would what still comes to us under the domestic, European, Greek, and Christian term of negative theology, of negative way, of apophatic discourse, be the chance of an incomparable translatability in principle without limit? Not of a universal tongue, of an ecumenism or of some consensus, but of a tongue to come that can be shared more than ever? One should wonder what signifies in this regard the friendship of the friend, if one withdraws it, like negative theology itself, from all its dominant determinations in the Greek or Christian world, from the fraternal (fraternalist) and phallocentric schema of *philia* or charity, as well as from a certain arrested form of democracy.

—Friendship and translation, then, and the experience of translation as friendship, that is what you seem to wish we were speaking about. It is true that one imagines with difficulty a translation, in the current sense of the term, whether it is competent or not, without some *philein*, without some love or friendship, without some "lovence" [*aimance*], as you would say, borne [*portée*] toward the thing, the text, or the other to be translated. Even if hatred can sharpen the vigilance of a translator and motivate a demystifying interpretation, this hatred still reveals an intense form of desire, interest, indeed fascination.

—Those are experiences of translation, it seems to me, that make up this "Colloquium," and almost all the authors even give this to be remarked. Let it be said in passing, a translation (the nonoriginal version of a textual event that will have preceded it) also shares that curious status of the *post-scriptum* about which we are going around in circles.

—In which, rather, we discuss [*nous débattons*], we flounder [*nous nous débattons*]. How does negative theology always run the risk of resembling an exercise of translation? An exercise and nothing but? And an exercise in the form of a *post-scriptum*? How would this risk also give it a chance?

—Let's start again from this proposition, if you like: "What is called 'negative theology,' in an idiom of Greco-Latin filiation, is a language [*langage*]."

—Only a language? More or less than a language? Isn't it also what questions and casts suspicion on the very essence or possibility of language? Isn't it what, in essence, exceeds language, so that the "essence" of negative theology would carry itself outside of language?

—Doubtless, but what is called "negative theology," in an idiom of Greco-Latin filiation, is a language, at least, that says, in one mode or another, what we have just specified about language, that is, about itself. How does one leap out of this circle?

—Consequently, to believe you, an admissible *disputing* [contestation *recevable*] of this proposition of the type S is P ("what is called 'NT' . . . is a language," etc.) could not take the form of a refutation. It could not consist in giving a critique of its falseness, but in suspecting its vagueness, emptiness, or obscurity, in accusing it of not being able to determine either the subject or the attribute of that judgment, of not even proving this learned ignorance, in the sense ennobled by Nicolas of Cusa or certain supporters of negative theology. The proposition ("What is called 'negative theology' . . . is a language") has no rigorously determinable reference: neither in its subject nor in its attribute, we just said, but not even in its copula. For it happens that, however little is known of the said negative theology . . .

—You avow then that we do indeed know something about it, we don't speak of it in the void, we come *after* this knowledge, however minimal and precarious. We preunderstand it . . .

—The preunderstanding then would be the fact from which we should indeed start, in relation to which we would be placed-after [*post-posés*]. We come *after the fact* [après le fait]: and the discursive possibilities of the *via negativa* are doubtless exhausted, that is what remains for us to think. Besides, they will be very quickly exhausted; they will always consist in an intimate and immediate exhaustion [*exhaustion*] of themselves, as if they could not have any history. That is why the slightness of the reference corpus (here *The Cherubinic Wanderer*, for example) or the rarefaction of examples should not be a serious problem. We are in absolute exemplarity as in the aridity of the desert, for the essential tendency is to formalizing rarefaction. Impoverishment is de rigueur.

—These discursive possibilities are exhausted as formal possibilities, no doubt, and if we formalize to the extreme the procedures of this theology. Which seems feasible and tempting. Then nothing remains for you, not even a name or a reference. You can speak of exhaustion [*d'épuisement*] only in the perspective of this complete formalization and in posing as extrinsic to this formal or conceptual completeness those "difficult metaphors . . . inclining almost to Godlessness," that poetic beauty, too, which Leibniz speaks about concerning Angelus Silesius. Thus you would oppose one form to the other, that of onto-logical formalism to that of poetics, and would remain prisoner of a problematic opposition between form and content. But this so traditional disjunction between concept and metaphor, between logic, rhetoric, and poetics, between sense and language, isn't it a philosophical prejudgment not only that one can or must deconstruct, but that, in its very possibility, the event named "negative theology" will have powerfully contributed to calling into question?

—I only wanted to recall that we preunderstood *already* and therefore that we write *after* preunderstanding negative theology as a "critique" (for the moment let's not say a "deconstruction") of the proposition, of the verb "be" in the third person indicative and of everything that, in the determination of the essence, depends on this mood, this time, and this person: briefly, a critique of ontology, of theology, and of language. To say "What is called 'negative theology', in an idiom of Greco-Latin filiation, is a language" is then to say little, almost nothing, perhaps less than nothing.

—Negative theology means (to say) very little, almost nothing, perhaps something other than something. Whence its inexhaustible exhaustion . . .

—That being the case, can one be authorized to speak of this apparently elementary *factum*, perhaps indeterminate, obscure, or void and yet hardly contestable, to wit, our preunderstanding of what is "called 'negative theology' . . . ," etc.? What we are identifying under these two words, today, isn't it first of all a corpus, at once open and closed, given, well-ordered, a set of statements [*un ensemble d'énoncés*] recognizable either by their family resemblance [English parenthetical gloss in the original—Ed.] or because they come under a regular logicodiscursive type whose recurrence lends itself to a formalization? This formalization can become mechanical . . .

—All the more mechanizable and easily reproducible, falsifiable, exposed to forgery and counterfeit since the statement of negative theology empties itself by definition, by vocation, of all intuitive plentitude. *Kenōsis* of discourse. If a phenomenological type of rule is followed for distinguishing between a full intuition and an empty or symbolic intending [*visée*] forgetful of the originary perception supporting it, then the apophatic statements *are, must be* on the side of the empty and then of mechanical, indeed purely verbal, repetition of phrases without actual or full intentional meaning. Apophatic statements represent what Husserl identifies as the moment of *crisis* (forgetting of the full and originary intuition, empty functioning of symbolic language, objectivism, etc.). But in revealing the originary and final necessity of this crisis, in denouncing from the language of crisis the snares of intuitive consciousness and of phenomenology, they destabilize the very axiomatics of the phenomenological, which is also the ontological and transcendental, critique. Emptiness is essential and necessary to them. If they guard against this, it is through the moment of prayer or the hymn. But this protective moment remains structurally exterior to the purely apophatic instance, that is, to *negative* theology as such, if there is any in the strict sense, which can at times be doubted. The value, the *evaluation*, of the quality, of the intensity, or of the force of events of negative theology would then result from this *relation* that articulates *this* void [*vide*] on the plentitude of a prayer or an attribution (theo-logical, theio-logical, or onto-logical) negated [*niée*], let's say denegated [*déniée*]. The criterion is the measure of a *relation*, and this relation is stretched between two poles, one of which must be that of positivity de-negated.

—From what does this redoubtable mechanicity result, the facility that there can be in imitating or fabricating negative theology (or, as well, a poetry of the same inspiration, of which we indeed have examples)? From the fact, I believe, that the very functioning of these statements resides in a formalization. This formalization essentially does without, tends essentially to do without all content and every idiomatic signifier, every presentation or representation, images and even names of God, for example, in this tongue or that culture. In brief, negative theology lets itself be approached (preunderstood) as a corpus largely archived with propositions whose logical modalities, grammar, lexicon, and very semantics are already accessible to us, at least for what is determinable in them.

—Whence the possibility of a canonizing monumentalization of works that, obeying laws, seem docile to the norms of a genre and an art. These works repeat traditions; they present themselves as iterable, influential or influenceable, objects of transfer, of credit and of discipline. For there are masters and disciples there. Recall Dionysius and Timothy. There are exercises and formations, there are schools, in the Christian mystical tradition as well as in an ontotheological or meontological (more Greek) tradition, in its exoteric or esoteric forms.

—Certainly, and he is already a disciple, however inspired, the one who wrote that not only God but the deity surpasses knowledge,

that the singularity of the unknown God overflows the essence and
the divinity, thwarting in this manner the oppositions of the negative
and the positive, of being and nothingness, of thing and nonthing—
thus transcending all the theological attributes:

Der unerkandte GOtt.

Was GOtt ist weiß man nicht: Er ist nicht Licht, nicht Geist,
Nicht Wonnigkeit, nicht Eins [Derrida's version: Nicht
     Wahrheit, Einheit, Eins], nicht was man Gottheit heist:
Nicht Weißheit, nicht Verstand, nicht Liebe, Wille, Gütte:
Kein Ding, kein Unding auch, kein Wesen, kein Gemütte:
Er ist was ich, und du, und keine Creatur,
Eh wir geworden sind was Er ist, nie erfuhr.

The unknowable God

What God is one knows not: He is not light, not spirit,
Not delight, not one [Not truth, unity, one], not what is
     called divinity:
Not wisdom, not intellect, not love, will, goodness:
No thing, no no-thing either, no essence, no concern:
He is what I, or you, or any other creature,
Before we became what He is, have never come to know.
                                                    (4: 21)

   —The following maxim [*sentence*] is precisely addressed to Saint
Augustine as if to someone close, a master and a predecessor that he
can amicably or respectfully challenge: "Stop, my *Augustine*: before
you have penetrated God to the bottom [*ergründen*], one will find the
entire sea in a small pit [*Grüblein*]" (4: 22).

   —Angelus Silesius had his own peculiar genius, but already he
was repeating, continuing, importing, transporting. He would transfer or translate in all the senses of this term because he already *was
post-writing*. This heir kept the archive, kept in memory the teaching
of Christoph Köler. He had read Tauler, Ruysbroeck, Boehme, and
above all Eckhart.

   —What we ought to start from, if I understand you rightly
(and this would be the *a priori* of our *a posteriori*, to wit, of this *post-*

scriptum we are engaged in), is this astonishing *fact* [fait], this *already done* [déjà fait], this *all done* [tout fait]: while negating or effacing all, while proceeding to eradicate every predicate and claiming to inhabit the desert . . .

—The desert is one of the beautiful and difficult metaphors that Leibniz was no doubt speaking of, but I am also struck by its recurrence, in other words, by the *typical striking* that reproduces the metaphor like a seal. Thus:

Man muß noch über GOtt.

. . . Wol sol ich dann nun hin?
Jch muß noch über GOtt in eine wüste ziehn.

One must go beyond God

. . . What should my quest then be?
I must beyond God into a desert flee.

(1: 7)

Or again:

Die Einsamkeit.

Die Einsamket ist noth: doch sey nur nicht gemein:
So kanstu überall in einer Wüsten seyn.

Solitude

Solitude is necessary, but be only not (in) public,
So you can everywhere be in a desert.

(2: 117)

And elsewhere it is a question of "desert times" (*in diser wüsten Zeit* [3: 184]). Isn't the desert a paradoxical figure of the *aporia*? No [*pas de*] marked out [*tracé*] or assured passage, no route in any case, at the very most trails that are not reliable ways, the paths are not yet cleared [*frayés*], unless the sand has already re-covered them. But isn't the uncleared way also the condition of *decision* or *event*, which consists in opening the way, in *(sur)passing*, thus in going *beyond?* In (sur)passing the aporia?

—Despite this desert, then, what we call negative theology grows and cultivates itself as a memory, an institution, a history, a discipline. It is a culture, with its archives and its tradition. It accumulates the *acts* of a tongue [*langue*]. That in particular is what the phrase "What is called 'negative theology,' in an idiom of Greco-Latin filiation, is a language" would suggest. However much one recalls (one precisely must recall and recall that that proves the possibility of the memory kept) that negative theology "consists," through its claim to depart from all consistency, in a language that does not cease testing the very limits of language, and exemplarily those of propositional, theoretical, or constative language . . .

—By that, negative theology would be not only a language and a testing of language, but above all the most thinking, the most exacting, the most intractable experience of the "essence" of language: a discourse on language, a "monologue" (in the heterological sense that Novalis or Heidegger gives to this word) in which language and tongue speak for themselves and record [*prennent acte de*] that *die Sprache spricht.* Whence this poetic or fictional dimension, at times ironic, always allegorical, about which some would say that it is only a form, an appearance, or a simulacrum. . . . It is true that, simultaneously, this arid fictionality tends to denounce images, figures, idols, rhetoric. An iconoclastic fiction must be thought.

—However much one says, then, that beyond the theorem and constative description, the discourse of negative theology "consists" in exceeding essence and language, by testifying it *remains.*

—What does "remain" mean here? Is it a modality of "being"?

—I don't know. Perhaps this, precisely, that this theology would be nothing . . .

—To be nothing, wouldn't that be its secret or declared vow? What do you believe you are thus threatening it with? Our discussion still supposes that this theology is something (determinable) and not nothing and wants to be or become something rather than nothing. Now we meant, just a moment ago too, to claim the contrary . . .

—A question of reading or hearing [*l'oreille*]. In any case, negative theology would be nothing, very simply nothing, if this excess or this surplus (with regard to language) did not imprint some mark on some singular events of language and did not leave some remains on the body of a tongue . . .

—A corpus, in sum.

—Some trace remains right in this corpus, becomes this corpus as *sur-vivance* of apophasis (more than life and more than death), survivance of an internal onto-logico-semantic auto-destruction: there will have been absolute rarefaction, the desert will have taken place, nothing will have taken place but this place. Certainly, the "unknowable God" ("*Der unerkandte GOtt*," 4: 21), the ignored or unrecognized God that we spoke about says nothing: of him there is nothing said that might hold . . .

—Save his name [*Sauf son nom*; "Safe, his name"] . . .

—Save the name that names nothing that might hold, not even a divinity (*Gottheit*), nothing whose withdrawal [*dérobement*] does not carry away every phrase that tries to measure itself against him. "God" "is" the name of this bottomless collapse, of this endless desertification of language. But the trace of this negative operation is inscribed *in* and *on* and *as* the *event* (what *comes*, what there is and which is always singular, what finds in this kenōsis the most decisive condition of its coming or its upsurging). *There is* this event, which remains, even if this remnance is not more substantial, more essential than this God, more ontologically determinable than this name of God of whom it is said that he names nothing that is, neither this nor that. It is even said of him that he is not what is *given there* in the sense of *es gibt:* He is not what gives, his is beyond all gifts ("*GOtt über alle Gaben*," 4: 30).

—Don't forget that that is said in the course of a prayer. What is prayer? No, one should not ask "What is prayer?," prayer in general. It is necessary to attempt to think prayer, in truth to test it out (to pray *it*, if one can say that, and transitively) through this particular prayer, this singular prayer in which or toward which prayer in general *strains itself*. For this particular prayer asks nothing, all the while asking more than everything. It asks God to give himself rather than gifts: "Giebstu mir dich nicht selbst, so hastu nichts gegeben"; "If you don't give yourself to me, then you have given nothing." Which interprets again the divinity of God as gift or desire of giving. And prayer is this interpretation, the very body of this interpretation. *In* and *on*, you said, that implies, apparently, some *topos* . . .

27. MARION

Dieu sans l'être: Hors texte (Paris: Presses Universitaires de France, 1991 [1982]), pp. 80–83, 86–91, 148–155, 197–203.

Trans. Thomas A. Carlson, *God Without Being* (Chicago: University of Chicago Press, 1991), pp. 53–60, 102–103, 104, 106–107, 139–144.

Jean-Luc Marion engages contemporary, and especially the deconstructive challenges to theology by arguing that they are anticipated by and already incorporated in traditional Christian negative theology, if this tradition is interpreted with sufficient subtlety. He defends this tradition as preserving the authentic sense of Christian revelation and its continued viability even in a radically secular age of culture today. This position has led Marion into direct debate with Derrida on questions of negative theology and particularly of the phenomenology of the "gift." For Marion, divinity is, in a miraculous manner, revealed in a givenness beyond description and in excess of intention, befuddling the ability of Logos to account for it. For Derrida, the impossibility of this givenness is what keeps open the messianic possibility and avoids the idolatry of proclaiming that the divine is actually present in something already here, rather than remaining always yet-to-be-given.[1]

In order to benefit from Marion's defense, theology must say nothing on its own but rather abandon itself entirely to the divine Word. Only this wholly other Word can communicate theological truth. Therefore theology must, in effect, say nothing and rather let itself *be* said by this unsayable Word (*Verbum indicible*)—just as the Word, as Christ, lets itself be said by the will of the Father in the silent suffering and mortification of its flesh. Marion thus presents Christian theology as a language of the ineffable Word that lets be said what it cannot itself say by letting *itself* be said—in the Incarnation—and finally by letting the Father's Will be done in offering itself up as a sacrifice for all ("Nevertheless not as I will, but as thou willst," Matthew 26:39).

---

1. See Marion's and Derrida's contributions to *God, the Gift, and Postmodernism*, ed. Caputo and Scanlon.

In a 1982 essay "La Vanité d'être et le nom de Dieu" (The Vanity of Being and the Name of God), Marion begins his reflections from Wittgenstein's invitation to silence, observing that Wittgenstein says nothing about the nature of this silence that would illuminate its sense.[2] What, Marion asks, is the sense of silence specifically about God, concerning whom there is much too much talk? Surely it is highly significant that in this case especially we talk so much about what we cannot talk about. The answer comes from an elucidation of the motivations for idolatry, since talk about the divine, by attributing to God some form or character as an object of discourse, is inherently idolatrous. Theism and atheism turn out to be equally idolatrous, for even the atheist must presuppose a concept of God in order to find it untrue. This is true even of Nietzsche's claim that all religious names and concepts are expressions of will to power, for "will to power" is a metaphysical notion that produces thousands of idols. If we are unable to keep silent about what we cannot say, as Wittgenstein bids us to do, this is because we always substitute for it some idol, and this *can* be talked about. What is beyond this idol, Marion proposes, can be signified best by crossing out the word—and with it even the concept—"G⊠d."[3]

Marion is interested in freeing theology from all metaphysical underpinnings, since they cannot but be idolatrous. He sees himself as extending Heidegger's effort to free theology from metaphysics, and he adopts Heidegger's proposal to eliminate the word "being" from theological discourse: "If I were yet to write a theology—as I sometimes feel tempted to do—the term *being* would in no wise appear in it. Faith has no need of the thought of being." Marion quotes this statement by Heidegger as an epigraph to *Dieu sans l'être*. But then he shows that Heidegger nevertheless does treat theology exclusively in relation to the question of being. Even the "gift" (the Incarnation) was interpreted by Heidegger as an equivalence for Being, which he interpreted as Giving (*Es gibt*). The domains of Being and the "gift" are exactly coterminus. Everything that is is "given."

---

2. "La Vanité d'être et le nom de Dieu," in *Analogie et Dialectique: Essais de théologie fondamentale*, ed. P. Gisel and P. Secretan (Geneva: Labor et Fides, 1982), pp. 17–49.

3. Marion writes the word "God" crossed out under a large **X**. See, further, Marion's "De la 'Mort de Dieu' aux Noms Divins: L'itinéraire théologique de la métaphysique," *Laval théologique et philosophique* 41/1 (1985): 25–41, for his critique of the inherent idolatry of all philosophical attempts to adjudicate theological questions merely by analysis of concepts. Both essays rework arguments of Marion's book *L'idole et la distance: Cinque études* (Paris: Bernard Grasset, 1977).

Genuinely freeing God from Being was already the project of Dionysius the Areopagite. Thomas Aquinas, regrettably in Marion's view, regressed from this position by taking Being as the proper name of God. For Dionysius, as for Plato before him, God or the Good was beyond Being. It was an object of the will but not of the intellect or of any kind of knowledge. Thomas Aquinas strove to demonstrate the priority of Being over the Good as the proper name of God, particularly in the *Summa Theologiae* Ia, q. 5, art. 2. He argued that Being, as the first intelligible, is the necessary and universal object of intellect, and that all the transcendentals (Being, Unity, Goodness, Beauty) presupposed Being in order to be apprehended by the intellect. Thus Being is always the first object in the order of conception: you must know that something *is* before you can know it as good or as true or as anything else. Against this Marion argues that although Being may be necessary in any human apprehension of an object, this does not make it the name of God. It says nothing about what is proper to God but only about how we approach and apprehend God. As Duns Scotus had maintained, although from the human point of view cognition of Being may be presupposed for any knowledge of God, this is not relevant to the divine names themselves and their relative order and dignity. Thus Thomas's position turns out to be idolatrous. He identifies what is but an image in our intellect—Being—with the invisible God.[4]

In the concluding segment of the 1982 "La Vanité" (not included in the revision for the book), Marion discusses scriptural passages that speak of Being in such a way as to subordinate it to God, the God "who calls the things that are not as though they were" (Romans 4:17). Scripture invokes God's absolute power over being and non-being, as opposed to ranging God among beings. Marion thereby employs Scripture to deconstruct ontology. No being by rights can glory in the face of God, for Being is nothing without God, who calls into being all beings, and who alone gives Being a meaning. The model provided by this scriptural God, furthermore, is not the self-sufficiency of a metaphysical hypostasis of Being but rather the self-giving of the Good. This is a goodness of gratuitous giving, unconditioned by anything that is. This God is rather the Creator of beings by the power of love as self-giving. This is the deeper doctrine of Scripture, which is more profound than any ontology. The absolute self-abandon effected in this originary gift of *agapè* renders the notion of the Being of beings vain and inert. Being is nothing without this power of love. Any revelation or remembrance of "God" requires that Being

---

4. My presentation of Thomas in volume 1 of this work offers another reading that avoids this conclusion.

be silenced in order to let this love speak. Even silence can be idolatrous. The silence that suits "God" is a silence motivated by love.

Thus, for Marion, Christianity offers a radically deeper interpretation of apophatic silence than that proposed by most postmodern theories and theologies. The sense of silence in the Christian tradition of negative theology is emphatically not agnostic but rather the apprehension of love that must be acted on and not said. Silence by and for love has a completely different sense from that of silence in the face of any kind of being. Only as filled with the love that is revealed eucharistically in the sacrifice of Christ can silence signify the unnameable and unsayable. If this silence is not to be just another form of idolatry directed toward the idea of some being exceeding description, it must be animated by the charity that only the Christ, the unsayable Word, "says" by relinquishing his own will for that of the Father: "Thy Will be done" (Matthew 6:11; cf. 26:39). The language of Scripture and revelation appeals in the name of love to those who are willing freely to respond and thereby to make a difference that is prior to any ontological difference between Being and beings. It is an appeal to a giving that gives being itself. This giving is God's own self-giving, and that is *agapè*.

What is unspeakable in words is spoken thus in self-giving. It is beyond what human words, with their division into sign and sense, can give. Only the language of Scripture, the Word of God, enables Marion to proffer this theology beyond logic. In Marion's language, the Logos is a self-giving to which the human "logos" can correspond in order to become "theo-logos." What is more, this can take place only through the Eucharist. In the Eucharist, the Word silently reveals itself in person as flesh and blood, giving thereby the key necessary to the interpretation of texts left as traces of the event of revelation. Only the gift of the body of Christ enables the Word to be more than the vanity of human words.

The following selection includes extracts from *God Without Being*, chapter 3, which is a revision of the article, "La Vanité d'être et le nom de Dieu," and the first section of chapter 5, "Of the Eucharistic Site of Theology." The latter piece moves beyond the dialogue with philosophers to an illustration of Marion's positive view of an unsayable Word that theology can let speak—or rather let itself be spoken by. This Word is unsayably distant from text and hermeneutics alike, but it can be experienced directly—in eucharistic community. A traditional Catholic sacramental rite, the Eucharist, together with the acts of charity which alone can validate it, thereby emerges as a way of exit from the impasses of postmodernism. Marion's negative theology of the Eucharist reveals the positive potential of apophasis to surpass the vanity of discourse disclosed by negative theology—and step beyond.

From *God Without Being,* chapter 3

The Crossing of Being

Thus, "what we cannot speak about we must pass over in silence—*darüber muss man schweigen.*" In other words, in passing from Wittgenstein to Heidegger, in speaking from the starting point of philosophy (or almost) and not from that of logic (or almost): "Someone who has experienced theology in his own roots, both the theology of the Christian faith and that of philosophy, would today rather remain silent about God [*von Gott zu schweigen*] when he is speaking in the realm of thinking."[1] Within such an improvised consensus, in spite or because of a judicious approximation, the two thinkers who dominate our epoch cross and meet. In it they radically determine, on the one hand, calculative thought and, on the other hand, meditating thought, and each their relations; such a consensus, however, does not restate, despite the evident similarity of terms, the caution that Ignatius of Antioch addressed to the overly prolix Christians: "It is better to keep silence and to be, than to speak without being."[2] If we are summoned to silence—if, as Aristotle says, we are "forced by the truth itself"[3] to keep silent with regard to something like God—this state of affairs nevertheless does not settle the fundamental question. For silence itself is expressed in several ways. We know silences of contempt and of joy, of pain and of pleasure, of consent and of solitude. Afforded by the concrete daily attitude and what it most rightly imposes is what one might call the theological attitude, which only bears on what Origen names the "dogmas to be kept in silence, *ta siōpōmena dogmata.*"[4] But what does this silence

1. L. Wittgenstein, *Tractatus Logico-philosophicus,* no. 7, *Schriften,* I (Frankfurt, 1980), p. 83 [trans. Pears and McGuinness]. And M. Heidegger, *Identität und Differenz,* p. 45 [trans. Stambaugh, pp. 54–55].

2. Ignatius of Antioch, *To the Ephesians,* XV, 1; also see XIX, 1, and *To the Magnesians,* VIII, 2, as well as, in *Die Apostolischen Väter, griechisch und deutsch,* ed. Joseph A. Fischer (Darmstadt, 1956), p. 157, n. 86.

3. Aristotle, *Metaphysics* A, 3, 984b10 [trans. Barnes, p. 1557].

4. Origen, *On the Song of Songs,* P.G. 17, 272a.

mean? To what silence are we summoned today? Death, preeminently, imposes silence; the emptiness of infinite spaces opposes its suffocating vacuity like an eternal silence; aphasia, desertlike, grows with its silence. Does this silence, which threatens modernity more than any other, have the least relation, as to something like God, with what Pseudo-Dionysius has in mind when he incites us to "honor the ineffable [things] with a wise silence"?[5]

In other words, the highest difficulty does not consist in managing to reach, with Wittgenstein or Heidegger, a guarded silence with regard to God. The greatest difficulty doubtless consists more essentially in deciding what silence *says:* contempt, renunciation, the avowal of impotence, or else the highest honor rendered, the only one neither unworthy nor "dangerous." But already we pay so much attention to securing the place where only silence is suitable that we do not yet try to determine the stakes and the nature of this silence. The silence concerning silence thus conceals from us that, finally, nothing demands more of interpretation than the nothingness of speech—or even that, to have done with silence, keeping silence does not suffice. Silence, precisely because it does not explain itself, exposes itself to an infinite equivocation of meaning. In order to keep silent with regard to God, one must, if not hold a discourse on God, at least hold a discourse worthy of God on our silence itself.

1—*The Silence of the Idol*

Let us take a moment to ascertain the seriousness of this new question, for a response is never worth more (and is often worth less) than the question that fostered it with a genuine questioning. A first indication clearly attests that, far from closing off a difficulty, silence opens one—the extreme difficulty that we experience in keeping silent before that about which, nevertheless, we simply cannot speak. There is nothing surprising in the fact that we may not be able to speak of God; for, if speaking is equivalent to stating a well-constructed

---

5. Denys, *Divine Names*, I, 3, P.G. 3, 589b. See IV, 22, 724b; *Mystical Theology* I, 1, 997a; *Celestial Hierarchy*, XV, 9: "to honor by our silence that which, hidden, surpasses us," 340b. Likewise Maximus Confessor: "only faith receives these things [the incarnation and its modalities], honoring the Word by one's silence," *Ambigua*, P.G. 91, 1057a.

proposition, then by definition that which is defined as ineffable, inconceivable, and unnameable escapes all speech. The surprising thing, therefore, is not our difficulty in speaking of God but indeed our difficulty in keeping silent. For in fact, with regard to God, overwhelmingly, we speak. In a sense we speak only about that, and much too much, with neither modesty nor precaution. . . . But whence comes the impotence to silence, or rather, our impotence to guard our silence instead of silencing that which our chattering assails?

Keeping our silence, in order precisely by this reserve to honor that which we would designate by silence—in other words, in this case, God—this would become thinkable only if God exposed himself to thought. The retreat of our eventual silence implies an absolute pole of reference around which a respectful desert might grow. The common idolatrous treatment of God prohibits straightaway the solitude of such an absolute pole of reference, since between our gaze or our speech and him, the idol interposes the invisible mirror where the first visible sends the thrust of this gaze back to itself. For what is characteristic of modernity, understood as the perfect completion of metaphysics, does not at all consist in a negation of God.

Such theoretical negation can be located easily in preceding centuries. Modernity is characterized first by the nullification of God as a question. Why does God no longer inhabit any process of questioning? Because the response to the question of his essence or existence (according to the strict metaphysical acceptation of these terms) becomes irrelevant. Not, undoubtedly, for ideological debate and according to the yardstick of the movement of ideas, but surely given a phenomenological reduction. What, then, is put at stake in a negation or an affirmation of God? Not God as such, but the compatibility or incompatibility of an idol called "God" with the whole of the conceptual system where beings in their Being make epoch. The gap between compatibility and incompatibility no doubt matters, but it matters infinitely less than the constant substitution, in one case and the other, of an absolute pole by an idol. Theism and atheism bear equally upon an idol. They remain enemies, but fraternal enemies, in a common and impassable idolatry. . . .

And so we understand why we manage so poorly to keep silent before that which we cannot express in a statement. What Wittgenstein indicates by the term of *das Mystische* we never have in view for itself, precisely because we always aim at it within our own aim.

Nobody demonstrates this better than Nietzsche, who, as by a phenomenological reduction *avant la lettre*, genealogically leads the
"gods"—all, without exception—back to the will to power. Now this
will to power speaks and produces, even if *das Mystische* appears
"dead" since the will to power indeed suffices as well to speak and to
produce it. That is, the "gods" can always be expressed, as genealogically recognized idols of the will to power. We never will have to keep
silent before that which we cannot say—because we never will have
anything to express other than idols of the will to power. Nothing is to
be said but the will to power, outside of which nothing *is*, not even the
nothing, since becoming itself passes, like being, to the will to power:
"Recapitulation: to impose upon becoming the character of Being—
that is the supreme will to power."[6] Hence we never will keep silent,
occupied with producing and expressing the thousand and one idols
at which the will to power, within and outside of us, will aim as so
many goals. Hence, not keeping silent, we will not point out, even by
a respectful silence, an absolute pole—absolved from the will to
power. Hence, by not keeping silent, by covering it with our busy
chattering, we silence that which silence alone, possibly, could have
honored—by attempting precisely not to say it, or even to aim at it.
Either to silence silence, by dint of words busied in declaring all the
idols and the thousand and one goals, or else to silence *oneself* in
order to let that very thing which silence honors be told.

But if our very silence does not succeed at keeping silent, the
fault does not return to some empirical behavior of "a public scoun-
drel" that the simple measures of an intellectual police would be able
to straighten out. Our silence either gives way to an indefinite chattering or no longer manages to honor, but simply passes under silence, because, fundamentally, it belongs, as do all of us, to the domain of nihilism, hence, of the play, finally laid bare, of the will to
power. Metaphysics comes to completion in the will to power that
does not cease to will itself, as well when it wills "gods" as when it
does not will them, and hence which wills only idols of itself,
and cannot but will such idols. And in this metaphysical completion, the western destiny of the Being of beings is consummated in its

6. *Wille zur Macht*, sec. 617 = Nietzsche, *Werke*, 7[154], VIII/1, p. 321
[trans. Kaufmann (modified)].

ultimate perfection, since "the innermost essence of Being is the will to power."[7]

We therefore must risk a question, already often approached, that has continued to appeal to us: in order to withdraw "God" from the idol, must we not undertake to think him—should we still say think?—starting from another instance than the one that reduces him to silence, or covers him over with idolatrous chattering? We identify this instance as the will to power, hence metaphysics in its completion, hence finally as Being itself envisaged as the Being of beings. To free "God" from his quotation marks would require nothing less than to free him from metaphysics, hence from the Being of beings. To free silence from its idolatrous dishonor would require nothing less than to free the word "God" from the Being of beings. But can one think outside of Being? And, in order to escape idolatry and to take away its quotation marks, does it suffice precisely no longer to mark them? . . .

5—The Inessential Name Thus First

It would remain only to go back to our initial question, if, however, a very pertinent objection did not stand out. We have just pointed out the excellence of the gift as if, necessarily, it went beyond Being/being, delivered and distorted it. But, on the contrary, must we not envisage the hypothesis that the gift does not strictly deploy Being/being as such? Or even more: that far from taking up the play between Being and being from a phantasmagorical "elsewhere," the gift does not rather deliver this play as such? In short: the gift still would belong to Being/being, precisely in that the gift would release its very opening. No one more than Heidegger allowed the thinking of the coincidence of the gift with Being/being, by taking literally the German *es gibt,* wherein we recognize the French *il y a,* there is: superposing one and the other, we would understand the fact that there should be (of course: being) as this fact that *it gives, ça donne.* Being itself is delivered in the mode of giving—from one end to the other along the path of his thought, from *Sein und Zeit* to *Zeit und Sein,* from 1927 to 1962, Heidegger did not cease to meditate on this equivalence.[8] Do we

7. *Wille zur Macht,* sec. 693 = Nietzsche, *Werke,* 14[8], VIII/3, p. 52 [trans. Kaufmann].

8. *Es Gibt* in *Sein und Zeit,* secs. 43, 44, etc.

not delude ourselves, then, by claiming to discover in the gift an instance anterior to Being/being that distorts the ontological difference of Being/being? Does not that which we apprehend as "otherwise than being" constitute precisely its most adequate and most secret thought? Indisputably—unless "gift" and "giving" can and must be understood in different ways, unless "gift" and "giving" are not determined here, always, despite the appearances, starting from Being/being. In fact, the gift can be understood in two so radically different ways that it will suffice to outline them here. On the one hand there is the sense of the gift that leads, in the *there is*, to the accentuating of the *it gives* starting from the giving itself, thus starting from giving insofar as it does not cease to give itself; in this case, the *it* that is supposed to give does not provide—any more than does the impersonal *il* on the threshold of the *il y a*—any privileged support. For it could appear, if thought began with it, only as a sort of being; with regard to "the enigmatic It [*ça/il*]" one would end up seeking what "indeterminate power" it masks; and one would miss precisely the whole stake of the gift, by a gross ontic and even causal regression. We therefore must leave the giver in suspension, even the very idea that a giver is necessary to the *it gives*, in order to interrogate the *it* solely "in light of the kind of giving that belongs to it: giving (*Geben*) as destiny, giving as a clearing porrection, *das Geben als Geschick, das Geben als lichtendes Reichen*."[9] . . ."it gives," with neither giver nor given, in a pure *giving*. . . .

On the other hand, the gift can be understood starting from giving—at least, as it is accomplished by the giver. The gift must be understood according to giving, but giving [*donation*] must not be understood as a pure and simple *giving* [*donner*]. Giving must be understood by reference to the giver. Between the gift given and the giver giving, giving does not open the (quadri-) dimension of appropriation, but preserves distance. Distance: the gap that separates definitively only as much as it unifies, since what distance gives consists in the gap itself.[10] The giving traverses distance by not ceasing to send the given back to a giver, who, the first, dispenses the given as such—a sending destined to a sending back. Distance lays out the intimate

---

9. Respectively, *Zur Sache des Denkens*, p. 17, then p. 19 [trans. Stambaugh (modified), pp. 17, 19].

10. See, for an essay on the "definition" of distance, in itself undefinable, *L'idole et la distance*, sec. 17.

gap between the giver and the gift, so that the self-withdrawal of the giver in the gift may be read on the gift, in the very fact that it refers back absolutely to the giver. . . . it is a ceaseless play of giving, where the terms are united all the more in that they are never confused. For distance, in which they are exchanged, also constitutes that which they exchange. . . .

. . . This journey, at once long and summary, which led us to the point of glimpsing the amplitude of what distance places in giving, allows us to outline a response. Every silence that remains inscribed in banality, in metaphysics, and even in Being/being, indeed, in a theology forgetful of the divine names, offers only mute idols. To remain silent does not suffice in order to escape idolatry, since, preeminently, the characteristic of the idol is to remain silent, and hence to let men remain silent when they no longer have anything to say—not even blasphemies. The silence that is suitable to the G⊗d who reveals himself as agape in Christ consists in remaining silent through and for agape: to conceive that if G⊗d gives, to say G⊗d requires receiving the gift and—since the gift occurs only in distance—returning it. To return the gift, to play redundantly the unthinkable donation, this is not said, but done. Love is not spoken, in the end, it is made. Only then can discourse be reborn, but as an enjoyment, a jubilation, a praise. . . . This silence, and no other, knows where it is, whom it silences, and why it must, for yet a time, preserve a mute decency—to free itself from idolatry. If we succeeded in glimpsing only the outline of that by which agape exceeds everything (and Being/being), then our silence could let us become, somewhat, "messengers . . . announcing the divine silence."[11]

---

11. Denys, *Divine Names*, IV, 2, P.G. 3, 696b.

From *God Without Being,* chapter 5

Of the Eucharistic Site of Theology

Theology can reach its authentically *theo*logical status only if it does not cease to break with all theo*logy*. Or yet, if it claims to speak of God, or rather of that G⊠d who strikes out and crosses out every divine idol, sensible or conceptual, if therefore it claims to speak of G⊠d, in such a way that this *of* is understood as much as the origin of the discourse as its objective (I do not say *object*, since G⊠d can never serve as an object, especially not for theology, except in distinguished blasphemy), following the axiom that only "God can well speak of God";[1] and if finally this strictly inconceivable G⊠d, simultaneously speaking and spoken, gives himself as the Word, as the Word given even in the silent immediacy of abandoned flesh—then there is nothing more suitable than that this theology should expose its logic to the repercussions, within it, of the *theos.*

1—Let It Be Said . . .

What, in fact, does theology—Christian theology—say? For in the end, what distinguishes Christian theology from every other does not stem from a singularity of meaning (as decisive as one would like) but from what, precisely, authorizes this eminent singularity, namely, the very position given to meaning, to its statement, and to its referent. Christian theology speaks of Christ. But Christ calls himself the Word. He does not speak words inspired by G⊠d concerning G⊠d, but he abolishes in himself the gap between the speaker who states (prophet or scribe) and the sign (speech or text); he abolishes this first gap only in abolishing a second, more fundamental gap, in us, men: the gap between the sign and the referent. In short, Christ does

---

1. Pascal, *Pensées,* Br. sec. 799, L. Sec. 303 [trans., Krailsheimer, p. 123]. With Athenagoras of Athens as counterproof: "each one thinking himself fit to know what concerns God not from God himself (*ou para theou peri theou*), but from himself alone," *A Plea Regarding Christians,* VII, P.G. 6, 904b.

not say the word, he says *himself* the Word. He says *himself*—the Word! Word, because he is said and proffered through and through. As in him coincide—or rather commune—the sign, the locutor, and the referent that elsewhere the human experience of language irremediably dissociates, he merits, contrary to our shattered, inspiring or devalued words, to be said, with a capital, the Word. To say that he says himself the Word already betrays that we stutter: for this "he says himself" already means to say—the Word. He says himself, and nothing else, for nothing else remains to be said outside of this saying of the said, saying of the said said par excellence, since it is proffered by the said-saying. In short the *dict* of the Said. He is said and all is said: all is accomplished in this word that performs, in speaking, the statement that "the Word pitched its tent among us" (John 1:14), because he has nothing to do, here, other than to say [himself]. That he simply should say [himself], and all is accomplished. That he should say [himself], and all is said. He only has to say [himself] in order to do. Better, he does not even have anything to say in order to say everything, since he incarnates the dict in saying it: no sooner said than done. And hence the Word, the Said, finally says nothing; he lets people speak, he lets people talk, "Jesus gave him no answer" (John 19:19 = Luke 23:9). And so he does by letting be said, and so he says by letting be done. So be it: "He says: all is finished" (John 19:30). The Word does not say [itself] as Word, or better: says [itself]—Word!—only by letting be said: which one can understand in a double sense. The Word, as Said of God, no man can hear or understand adequately, so that the more men hear him speak their own words, the less their understanding grasps what the said words nevertheless say as clear as day. In return, men cannot render to the Word the homage of an adequate denomination; if they can—by exceptional grace—sometimes confess him as "Son of God," they do not manage (nor ever will manage) to say him as he says himself. The Word is not said in any tongue, since he transgresses language itself, seeing that, Word in flesh and bone, he is given as indissolubly speaker, sign, and referent. The referent, which here becomes locutor, even if he speaks our words, is not said in them according to our manner of speaking. He proffers himself in them, but not because he says them; he proffers himself in them because he exposes himself in them; and exposes himself less as one exposes an opinion than as one exposes oneself to a danger: he exposes himself by incarnating himself. Thus speaking our words, the Word redoubles his incarnation, or rather accomplishes it absolutely, since language constitutes us more carnally than our flesh. Such an incarnation in our words can be undertaken only by the Word, who comes to us before our words. We, who on the contrary occur only in the words, we cannot freely carry out this incarnation. Incarnate in our words, the Word acquires in them a new unspeakableness, since he can be spoken in them only by the movement of incarnation that is, so to speak, anterior to the words, which he speaks and which he lets speak him. Any speech that speaks only from this side of language hence cannot reach the referent, which, alone and in lordly manner, comes nevertheless, in language, to meet us. Before our words, the Word lets people talk, thus manifesting that he cannot be spoken in them, but that, by the lordly freedom of this redoubled incarnation, he gives himself in them to be spoken. What is unheard of in the Word stems from the fact that he only says [himself] unspeakably (gap Word/words), but that in this very unspeakableness he is said nevertheless perfectly (the gap traversed by redoubled incarnation). The Word says [himself] absolutely though unspeakably, unless he is only absolved from unspeakableness in traversing it by a perfect incarnation. He is unspeakable, not simply like an overly high note that no throat can sing, by default of speech: it is not only a question of speech, but especially of the sign and meaning. He is unspeakable also, but not only, like the untenable thought of the abyss, where Zarathustra founders, because it opens to the terror of an unfurling of divinity: for it is not a question here first of a thought, but of a referent, in flesh and bone, of the Word whose incarnation occupies and transgresses at once the order of speech and of meaning. No human tongue can say the Said of God. For to say it, one must speak as He alone speaks, with *exousia* (Mark 1:22, etc.), with that sovereign freedom, whose (super-) natural ascendancy impresses all as an omnipotence so great that it only has to speak in order to be admitted. The Word says itself, it therefore becomes unspeakable to us; labile inhabitant of our babble, it inhabits our babble nevertheless as referent. The Word, as Son, receives from the Father the mandate and the injunction (*entolē*) to say; but, when he becomes the locutor, this message already coincides otherwise (or precisely: not otherwise) with that message which the paternal illocution eternally realizes in him as Word; such that he can legitimately transfer, in the very act of his statement—the incarnation—not only the

474   THE UNUTTERABLY OTHER

message spoken by him, but the speaker who, with and before him, speaks it, him, the unspeakable Said, as such—*Verbum Dei*. When he speaks the words of the Father, he lets himself be spoken by the Father, as his Word. Thus *the Word is said as it is given:* starting from the Father and in return to the Father. This very transference designates the Spirit. Or rather the Spirit takes the turn to speak in order to designate this transference of the speaker (Jesus) in the sign (the text of the divine will) as that of which the Spirit trinitarily offers the referent—"A voice came from heaven; I glorified you and I will glorify you" (John 12:28), the voice where Spirit speaks (at the baptism; Matt. 3:16), in the name of the Father (transfiguration, Mark 9:7) who speaks the Son as such. In other words: I hold this one as my preferred son in whom I proffer myself, the proffered that, of all the proffered, I prefer because he prefers to proffer me, rather than himself. Preferred, proffered: the Word, beloved Son. The Word lets himself be said by the Father—in the Spirit that consists, in a sense, only in this—exactly as he lets his will do the will of the Father. Thus appears the Said of the Father: the Word seems to be the Said, when he appears as the Son of the Father. Said of the Father: the Word proffered by the breath of the paternal voice, breath, Spirit. Upon the Cross, the Father expires as much as the Word—since they expire the same Spirit. The Trinity respires from being able to breathe among us.

Of such a Word, of such a *logos*, a discourse becomes legitimate, hence possible, only if it receives and maintains the repercussion of that which it claims to reach. To justify its Christianity, a theology must be conceived as a *logos* of the *Logos*, a word of the Word, a said of the Said—where, to be sure, every doctrine of language, every theory of discourse, every scientific epistemology, must let itself be regulated by the event of its redoubling in a capital, intimate, and anterior instance. It is not simply a question of making a concession, for example, of admitting that, given the event of Christ, certain conditions of linguistics, of hermeneutics, and of the methods of human sciences have to undergo a few modifications, even exceptions. For here, the Word arises short of the field of possible objects for given methods: one can well attempt (in fact though, one cannot) to do "theologies" of labor, of nonviolence, of progress, of the middle class, of the young, and so on, where only the complement of the noun changes; but one could not do a "theology of the Word," because if a *logos* pretends to precede the *Logos*, this *logos* blasphemes the Word (of) G⊗d. Only the Said that lets itself be said by the Father can assure the pertinence of our *logos* concerning him, in teaching it also to let itself be said—said by the Word made flesh, unspeakable and silent. Theology: most certainly a human *logos* where man does not master language but must let himself be governed by it (Heidegger); but above all, the only *logos* of men that lets itself be said—remaining human *logos* more than ever—by the *Logos*. To do theology is not to speak the language of gods or of "God," but to let the Word speak us (or make us speak) in the way that it speaks of and to G⊗d: "Receive the spirit of filiation, in which we cry, 'Abba, Father'" (Rom. 8:15), "You then, pray thus: Our Father who art in heaven . . ." (Matt. 6:9).[2] Theology: a *logos* that assures its pertinence concerning G⊗d to the strict degree that it lets the *Logos* be said in itself, *Logos* itself understood (strictly: heard) as he who alone can let himself be said perfectly by the Father: for in order to say G⊗d one first must let oneself be said by him to the point that, by this docile abandon, G⊗d speaks in our speech, just as in the words of the Word sounded the unspeakable Word of his Father. It is not a question, for the "theologian," of reaching that which his discourse speaks (well or poorly—what does it finally matter, for what norm in this world would decide?) of G⊗d, but of abandoning his discourse and every linguistic initiative to the Word, in order to let himself be said by the Word, as the Word lets himself be said by the Father—him, and in him, us also. In short, our language will be able to speak of G⊗d only to the degree that G⊗d, in his Word, will speak our language and teach us in the end to speak it as he speaks it—divinely, which means to say in all abandon. In short, it is a question of learning to speak our language with the accents—with the accent of the Word speaking it. For the Word, by speaking our words, which he says word-for-word, without changing anything of them (not an *iōta* Matt. 5:18), takes us at our word, literally: since

---

2. *Father* constitutes the first word that we say to G⊗d in the very sense that G⊗d says it (to G⊗d, as Son to Father, precisely): "But, one day, somewhere, he was praying. When he had finished, one of his disciples asked him: 'Lord, teach us to pray, as John taught it to his disciples.' He said to them: 'When you pray, say: Father . . .'" (Luke 11:1–2). *Father*, we cry (Romans 8:15; Galatians 4:16), only because first Christ says it himself (Mark 14:36; Matthew 11:25; 26:39; Luke 23:34, 46; John 11:41; 12:27, 28; 17:1, 5, 11, 21, 24, 25; etc.).

he speaks what we speak, but with an entirely different accent, he promises us the challenge, and gives us the means to take it up—to speak our word-for-word with his accent, the accent of a God. The theologian lets himself say (or be said by) the Word, or rather lets the Word let him speak human language in the way that God speaks it in his Word.

PERMISSIONS AND ACKNOWLEDGMENTS

1. Hölderlin. *Friedrich Hölderlin: Poems and Fragments.* Trans. Michael Hamburger. Ann Arbor: University of Michigan Press, 1967. Reprinted by permission of University of Michigan Press.

2. Schelling. Original translation from *Philosophie der Offenbarung*, in *Sämtliche Werke*. Ed. Karl Friedrich August Schelling. Stuttgart: Cotta, 1856–71.

3. Kierkegaard. *Fear and Trembling.* Trans. Howard V. Hong and Edna H. Hong. Princeton: Princeton University Press, 1983. Copyright (c) 1983 by Princeton University Press. Reprinted by permission of Princeton University Press.

4. Dickinson. *The Poems of Emily Dickinson.* Ed. Thomas H. Johnson. Cambridge, Mass.: The Belknap Press of Harvard University, 1955. Copyright (c) 1951, 1955, 1979 by the President and Fellows of Harvard College. Reprinted by permission of the publishers and the Trustees of Amherst College.

5. Hofmannsthal. *The Lord Chandos Letter.* Trans. Michael Hofmann. London: Syrens, 1995. Copyright (c) 1995 by Michael Hofmann. Reprinted by permission of Penguin Books Ltd.

6. Rilke. *Duino Elegies and The Sonnets to Orpheus.* Trans. A. Poulin, Jr. Boston: Houghton Mifflin, 1977. Copyright (c) 1975, 1976, 1977 by A. Poulin, Jr. Reprinted by permission of Houghton Mifflin Company. All rights reserved.

7. Kafka. "On Parables" and "The Silence of the Sirens," in *Franz Kafka: The Complete Short Stories.* Ed. Nahum N. Glatzer, trans. Willa and Edwin Muir. Copyright (c) 1946, 1947, 1948, 1949, 1954, 1958, 1971 by Schocken Books. Used by permission of Schocken Books, a division of Random House, Inc.

8. Benjamin. "The Task of the Translator," from *Illuminations* by Walter Benjamin, copyright (c) 1955 by Suhrkamp Verlag, Frankfurt a.M. English trans. by Harry Zohn, copyright (c) 1968 and renewed 1996 by Harcourt, Inc. Reprinted by permission of Harcourt, Inc.

9. Rosenzweig. *The Star of Redemption*. Trans. William W. Hallo. Notre Dame: University of Notre Dame Press, 1985.

10. Wittgenstein. "Lecture on Ethics," in *Philosophical Occasions 1912–1951*. Ed. James C. Klagge and Alfred Nordmann. Indianapolis and Cambridge: Hackett, 1993. Copyright (c) 1965 by *The Philosophical Review*. Public domain.
    Tractatus, 6.4 to 7.1. From *Tractatus Logico-Philosophicus*. Trans. C. K. Ogden, with introduction by Bertrand Russell. London: Routledge, 1992.

11. Heidegger. "Words." Trans. Joan Stambaugh. In *On the Way to Language*. New York: Harper & Row, 1971. Copyright (c) 1971 in the English translation by Harper & Row Publishers, Inc. Reprinted by permission of HarperCollins Publishers, Inc.

12. Weil. "He Whom We Must Love Is Absent." Trans. Emma Craufurd. In *Gravity and Grace*. London: Routledge and Kegan Paul, 1952.

13. Malevich. "God Is Not Cast Down," in *Essays on Art, 1915–1933*, vol. 1. Trans. Xenia Glowacki-Prus and Arnold McMillin. Copenhagen: Borgens Forlag, 1968. Ed. Troels Andersen.

14. Schoenberg. *Moses and Aaron. Opera in Three Acts*. Trans. Allen Forte, Miniature Score. Recorded by Chicago Symphony Orchestra and Chorus, Sir Georg Solti, Orchestra Hall, Chicago, April–May 1984. London: Decca Record Company, 1985.

15. Adorno. "Music and Language: A Fragment," in *Quasi una fantasia: Essays on Modern Music*. Trans. Rodney Livingstone. London–New York: Verso, 1992. Reprinted by permission of Verso.
    Negative Dialectics. Trans. E. B. Ashton. New York: Continuum, 1973. Reprinted by permission of The Continuum International Publishing Group, Inc.

16. Cage. "Lecture on Nothing," in *Silence*. Middletown, Conn.: Wesleyan University Press, 1939–61. Reprinted by permission of the Wesleyan University Press.

17. Jankélévitch. "Music and Silence," in *Music and the Ineffable*. Trans. Carolyn Abbate. Princeton: Princeton University Press, 2003. Copyright (c) 2003 by Princeton University Press. Reprinted by permission of Princeton University Press.

18. Beckett. *The Unnamable*. New York: Grove Press, 1958. Reprinted with permission by Grove/Atlantic, Inc. and Calder Publications.
    "Texts for Nothing," #8, in *Stories and Texts for Nothing*. New York: Grove, 1967. Reprinted with permission by Grove/Atlantic, Inc. and Calder Publications.

19. Steiner. "Silence and the Poet," in *Language and Silence: Essays on Language, Literature, and the Inhuman.* New York: Atheneum, 1967. Copyright (c) 1958, 1967 by George Steiner. Reprinted by permission of Georges Borchardt, Inc., for the author.

20. Philip. *Looking for Livingstone: An Odyssey of Silence.* Stratford, Ontario: The Mercury Press, 1991. Reprinted by permission of the author.

21. Bataille. *Inner Experience.* Trans. Leslie Anne Boldt-Irons. Reprinted by permission from the State University of New York Press. Copyright (c) 1988 State University of New York. All rights reserved.

22. Jabès. *The Book of Questions: El, or the Last Book.* Trans. Rosmarie Waldrop. Middleton, Conn.: Wesleyan University Press, 1984. Reprinted by permission of University Press of New England.
   The Book of Resemblances. Trans. Rosmarie Waldrop. Middleton, Conn.: Wesleyan University Press, 1990. Reprinted by permission of University Press of New England.

23. Celan. German texts from *Paul Celan, Werke Band 2 und 3* reprinted by permission of Suhrkamp Verlag Frankfurt am Main. Copyright (c) 1983. Trans. Michael Hamburger, *Poems of Paul Celan.* New York: Persea Books, 1995. Reprinted by permission of Persea Press.

24. Levinas. *Otherwise than Being or Beyond Essence.* Trans. Alphonso Lingis. Dordrecht: Kluwer, 1991. Reprinted with kind permission of Kluwer Academic Publishers.

25. Blanchot. "How to Discover the Obscure?" in *The Infinite Conversation.* Trans. Susan Hanson. Minneapolis: University of Minnesota Press, 1993. English language edition copyright (c) 1993 of the University of Minnesota. Original French edition, *L'entretien infini,* copyright (c) 1969 by Editions Gallimard.

26. Derrida. "Sauf le nom (Post-Scriptum)" in *On the Name.* Trans. John P. Leavey, Jr. Stanford: Stanford University Press, 1995. Ed. Thomas Dutoit. Copyright (c) 1995 English translation by the Board of Trustees of the Leland Stanford Jr. University. Used with the permission of Stanford University Press, www.sup.org.

27. Marion. *God Without Being.* Trans. Thomas A. Carlson. Chicago: University of Chicago Press, 1991. Copyright (c) 1991 by University of Chicago Press. Reprinted with permission of University of Chicago Press.

Unless otherwise indicated, notes to the excerpted readings are a selection, sometimes shortened or slightly abridged, of the notes in the English-language editions of the source texts at the beginning of each section.

A fragment of the general introduction appeared as "Franz Rosenzweig and the Emergence of a Post-Secular Philosophy of the Unsayable," *International Journal for Philosophy of Religion* 58/3 (2005): 151–180. Another part is forthcoming in *Modernism/Modernity*. An article on "Emily Dickinson's Apophatic Poetics" incorporating some paragraphs and sentences from that section is forthcoming in *Spiritus*.